RELIGION AND POLITICS IN URBAN IRELAND, *c*.1500–*c*.1750

Religion and Politics in Urban Ireland,
c.1500–*c*.1750

Essays in Honour of
COLM LENNON

Salvador Ryan & Clodagh Tait

EDITORS

FOUR COURTS PRESS

Set in 10.5 pt on 12.5 pt Ehrhardt for
FOUR COURTS PRESS LTD
7 Malpas Street, Dublin 8, Ireland
www.fourcourtspress.ie
and in North America for
FOUR COURTS PRESS
c/o ISBS, 920 N.E. 58th Avenue, Suite 300, Portland, OR 97213.

© The various contributors and Four Courts Press, 2016

A catalogue record for this title
is available from the British Library.

ISBN 978–1–84682–574–3

All rights reserved. No part of this publication may be
reproduced, stored in or introduced into a retrieval
system, or transmitted, in any form or by any means
(electronic, mechanical, photocopying, recording or
otherwise), without the prior written permission of
both the copyright owner and the publisher of this book.

Printed in England
by Antony Rowe Ltd, Chippenham, Wilts.

Contents

LIST OF ABBREVIATIONS	7
PREFACE *Salvador Ryan & Clodagh Tait*	9
Colm Lennon as educator and colleague: an appreciation *Jacqueline Hill & Mary Ann Lyons*	13
The research and scholarly writings of Professor Colm Lennon *Steven G. Ellis*	17
Select list of the publications of Colm Lennon to 2015 Compiled by *Bernadette Cunningham & Raymond Gillespie*	21
The religious guild of St George Martyr, Dublin *Mary Esther Clark & Gael Chenard*	31
Tudor reformations in Cork *Henry A. Jefferies*	51
The limits of Old English liberty: the case of Thomas Arthur, MD (1593–1675), in Limerick and Dublin *Mary Ann Lyons*	70
Henry Burnell and Richard Netterville: lawyers in civic life in the English Pale, 1562–1615 *Nessa Malone*	89
Goliath and the boy David: Henry Fitzsimon, James Ussher and the birth of Irish religious debate *Alan Ford*	108
The dissolution of the monasteries and the parishes of the western liberty of Meath in the seventeenth century *Rory Masterson*	134
Nuns and their networks in early modern Galway *Bernadette Cunningham*	156

Religion and politics in a provincial town: Belfast, 1660–1720   173
  Raymond Gillespie

Oaths and oath-taking: the civic experience in Dublin, 1660–1774   193
  Jacqueline Hill

Catholic and Protestant Dublin weavers before the Spanish
Inquisition, 1745–54   210
  Thomas O'Connor

A saint for eighteenth-century Dublin? Father John Murphy   225
  Toby Barnard

Sir John Gilbert (1829–98): historian of the Irish bourgeoisie   249
  Ciaran Brady

LIST OF CONTRIBUTORS   275

INDEX   277

Abbreviations

CARD	*Calendar of ancient records of Dublin*, ed. J.T. & R.M. Gilbert (19 vols, Dublin, 1889–1944)
CSPI	*Calendar of the state papers relating to Ireland, 1509–73* [etc.] (24 vols, London, 1860–1911)
DIB	James McGuire & James Quinn (eds), *Dictionary of Irish biography* (Cambridge, 2009) and online edition
EHR	*English Historical Review* (London, 1886–)
IHS	*Irish Historical Studies: the Joint Journal of the Irish Historical Society and the Ulster Society for Irish Historical Studies* (Dublin, 1938–)
JCHAS	*Journal of the Cork Historical and Archaeological Society* (Cork, 1892–)
JGAHS	*Journal of the Galway Archaeological and Historical Society* (Galway, 1900–)
JRSAI	*Journal of the Royal Society of Antiquaries of Ireland* (Dublin, 1892–)
ODNB	*Oxford dictionary of national biography* (Oxford, 2004) and online edition
PRIA	*Proceedings of the Royal Irish Academy* (Dublin, 1836–)

Preface

SALVADOR RYAN & CLODAGH TAIT

Urbanus et instructus: this Latin expression perhaps captures as best as one can the character of this volume's honoree: a gentleman and a scholar; not merely a 'gentleman', in a narrow sense, but, more importantly, a 'gentle man'. For those of us who have sat at his feet, either in the context of formal university lectures or during his frequent presentations at academic conferences, who have been directed by him in postgraduate or postdoctoral work, collaborated with him on various scholarly projects, or who have simply experienced his invariably pleasant and encouraging demeanour in passing encounters, the impression that remains is of a scholar who, while deeply learned, widely respected and quietly confident in his professional craft, nevertheless wears such distinction lightly and with a genuine humility that is not always found among those who tread the halls of academe. The story of his treatment of a third year BA student is a case in point. The student, who was taking Colm's course on the history of Dublin in the late medieval and early modern period, handed in a paper on the religious guild of St Anne in St Audoen's Church, an area on which Colm had already done some significant research. When the student returned, Colm carefully took the student through his paper and complimented him on his efforts before remarking 'you went much further than I did in my own studies of St Anne's'. This remark reflects not so much the quality of the student's paper as Colm's eagerness to encourage him in his endeavours and to show that valuable historical discoveries need not be the sole preserve of tenured academic teaching staff. Those who have had the pleasure of experiencing Colm's gentle yet purposeful scholarly guidance over the years will recognize in this story those signature traits of respect, courtesy and confidence-building which were an important part of Colm's approach to teaching and supervision and, indeed, central to his dealings with others more generally.

Colm joined the Department of History at Maynooth on 1 October 1978 and gave over thirty years' service to the department as an educator, a colleague, and a scholar of international repute, before retiring in September 2010. Plans were already afoot, even at that stage, to mark Colm's significant contribution to Irish historical scholarship and to the teaching of history over a long and distinguished career. It was with the utmost pleasure that we, as editors, assumed the responsibility of bringing this volume to birth. We are honoured to be joined in this enterprise by a number of Colm's colleagues and former students, each of whom responded with great enthusiasm to our invitation to contribute articles and tributes: if the very word *festschrift* means a writing in celebration of someone or something, there cannot be any doubt as to the worthiness of the recipient of this particular celebratory collection. Given Colm's various teaching and research interests, the immediate challenge was to find a coherent theme which might draw some of the more significant of these interests together. And thus was it decided to focus on religion and politics in urban Ireland in the early modern period. Each of the essays in the collection focuses on some aspect of this theme, beginning with Mary Clark and Gael Chenard's contribution on the guild of St George, a piece which, admittedly, launches the volume from a late medieval perspective (but this too reflects Colm's own work on late medieval Dublin) and concludes with an essay by Ciaran Brady on that other great historian of Dublin, Sir John T. Gilbert. While these two pieces, which bookend the volume, might be seen as strictly overstepping the stated chronology, there is something fitting in this, too, for Colm's historical research never limited itself to forced chronologies, but always seemed to manage to be expansive and forensic at the same time.

Urban studies held a particular interest for Colm. Prior to his pioneering work on Irish urban centres like Dublin and Limerick, publications on urban centres were rare, and often antiquarian in their nature. While several histories of individual towns had been produced in the nineteenth century, these tended to chronicle long periods of time, often in somewhat uneven detail. Articles in numerous local history journals and elsewhere often took as their theme the rapidly vanishing built heritage – especially the ecclesiastical buildings – of the Irish towns. The rich documentary heritage of the towns was recognized in the publication of many of the surviving corporation records, especially by Richard Caulfield and J.T. Gilbert, whose career as historian of Dublin is charted in this volume by Ciaran Brady, as mentioned above. However, H.F. Berry's diligent collection of many of the surviving guild records into the Dublin Public Record Office ensured their destruction alongside some countless other irreplaceable documents like wills and parish registers in 1922. This disaster, alongside other losses of documents noted as being extant in the nineteenth century, such as the Red Book of Kilkenny, as well as a valorization of Gaelic rather than Old English history, contributed to a decline in publications about the Irish early modern towns, apart from those appearing periodically in local history journals such as the *Dublin Historical Review*. Relatively few pages were devoted to urban communities in the *New History of Ireland*, volume 3, largely in the context of demographic, economic and social history, rather than religion and politics. Only in the 1980s, led by Colm's studies of Richard Stanihurst 'the Dubliner' in 1981, and of Dublin's office-holders in 1989, as well as the establishment of the Irish Historic Towns Atlas project, and the work of Anthony Sheehan and Brendan Bradshaw, did early modern urban history begin to attract more attention.

Preface

But how was urban history to be written in the light of limited source material? With *The lords of Dublin in the age of Reformation*, Colm provided new perspectives on Dublin through a forensic study of its elite, revealing the working of its corporation and the religious lives of its citizens. He pioneered effective methodologies, such as prosopography, for dealing with the scattered information available on his subjects. His account of the patrician families of early modern Limerick used a wide range of sources, material culture as well as documents, to emphasize how their 'sense of themselves as an elite' was created through the use of building, burial, genealogy and history. His work on topics like poverty meanwhile has shown how the surviving corporation, ecclesiastical and guild records can throw light on the lower as well as the upper sections of society. Colm has also contributed to making valuable primary sources available in print – these include ecclesiastical records such as the *Christ Church deeds*; a new calendar of the state papers of the reign of Edward VI; and the surviving records of the guilds of St Anne and St Sythe. Finally, as with other publications in the series, his Irish Historic Towns Atlas (*Dublin, Part II, 1610–1759*) has used maps and geographical as well as historical methodologies to reveal the landscape of early modern Dublin.

The wider context in which the communities of individual towns operated has been a key part of Colm's work. Whereas towns had previously largely been considered as discrete units, he has highlighted common issues faced by the townspeople throughout Ireland, such as the negotiation of relationships with neighbouring gentry and aristocratic families, Old English, Gaelic and New English (one of Colm's own current projects is a book on the gentry of the Pale). His work on Richard Stanihurst emphasized that Old English Dublin writer's understandings of Gaelic Ireland, as well as his own community. His books on Stanihurst and Richard Creagh, Limerick citizen and Catholic archbishop of Armagh, used their biographies to illustrate wider political and religious influences affecting the inhabitants of Ireland in this period. Furthermore, his reconstructions of Creagh and Stanihurst's continental connections and international adventures emphasize the wider European circles in which many Irish people, urban and rural, Catholic and Protestant, moved.

Colm has also made some key interventions regarding the broader course of religious history in early modern Ireland. His nuanced studies of Catholic religiosity have argued for a gradual and relatively slow Counter-Reformation and have greatly influenced debates about why and when the Reformation failed in Ireland. His focus on changes in Catholic religious practice and in the development of Catholic recusancy has caused him to highlight this community's dynamism rather than its conservatism. He has also paid close attention to religious controversy, conflict, violence and martyrdom. In all of this, Colm has noted the role of women, particularly as patrons of the personnel of the Catholic church and participants in its rituals, as well as within the religious confraternities and sodalities that were so important to sustaining domestic Catholic practice.

The essays in this volume adopt some of Colm's methodologies and concerns. We offer them in gratitude to a scholar and a gentleman who has touched all of our lives in different ways.

Finally, the editors would like to thank the Department of History, Maynooth University, for funding this publication and the staff at Four Courts Press for seeing this volume to print with their customary professionalism and efficiency.

Colm Lennon as educator and colleague: an appreciation

JACQUELINE HILL & MARY ANN LYONS

Colm Lennon taught for a number of years at second level and at University College Dublin before joining the staff of the History Department at Maynooth in 1978. From then until his retirement in 2010, Colm made an outstanding contribution to the success of the department, not only through his delivery of excellent courses and provision of expert supervision in early modern Irish and European history, but also through his role in shaping the department's ethos, most especially its strongly pastoral approach to students and their learning.

Colm joined what was then a small department in the NUI sector of St Patrick's College, Maynooth. The late Monsignor Patrick Corish was head of the department, and the other full-time members were Mary Cullen, Vincent Comerford and Jackie Hill. This unchanged five-person team constituted the departmental establishment until Professor Corish's retirement in 1988. Elma Collins and Christopher Woods supplemented the department's teaching in their capacity as tutors.

With his experience of secondary level teaching, Colm proved to be an inspiring lecturer. This, combined with genuine courtesy and interest in the students' progress, meant that his elective classes were always over-subscribed. During the early part of his career, Colm taught an undergraduate survey module on Renaissance and Reformation Europe with characteristic enthusiasm and innovation, drawing extensively on works of art, sculpture, architecture and literature to stir students' curiosity, enrich exploration and stimulate further independent study of that era. Thereafter, through his contributions to the university's European studies programme, of which he was director for a time, Colm continued to share his passion for early modern and indeed modern European history with his students whom he accompanied on annual field trips to Belgium. Always a progressive and outward-looking educator, he was also a very active participant in several European student exchange programmes, particularly ERASMUS, ECTS, and CLIOH, and he served as the department's international coordinator at a time when the Erasmus exchange scheme was being set up, a key role that involved considerable overseas travel. His courses were particularly popular with visiting students from abroad who were especially appreciative of his accessible teaching style and his warm, welcoming approach.

It was his core module on sixteenth-century Ireland, taught to ever-growing numbers of first year students, which ensured that over many years, all history students encountered his quiet but authoritative, fluent and engaging manner. For the majority, this was their first foray into a very unfamiliar period of Irish history but Colm's expert understanding of the period combined with his pedagogical excellence made this challenging encounter an enjoyable and illuminating learning experience. Drawing upon a wealth of teaching experience in the field, he published the popular textbook, *Sixteenth-century Ireland: the incomplete conquest* (Dublin, 1994; 2nd edn, 2005), which was widely praised and particularly commended for bringing alive the physical and mental complexities of the island with which the Tudor administrators repeatedly wrestled. In producing this text, he performed a great service in promoting and enhancing the teaching and study of early modern Irish history in Ireland and abroad for many years to come.

In tandem with his burgeoning research output in the field of urban historical studies, Colm developed several innovative specialist modules on urban history in an Irish context. Final year history students were especially fortunate in having the unique opportunity to take a course with Colm on the development of his native Dublin during the period 1450 to 1700. Under his expert tutelage, they traced the evolutionary stages from medieval town to capital city through his classes and the many walking tours of the city that he led, and by completing independent research projects under his close supervision. Colm's passion for the study of printing and reading in early modern Ireland and Europe was the inspiration for a third strand to his teaching profile. His second year module titled 'Printers and readers: the culture of the printed book in the early modern world' was exceptionally popular with students who derived particular pleasure and learned a great deal from their visits to the National Print Museum and the Russell Library, Maynooth – evidence of Colm's appreciation for encouraging his students to be active participants in their learning. What made him an exceptional educator, as his students will testify to, was his unique style of teaching and interaction with students at all levels. While demanding very high standards, Colm was always a source of steady and gentle support to students. He was affirmative, constructively critical, attentive to individual students' aptitudes and potential, always mindful of their confidence, willing to give of his time to listen to and advise them, and sensitive to their broader development as people. As those fortunate enough to have been educated by him will testify, Colm Lennon clearly understood that 'the secret in education lies in respecting the student' (Ralph Waldo Emerson).

The result was that a steady stream of students enrolled to undertake research degrees under his able supervision. Colm was a diligent and conscientious supervisor, whose students invariably completed their theses, frequently leading to publication, and, in some cases, to academic posts. With his expertise in the field, he was successful in attracting IRCHSS funding for two projects, one on Irish confraternities to 1700, followed by another examining religion and social identity in Ireland at parish level in the period 1775–1965, which provided employment for several post-doctoral fellows, and led to publication.

Within the department, Colm was always willing to take on any of the various administrative responsibilities. For many years he filled the role of examinations coordinator, and external examiners knew that they could rely on him to have everything in order when they came to deliver their verdicts on the scripts. He was a strong supporter of the undergraduate students' History Society, and frequently attended the annual conferences of the Irish History Students' Association. On several occasions he served as acting head of department. Outside the History Department, Colm helped to establish the BA in European Studies, and became its first director. He regularly attended Faculty meetings, and served as secretary to the Faculty of Arts. In addition, he frequently gave talks to the Dublin branch of the History Teachers' Association of Ireland. Colm continues to provide lectures and tours for students who come to Maynooth from SUNY Brockport for summer courses.

Given his strong interest in the religious history of the early modern period, in 1981 Colm joined Monsignor Corish in his work for the Diocesan Commission for Causes, comprised of a number of professional historians whose brief was to determine with all possible accuracy the facts of the life and death of seventeen individuals who, in 1988, would be officially recognized as martyrs by the Roman Congregation for the Causes of Saints. These seventeen 'Irish martyrs' were beatified by Pope John Paul II in St Peter's Square on 27 September 1992. Colm had special responsibility for establishing the biographical data for the martyrdom of Richard Creagh (1523–86) and his research on Creagh led to the publication of *An Irish prisoner of conscience of the Tudor era: Archbishop Richard Creagh of Armagh, 1523–86* by Four Courts Press in 2000.

Colm was also an active member for many years of the Irish Committee of Historical Sciences (the national branch of the Comité International des Sciences Historiques (CISH)), which represents the interests of historians in Ireland, north and south. He represented the committee at several international congresses of the CISH; he helped to organize the 23rd Irish Conference of Historians, held in Maynooth in 1997, and he was co editor of the papers delivered at the conference, which were published under the title *Luxury and austerity* by UCD Press in 1999.

All this was undertaken while Colm was continuing to publish regularly. He is also a painter of note: one of his paintings was presented to former NUIM President Tom Collins on the occasion of his leaving Maynooth.

We are delighted to be involved in this collective effort by Colm's former students, colleagues and friends, to celebrate what we all owe to this most gifted, generous and always approachable scholar.

The research and scholarly writings of Professor Colm Lennon

STEVEN G. ELLIS

Professor Colm Lennon's research and writing has established him as one of the most distinguished and prolific historians of early modern Ireland. In a long career extending to date over forty years, he has published seven monographs, five co-edited volumes, and a fine collection of insightful scholarly papers. A major focus of his research has been on the development of the Pale community around Dublin, its religion and identity, set within the context of the wider response in Ireland to the developments now known to historians as the Tudor conquest. To appreciate the extent of his achievement, however, it is important to draw attention to the changing expectations held of academic historians during the period from the 1970s onwards.

Lennon's appointment in 1978 to a university lectureship at what later became NUI Maynooth was, besides a recognition of his teaching experience, a reflection of the high regard in which the research for his Master's thesis was held. By then, parts of his dissertation, 'Conflict and change in Old English society: the testimony of Richard Stanihurst's life and works' (NUI, 1975), were already beginning to appear in published papers. This was well before the concept of 'research-led teaching' had entered the academic vocabulary and had been added to a lecturer's responsibilities. A lecturer's main responsibility was then still to the teaching of undergraduates. This was an era in which the occasional publication emanating from a lecturer's research and writing was more a cause for celebration than a recognition of his normal duties; and the stale and underdeveloped state of historical research and writing on sixteenth-century Ireland was quite apparent from a comparison of the Tudor and Stuart sections of volume 3 (1534–1691) of the unfortunately named *A new history of Ireland* (Oxford, 1976). The NUI was also among the last universities to retain the old concept of an extended Master's thesis which was akin to, and longer than, the present doctoral dissertation. Lennon's thesis thus provided the basis for some scholarly articles, of which 'Richard Stanihurst and Old English identity' in *Irish Historical Studies*, 21 (1978) was probably the most influential. In addition, the thesis was itself soon revised for publication as *Richard Stanihurst the Dubliner, 1547–1618* (Dublin, 1981). Essentially, this monograph addressed the response of the Old English elite to its gradual displacement by New English soldier-administrators, offering a case study of a major theme of the Tudor conquest to which Lennon was to return in many of his later writings.

By then, Lennon's pursuit of scholarship had driven him to embark on a doctorate, the research for which had mostly to be squeezed into long vacations and hasty visits to record offices in time stolen out of the teaching year. The project was eventually published in revised format as *The lords of Dublin in the age of Reformation* (Dublin, 1989). To some extent, *The lords of Dublin* broadened perspectives outlined in *Richard Stanihurst*, but essentially this was a pioneering and wholly convincing attempt to replace, in the case of Tudor Dublin, the traditional, largely antiquarian approach to towns and cities in Ireland which then obtained with the kind of urban history which had recently been written by academic historians in respect of towns and cities in Tudor England. A particular feature of Lennon's study was its use of a range of new types of sources: these offered some balance to the traditional heavy reliance on the state papers with their ex parte statements which to date had, unfortunately, formed the basis of too much historical writing on Tudor Ireland. A decade later, he published, with James Murray, a scholarly edition of just one of these sources, *The Dublin City Franchise Roll, 1468–1512* (Dublin, 1998), which elucidated a slightly earlier period of the city's history. More generally, this research led him to study such topics as the guild structure of Tudor Dublin and the (self) government of the city, topics which were further developed in later writings which broadened the approach both geographically and chronologically. Geographically, his research included some notable short studies of Limerick, including the 28th O'Donnell Lecture, delivered in 1999 (the first such lecture delivered at NUI Maynooth) and published as *The urban patriciates of early modern Ireland: a case-study of Limerick* (Dublin, 2000). Chronologically, this included, most notably, a recent volume in the Irish Historic Towns Atlas series on *Dublin, 1610–1756: the making of the early modern city* (Dublin, 2009) which looked at the city's development in more modern times to the mid-eighteenth century.

By the time *The lords of Dublin* was published in the late 1980s, the Revisionist Debate was raging; and it was in this highly charged atmosphere that Lennon wrote what became the standard survey of Ireland in the sixteenth century. *Sixteenth-century Ireland: the incomplete conquest* (Dublin, 1994; rev. ed., Dublin, 2005) in the New Gill History of Ireland series offered a fresh, even-handed, and much more wide-ranging survey than its predecessor in the Gill series, and it was also remarkably free of the rancour which characterized much of that debate. It is indeed a feature of Lennon's research and writing that he consistently avoids anything which smacks of controversy: his style is clear and non-judgmental, allowing the facts to speak for themselves. This is true also of his footnote citations, which reference facts rather than interpretations, and so sometimes cite without comment conflicting statements by historians with very different views on the progress of the

Tudor conquest. His own views are of course obliquely indicated in the text, if in no other way than by his choice of concepts and terminology: 'Anglo-Norman', 'Anglo-Irish', 'Old English' and 'old colonials' for the English of Ireland; 'Gaelic', 'Irish' and 'Scots' for the *Gaedhil*; 'nationwide' and 'national' as a collective. Yet no historian can hope to cover adequately all the various aspects of what for Tudor officials passed as Ireland's 'reduction to civility'. Lennon's survey displays an impressive command of the printed literature, with a focus on the towns, trade and urban culture. Another evident strength of his survey is its detailed, often quite vivid, picture of what Tudor reform actually meant at local level and how the various strategies translated into practice, notably in the volume's very imaginative four chapters which describe developments in each of Ireland's four provinces, *c.*1560–1600. For the chapter on Leinster, moreover, Lennon also makes use of research by his own students.

Sixteenth-century Ireland is also particularly impressive and sure-footed in its treatment of the religious changes of the sixteenth century. This has always been one of the strengths we have come to associate with Lennon's scholarship; but the volume also offers an early insight into the author's views (developed in his later writings) on other aspects of traditional Christianity as reshaped under the impact of Tudor reform. A particularly striking aspect of this later work was his pioneering studies of the late medieval chantries and religious guilds and confraternities. These survived the Tudors, in part by reason of the regime's surprising failure – as Lennon has shown – to enact an Irish equivalent of the English Chantries Act. They thus provided a vital element of continuity between pre-Reformation piety in English Ireland and Counter-Reformation Catholicism. More recently, Lennon's views on sixteenth-century religious life have been rounded out both with studies of the ministry and the lay community of the Church of Ireland and an edition and a commentary on aspects of the rich surviving records of Christ Church Cathedral, Dublin.

Concurrently, Lennon has continued his studies of the development of Catholic recusancy and the Counter-Reformation movement in Ireland which had long been a feature of his research and writing. These included some short studies of Catholic martyrs, of the emergence of Irish Catholic ideology, and of the origins of Catholic nationalism. The most important work in this genre, however, was a fine, insightful biography of *An Irish prisoner of conscience of the Tudor era: Archbishop Richard Creagh of Armagh, 1523–1586* (Dublin, 2000) whose example early in Elizabeth's reign did much to persuade the citizens of Limerick and Dublin in their Catholicism and to detach them from Protestant worship.

Colm Lennon's research and writing on early modern Ireland has always set high standards, but the increasing tempo of his scholarly output over the past fifteen years probably also reflects the increasing pressures at this time on university lecturers to publish. Certainly, in terms of scholarly articles and books Lennon's output more than doubled in the ten years from 2000 by comparison with the previous decade. The increasing globalization of the academic community has also fostered his growing international reputation. In line with the heightened expectations of a university lecturer in this field, this has also been registered in a stream of scholarly articles and chapters emanating from foreign presses. By the time he retired in 2010, around a quarter of his work was being published abroad, including occasional papers in French and Italian. It is not too much to say that our understanding of sixteenth-century Ireland has been transformed in the period of Colm Lennon's academic career by a veritable explosion of research and writing affecting almost all aspects of the subject. In large measure, the responsibility for shaping that transformation rests with Lennon himself.

Select list of the publications of Colm Lennon to 2015

COMPILED BY BERNADETTE CUNNINGHAM
& RAYMOND GILLESPIE

BOOKS / EDITIONS

1981
Richard Stanihurst the Dubliner, 1547–1618: a biography with a Stanihurst text on Ireland's past (Dublin: Irish Academic Press, 1981).

1989
The lords of Dublin in the age of reformation (Dublin: Irish Academic Press, 1989).

1990
edited with R.V. Comerford, Mary Cullen and Jacqueline R. Hill, *Religion, conflict and coexistence in Ireland: essays presented to Monsignor Patrick Corish* (Dublin: Gill & Macmillan, 1990).

1994
Sixteenth-century Ireland: the incomplete conquest. New Gill History of Ireland, 2 (Dublin: Gill & Macmillan, 1994).

1998
edited with Raymond Refaussé, *The registers of Christ Church Cathedral, Dublin.* A history of Christ Church, Dublin, documents, 4 (Dublin: Four Courts Press, 1998).

with James Murray, *The Dublin city franchise roll, 1468–1512* (Dublin: Dublin Corporation, 1998).

1999
The urban patriciates of early modern Ireland: a case-study of Limerick. O'Donnell Lecture series (Dublin: National University of Ireland, 1999).

edited with Jacqueline R. Hill, *Luxury and austerity: Historical Studies XXI. Papers read before the 23rd Irish Conference of Historians held at St Patrick's College, Maynooth, 16–18 May 1997.* Historical Studies Irish Conference of Historians, 21 (Dublin: University College Dublin Press, 1999).

2000
An Irish prisoner of conscience of the Tudor era: Archbishop Richard Creagh of Armagh, 1523–1586 (Dublin: Four Courts Press, 2000).

2008
Dublin. Part 2, 1610–1756. Irish Historic Towns Atlas, 19 (Dublin: Royal Irish Academy in association with Dublin City Council, 2008).

2010
Dublin's civic buildings in the early modern period: the Sir John T. Gilbert commemorative lecture, 2009 (Dublin: Dublin City Public Libraries, 2010).

with John Montague, *John Rocque's Dublin: a guide to the Georgian city* (Dublin: Royal Irish Academy, 2010).

2012
Editor, *Confraternities and sodalities in Ireland: charity, devotion and sociability* (Dublin: Columba Press, 2012).

2014
That field of glory: the story of Clontarf from battleground to garden suburb (Dublin: Wordwell, 2014)

2015
Calendar of state papers Ireland: Tudor period, 1547–1553 (Dublin: Irish Manuscripts Commission, 2015)

ARTICLES, BOOK CHAPTERS AND DICTIONARY ENTRIES

1975
'Recusancy and the Dublin Stanyhursts', *Archivium Hibernicum*, 33 (1975) 101–10.

1978
'Richard Stanihurst (1547–1618) and Old English identity', *Irish Historical Studies*, 21:82 (1978), 121–43.

1979
'Reform ideas and cultural resources in the inner Pale in the mid-sixteenth century', *Stair: Journal of the History Teachers' Association of Ireland*, 2 (1979), 3–9.

1983
'Civic life and religion in early seventeenth-century Dublin', *Archivium Hibernicum*, 38 (1983), 14–25.

1986
'The Counter-Reformation in Ireland 1542–1641' in Ciarán Brady and Raymond Gillespie (eds), *Natives and newcomers: essays on the making of Irish colonial society, 1534–1641* (Dublin: Irish Academic Press, 1986), pp 75–92, 221–4.

1987
'Civic privilege and state power in Dublin, 1534–1613', *Rostrum* (1987), 107–14.

1988
'The great explosion in Dublin, 1597', *Dublin Historical Record*, 42:1 (1988), 7–20.

'"The beauty and eye of Ireland": the sixteenth century' in Art Cosgrove (ed.), *Dublin through the ages* (Dublin: College Press, 1988), pp 46–62.

1989
'The rise of recusancy among the Dublin patricians, 1580–1613' in W.J. Sheils and Diana Wood (eds), *The churches, Ireland and the Irish: papers read at the 1987 Summer Meeting and the 1988 Winter Meeting of the Ecclesiastical History Society.* Studies in Church History, 25 (Oxford and New York: Blackwell Publishers, 1989), 123–32.

1990
'The chantries in the Irish Reformation; the case of St Anne's Guild, Dublin, 1550–1630' in R.V. Comerford, Mary Cullen, Jacqueline R. Hill and Colm Lennon (eds), *Religion, conflict and coexistence in Ireland: essays presented to Monsignor Patrick Corish* (Dublin: Gill & Macmillan, 1990), pp 6–25; 293–7.

1991
'The sixteenth century' in Réamonn Ó Muirí (ed.), *Irish church history today* (Armagh: Cumann Seanchais Árd Mhacha [1991]), pp 27–41.

1992
'"The bowels of the city's bounty": the municipality of Dublin and the foundation of Trinity College in 1592', *Long Room*, 37 (1992), 10–16.

1994
'The foundation charter of St Sythe's guild, Dublin, 1476', *Archivium Hibernicum*, 48 (1994), 3–12.

1995
'Dublin's great explosion of 1597', *History Ireland*, 3:3 (1995), 29–34.

'The survival of the Confraternities in Post-Reformation Dublin', *Confraternitas*, 6:1 (1995), 5–12.

1996
'Edmund Campion's Histories of Ireland and reform in Tudor Ireland' in Thomas M. McCoog (ed.), *The reckoned expense: Edmund Campion and the early English Jesuits: essays in celebration of the first centenary of Campion Hall, Oxford (1896–1996)* (Woodbridge and Rochester (NY): Boydell, 1996), pp 67–84 (2nd ed., Rome: Institutum Historicum Societatis Iesu, 2007), pp 75–96.

1997
'Primate Richard Creagh and the beginnings of the Irish Counter-Reformation', *Archivium Hibernicum*, 51 (1997), 74–86.

with Raymond Gillespie, 'Reformation to restoration' in Seán Duffy (ed.), *Atlas of Irish history* (Dublin: Gill & Macmillan, 1997), pp 50–69; (2nd ed., Dublin: Gill & Macmillan, 2000), pp 50–69.

1999
'Dives and Lazarus in sixteenth-century Ireland' in Jacqueline R. Hill and Colm Lennon (eds), *Luxury and austerity*. Historical Studies XXI (Dublin: University College Dublin Press, 1999), pp 46–65.

'Political thought of Irish Counter-Reformation churchmen: the testimony of the "Analecta" of Bishop David Rothe' in Hiram Morgan (ed.), *Political ideology in Ireland, 1541–1641* (Dublin: Four Courts Press, 1999), pp 181–202.

2000
'"A dangerous man to be among the Irish": Archbishop Richard Creagh and the early Irish Counter-Reformation', *History Ireland*, 8:3 (2000), 27–31.

'The beatified martyrs of Ireland (8): Francis Taylor', *Irish Theological Quarterly*, 65:4 (2000), 353–62.

'Mass in the manor house: the Counter-Reformation in Dublin, 1560–1630' in James Kelly and Dáire Keogh (eds), *History of the Catholic diocese of Dublin* (Dublin: Four Courts Press, 2000), pp 112–26.

2001
'The changing face of Dublin, 1550–1750' in Peter Clark and Raymond Gillespie (eds), *Two capitals: London and Dublin, 1500–1840*. Proceedings of

the British Academy, 107 (Oxford and London: Oxford University Press for the British Academy, 2001), pp 39–52.

'Irish Confraternities, 1400–1700', *Confraternitas*, 12:2 (2001), 36–9.

'The Nugent family and the diocese of Kilmore in the sixteenth and early seventeenth centuries', *Breifne: Journal of Cumann Seanchais Bhréifne*, 9:37 (2001), 360–74.

'Le guerre di religione in Irlanda: colonizzazioni protestanti e martiri della Chiesa cattolica' in Luciano Vaccaro and Carlo Maria Pellizzi (eds), *Storia dell'Irlanda* (Milan: Centro Ambrosiano, 2001), pp 195–212.

2002
'Religious wars in Ireland: plantations and martyrs of the Catholic church' in Brendan Bradshaw and Dáire Keogh (eds), *Christianity in Ireland: revisiting the story* (Dublin: Columba Press, 2002), pp 86–95.

'Richard Stanihurst's "Spanish Catholicism": ideology and diplomacy' in Enrique García Hernán (ed.), *Irlanda y la monarquía hispánica: Kinsale 1601–2001 – guerra, política, exilio y religión* (Madrid: Consejo Superior de Investigaciones Científicas, 2002), pp 75–88.

'The shaping of a lay community in the Church of Ireland, 1558–1640' in Raymond Gillespie and W.G. Neely (eds), *The laity and the Church of Ireland, 1000–2000: all sorts and conditions* (Dublin: Four Courts Press, 2002), pp 49–69.

2003
'Taking sides: the emergence of Irish Catholic ideology' in Vincent Carey and Ute Lotz-Heumann (eds), *Taking sides?: colonial and confessional mentalités in early modern Ireland: essays in honour of Karl S. Bottigheimer* (Dublin: Four Courts Press, 2003), pp 78–93.

'Richard Stanihurst (1547–1618)' in Edward A. Malone (ed.), *Dictionary of literary biography: vol. 281: British rhetoricians and logicians, 1500–1660* (Farmington Hills, ML, 2003), pp 296–303.

2004
'Bagenal [Bagnal], Sir Nicholas (d. 1590/91), soldier'
'Burke, Richard, fourth earl of Clanricarde and first earl of St Albans (1572–1635), politician'
'Cosby, Francis (d. 1580), soldier and planter in Ireland'
'Creagh [Crevagh], Richard (c.1523–1586?), Roman Catholic archbishop of Armagh'
'Eustace, James, third Viscount Baltinglass (1530–85), nobleman and rebel'

'Gilbert, Sir John Thomas (1829–1898), historian and antiquary' [*revision*]
'Graham, John (1776–1844), historian' [*revision*]
'Hartry, Malachy [formerly John] (b. 1580? d. in or after 1651), historian'
'Molyneux, Thomas (1531–97), administrator'
'Moore, Sir Edward (*c*.1530–1602), administrator'
'Netterville, Nicholas, first Viscount Netterville of Dowth (1581–1654), politician'
'Nugent, Christopher, fifth Baron Delvin (1544–1602), nobleman'
'Nugent, Nicholas (d. 1582), judge'
'Rothe, David (*c*.1573–1650), Roman Catholic bishop of Ossory'
'St Lawrence, Christopher, seventh Baron Howth (d. 1589), nobleman'
'St Lawrence, Christopher, ninth Baron Howth (d. 1619), soldier and informer'
'Stanihurst [Stanyhurst], Richard (1547–1618), literary scholar and translator'
'Ussher, Henry (*c*.1550–1613), Church of Ireland archbishop of Armagh'
'White, Peter (fl. 1551–*c*.1570), Church of Ireland dean of Waterford'
'White, Stephen (b. *c*.1574, d. in or after 1646), scholar and theologian'
in Colin Mathew (ed.), *Oxford dictionary of national biography* (60 vols, Oxford: Oxford University Press, 2004).

2005
'Francis Taylor' in Patrick J. Corish (ed.), *The Irish martyrs* (Dublin: Four Courts Press, 2005), pp 138–47.

2006
'Bishops in contention: secular and ecclesiastical politics in later sixteenth-century Clogher', *Clogher Record: Journal of the Clogher Historical Society*, 20:1 (2006), 1–12.

'The Book of Obits of Christ Church Cathedral, Dublin' in Raymond Gillespie and Raymond Refaussé (eds), *The medieval manuscripts of Christ Church Cathedral, Dublin* (Dublin: Four Courts Press, 2006), pp 163–82.

'The confraternities and cultural duality in Ireland, 1450–1550' in Christopher F. Black and Pamela Gravestock (eds), *Early modern confraternities in Europe and the Americas: international and interdisciplinary perspectives* (Aldershot; Burlington, VT: Ashgate, 2006), pp 35–52.

'The dawn of the Reformation in Ireland' in J.R. Bartlett and Stuart Kinsella (eds), *Two thousand years of Christianity and Ireland: lectures delivered in Christ Church Cathedral Dublin, 2001–2002* (Dublin: Columba Press, 2006), pp 105–18.

'Recusancy and Counter-Reformation' in J.R. Bartlett and Stuart Kinsella (eds), *Two thousand years of Christianity and Ireland: lectures delivered in Christ Church Cathedral Dublin, 2001–2002* (Dublin: Columba Press, 2006), pp 119–32.

'The FitzGeralds of Kildare and the building of a dynastic image, 1500–1630' in William Nolan and Thomas McGrath (eds), *Kildare: history and society. Interdisciplinary essays on the history of an Irish county* (Dublin: Geography Publications, 2006), pp 195–212.

'Fraternity and community in early modern Dublin' in Robert Armstrong and Tadhg Ó hAnnracháin (eds), *Community in early modern Ireland* (Dublin: Four Courts Press, 2006), pp 167–78.

with Ciaran Diamond, 'The ministry of the Church of Ireland, 1536–1636' in T.C. Barnard and W.G. Neely (eds), *The clergy of the Church of Ireland, 1000–2000: messengers, watchmen and stewards* (Dublin: Four Courts Press, 2006), pp 44–58.

'The print trade, 1550–1700' in Raymond Gillespie and Andrew Hadfield (eds), *The Irish book in English, 1550–1800*. The Oxford History of the Irish Book, 3 (Oxford: Oxford University Press, 2006), pp 61–73.

'The print trade, 1700–1800' in Raymond Gillespie and Andrew Hadfield (eds), *The Irish book in English, 1550–1800*. The Oxford History of the Irish Book, 3 (Oxford: Oxford University Press, 2006), pp 74–87.

2007
'Pedagogy and reform: the influence of Peter White on Irish scholarship in the Renaissance' in Thomas Herron and Michael Potterton (eds), *Ireland in the Renaissance, c.1540–1660* (Dublin: Four Courts Press, 2007), pp 43–51.

2008
'Ossory and the Reformation: the testimony of Carrigan's *History and antiquities*', *Ossory, Laois and Leinster*, 3 (2008), 73–86.

'The parish fraternities and County Meath in the late Middle Ages', *Ríocht na Mídhe*, 19 (2008), 85–101.

Principal investigator. Website: 'Religious and social identities in Ireland: the role of parish confraternities and associations, 1775–1965' (Maynooth: National University of Ireland Maynooth. Department of History) (2008–). See http://archive-ie.com/page/174563/2012-07-21/http://www.irishconfraternities.ie/.

2009
'The dissolution to the foundation of St Anthony's College, Louvain, 1534–1607' in Edel Bhreathnach, Joseph MacMahon and John McCafferty (eds), *The Irish Franciscans, 1534–1990* (Dublin: Four Courts Press, 2009), pp 3–26.

'From Speed to Rocque: the development of early modern Dublin', *Dublin Historical Record*, 62:1 (2009), 2–15.

'The medieval town in the early modern city: attitudes to Dublin's immediate past in the seventeenth and eighteenth centuries' in John Bradley, Alan J. Fletcher and Anngret Simms (eds), *Dublin in the medieval world: studies in honour of Howard B. Clarke* (Dublin: Four Courts Press, 2009), pp 435–47.

'Peter White – a Renaissance schoolmaster in Kilkenny' in John Bradley and Michael O'Dwyer (eds), *Kilkenny through the centuries: chapters in the history of an Irish city* (Kilkenny: Kilkenny Borough Council, 2009), pp 130–9.

'Religious and social change in early modern Limerick: the testimony of the Sexton family papers' in Liam Irwin and Gearóid Ó Tuathaigh (eds), *Limerick: history and society. Interdisciplinary essays on the history of an Irish county* (Dublin: Geography Publications, 2009), pp 113–28.

'The Richard Stanihurst–Justus Lipsius friendship: scholarship and religion under Spanish Habsburg patronage in the late sixteenth century' in Jason Harris and Keith Sidwell (eds), *Making Ireland Roman: Irish neo-Latin writers and the Republic of Letters* (Cork: Cork University Press, 2009), pp 48–58.

'Creagh, Richard (*c*.1523–*c*.1588), Catholic archbishop of Armagh'
'Stanihurst, Richard (1547–1618), scholar and diplomat'
in James McGuire and James Quinn (eds), *Dictionary of Irish biography* (9 vols, Cambridge: Cambridge University Press, 2009).

2010
'The flight of the earls in British-Spanish diplomacy' in Thomas O'Connor and Mary Ann Lyons (eds), *The Ulster earls and baroque Europe: refashioning Irish identities, 1600–1800* (Dublin: Four Courts Press, 2010), pp 77–87.

2011
'Bridging division or bonding faction? Civic confraternity and religious sodality in seventeenth-century Ireland' in Stafania Pastore, Adriano Prosperi and Nicholas Terpstra (eds), *Brotherhood and boundaries: fraternità e barriere* (Pisa: Edizioni della Normale, 2011), pp 509–18.

'The political context at home and abroad for Ó Cianáin's work' in Fearghus Ó Fearghail (ed.), *Tadhg Ó Cianáin: an Irish scholar in Rome* (Dublin: Mater Dei Institute of Education, 2011), pp 34–47.

'Francisco de Borja and the Irish mission of the Society of Jesus' in Enrique García Hernán and María del Pilar Ryan (eds), *Francisco de Borja y su tiempo: política, religion y cultura en la edad moderna* (Valencia: Albatros, 2011), pp 457–64.

2012

'Confraternities in Ireland: a long view' in Colm Lennon (ed.), *Confraternities and sodalities in Ireland: charity, devotion and sociability* (Dublin: Columba Press, 2012), pp 15–34.

with Robin Kavanagh, 'The flowering of the confraternities and sodalities in Ireland, c.1860–c.1960' in Colm Lennon (ed.), *Confraternities and sodalities in Ireland: charity, devotion and sociability* (Dublin: Columba Press, 2012), pp 76–96.

'The medieval manor of Clontarf, 1171–1540' in Seán Duffy (ed.), *Medieval Dublin XII: proceedings of the Friends of Medieval Dublin Symposium 2010* (Dublin: Four Courts Press, 2012), pp 189–206.

'The fraternity of St Anne in St Audoen's parish, Dublin' in Salvador Ryan and Brendan Leahy (eds), *Treasures of Irish Christianity [volume I]: people and places, images and texts* (Dublin: Veritas, 2012), pp 116–18.

2013

'Ireland in the Renaissance: recent work and new directions', *Renaissance Quarterly*, 66 (2013), 568–80.

'Ireland' in Paulina Kewes, Ian W. Archer and Felicity Heal (eds), *The Oxford Handbook of Holinshed's Chronicles* (Oxford: Oxford University Press, 2013), pp 663–78.

'Maurice O'Fihely and the coming of the printed word' in Salvador Ryan and Brendan Leahy (eds), *Treasures of Irish Christianity, volume II: a people of the word* (Dublin: Veritas, 2013), pp 98–100.

'Mayor Francis Taylor (1595–6), the martyred mayor' in Ruth McManus and Lisa-Marie Griffith (eds), *Leaders of the city: Dublin's first citizens, 1500–1950* (Four Courts Press: Dublin, 2013), pp 35–43.

'Trades and services' in H.B. Clarke and Sarah Gearty (eds), *Maps & texts: exploring the Irish Historic Towns Atlas* (Dublin: Royal Irish Academy, 2013), pp 183–96.

2014

'The man of law's tale' in Sparky Booker and Cherie Peters (eds), *Tales of medieval Dublin* (Dublin: Four Courts Press, 2014), pp 149–60.

'The making of the Geraldines: the Kildare FitzGeralds and their early historians' in Patrick Cosgrove, Terence Dooley and Karol Mullaney Dignam (eds), *Aspects of Irish aristocratic life: essays on the FitzGeralds and Carton House* (Dublin: University College Dublin Press, 2014), pp 71–8.

'The battle of Clontarf, 1014: a millennium of historical perspectives', *Dublin Historical Record*, 67 (2014), 26–38.

'The battle of Clontarf in the classroom: a millennium perspective', *Stair: Journal of the History Teachers' Association of Ireland* (2014), 11–15.

2015
'L'état, les lois pénales et exilés religieux: Irlande, xvie-xviie siècles' in Isabelle Poutrin and Alain Tallon (eds), *Les expulsions de minorités religieuses dans l'Europe des XIIIe-XVIIe siècles* (Paris, 2015), pp 117–28.

The religious guild of St George Martyr, Dublin

MARY ESTHER CLARK & GAEL CHENARD

Religious guilds played an important part in the social fabric of Dublin city and county during the later Middle Ages. These were organisations consisting of lay men and women which were established by royal charters during the fourteenth and fifteenth centuries to foster the spiritual welfare of their members. Religious guilds were generally organized on the model of trade and craft guilds and were usually governed by a master and two wardens elected by the members.[1] Dublin had at least eleven religious guilds, seven in the city and four in the county. The primary function of the religious guild was to maintain a chantry of one or more priests to sing or chant Mass for deceased guild members and to support the fabric of the chapel housing these devotions.

The religious guild provided an opportunity for ordinary citizens to come together by supporting their own chantry and chapel. To finance this very expensive undertaking, guilds were allowed under their charters to acquire lands for investment purposes, and this landbank was supplemented by endowments and bequests from guild members. The relative importance of Dublin's religious guilds may be assessed by a comparison of the value of lands which they were permitted to obtain. St George Martyr, created in 1426 as the guild of the municipal authority, the Dublin City Assembly, held lands worth £100 yearly; St Anne's guild, established in 1430, held lands worth £66 yearly; the lands of Corpus Christi (created 1444) and of St Sythe (created 1476) were each worth £40 yearly; while the lands of St Mary's chantry in the church of St Nicholas Within (created 1470) were worth £13 6s. 8d.

In the late sixteenth century, the religious guilds of Dublin acquired increased importance as strongholds of the Counter-Reformation. In England, religious guilds were abolished under the Chantries Act of 1547, and the first Reformation archbishop of Dublin, George Browne, suggested that religious guilds should also be suppressed in Ireland and that their revenues should be

---

Mary Esther Clark is the Dublin City Archivist and has researched and written this introductory essay which expands on her work on the guild in M. Clark and R. Refaussé, *Directory of historic Dublin guilds* (Dublin, 1993); Gael Chenard is the Directeur des Archives Departmentales des Hautes-Alpes. He prepared these transcripts of the Guild of St George documents during an internship at Dublin City Archives in 2006.
1 Colm Lennon, 'The chantries in the Irish Reformation: the case of St Anne's guild, Dublin, 1550–1630' in R.V. Comerford et al. (eds), *Religion, conflict and coexistence in Ireland* (Dublin, 1990), pp 6–25.

seized to maintain schools. These proposals were never implemented, and many of Dublin's religious guilds survived as bulwarks of the Roman Catholic community, protected by their charters and their investments, while paradoxically continuing to maintain their chantry chapels within the parish churches of the Church of Ireland. St George's Chapel was built in the late twelfth century to the east of Dublin, outside the city walls. This vulnerable location may have been chosen because it was near the site of a holy well, and in consequence the road where the chapel stood was called St George's Lane (now called South Great George's Street).[2] The chapel stood on the west side of the lane, while the holy well was opposite on its east side. St George's Chapel was rebuilt in 1213, and during the episcopate of Henry de Loundres, archbishop of Dublin (1213–1228) it was given to All Hallows' priory in exchange for St Paul's Church.[3]

According to the historian Richard Stanihurst, writing in 1577, 'in old time ... the better part of the suburbs of Dublin should seem to have stretched' along St George's Lane – therefore the chapel must originally have served a growing population.[4] This eastern suburb of Dublin was under constant attack by Irish clans from the Wicklow Mountains and eventually the inhabitants abandoned their houses 'and embaied themselves within the citie walls'.[5] In 1423 the lands of All Hallows' priory were seized and laid waste and it would appear that St George's Chapel was either damaged or – more likely – completely destroyed during this raid. Permission to reconstruct the chapel was secured in February 1426, when Henry VI issued letters patent to the mayor of Dublin, Sir Walter Terrell, and to other Dublin citizens, allowing them to build a chapel to the honour of the Virgin Mary and St George the Martyr within the city franchises.[6] Four months later, on 27 June 1426, the king issued letters patent granting permission for the creation of a fraternity or guild in Dublin in honour of St George Martyr, to be based in the chapel with one or more priests to celebrate divine services every day forever.[7] The guild was almost certainly instituted as a means of financing the rebuilding and subsequent maintenance of the chapel, which was still owned by All Hallows' priory. The chapel must have been rebuilt by June 1433,

---

2 In 1617, the Dublin City Assembly ordered the inhabitants of St George's Lane to pay for the repair of an 'auncient well' which had been stopped up – a fate which was visited on many holy wells at the time of the Reformation. *CARD*, 3, p. 80. An authority on the underground rivers and wells of Dublin has noted that a well is still in existence underneath the gates of the present South City Markets in South Great George's Street. See Clair L. Sweeney, *The rivers of Dublin* (Dublin, 1991), p. 108.   3 Myles V. Ronan, 'Religious customs of Dublin medieval guilds', *Irish Ecclesiastical Record*, 5th series, 26 (1925), 375.   4 From Stanihurst's 'Description of Dublin, 1577', reprinted in *CARD*, 1, pp 548–9.   5 Stanihurst, 'Description of Dublin', p. 549.   6 Dublin City Archives, C1/02/04 Recorder's Book, pp 462–4, entry no. 177.   7 Dublin City Archives, RG/01/01 Guild of St George Martyr, document no. 1.

when Thomas Lawless was appointed as guild chaplain for life at a yearly stipend of six marks.[8]

St George Martyr became the religious guild of the Dublin City Assembly with the outgoing mayor and bailiffs of Dublin acting as the guild master and wardens for a period of one year. Women were also permitted to become members of St George Martyr, since the foundation document of the guild refers to 'fratres et sorores'.[9] No further information is available, but it is probable that the wives of members of the City Assembly made up the female members of the guild. The guild was also permitted to acquire lands to the value of £100 and it derived an income from issuing leases of its property. Other sources of income were also explored. In 1448, the City Assembly ruled that the guild could choose one good cow out of cattle taken in raids by the mayor, bailiffs and commons.[10] This idea was adopted by the Irish Parliament, which in 1457 gave St George's Chapel a grant of one cow in every forty out of cattle seized in raids against the Irish or else 5s. as an alternative payment.[11]

In the late fifteenth century, the guild of St George Martyr was drawn into politics and was assigned a military role in the defence of the Pale. The first Tudor king, Henry VII, regarded the guild as an old Lancastrian foundation, whose loyalty could be relied on in the face of residual claims to the throne from the Yorkist faction. This came to a head in 1493, when the monarch's authority in Ireland was threatened by external attack and internal collapse. The Pretender Perkin Warbeck, who claimed to be Richard, duke of York (one of the 'Princes in the Tower'), was poised to invade Ireland from Flanders; and within the Pale, the power of Gerald FitzGerald, eighth earl of Kildare, rivalled that of the crown. In September 1493 the lord deputy Walter FitzSimon, archbishop of Dublin, secured the support of St George Martyr by granting the guild an annuity of eight marks of silver. It was specified that 40s. from this grant was to be spent by the guild on the purchase of bows and arrows to be distributed among the commons of Dublin for expeditions and hostings against Irish and English rebels. Nor was this an empty threat – the mayor and commons of Dublin formed part of an army raised within the Pale that inflicted a decisive defeat on Clanricard and O'Brien at the Battle of Knockdoe, Co. Galway in 1504. In an attempt to forge links between the diocese of Dublin and the guild, five marks from the grant were assigned to the four minor canons in St Patrick's Cathedral,

---

8 Dublin City Archives, RG/01/02 Guild of St George Martyr, document no. 2.   9 Dublin City Archives, RG/01/02 Guild of St George Martyr, document no. 2. Colm Lennon has noted that women wielded remarkable economic power in late fifteenth century Dublin and just under one-fifth of the free citizens admitted between 1468 and 1512 were female. Colm Lennon and James Murray (eds), *The Dublin City Franchise Roll, 1468–1512* (Dublin, 1998), p. xxiii.   10 *CARD*, 1, p. 272.   11 Ronan, 'Religious guilds', p. 375.

Dublin, on condition that they celebrated divine service on Sundays in St George's Chapel.[12]

By the early sixteenth century, the threat to the Pale had been repulsed and the guild of St George Martyr could return to peaceful pursuits. In 1506 its annuity of eight marks was converted into a yearly grant, issued without conditions. From this grant, the guild reserved four marks as a stipend for 'an honest chapleyn to say Masse and other divine service in [St George's] chapel on Sundays and feast-days and every Wednesday, Friday and Saturday'.[13] A member of All Hallows' priory performed this function until the monastery was suppressed in 1538.

In addition to its religious and military functions, the guild was responsible for the annual pageant held on St George's day, 23 April. The earliest reference to this pageant occurs in 1466, when it is mentioned as an existing entity and it may well have been instituted to mark the restoration of the chapel in 1433. A similar pageant was organized in Norwich by its local guild of St George and this may have inspired the Dublin pageant. The theme was the story of St George and the dragon, with the mayor of Dublin, his immediate predecessor and the two city bailiffs selecting players for the principal roles, while the guild of St George paid the players' wages. The pageant concluded at St George's Chapel, which was decorated with damasks on the walls, cushions on the church benches and rushes on the floor.[14] The dragon made a second appearance later in the year in the Corpus Christi pageant, when it was carried by the haggardmen and husbandmen – they were also charged with repairing it as necessary.[15] A husbandman was someone who tilled and cultivated the soil, usually a freeholder – a peasant who owned his own land. A haggardman was someone who stored the produce of harvest in a haggard or stackyard. It is of interest to note the involvement of these rural workers in what were essentially urban pageants, designed to celebrate the Dublin City Assembly and the Dublin craft guilds.

St George's day also saw the annual muster of the military guild or brotherhood of St George, a parallel but separate organization. In 1473, two royal commissioners, Sir Gilbert Debenham and James Norris, were sent to Ireland by Edward IV to inspect and evaluate the current arrangements for the defence of the Pale.[16] Arising from this inspection, the Brotherhood of Arms of St George was established by the Irish Parliament on 18 March 1474 to act as an auxiliary army. This military guild consisted of thirteen magnates from the Pale, presided over by the lord deputy. The brotherhood met in Dublin each year on 23 April to elect its captain who was provided with a retinue of

12 *CARD*, 1, pp 141–2.   13 Dublin City Archives, C1/02/04 Recorder's Book, p. 300, entry no. 137.   14 *CARD*, 1, p. 324. For a full description of the pageant, see Alan J. Fletcher, *Drama, performance and polity in Pre-Cromwellian Ireland* (Cork, 2000), pp 138–41, 154, 158–9, 177.   15 *CARD*, 1, pp 239–41.   16 Steven G. Ellis, *Tudor Ireland* (London, 1985), p. 58.

120 mounted archers, forty men-at-arms and forty pages. It was financed by revenues raised from poundage but in practice the cost of maintaining the military guild far exceeded the moneys raised and both guild and tax were suspended in 1476. The brotherhood was restored by order of Edward IV in 1479, but its size was restricted to the numbers which could be supported by poundage. It survived in this truncated form until 1494, when it was finally abolished by Henry VII.

Under the Reformation of Henry VIII the priory of All Hallows was suppressed in 1538 and its property and lands were granted to the municipal authority, Dublin Corporation, in the following year.[17] St George's Chapel thus came into the city's possession since until then it had been the property of the priory even though it was maintained by the guild. The chapel was then over a hundred years old and it was in need of repair. At Christmas 1552, the City Assembly granted a lease of its churchyard to Patrick Uriell, on condition that he maintain the chapel and its little tower 'stiff and staunch' and that he re-slate and lathe the chapel roof.[18] These emergency measures were not sufficient and two years later, in 1554, the City Assembly asked Robert Cusack to re-build the chapel, apparently with stones taken from All Hallows' priory.[19] Instead, Cusack removed stones and timber from St George's Chapel and used them to build a bread oven, thus converting, as the historian Richard Stanihurst remarked, 'the ancient monument of a doutie, adventurous and holie knight [St George] to the colerake sweepings of a pufloafe baker'.[20] At the next meeting of the City Assembly, several of the aldermen interceded for Cusack, pointing out how useful the oven was. Cusack was not only pardoned but was also expressly relieved of any obligation to rebuild the chapel.[21]

In 1565, Richard Core was granted a lease of St George's churchyard for fifty-one years. Although the chapel was in ruins, parts of it were still standing, and Core was forbidden to diminish the walls or to remove the stones lying within the churchyard. It was also agreed that if the chapel were to be rebuilt, then the lease would become void and the churchyard would revert to its original use.[22] Here, the City Assembly was clearly reserving its position in case the Reformation should be reversed. However, the excommunication of Elizabeth I by Pope Pius V in 1570 sharpened religious divisions, and the City Assembly then adopted a more ruthless attitude towards St George's, allowing one of the chapel bells to be built into a clock over the

---

[17] Dublin City Archives, Royal Charter No. 73: 30 Henry VIII, dated 27 Nov. 1538, is an inspeximus of the voluntary surrender of the priory and lands of All Hallows by Prior Walter Handcocke to Henry III. Royal Charter No. 74, dated 4 Feb. 1538/9, is the grant of the house and lands of All Hallows to the mayor, bailiffs, commons and citizens of Dublin in recognition of their defence of the city against attacks by [Silken] Thomas FitzGerald.   [18] *CARD*, 1, p. 324.   [19] *CARD*, 1, p. 431.   [20] From Stanihurst, 'Description of Dublin', p. 549.   [21] *CARD*, 1, p. 447.   [22] *CARD*, 2, pp 36–7.

Bridge Gate in the city walls.[23] This decision sealed the fate of the chapel, which was never rebuilt. It had almost certainly been demolished by 1607, when Nicholas Stephens was granted a lease of 'a void garden in Saint George's Lane, called Saint George's Church yarde'.[24] The former churchyard was subsequently leased to Thomas Browne in 1670.[25]

St George's pageant, with its superstitious content, seems to have been suspended during the reign of Edward VI and was not revived during the tenure of his Catholic half-sister Mary Tudor. In 1558, the year of Elizabeth's accession to the throne, the dragon's harness was discovered in Tailors' Hall, along with red and white flags carried by footmen and two standards borne by horsemen during the pageant.[26] This find led to a brief revival of the pageant, and early in 1559 the City Assembly ordered that the dragon was to be repaired and maintained on a regular basis.[27] The last recorded performance of the pageant was in 1567 and the hardening of religious attitudes after 1570 may have led to its demise.

While the chapel and the pageant were both suppressed, the guild of St George Martyr continued, although after 1570 it was reduced largely to acting as a vehicle for issuing leases of its own property. In 1577, the City Assembly reaffirmed the tradition that the outgoing mayor and sheriffs (formerly bailiffs) of Dublin should be master and wardens of the guild for the following year.[28] Under James I, an official attitude of hostility was adopted towards all elements of the Roman Catholic faith and within weeks of the king's accession in March 1603, the City Assembly moved to abolish the guild of St George Martyr. The mayor and constables of the Dublin Staple took over the functions of master and wardens of the guild, a legal nicety that enabled leases of the guild property to be issued.[29] From then on, the guild's property was treated as part of the city's possessions, but the revenues raised by leases were itemized separately in the city treasurer's accounts.

Effectively, St George was the patron saint of Dublin for 177 years, from 1426 until 1603. This is best illustrated by an illumination to a charter issued by Edward VI in 1548.[30] Here, the traditional emblem of the city, three watchtowers atop one of the city gates, defended by archers with crossbows, as engraved on the medieval Dublin city seal, has been subverted. The archers and crossbows have been replaced by flags of St George, illustrating the defensive role of his guild which for so long had helped to provide security and a sense of civic identity for Dublin.

23 *CARD*, 2, p. 69.   24 *CARD*, 2, pp 474, 497–8.   25 *CARD*, 4, pp 518–19; also Dublin City Archives, Expired Leases, no. 528.   26 *CARD*, 1, p. 476.   27 *CARD*, 2, pp 3–4.   28 *CARD*, 2, p. 119.   29 *CARD*, 2, p. 405.   30 Dublin City Archives, Royal Charter No. 79: 2 Edward VI, dated 21 Apr. 1548.

GUILD OF ST GEORGE MARTYR 1

RG1/01/01: Foundation charter of the Dublin Guild of St George, issued by Henry VI

Dublin, 27 June 1426

Formerly sealed on scrip of parchment, white wax

Henricus Dei gracia rex Anglie et Ffrancie et dominus Hibernie omnibus ad quos presentes littere pervenerint salutem. Sciatis quod de gracia nostra speciali, de assensu carissimi consanguinei nostri Jacobi le Botiller, comitis de Ormond, justiciarii nostri terre nostre Hibernie, et consilii nostri in eadem terra nostra, concessimus et licentiam dedimus pro nobis, heredibus et successoribus nostris quantum in nobis est, dilectis nobis Jacobo le Botiller, comiti de Ormond, Johanni domino Talbot et Ffurnyvall, Hugoni Banent, clerico, thesaurario nostro in Hibernia, Waltero Tirrell, militi, majori civitatis nostre Dublini, Johanni Blakenay, Reginaldo Suyterby, Willemo Tynbegh, Johanni Drake, Thome Cusak, Luco Dowedale, Roberto Gallan, Johanni Fil Hugonis Whits, Thome Shortales, Johanni Kilbery, Johanni Barret, Richardo Gustats, Ricardo Bone, Radulpho Pembroke, Johanni Coryngham, Roberto d'Irland, Johanni Elys, civibus civitatis nostre predicte, quod ipsi vel illi qui de ipsis supervixerint, ordinare possint quondam capellam ad laudem Dei et beate Marie virginis et honorem sancti Georgii martiris, in aliquo certo loco infra ffranchesiam aut libertatem civitatis nostre Dublini ubi melius et convenientius juxta discrecionem et ordinacionem eorumdem comitis, Johannis, Hugonis, Walteri, Johannis, Reginaldi, Willemi, Johanni, Thome, Luce, Roberti, Johannis, Thome, Johannis, Johannis, Richardi, Ricardi, Radulphi, Johannis, Roberti et Johannis vel alicujus eorumdem qui de ipsis supervixerint melius videbitur expedire. Et quod dicti comes, Johannes, Hugo, Walterus, Johannes, Reginaldus, Willemus, Johannes, Thomas, Lucas, Robertus, Johannes, Thomas, Johannes, Johannes, Richardus, Ricardus, Radulphus, Johannes, Robertus et Johannes aut illi qui de se ipsis supervixerint, ad laudem Dei ac beate Marie virginis et honorem dicti sancti Georgii, ut prefertur, quandam fraternitatem sive gildam successive et in successionem perpetuam de se ipsis ac aliis personis, tam hominibus quam mulieribus, in dicta capella sancti Georgii acceptare possint, et quod fratres fraternitatis aut gilde predicte sic incepte, inchoate, inite, facte, fundate, ordinate et stabilite, singulis annis duos magistros de se ipsis qui regimen, gubernacionem et supervisum fraternitatis sive gilde hujusmodi ac custodiam omnium terrarum, tenementorum, redditum, serviciorum, possessionum, bomorum et catallorum qui eidem fraternitati vel gilde exuunt adquiri, dari, concedi aut assignari vel ad eandem fraternitatem sive gildam pertineri contigit, habeant singulis annis plenam potestatem eligere, ordinare et successive constituere ac illos magistros de anno in annum et tempore in tempus cum opus et necesse fuerit de officiis predictis amonere et exonerare ac quosdam alios suis loco et nomine prout eis placuerit ponere, substituere et subrogare necnon fraternitatem vel gildam perpetuam inter se et de ipsis facere inchoare et inire, ac sigillum commune pro negociis et agendas ad eandem fraternitatis sive gildam exuunt spectantibus deserviturum, habere et exidere possint ac eciam quod magistri predicti et successores sui magistri ibidem qui pro tempore fuerint pro fraternitate vel gilda illa ac pro terries, tenementis, redditibus, serviciis, possessionibus, bonis et catallis ejusdam fraternitatis aut gilde in quibuscumque accionibus, causis, querelis, demandis et plitis tam realibus et personalibus quam mixtis cujuscumque generis fuerint vel nature, per nomen magistrorum fraternitatis sive gilde sancti Georgii Dublini coram judicibus secularibus et ecclesiasticis quibuscumque implicent et implicentur, respondeant et respondeantur ac implicare et implicari necnon respondere et responderi possint et debeant. Et quod idem comes, Johannes, Hugo, Walterus, Johannes, Reginaldus, Willemus, Johannes, Thomas, Lucas, Robertus, Johannes, Thomas, Johannes, Johannes, Richardus, Ricardus, Radulphus, Johannes, Robertus et Johannes ac singuli fratres fraternitatis vel gilde predicte et successores sui magistri et fratres ejusdem fraternitatis sive gilde convenient et convenire valeant locis temporibus congruis et oportunis quociens et quando eis melius placuerit ad tractandum, concordandum et communicandum inter se ipsos una cum aliis pro consilio et avisamento habendis pro statu et bono regimine dicte fraternitatis vel gilde ac fratrum et sororum ejusdem fraternitatis aut gilde et successorum suorum, ordinacionesque licitas et honestas ad laudem Dei ac beate Marie virginis et honorem dicti sancti Georgii, pro bona gubernacione dicte fraternitatis sive gilde, de anno in annum et tempore in tempus faciendas, et easdem ordinaciones similiter de tempore in tempus cum opus et necesse fuerit augmentare vel minuere secundum discrecionem ipsorum magistrorum et fratrum fraternitatis vel gilde predicte et successorum suorum magistrorum et fratrum dicte fraternitatis aut gilde imperpetuum. Ulterius, quod de uberiori gracia nostra speciali concessimus dictis comiti, Johanni, Hugoni, Waltero, Johanni, Reginaldo, Willemo, Johanni, Thome, Luco, Roberto, Johanni, Thome, Johanni, Johanni, Richardo, Ricardo, Radulpho, Johanni, Roberto, Johanni quod ipsi vel illi qui de ipsis supervixerint, ad laudem Dei ac beate Marie virginis et honorem predicti sancti Georgii facere, ordinare et stabilire possint juxta discrecionem ordinacionem et provisionem ipsorum comitis, Johannis, Hugonis, Walteri, Johannis, Reginaldi, Willemi, Johannis, Thome, Luce, Roberti, Johannis, Thome, Johannis, Johannis, Richardi, Ricardi, Radulphi, Johannis, Roberti et Johannis vel alicujus eorumdem qui de ipsis supervixerint quondam cantariam unius capellani vel plurimorum capellanorum divina singulis diebus in supradicta capella imperpetuum celebraturorum pro salubri statu nostro ac Jacobi le Botiller, comitis de Ormond, prefati justiciarii nostri, necnon Johanne, consortis ipsius comitis, et liberorum suorum, et predicti Johannis, domini Talbot et Furnyvall, necnon Margarete, consortis ipsius Johannis, et liberorum suorum, et predicti thesaurarii nostri ac majoris et concivium antedictorum ac fratrum et sororum fraternitatis sive gilde quamdiu vixerint, et pro animabus carissimi patris nostri ac nobelium progenitorum nostrorum, necnon omnium et singulorum superius expressatorum cum ab hac luce migraverint et fratrum et sororum dicte fraternitatis vel gilde ac eorum successorum (...) ac omnium fidelium defunctorum imperpetuum, et quod predicti magistri ac fratres et sorores fraternitatis aut gilde predicte qui pro tempore fuerint, predictos capellanum seu capellanos de anno in annum et tempore in tempus deponere possint et amonere, et alios idoneos (...) possint prout eis placuerit et quod dicti magistri ac fratres et sorores et eorum successores, magistri ac fratres et sorores ejusdem fraternitatis sive gilde convenire possint locis et temporibus oportunis quando eis melius placuerit ad tractandum et ordinandum pro can(...) ordinacionem in hac parte facienda. Et insuper concessimus et licenciam dedimus prefatis magistris, fratribus et sororibus dicte fraternitatis sive gilde et successoribus suis pro tempore existentibus cum dicta fraternitas vel gilda sit facta vel ordinata et stabilita, ut prefert, quod ipsi acquirere possint terras, tenementa, redditus, servicia et advocaciones ecclesiarum sive capellarum, tam in dominico et feodo quam in reversione, cum pertinenciis usque ad valorem centum librarum per annum ultra onera et reprisas, licet de nobis in capite seu de aliis tenentur habenda et tenenda sibi et successoribus suis magistris ac fratribus et sororibus ejusdem fraternitatis aut gilde imperpetuum de capitalibus dominis feodorum per servicia inde debita et de jure consueta, ad inveniendum, supportandum et sustenandum omnia dicte cantarie unius, capellani vel plurimorum cappelanorum divina in dicta cantaria, ut predictum est, celebraturorum ac alia opera pietatis pro statu et animabus antedictis facienda imperpetuum. Statuto de terris, tenementis ad manum mortuam non ponendum edito seu aliis statutis vel ordinacionibus quibuscumque, ante hec tempora in contrarium similiter dictis non obstentibus. Volentes quod predicti comes, Johannes, Hugo, Walterus, Johannes, Reginaldus, Willemus, Johannes, Thomas, Lucas, Robertus, Johannes, Thomas, Johannes, Johannes, Richardus, Ricardus, Radulphus, Johannes, Robertus et Johannes vel heredes sui seu magistri dicte fraternitatis sive gilde aut fratres et sorores ejusdem fraternitatis aut gilde vel eorum successores racione statutorum, ordinacionum aut aliorum premissorum per nos, heredes vel successores nostros, justiciarios, escaetores, vicecomites aut alios ballivos seu ministros nostros vel heredum nostrorum seu successorum nostrorum nuper regum Anglie aut alios quoscumque inde occasionentur, inquietentur, molestentur in aliquo seu graventur. In cujus rei testimonium has litteras nostras fieri fecimus patentes, teste prefato justiciario nostro, apud Dublinum vicesimo septimo die junii anno regni nostri quarto.

GUILD OF ST GEORGE MARTYR 2

R1/01/02: Appointment of Thomas Lawless as chaplain to the Guild of St George

Dublin, 27 June 1426

Formerly sealed on scrip of parchment, white wax

Henricus Dei gracia rex Anglie et Francie et dominus Hibernie omnibus ad quos presentes littere pervenerint salutem. Sciatis quod de gracia nostra speciali, de assensu carissimi consanguinei nostri Jacobi le Botiller, comitis de Ormond, justiciarii nostri terre nostre Hibernie, et consilii nostri in eadem terra nostra, concessimus et licentiam dedimus pro nobis, heredibus et successoribus nostris quantum in nobis est, dilectis nobis Jacobo le Botiller, comiti de Ormond, Johanni domino Talbot et Ffurnyvall, Hugoni Banent, clerico, thesaurario nostro in Hibernia, Waltero Tirrell, militi, majori civitatis nostre Dublini, Johanni Blakenay, Reginaldo Suyterby, Willemo Tynbegh, Johanni Drake, Thome Cusak, Luco Dowedale, Roberto Gallan, Johanni Fil Hugonis Whits, Thome Shortales, Johanni Kilbery, Johanni Barret, Richardo Gustats, Ricardo Bone, Radulpho Pembroke, Johanni Coryngham, Roberto d'Irland, Johanni Elys, civibus civitatis nostre predicte, quod ipsi vel illi qui de ipsis supervixerint, ordinare possint quondam capellam ad laudem Dei et beate Marie virginis et honorem sancti Georgii martiris, in aliquo certo loco infra ffranchesiam aut libertatem civitatis nostre Dublini ubi melius et convenientius juxta discrecionem et ordinacionem eorumdem comitis, Johannis, Hugonis, Walteri, Johannis, Reginaldi, Willemi, Johanni, Thome, Luce, Roberti, Johannis, Thome, Johannis, Johannis, Richardi, Ricardi, Radulphi, Johannis, Roberti et Johannis vel alicujus eorumdem qui de ipsis supervixerint melius videbitur expedire. Et quod dicti comes, Johannes, Hugo, Walterus, Johannes, Reginaldus, Willemus, Johannes, Thomas, Lucas, Robertus, Johannes, Thomas, Johannes, Johannes, Richardus, Ricardus, Radulphus, Johannes, Robertus et Johannes aut illi qui de se ipsis supervixerint, ad laudem Dei ac beate Marie virginis et honorem dicti sancti Georgii, ut prefertur, quandam fraternitatem sive gildam successive et in successionem perpetuam de se ipsis ac aliis personis, tam hominibus quam mulieribus, in dicta capella sancti Georgii acceptare possint, et quod fratres fraternitatis aut gilde predicte sic incepte, inchoate, inite, facte, fundate, ordinate et stabilite, singulis annis duos magistros de se ipsis qui regimen, gubernacionem et supervisum fraternitatis sive gilde hujusmodi ac custodiam omnium terrarum, tenementorum, redditum, serviciorum, possessionum, bomorum et catallorum qui eidem fraternitati vel gilde exuunt adquiri, dari, concedi aut assignari vel ad eandem fraternitatem sive gildam pertineri contigit, habeant singulis annis plenam potestatem eligere, ordinare et successive constituere ac illos magistros de anno in annum et tempore in tempus cum opus et necesse fuerit de officiis predictis amonere et exonerare ac quosdam alios suis loco et nomine prout eis placuerit ponere, substituere et subrogare necnon fraternitatem vel gildam perpetuam inter se et de ipsis facere inchoare et inire, ac sigillum commune pro negociis et agendas ad eandem fraternitatis sive gildam exuunt spectantibus deserviturum, habere et exidere possint ac eciam quod magistri predicti et successores sui magistri ibidem qui pro tempore fuerint pro fraternitate vel gilda illa ac pro terries, tenementis, redditibus, serviciis, possessionibus, bonis et catallis ejusdam fraternitatis aut gilde in quibuscumque accionibus, causis, querelis, demandis et plitis tam realibus et personalibus quam mixtis cujuscumque generis fuerint vel nature, per nomen magistrorum fraternitatis sive gilde sancti Georgii Dublini coram judicibus secularibus et ecclesiasticis quibuscumque implicent et implicentur, respondeant et respondeantur ac implicare et implicari necnon respondere et responderi possint et debeant. Et quod idem comes, Johannes, Hugo, Walterus, Johannes, Reginaldus, Willemus, Johannes, Thomas, Lucas, Robertus, Johannes, Thomas, Johannes, Johannes, Richardus, Ricardus, Radulphus, Johannes, Robertus et Johannes ac singuli fratres fraternitatis vel gilde predicte et successores sui magistri et fratres ejusdem fraternitatis sive gilde convenient et convenire valeant locis temporibus congruis et oportunis quociens et quando eis melius placuerit ad tractandum, concordandum et communicandum inter se ipsos una cum aliis pro consilio et avisamento habendis pro statu et bono regimine dicte fraternitatis vel gilde ac fratrum et sororum ejusdem fraternitatis aut gilde et successorum suorum, ordinacionesque licitas et honestas ad laudem Dei ac beate Marie virginis et honorem dicti sancti Georgii, pro bona gubernacione dicte fraternitatis sive gilde, de anno in annum et tempore in tempus faciendas, et easdem ordinaciones similiter de tempore in tempus cum opus et necesse fuerit augmentare vel minuere secundum discrecionem ipsorum magistrorum et fratrum fraternitatis vel gilde predicte et successorum suorum magistrorum et fratrum dicte fraternitatis aut gilde imperpetuum. Ulterius, quod de uberiori gracia nostra speciali concessimus dictis comiti, Johanni, Hugoni, Waltero, Johanni, Reginaldo, Willemo, Johanni, Thome, Luco, Roberto, Johanni, Thome, Johanni, Johanni, Richardo, Ricardo, Radulpho, Johanni, Roberto, Johanni quod ipsi vel illi qui de ipsis supervixerint, ad laudem Dei ac beate Marie virginis et honorem predicti sancti Georgii facere, ordinare et stabilire possint juxta discrecionem ordinacionem et provisionem ipsorum comitis, Johannis, Hugonis, Walteri, Johannis, Reginaldi, Willemi, Johannis, Thome, Luce, Roberti, Johannis, Thome, Johannis, Johannis, Richardi, Ricardi, Radulphi, Johannis, Roberti et Johannis vel alicujus eorumdem qui de ipsis supervixerint quondam cantariam unius capellani vel plurimorum capellanorum divina singulis diebus in supradicta capella imperpetuum celebraturorum pro salubri statu nostro ac Jacobi le Botiller, comitis de Ormond, prefati justiciarii nostri, necnon Johanne, consortis ipsius comitis, et liberorum suorum, et predicti Johannis, domini Talbot et Furnyvall, necnon Margarete, consortis ipsius Johannis, et liberorum suorum, et predicti thesaurarii nostri ac majoris et concivium antedictorum ac fratrum et sororum fraternitatis sive gilde quamdiu vixerint, et pro animabus carissimi patris nostri ac nobelium progenitorum nostrorum, necnon omnium et singulorum superius expressatorum cum ab hac luce migraverint et fratrum et sororum dicte fraternitatis vel gilde ac eorum successorum (...) ac omnium fidelium defunctorum imperpetuum, et quod predicti magistri ac fratres et sorores fraternitatis aut gilde predicte qui pro tempore fuerint, predictos capellanum seu capellanos de anno in annum et tempore in tempus deponere possint et amonere, et alios idoneos (...) possint prout eis placuerit et quod dicti magistri ac fratres et sorores et eorum successores, magistri ac fratres et sorores ejusdem fraternitatis sive gilde convenire possint locis et temporibus oportunis quando eis melius placuerit ad tractandum et ordinandum pro can(...) ordinacionem in hac parte facienda. Et insuper concessimus et licenciam dedimus prefatis magistris, fratribus et sororibus dicte fraternitatis sive gilde et successoribus suis pro tempore existentibus cum dicta fraternitas vel gilda sit facta vel ordinata et stabilita, ut prefert, quod ipsi adquirere possint terras, tenementa, redditus, servicia et advocaciones ecclesiarum sive capellarum, tam in dominico et feodo quam in reversione, cum pertinenciis usque ad valorem centum librarum per annum ultra onera et reprisas, licet de nobis in capite seu de aliis tenentur habenda et tenenda sibi et successoribus suis magistris ac fratribus et sororibus ejusdem fraternitatis aut gilde imperpetuum de capitalibus dominis feodorum per servicia inde debita et de jure consueta, ad inveniendum, supportandum et sustenandum omnia dicte cantarie unius, capellani vel plurimorum cappelanorum divina in dicta cantaria, ut predictum est, celebraturorum ac alia opera pietatis pro statu et animabus antedictis facienda imperpetuum. Statuto de terris, tenementis ad manum mortuam non ponendum edito seu aliis statutis vel ordinacionibus quibuscumque, ante hec tempora in contrarium similiter dictis non obstentibus. Volentes quod predicti comes, Johannes, Hugo, Walterus, Johannes, Reginaldus, Willemus, Johannes, Thomas, Lucas, Robertus, Johannes, Thomas, Johannes, Johannes, Richardus, Ricardus, Radulphus, Johannes, Robertus et Johannes vel heredes sui seu magistri dicte fraternitatis sive gilde aut fratres et sorores ejusdem fraternitatis aut gilde vel eorum successores racione statutorum, ordinacionum aut aliorum premissorum per nos, heredes vel successores nostros, justiciarios, escaetores, vicecomites aut alios ballivos seu ministros nostros vel heredum nostrorum seu successorum nostrorum nuper regum Anglie aut alios quoscumque inde occasionentur, inquietentur, molestentur in aliquo seu graventur. In cujus rei testimonium has litteras nostras fieri fecimus patentes, teste prefato justiciario nostro, apud Dublinum vicesimo septimo die junii anno regni nostri quarto.

GUILD OF ST GEORGE MARTYR 3

RG/01/03:
Lease of a garden in the parish of St Mary del Dam, Dublin, to John West and John Fyan, merchants

24 June 1479

Formerly sealed of two seals on scrip of parchment, red wax

Chirograph

Hec indentura facta inter Nicholaum Bourke et Ricardum Arland, magistros gilde sive ffraternitatis sancti Georgii martiris in suburbio civitatis Dublini, et Thomam Ussher et Reginaldum Talbot, gardianos ejusdem gilde sive ffraternitatis, ac fratres et sorores dicte gilde sive ffraternitatis ex una parte, et Johannem Weste et Johannem Ffuyaun, cives et mercatores dicte civitatis ex parte altera, testatur quod predicti magistri, gardiani, fratres et sorores, ex ipsorum unanimi assensu, concesserunt et ad firmam dimiserunt predictis Johanne Weste et Johanni Ffuyaun unum gardinum cum pertinenciis in parochia sancte Marie de la Dam prout jacet inter terram abbatie et conventus domus sive monasterii sancti Thome martiris juxta Dublinum ex parte orientali, terram prioris et ffratrum hospitalis sancti Johannis Baptiste extra portam novam civitatis Dublini ex parte occidentali, regiam feratam que ducit ibidem ad castrum regium ejusdem civitatis ex parte australi et terram domine Johanne Sueterbis ex parte boriali, habendum et tenendum dictum gardinum cum omnibus pertinenciis, prefatis Johanni Weste et Johannie Ffuyaun, heredibus et assigatis suis a die confectionis presentium usque ad finem termini duodecim annorum proximorum tunc sequentum plenarie complendorum, reddendo inde annuatim iidem Johannes Weste et Johannes Ffuyaun, heredes et assignati sui dictis magistris, gardianis, fratribus et sororibus dicte gilde sive ffraternitatis et successoribus suis sex solidos et octo denarios argenti ad duos anni terminos, videlicet ad festa nativitatis Domini et nativitatis sancti Johannis Baptiste per equales porciones durante termino dictorum duodecim annorum. Et prefati magistri, gardiani, fratres et sorores dicte gilde sive ffraternitatis, dictum gardinum cum omnibus suis pertinenciis prefatis Johanni Weste et Johanni Ffuyaun, heredibus et assignatis suis in forma predicta contra omnes gentes warantizabunt, acquietabunt et defendent per presentes. In cujus rei testimonium tam sigillum commune dicte gilde sive ffraternitatis quam sigilla dictorum Johannis Weste et Johannis Ffuyaun presentibus indenturis alternatim sunt appenda. Datum in festo sancti Johannis Baptiste anno regni regis Edwardi quarti decimo nono.

GUILD OF ST GEORGE MARTYR 4

RG/01/04: Lease of St George's Lane, Dublin, to Richard Arland, merchant

2 May 1480

Sealed on scrip of parchment, red wax

Chirograph

Hec indentura facta inter Nicholaum Bourke, magistrum gilde sive ffraternitatis sancti Georgii juxta Dublinum, et Thomam Ussher et Reginaldum Talbot, gardianos ejusdem gilde sive ffraternitatis ex una parte, et Ricardum Arland, civem et mercatorem dicte civitatis ex altera parte, testatur quod predicti magistri, gardiani, fratres et sorores, ex ipsorum unanimi concensu et assensu, concesserunt et ad firmam dimiserunt predicto Ricardo unam venellam sancti Georgii cum pertinenciis in vulgo *le grendlane* vocatam, prout primo se extendit a venella que ducit ad ecclesiam sancti Georgii predicte versus occidentem, usque ad viretum de *le Hogges* versus orientem, jacens inter *le chekkerzardes* versus aquilonem et gardinum quem Johannes White Deyer modo occupat versus australem, prout jacet in latitudine inter parcam ffratrum carmelitarum dicte civitatis ex parte orientali, et gardinos quos dictus Johannes Whits, Walterius Russell, Thomas Pott et alii modo occupant ex parte occidentali, et secundo se extendit in longitudine a predicto *le chekkerzardes* versus aquilonem usque viam que ducit ad domum leprosorum sancti Stephani versus australem, habendam et tenendam predictam venellam, alias *le grendlane* vocatam, prefato Ricardo, heredibus et assignatis suis a die confectionis presentium usque ad finem termini duodecim annorum proximorum tunc sequentum plenarie complendorum, reddendo inde annuatim idem Ricardus, heredes et assignati sui dicto magistro, gardianis, fratribus et sororibus dicte gilde sive ffraternitatis et successoribus suis, magistris, gardianis, fratribus et sororibus dicte gilde sive ffraternitatis, duos solidos argenti ad duos anni terminos, videlicet ad festa sancti Michaelis archangeli et Pasche per equales porciones durante termino dictorum duodecim annorum. Et prefati magister, gardiani, fratres et sorores dicte gilde sive ffraternitatis, dictam venellam cum pertinenciis prefato Ricardo, heredibus et assignatis suis, modo et fforma predicta contra omnes gentes warantizabunt, acquietabunt et per presentes defendent durante termino dictorum duodecim annorum. In cujus rei testimonium tam sigillum commune dicte gilde sive ffraternitatis quam sigillum dicti Ricardi hiis indenturis alternatim sunt appenda. Datum secundo die maii anno regni regis Edwardi quarti vicesimo.

GUILD OF ST GEORGE MARTYR 5

RG/01/05: Lease of cellar in Bernelle's Lane, Dublin, to William Newman merchant

24 August 1536

Formerly sealed on scrip of parchment, red wax

Chirograph

This indenture, made the xxiiii[th] day of August the xxviii year of the beyng of our soverayn, lord kyng Henri the viii, betwix Thomas Stephyns and Robert Shyllyngford, masteris of fraternite and yeld of seynt Gorges Churchof Dublin, John Mony and Henri Plunket, wardynges of the same yeld of the one party, and William Newman of Dublin, merchant, of the other party, wittenissith that the said masteris and wardynges, by the assent and consent of the brether and sisteris of the said yeld, hav lett and set to ferme unto the said William a siller in Bernelles lane, belonging to Seynt Gorge, which siller landyth unto Seynt Gorgeis grown on the este side, and to the payment callyd Burnellis lane un the west side, and to seynt Gorgeis land un the southe side and unto Willamis land un the north side, to have and to hold the said siller unto the said William, his heirs, executoris ans assignis for terme of one and thyrtty yers next ensuying the date above wryttyn, paying the fee yerly duryng the said terms to the said masteris and wardynges and to ther successores [...] sillyinges of lesfull mony of Irland to be payd att two festes of the yer, that is to say att the fest of seynt Mychell th'archangill and Ester by even porcionis, and the said William and his heirs or assignis shall repair and uphold the said siller bothe wallis tos[...] tenantable all tyme duryng the said terme and att the [...] hew [...] sufficient byldyd and reparyd. And the said masteris and wardynges and ther successoris shall warrand, acquit and defend the said siller [...] duryng the said terme. For wittenis wher of to this parte of the indenture [...] in the custody of the said masteris and wardinges the said William [...] the day and yere above wryttyun.

GUILD OF ST GEORGE MARTYR 6

RG/01/06: Lease of a cellar, loft and garden in Cusack Lane, Dublin, to Alderman Edward Barrane

14 August 1573

Formerly sealed on scrip of parchment, red wax

Chirograph

This indenture, made the fourtenth daye of Auguste in the year of our lord and God a thousande fyve houndred seventy three, betwixt master Patricke Dowdall and master Thomas FfitzSimons, masteris of ther ffraternytie or yeald of Seynt George of the cyttie of Dublin, Symon Growe and Androwe Luttrell, wardens of the same ffraternytie or yeald of th'one parte, and master Edward Barrane of the same cyttie, alderman, of th'other partyie, witnessith that the said masteris and wardinges, with th'assent and consent of the breatherne and systres of the said ffraternytie or yeald, have dymysed, sell and lett to ferme by this presents to the said Edward, a seller and lofte on the same and a gardenie in the Backesyde theirof with their appartemants in the lane called Cusak lane, going to the keyes of the cyttie of Dublin from the cokestreate, which seller, lofte and gardenie master Johne Spencfeld, late of Dublin alderman deceased, hold by lease of the said yeald for yeares non exspired, to have and to hold the said seller and outher the premysses with the appartemants to the said Edward, his executoris and assignes in as lardge and ample maner as the said Johne Spencefeld hold and ocupied the same, from the feast of seynt Mychaell th'archangell next ensuinge the date hereof, during and unto th'ende of the terme and for the terme of threscore and one yeres then next ensuinge fully to be completed and ended, the said Edward, his executoris and assignes yelding and paieng therfor yearly to the said masteris and wardinges and their successoris fyfftye shilling lawfull money of Irland at the feast of Easter and seynt Michaell th'archangell by equall porcions during the said terme. And the same Edward, his executoris and assignes shall repaire, kepe and maintaine the roufe, lofte, wals and speers of the said seller trong, tyffe, stanch and tennantable during the said terme and so shall leave the same at th'end of the said terme upon the papre, cost and chardge of the said Edward, his executoris and assignes. And yf it fortune the said rent be behind unpaied, in parte or in the whole, during the space of two monethes next after enny of the said feast aforesaid being lawfully demanded, that then yt shalbe lawfull unto the said masteris and wardinges and their successoris to enter in the premisses and to dystrenie and the dystres so taken with them to retaine tyll such tyme as they be fully sattisfied and paied of the said rent and the rerages therof, and yf no sufficient dystres in all the premysses maye be found, that it shalbe lawfull unto the said masteris and wardinges and to their successoris in all the premisses to reenter and the same to have againe this presente lease not with standing. And the said masteris and wardinges covenanteth and grannteth for them and their successoris to and with the said Edward, his executoris and assignes to warant, acquite and defend the said seller and gardenie and outher the premysses with their appartemants to the said Edward, his executoris and assignes against all people by theise presents during the said terme. In witnes wherof the said Edward, to this parte of theise indentures remaining in the custodye of the said masteris and wardinges, have sell his seale. Dated the daye and yere above wrytten.

GUILD OF ST GEORGE MARTYR 7

RG/01/07: Fee-farm grant of one house or tenement in Shippers' Lane, Dublin, to Thomas Gumesby

17 April 1618

Formerly sealed on scrip of parchment

Chirograph

On the back: Signed, sealed and delivered in the presence of us: James Carroll, Richard Forcter, Edward Ball.

This indenture, made the xvii[th] day of Apriell in the yeare of our lord and God 1618, between sir James Carroll, knight, major of the cittie of Dublin, master William Bushopp, Robert Lynaker, shirives of the said cittie, the commons and the cittizens of the said cittie of th'one parte, and Thomas Gumesby of Dublin, upholster, of th'other parte, witnesseth that the said major, shirives, commons and cittizens, of theire whole assents and conssents, have demised, grannted, sell and lett fearme unto the said Thomas Gumesby, one howse or tenement in shippeurs late within the cittie of Dublin, parcell of the lands of saint Georges now in the holding of master John Goodering of Dublin, elderman, to have and to hold, possesse and anjoy the said howse or tenement with th'appartements, containing in leingth from the south to the north twentie six foote in the forstreet, and in the backe syde of the said howse or tenement twentie and foure foote, and in the breadth from east to west eigtheene foote and five inches, unto the said Thomas Gumesby, his executours and assignes for and duryng the time tearme and space of threescore and one yeares fully to be compleat and ended the said tearme to begin imediatly after the expiration, surrender or avoydance of the said John Woodiringes lease being yet in being for eight yeares from the twentieth day of the next Maii, the said Thomas Gumesby, his executours and assignes yealding and paieing to the threasurer of this cittie, immediatly dureing the said eight years of master Gooderinges lease, the anuall rent of twentie seaven shillings six spence sterling current mony in England, at Michaelmas and Easter yearely by equall sportions. And the said eight yeares be the said Thomas, his executours and assignes yealding and paieing therefore and thereout unto the said major, shirives, commons and cittizens and theire successours, to the hands of the threasurer of the same cittie for the time being, for the use of the same cittie dureing the threescore and one yeares in revertion grannted by this lease the annuall rent of fiftie shillings sterling current mony in England at the feast of saint Michell the archangell and Easter yearely by equall portions. And yf it fortune the said yearely rent or any parte thereof to be behind and unpaid in parte or in the whole the same, being lawfully demanded by the space of six weeks next after any of the said feasts where at the same ought to be paid, and noe sufficient distresses to be found uppon the premisses here by demises after the same doth come unto the said Thomas Gumesby that then this lease to cease and be meerely voyd at the ellection and choyce of the said major, shirives, commons and cittizens and their successours any thing here in contained to the contrary not with standing. And the said Thomas Gumesby fore his, his executours and assignes covenanteth and grannteth to and with the said major, shirives, commons and cittizens and theirs successours the said howse tenement with the appartemants to maintain, repaire and keepe upp from tyme to time and at all tymes hereafter dureing the said tearme stiffe, stanth and tenantable and so to lease the same at the end thereof. And the said major, shirives, commons and cittizens, fore them and theire successours, covenanteth and grannteth to and with the said Thomas Gumesby, his executours and assignes the said howse or tenement with the appartemants unto the said Thomas Gumesby, his executours and assignes, against them and theire successours and any of ther clayming by or under them or there estate, to warrant, acquit and defend dureing the tearme and yeares afore said by theis presents. In witness whereof to this parte of the indenture remaining with the said major, shirives, commons and citizens, the said Thomas Gumesby hath putt his hand and seale. Dated the day and yeare first above written.

Signed: Thomas Gumesby

GUILD OF ST GEORGE MARTYR 8

RG/01/08: Grant of four marks of silver to the Priory [of All Hallows] for the provision of a chaplain to the Guild of St George

September 1506

Formerly sealed on scrip of parchment; damaged; portions missing

Chirograph

[...] betwex Thomas [...] of the yelde in the honour of seynt George the marter [...] the cytte of Dublin moryo [...] theof at[...] of the said [...] and say this prior [...] the house of all seynts by sides [...]witnenth that [...] wardens and there successours by the [...]-ly assent and consent of all the ffraternite of the [...] and appartenants [...] prior and covent and there successours four marke of sylver of lawfull money to be paid to the [...] prior and convent and ther successours [...] houds of the said masters and wardens that now been or for tyme shalbe at the feste of Easter and seynt Michell th'archangell by equal porcyons yerly for the [...]-cion and wages of a honest chapleyn to say masse and other divyne servis in the said [...]-ondares and fested and thries [...] wedynsday, ffriday and saterday [...] by the same and to h[...] to the said prior and covent ant ther successours in forme foresaid as long as the said masters and wardens and ther successours [...] and enjoyeth and shall have [...] grannteds by the king to the said masters, wardens and ther successours to f[...] –eyn a prest at the plesure of [...] aforesaid provideds that as [...] covent and ther successours [...] duy defalt in the servis [...] to [...]-miss that then the said prior [...] defalt of every day and that [...] the masters and wardens for the tyme [...] the money [...] In witnes wherof the [...] use of the said prior [...] endenture remaining [...] masters and wardens is put [...] of september the yere [...] Henry the vii[th] [...] the yere of our [...] a m v[c] and vi.

GUILD OF ST GEORGE MARTYR 9

RG/01/09: Lease of premises to Laurence [surname missing]

Chirograph; document damaged; portions missing

[...] imperpetuum et [...] Laurencio, heredibus [...] sancto Georgio et fraternitati [...] datum confectionis [...] vel assignati sui prefatis magistro [...]

decem solidos [...] bone et legalis monete ad duos anni terminos ad ffesta Pasche et sancti Thome equis porcionibus. Et si contingat quod [...] decem solidorum in [...] non solvat per sex septimanas post aliquem terminum festorum predictorum, [...] valeant bene [...] in dictam domum distringere et districciones [...] et [...]-ciis ejusdem parte [...] fuerit sattisfactus. Et si contingat quod [...] vel [...] fore [...] non [...] septimanas proximas sequentes [...] intrare et eam [...] heredes et assignati [...] in adeo bono statu [...] partes predicte [...]

Tudor reformations in Cork

HENRY A. JEFFERIES

On 14 July 1644, all Catholics in Cork 'by beat of drum and on pain of death [were] expelled out of the city and suburbs, and their houses *et cetera* in the city and suburbs seized'.[1] Thereafter Cork became an aggressively Protestant city. Its New English elite 'imposed their own image on Cork by obliterating the physical fabric of its medieval past and by building a "New Jerusalem" upon it'.[2] With changes to the cityscape came changes to the churches. All of Cork's medieval churches were dismantled in the eighteenth century and virtually all of their medieval and early modern furnishings and funerary monuments were discarded. No other city in Ireland suffered such a cataclysmic disruption, with the result that hardly anything survives of Tudor Cork above the ground. Added to this is the fact that the documentary record for the years prior to the seventeenth century is incredibly depleted. It is impossible even to try to emulate Colm Lennon's incomparable study of Dublin.

REFORMATION CORK

In 1574 David Wolfe S.J. stated: 'Touching the city of Cork ... in Desmond [it] may contain about 800 inhabitants, all merchants, fishermen and artisans'.[3] That figure compares with his estimates of 800–900 for Limerick and 1,000 for Waterford. Wolfe's estimate is low, probably an underestimate, but in the absence of data any attempt to define Cork's population during the Tudor period would now be so speculative as to be worthless. The *Pacata Hibernia* map of 1587 confirms Cork's small size. It shows two islands near the mouth of the River Lee enclosed by castellated city walls and twenty mural towers, several with cannons issuing from their windows. Cork's quays were located inside the city walls, behind a portcullis gateway between the King's Castle and the Queen's Castle – a scene reminiscent of Cork's coat of arms. Some heads are shown on spikes above the two gates to the city to warn visitors with evil intent of the fate that awaited serious malefactors. Richard

---

1 Cited in Mark McCarthy, 'The historical geography of Cork's transformation from a late medieval town into an Atlantic sea-port, 1600–1700' (PhD, UCC, 1997), p. 290. For the wider context see John A. Murphy, 'The expulsion of the Irish from Cork in 1644', *JCHAS*, 69 (1964), passim. 2 Henry A. Jefferies, *Cork: historical perspectives* (Dublin, 2004), p. 134. 3 *Calendar of state papers. Rome, ii, 1572–8*, ed. J.M. Rigg (London, 1926), no. 293.

Stanihurst wrote that even in Elizabeth's reign the citizens 'are so encumbered with evil neighbours, the Irish outlaws, that they are fain to watch their gates hourly to keep them out at service time, at meals, from sun to sun, nor suffer any stranger to enter the city with his weapon but the same to leave at a lodge appointed. They walk out at seasons for recreation with power of men furnished [i.e. with armed escorts]'.[4] William Camden observed that the citizens were 'so beset with rebel enemies on all sides that they are obliged to keep constant watch as if the town was constantly besieged'.[5]

However, the citizens of Cork were not forever confined behind the city walls. Traders, and the citizens employed in processing agricultural goods, depended on the countryside for their livelihoods, and several of the elite felt confident enough to lend credit to lords across southern Munster.[6] Many of the elite owned properties not just beyond the walls but around Cork harbour generally.[7] The establishment of the provincial presidency in Cork in 1571, with the president resident in Shandon Castle with a garrison of soldiers, brought royal authority to bear in Cork's hinterland. Lord Deputy Sidney visited Cork in December 1575 and was struck by the greatly improved conditions within the city: 'The good estate and flourishing of that city well approves the good effect of resident authority amongst them, for it is so amended as in so few years I have seldom seen any town'.[8] The maps of Cork in the Hardiman Atlas, one dated to c.1601 and the second to 1602, show suburban development north and south of the Lee. Mark McCarthy counted the houses shown on the 1602 map and found 354 dwellings drawn inside the city walls, and 93 in the suburbs and estimated Cork's population at 2,906 at the turn of the century.[9] While one must be very cautious in dealing with early, impressionistic maps, the scale of suburban development in Cork over the last quarter of the sixteenth century seems to have been significant.

Throughout the Tudor period, Cork was dominated by an oligarchy of merchants who were far wealthier than the bulk of the inhabitants.[10] They were predominantly but not exclusively English by descent. They were endogamous: Camden wrote that they 'dare not marry their daughters in the country, but contract [marriages] one with another amongst themselves, whereby all the citizens are related in some degree or other'.[11] They dominated the city's economy, and the corporation.

---

4 Richard Stanihurst, 'Description of Ireland' in Raphael Holinshed, *The chronicles of England, Scotlande and Irelande* ... 6 (London, 1807–8 [1577]), p. 30.   5 William Camden, *Brittania* (1753, 3rd ed.), p. 979.   6 See, for example, the will of Nicholas Faggan, dated 26 Mar. 1578: Richard Caulfield, 'Wills and inventories, Cork, *temp.* Mary and Elizabeth', *Gentleman's Magazine* (July 1861), 36.   7 A.F. O'Brien, 'Politics, economy and society: the development of Cork and the Irish south coast region, c.1170 to c.1583' in Patrick O'Flanagan and Cornelius G. Buttimer (eds), *Cork: history and society* (Dublin, 1993), p. 141.   8 F.H. Tuckey, *The county and city of Cork remembrancer* (Cork, 1837), p. 56.   9 McCarthy, 'Historical geography', p. 216.   10 Jefferies, *Cork*, pp 75, 91–5.   11 Camden,

Maritime trade was very modest before the mid-sixteenth century.[12] Its scale is reflected in the archaeological record in Cork.[13] Records from Bristol, by far the most important English port handling southern Irish trade in the Tudor period, show only one to three ships a year either arriving at Bristol from Cork, or departing for Cork.[14] There may have been some coasting trade, but not enough significantly to alter the fact that the cross-channel trade centred on Cork was small. If Wendy Childs' estimates of Iberian traffic are at all correct, the number of ships from mainland Europe docking in Cork each year may have been something of the same order as English ships.[15] That would explain how Cork's relatively short stretch of quays was able to accommodate the ships carrying the city's maritime trade.

With Cork's modest trade focused on the conservative west of England, and with France and the Spanish territories, it is hardly surprising that Lutheranism made little impact on the citizens of Cork. The impression one gains from the surviving evidence is that the people of Cork were very attached to the Catholic religion before Henry VIII's breach with Rome. The two parish churches within the city walls were shown as very commodious buildings in the Hardiman Atlas. St Peter's Church extended back quite some distance from the North Main Street. It housed many chantry chapels in which priests celebrated Masses for the souls of the founders and their families, of which the Lady Chapel was the best endowed.[16] For example, an inquisition of 1578 found that one Robert Gould, at some distant date, had granted two messuages and a garden worth 6s. 8d. per annum, besides reprises, to maintain a priest to celebrate the Mass for the souls of deceased members of his family in St Peter's Church.[17]

Christ Church was the civic church and was more impressive than St Peter's. The map of 1601 shows it with north and south aisles and a square tower at its north-western corner. It too had a Lady Chapel and an array of chantry chapels, like St James' Chapel to which Edmond White made a small bequest in his will of 7 June 1582.[18] An inquisition of 1578 found that a chantry had, at some distant date, been founded in Christ Church, to which one James White had granted the church of St Lawrence (also within the walls) and three messuages adjacent to it worth 3s. 4d. per annum. James Milton had likewise granted it a carucate of land worth 6s. per annum.[19] The inquisition also investigated the residential college that Philip Gould had

Brittania, p 979.   12 Jefferies, *Cork*, pp 84–7.   13 Dermot Twohig, 'Archaeological heritage', *Cork Examiner*, 27 Mar. 1985.   14 William O'Sullivan, *The economic history of Cork city from earliest times to the act of Union* (Cork, 1937), p. 74.   15 Wendy Childs, 'Ireland's trade with England in the later Middle Ages', *Irish Economic and Social History*, 9 (1982), 10.   16 Evelyn Bolster (ed.), 'A landgable roll of Cork city', *Collectanea Hibernica*, 13 (1970), 7–18.   17 J. Windele, *Historical and descriptive notices of the city of Cork from its foundation to the middle of the nineteenth century* (Cork, 1973), p. 49.   18 *Gentleman's Magazine* (June 1862), 713.   19 Windele, *Cork*, p. 46.

founded to house Christ Church's chantry priests in 1483. The college was excavated in 1975 and was found to measure 28 x 7 metres on an east–west axis, but very few details of the excavation were preserved.[20]

The surviving wills of the sixteenth century, published in the *Gentleman's Magazine* by Richard Caulfield in 1861, give no indication that there was any problem with the fabric of the parish church buildings. The wills themselves date mainly from the late 1560s to the early 1580s, but in form and content they are very similar to de Wynchedon's will of 1306 and the Tyrry wills of the mid-fifteenth century, and generally include modest bequests of cash to the church. Not included in the wills were the significant sums which had to be paid to the church in association with funerals. There were fees for the administration of the last rites, for funeral services and for the grave. For example, Daniel Conwey, an Irishman living in Cork, set aside £1 for his burial at Kilcrea Friary in 1571.[21] The best clothes of the deceased were also claimed by the parish clergy as a 'mortuary', and a 'canonical portion' (amounting to an onerous 29 per cent in Armagh diocese and 33 per cent in Dublin diocese, for instance) was levied on the moveable goods of the deceased.[22] Such fees and levies caused some resentment among the laity, as is shown in the presentments made by several juries in south-eastern Ireland in 1537.[23] Therefore the additional, voluntary, bequests recorded in the wills may be taken as evidence of people's positive disposition towards the church.[24]

Cork's elite had themselves buried under the floors of their parish churches. Their wills typically direct that their bodies be buried either in Christ Church or St Peter's Church, often specifying that they be buried in a chantry chapel, as did the will of George Galwey, written on 30 April 1579, which directed that he be buried in St Katherine's Chapel in St Peter's.[25] In 1580 Andrew Galwey's will requested burial 'in the chauntry of my parish church of Saincte Peters',[26] while Edmond White's will of 7 June 1582 asked that he be buried where his 'ancestors' lay in St James' Chapel in Christ Church.[27] Andrew Roche, in his will of 5 December 1618, bequeathed his

---

20 A. Gwynn and R.N. Hadcock, *Medieval religious houses: Ireland* (London, 1970), p. 359; Dermot Twohig, 'Archaeological excavations' in *Cork Examiner*, 27 Mar. 1985; Rose Cleary, 'The excavations' in R.M. Cleary, M.F. Hurley and E. Shee Twohig (eds), *Excavations by D.C. Twohig at Skiddy's Castle and Christ Church, Cork, 1974–77* (Cork, 1997), p. 95.   21 *Gentleman's Magazine* (July 1861), 35.   22 H.A. Jefferies, *Priests and prelates of Armagh in the age of reformations* (Dublin, 1997), p. 31.   23 Presentments from south-eastern Ireland, 1537 (PRO, SP 60/5/60; SP 60/5/64; SP 60/5/78; SP 60/5/85). See also, Jefferies, 'The role of the laity', *Archivium Hibernicum*, 52 (1998), 78–9.   24 To understand the Cork wills in their wider context, see Clodagh Tait, *Death, burial and commemoration in Ireland, 1550–1650* (Basingstoke, 2002).   25 *Gentleman's Magazine* (Sept. 1861), 257.   26 *Gentleman's Magazine* (Sept. 1861), 257–8.   27 *Gentleman's Magazine* (June 1862), 713. David Tyrry, in his will of 13 Mar. 1570, directed that his body be buried under the chancel, close to the main altar: *Gentleman's Magazine* (Apr. 1862), 443.

grave in the Lady Chapel in Christ Church to his sons so that 'my own children shall be buried there and none other'.[28] It was common for testators to decree that their body be buried with late family members. William Galwey directed that he be buried with his father and his first wife, Margaret Gould.[29] Alderman Andrew Galwey, 9 February 1580, wished to be buried in the same grave as his second wife, Catherine Roche, daughter of Alderman James Roche.[30] In her will of 22 June 1582 Genet Galwey, wife of the late Alderman John Gould, asked to be buried with her husband 'if possible'.[31] Alderman Christopher Galwey directed that his body be buried with his father and mother in St Peter's Church.[32]

Until its demolition in the eighteenth century St Peter's had funerary monuments dating back to 1500.[33] The monuments were discarded, with several ending up incorporated into the walls of buildings in the area of Grattan Street.[34] John Windele recorded the existence of a couple of those stones, together with 'an ancient sculptured head cut in limestone' in a wall at the corner of Peter's Street. Part of the crypt of the medieval Christ Church survived its demolition and houses a small collection of burial monuments dating back to the early Tudor period, and a stone effigy dating as far back as the thirteenth century.[35] The chantries and the funerary monuments reflect the attachment of the elite to the Catholic church and its doctrines. They 'must also reflect similar attitudes in the local community in general since investments of this kind were undoubtedly expected to yield dividends in the currency of public estimation'.[36]

The Augustinian, Dominican and Franciscan orders each had a friary in Cork, and the friars played an important role in supplementing the pastoral care provided by the parochial clergy with expert preaching. The friars were wholly dependent upon voluntary donations and bequests, and not only were three communities maintained in Cork, but there is evidence of expensive building work having been carried out at both the Augustinian and Dominican friaries before the Reformation – an indirect indication of their popularity.[37] The surviving tower of Red Abbey, an Augustinian friary

---

28 *Gentleman's Magazine* (Apr. 1861), 441.   29 *Gentleman's Magazine* (Sept. 1861), 257.
30 *Gentleman's Magazine* (Sept. 1861), 257–8.   31 *Gentleman's Magazine* (Sept. 1861), 261.   32 *Gentleman's Magazine* (Sept. 1861), 261.   33 Windele, *Cork*, p. 49.   34 Windele, *Cork*, p. 27.   35 J. Bradley, A. Halpin and H. King, *Cork city* (Urban Archaeology Survey, 14, 2 1985), pp 59–65.   36 Brendan Bradshaw, 'The Reformation in the cities: Cork, Limerick and Galway' in John Bradley (ed.), *Settlement and society in medieval Ireland: studies presented to F.X. Martin, OSA* (Kilkenny, 1998), p. 450.   37 Colin Rynne, *The archaeology of Cork city and harbour from the earliest times to industrialization* (Cork, 1993), p. 57; Maurice F. Hurley and Cathy M. Sheehan, *Excavations at the Dominican priory, St Mary's of the Isle, Cork* (Cork, 1995), pp 28–40, 48–51; Bradshaw, 'The Reformation in the cities', p. 450. This is not to imply that the Franciscans were unable to engage in building work; the evidence is simply not available at the moment to determine what developments occurred at their friary.

founded late in the thirteenth century,[38] dates from the fifteenth century, and archaeologists found evidence for a tower of similar date incorporated into the Dominican friary of St Mary's of the Isle, together with a south aisle added to its church.[39] A new dormitory had been built for the Augustinian friary shortly before it was dissolved by Henry VIII in 1541, an indication of a strong community in good order.[40] Cork's Augustinians embraced a very strict reform movement called Observantism between 1472 and 1484, and the Dominicans followed in 1484 and the Franciscans in 1500.

It is impossible to define the state of the church or religion in Cork before the Reformation with any great degree of precision. Yet the investment of the lay patricians in chantries, Philip Gould's foundation of the chantry college by Christ Church in 1483, and the money given to the friars in Cork may be taken as reflections of the elites' commitment to the Catholic order before the Reformation.[41] While there is no way of determining levels of Mass attendance in Cork on the eve of the Reformation, nor the depths of religious convictions among its varied inhabitants, the indications are that the institutional church enjoyed significant support in Cork. The evidence available for Cork is consistent with a general pattern emerging from across Ireland, which suggests that the church was in reasonably good order and enjoyed much support on the eve of the Reformation.[42] Such support 'did not, of itself, guarantee the survival of the Church, nor did it make the failure of the reformations inevitable. Nonetheless, it is clear that historians must take greater account of the strength and popularity of the Catholic Church in future studies of the history of religion in sixteenth-century Ireland'.[43] There is no question but that Henry VIII's breach with Rome initially aroused much opposition in Ireland – demonstrated most starkly during the Kildare rebellion.[44] However, at least one of Cork's elite showed positive enthusiasm for the ecclesiastical revolution. William Sarsfield, citizen of Cork, in a notorial document drawn up in Cork in 1537, made a gratuitous reference to 'King Henry VIII, orthodox Defender of the Faith, Supreme Head under Christ of the Churches of England and Ireland, our invincible prince'.[45] This enthusi-

---

[38] Rynne, *Archaeology of Cork*, p. 57. [39] Hurley and Sheehan, *Dominican priory*, pp 48–51. [40] N.B. White (ed.), *Extents of Irish monastic possessions, 1540–1* (Dublin, 1943), p. 140. [41] For the college see Aubrey Gwynn and R.N. Hadcock, *Medieval religious houses: Ireland* (London, 1970), p. 359; Twohig, 'Archaeological heritage'. [42] Colm Lennon, *The lords of Dublin in the age of Reformation* (Dublin, 1989), pp 34, 130–4, 146–7; Jefferies, *The Irish church and the Tudor reformations* (Dublin, 2010), pp 15–68. [43] Jefferies, 'Role of the laity', p. 83. [44] While its leader was not motivated primarily by religious concerns, he was able to harness the widespread opposition to Henry VIII's schism to garner support for his cause: S.G. Ellis, 'The Kildare rebellion and the early Henrician Reformation', *Historical Journal*, 23 (1980), 497–519; Laurence McCorristine, *The revolt of Silken Thomas: a challenge to Henry VIII* (Dublin, 1987); Jefferies, 'The Kildare rebellion: accident or design?', *Journal of the County Kildare Archaeological Society*, 19 (2004–5), 447–59. [45] Marsh's Library, Dublin, MS C.I.13.

astic formula was not a standard requirement but reflected Sarsfield's sentiments in endorsing the Henrician Reformation.[46] There is no way of knowing if Sarsfield's sentiments were widely shared, but they do warn against simplistic assumptions about the likely outcome of the Reformation in Cork. On the other hand, it is important to bear in mind that while Henry VIII reigned the doctrines promulgated from the pulpits across the Tudor dominions remained essentially Catholic, and the liturgy continued to be celebrated in Latin. The people of Cork were not being asked to accept Protestantism but to accept, at least nominally, the king as head of a schismatic but conservative church.

On 20 September 1536, Henry VIII directed that Dominick Tyrry, the rector of Shandon, be made bishop of Cork and Cloyne. The new bishop acknowledged Henry VIII as supreme head of the Irish church, and he renounced the authority of the pope.[47] At first the papacy was cautious, but from 1539 a series of Roman Catholic bishops was appointed to Irish dioceses occupied by prelates who acknowledged the royal supremacy. In September 1540 a Franciscan friar was provided to Cork, but he died in Rome.[48] In November the pope provided John O'Heyne as papal bishop of Cork and Cloyne. Bishop O'Heyne informed the papacy that he had failed to establish himself at Cork because of the 'schismatics' and 'lapsed Catholics' there.[49] In February 1545 Pope Paul III appointed him to Elphin for a trial period of six months.[50] O'Heyne met with failure there too and, as late as 1557, after Tyrry's death, he tried again (in vain) to make his episcopacy effective in Cork.[51] The fact was that Cork's elite preferred to have one of their own as bishop of Cork – Dominic Tyrry was followed by Roger Skiddy, another member of a local patrician family – than a papally appointed Irishman.

The willingness of Cork's elite to collaborate with the Henrician Reformation is more strikingly revealed by the fate of the religious communities in the city. In February 1541 Walter Cowley and James White, two government officials, arrived in Cork to supervise the dissolution of the religious houses there.[52] Inquisitions were conducted by a jury comprised of some of the leading citizens of the city, including Patrick Coppinger, Walter Galwey, Richard Gould and John Skiddy.[53] The jurors found that the abbey of the cave of St Finbarr, or Gill Abbey, had a single monk only in its community and no chapel in use. It was quickly suppressed.[54] The Cork jurors

---

[46] The public notary is most unlikely to have imposed his own sentiments on Sarsfield's document. [47] William M. Brady, *Clerical and parochial records of Cork, Cloyne and Ross* (3 vols, Dublin, 1863), 3, pp 45–6. [48] Bolster, *Diocese of Cork*, p. 3. [49] Ibid. [50] F.X. Martin, 'Bernard O'Higgin, OSA, bishop of Elphin' in A. Cosgrove and D. McCartney (eds), *Studies in Irish history in honour of R. Dudley Edwards* (Dublin, 1979), pp 59–75, especially p. 64. [51] BL, Cotton, Titus B. xi, Plut. xxv D., f. 489. [52] Bradshaw, *The dissolution of the religious orders in Ireland under Henry VIII* (Cambridge, 1974), pp 153–5. [53] *Extents of Irish monastic possessions*, pp 138–43. [54] Ibid., pp 141–3.

had no hesitation in suggesting that the churches, chapels and belfries of the Augustinian, Dominican and Franciscan friaries might be demolished and the remainder of their properties secularised.[55] The friars of Cork appear to have dispersed. Brendan Bradshaw was struck by the 'alacrity' with which local merchants took up leases and purchased former religious properties 'indicating a lack of popular support for the mendicants in Cork'.[56] It certainly suggests a lack of scruple concerning church property, and a readiness to accept the breach from the papacy as final. The dissolution campaign in Cork city was financially unrewarding for the crown,[57] but politically it was a great success. It consolidated the Henrician Reformation by giving some important citizens in Cork a stake in the success of that policy. As an 'act of state', the Reformation made significant progress.

No evidence survives about Edward VI's Reformation in Cork but popular sentiment, lay and clerical, led to the immediate restoration of the Mass after Mary Tudor became the queen in August 1553.[58] On the other hand, there was no restoration of the religious houses. Local merchants secured the queen's confirmation for their retention of the former religious properties.[59] Efforts by the earl of Desmond and the Dominican prior at Youghal to have the friary of St Mary's of the Isle in Cork restored were unsuccessful.[60] In any event, the Marian restoration proved to be short-lived as Mary died and was succeeded by her half-sister, Elizabeth, in November 1558. The Irish parliament of 1560 speedily acknowledged Elizabeth as 'supreme governor of this realm ... as well in all spiritual or ecclesiastical things or causes, as temporal'.[61]

Roger Skiddy, dean of Limerick but a member of Cork's mercantile elite, had been nominated to be the bishop of Cork and Cloyne by Mary but he was not consecrated before her death.[62] In fact, it was not until 29 October 1562 that Elizabeth confirmed his appointment as bishop.[63] Henry Cotton stated that he was consecrated *papali ritu*.[64] Although he acquiesced in the royal supremacy he did not embrace Protestantism and his resignation as bishop on 18 March 1567, coinciding as it did with the visit of Lord Deputy Sidney to the city, probably had something to do with his failure to promote the Reformation in Cork. Instead, Skiddy was appointed as warden to the collegiate church at Youghal, an office in which he could enjoy a reasonably good salary out of harm's way. He died *c*.1588, after transferring certain items of the plate of St Fin Barre's Cathedral to Philip Gould, archdeacon of Cork.[65] In June 1570 one of Sidney's chaplains, an Englishman named

---

55 Ibid.   56 Bradshaw, *Dissolution*, p. 155.   57 Ibid.   58 Jefferies, *Irish church*, pp 104–15.   59 Bolster, *Diocese of Cork*, pp 44–5.   60 Ibid., p. 45.   61 Jefferies, 'The Irish parliament of 1560: the Anglican reforms authorised', *Irish Historical Studies*, 26 (1988).   62 Bolster, *Diocese of Cork*, p. 49. Skiddy was appointed as executor by his brother, William Skiddy, by his will proved on 5 Apr. 1578: *Gentleman's Magazine* (Apr. 1862), 443.   63 Bolster, *Diocese of Cork*, p. 59.   64 Henry Cotton, *Fasti Ecclesiae Hibernicae* (6 vols, Dublin, 1848–51), 6, Appendix, p. xxiii.   65 Bolster, *Diocese of Cork*, p. 60.

Richard Dixon, was appointed as the queen's bishop of Cork, but he was deposed one year later for bigamy.[66]

In February 1568 the papacy provided Nicholas Landes as the Catholic bishop of Cork but he failed to become established in the diocese.[67] His successor, Edmund Tanner, was provided in November 1574.[68] Tanner arrived in Ireland in 1576 but was soon detained. He was released in 1577 after agreeing not to enter the city of Cork. Tanner is interesting as one of a new breed of Catholic priest. He was trained by the Society of Jesus, a society founded in 1540 for converting the 'heathen'. The zeal and quality of the Jesuit priests made them invaluable in the Catholic church's war with Protestantism, but Tanner's influence in Cork is indeterminate.

In 1574 David Wolfe, another Jesuit priest, wrote a description of Ireland in which he claimed that everyone in Cork was Catholic.[69] That may not have been entirely true. In July 1569, James Fitzmaurice Fitzgerald had demanded of the mayor and corporation of Cork that they 'abolish out of that city that old heresy newly raised and invented', and banish from the city Barnaby Daly and all other Protestants (whom he denoted by the French term 'Huguenots'), both male and female. It may be, though, that those 'other' Protestants were English. Brendan Bradshaw made the point that 'It is possible, of course, that by the time Wolfe wrote in 1574 the reformers had bowed to pressure and left the city'. However, Nicholas Pett, provost marshall of Munster, left his Protestant service book to his 'friend', Barnaby Daly, in his 1572 will, which was written in Cork.[70]

Despite their preference for Catholicism, Wolfe revealed that citizens of Cork attended the Protestant church services in 1574. There was no sign yet of open resistance to the Church of Ireland in the city. Interestingly, Wolfe testified to the zeal of the Church of Ireland bishop of Cork in preaching to the citizens. That bishop was Mathew Sheyne, a Tipperary man, appointed to Cork diocese by Elizabeth in May 1572. Sheyne had been recommended by the 'godly' of Cork, i.e., local Protestants, and Wolfe's testimony suggests that they chose well.[71] Sheyne hit the 'headlines' in October 1578 when he publicly burned a venerated statue of St Dominic at the market cross in the city, 'to the great grief of the superstitious people of that place'.[72] One can only wonder whether the bishop was supported by the civic authorities in carrying out the burning of the relic in the heart of the walled city, or

---

66 *CSPI, 1509–73*, p. 444; James Morrin (ed.), *Calendar of patent and close rolls of chancery in Ireland, Henry VIII to 18th Elizabeth* (Dublin, 1861), p. 539; Brady, *Clerical and parochial records*, 3, p. 47; Bolster, *Diocese of Cork*, 2, pp 71–2. 67 Bolster, *Diocese of Cork*, 2, p. 63. 68 Ibid., pp 73–9. 69 J. Begley, *The diocese of Limerick in the sixteenth and seventeenth centuries* (Dublin, 1927), appendix, pp 494–515. 70 Bradshaw, 'Reformation in the cities', p. 475, n. 59; *Gentleman's Magazine* (Feb. 1862), p. 165. 71 Bolster, *Diocese of Cork*, 2, p. 72. 72 Walter Harris (ed.), *The whole works of Sir James Ware concerning Ireland* (2 vols, Dublin, 1739), 1, p. 564.

whether he had to rely on the English garrison supporting the president of Munster at Shandon. At the same time as the statue of St Dominic was destroyed in 1578, inquisitions were held in Cork regarding the chantries and their endowments were confiscated by the crown. The Reformation had truly arrived. However, Sheyne discredited his cause when he had to confess from the pulpit of St Finbarr's Cathedral that he had sold benefices, a sin known as simony, in order to supplement his income.[73] Eoghan Ó Dubhthaigh castigated Sheyne and the two other Irish Protestant bishops in Munster for 'corruption'.[74] One cannot rule out the possibility of local support for him, however, because when Sheyne died in 1582–3 Patrick Galwey, the mayor of Cork, recommended a zealous Protestant, William Lyon, to succeed him.[75]

THE WILLS OF CORK'S CITIZENS

It is difficult to discern what the people in Cork thought about the religious struggle being waged for their hearts and souls. Twenty-five published wills from 1567 to the early 1580s offer tantalizing glimpses into the religious outlooks of some wealthier citizens who had property enough to bequeath. Wills have been used extensively in England to trace the progress of the Tudor reformations. Unfortunately, the sample of Cork wills is very small and cannot form the basis of confident assertions about the Reformation in Cork. What is offered here is an impressionistic survey to see what they may suggest about religious feeling in Cork about the time of Bishop Sheyne's episcopate.

Adam Gould, whose will was dated 26 November 1571, bequeathed five marks to Christ Church 'so that the olde faith be set up' – an exceptionally explicit statement of support for the Catholic faith, albeit from an early stage in the Elizabethan Reformation, and probably by an older man.[76] Another will from that time, from Patrick Meade, bore the following declaration: 'I do commit my soul onto the hands of Almighty God, and to his mother Saint Mary, and to his blessed company of all the angels and saints in heaven'.[77] A similarly Catholic declaration was made by Alderman Andrew Galwey in his will dated 9 February 1580, which dedicated his soul to 'Almighty God, and to his blessed mother, Mary, and to all of the company of heaven'.[78] Yet, indicative though such declarations are of Catholic commitment, those are the only three of the sample of twenty-five wills from Elizabethan Cork to be explicitly Catholic. At the same time, there are signs that alternative expressions of Catholic belief might be displayed in domestic settings. An Elizabethan fireplace in Cork bears this inscription:

73 W.M. Brady, *State papers concerning the Irish church* (London, 1868), no. xix.
74 Marc Caball, *Poets and politics: continuity and reaction in Irish poetry, 1558–1625* (Cork, 1998), pp 78–9.   75 *Works of Ware*, i, p. 565.   76 *Gentleman's Magazine* (Nov. 1861), 501.
77 *Gentleman's Magazine* (Jan. 1862), 31.   78 *Gentleman's Magazine* (Sept. 1861), 257–8.

Made at Cork i anno dni. 1586 xxiii June.

Thy sugred name O Lord, engrave within my brest,
Sith therein doth consist my weal and onelie rest.
I.H.S.

The reference here to the 'sugred name' invokes Catholic devotion to the name of Jesus, and would have made a definite statement about the houseowner's religious convictions.[79]

By contrast, in his will Nicholas Pett, the English provost marshall of the province of Munster, dedicated his soul to solely to 'Almighty God'.[80] William Skiddy, brother of the first Elizabethan bishop of Cork, in his will dated 5 April 1578, also dedicated his soul to 'Almighty God',[81] as did Genet Creagh, in her will of 5 March 1582.[82] Pett was certainly a Protestant and, while dedicating one's soul to God alone was not an exclusively Protestant formula in wills, its use by Skiddy and Creagh may conceivably betoken some degree of Protestant influence – though I am not so bold as to propose that as a probability.

As well as the three explicitly Catholic wills, and the two wills which may reflect at least a hint of Protestant influence, there are twenty others that may be characterized as fairly neutral in terms of denomination. Fifteen of the wills (60% of the sample) make no religious reference other than the standard formula: 'In the name of God, Amen' or its Latin equivalent, 'Nomine Dei, Amen'. A further two (8%) open with the variant: 'In the name of the Father, Son and Holy Ghost'.[83] The remaining three are little different to the rest, with the standard formula being complemented in the course of the wills with a stated concern for the testator's soul,[84] a plea for God's mercy,[85] and an interesting provision in Richard Tirry's will, dated 14 April 1582, that the money set aside for his daughter's dowry [£40] should be divided between the two city parish churches 'if it should please God to call her out of this life before she be preferred'.[86] Strikingly, Tirry made no other bequest to the church other than that very provisional proviso.

In fact, in ten of the wills (40%) there is no bequest of a religious nature. In addition, Daniel Conwey's bequest of 20s. for his burial and a black cassock to a priest were no more than the obligatory burial costs and mortuary

---

79 Windele, *Cork*, p 27; R. Lutton, '"Love this name that is IHC": vernacular prayers, hymns and lyrics to the holy name of Jesus in pre-Retormation England' in E. Salter and H. Wicker (eds), *Vernacularity in England and Wales, c.1300–1550* (Turnhout, 2011), pp 129–40, 144–5. I am grateful to Clodagh Tait for bringing this reference to my attention. 80 *Gentleman's Magazine* (Feb. 1862), 165. 81 *Gentleman's Magazine* (Apr. 1862), 443. 82 *Gentleman's Magazine* (July 1861), 34. 83 *Gentleman's Magazine* (Sept. 1861), 257; (Apr. 1862), 443. 84 *Gentleman's Magazine* (May 1861), 532. 85 *Gentleman's Magazine* (July 1861), 36. 86 *Gentleman's Magazine* (June 1862), 710.

that testators did not normally record in their wills.[87] Conwey may have been too poor to make further bequests, and the widows, Ellen Ní Connyly and Genet Galwey, may also have been fairly poor, but poverty does not explain why Alderman George Galwey, Alderman William Sarsfield or Nicholas Faggan, a merchant whose Catholic tombstone is still extant, made no bequests to the church in their wills. The number of testators who made no bequests to the church seems surprising but, in the absence of a sample of pre-Reformation wills, it is may be unwise to speculate whether people were less inclined to make bequests to the church during the course of the Reformations. On the other hand, the fact that most churches in the Pale were allowed to fall into ruin after they were Protestantized suggests that some withdrawal of financial support for the churches in Cork is likely.

Of the bequests made to the church the most generous was that of the staunchly Catholic Alderman Andrew Galwey in his will of 9 February 1580.[88] He made an endowment to finance two priests in St Peter's Church, and another in Christ Church. He bequeathed £3 for the maintenance of St Peter's, and £2 6s. 8d. for Christ Church, along with a donation of 13s. 4d. for the maintenance of the Poor Men's house, and lesser gifts to St Fin Barre's Cathedral and other churches near the city. He also made provision for 3s., either in cash or iron, to be given towards the cost of each church being built in Cork diocese. He set aside £2 to be given to the poor of Cork one month after his death. His will reflected a very pious disposition, yet it was quite exceptional. It is significant too that Galwey, despite his Catholic sentiments, invested so much money in his parish church two decades after it had been officially transformed into a Protestant establishment. The three chaplains financed by Galwey remind one of the chantry chaplains of former days, and one wonders what function they served in a church reformed according to the Elizabethan settlement.

Alderman Christopher Galwey's will, dated 12 September 1582, has no Catholic dedications. He provided 30s. for the maintenance of St Peter's and Christ Church, 5s. 8d. for St Fin Barre's and 4s. for Holy Rood.[89] He bequeathed £1 to the Vicar David Tirry, and 3s. to three other priests. None of those bequests was distinctively Catholic, though his traditional beliefs are reflected in his gift of 3s. to be paid to Thomas Moyrane, a priest, 'in remembrance of me' – a phrase which calls to mind the purpose of the former chantries. William Verdon, whose will was dated 3 March 1567, bequeathed £1 to Rector Coppinger and two other priests, as well as £1 for the Lady Chapel in Christ Church.[90] John Tadhg MacCarthy, whose will is dated 23 December 1577, bequeathed two barrels of barley for the mainte-

---

87 *Gentleman's Magazine* (July 1861), 35. 88 *Gentleman's Magazine* (Sept. 1861), 257–60. 89 *Gentleman's Magazine* (Nov. 1861), 261–2. 90 *Gentleman's Magazine* (June 1862), 711–12.

nance of Christ Church and he directed that 12*d*. be paid to every poor priest there.[91] William Galwey, whose will was dated 20 July 1581, made no Catholic declarations though he bequeathed 5*s*. per annum to the priests of Christ Church.[92] Edmond White, in his will dated 7 June 1582, bequeathed 6*d*. to three priests in Christ Church, along with 3*s*. 4*d*. for the maintenance of the nave and a further 3*s*. 4*d*. for candles, the latter gift showing his traditionalist sympathies.[93]

One wonders whether the 'poor priests' attached to the city's parish churches somehow continued to maintain the function of the chantry chaplains after the chantries were dissolved in 1578,[94] conducting services in memory of the deceased patricians employing the Latin edition of the *Book of Common Prayer*. In any event the money bestowed on the supernumerary chaplains in Christ Church and St Peter's and on the fabric of the churches themselves was often given by people who favoured the old faith but were reluctant to sever long-standing and intimate ties with their parish churches or chapels even when they were 'reformed' at the queen's command.

COUNTER-REFORMATION CORK

The wills from the middle of Elizabeth's reign give no grounds for thinking that the Reformations had made significant progress in winning people's adherence in Cork, but it does seem that people's attachment to Catholicism may have been weakened. The wills certainly do not convey an impression of a general religious enthusiasm, either among men or women. The wills – and it has to be borne in mind that they are a very small sample indeed, no more than a palimpsest – seem to show that a small minority were very committed Catholics, and that Protestantism had few if any adherents (at least among the older age group most likely to make wills), but the majority of people (though many were clearly inclined to the religion of their forebears) were willing to conform to the Elizabethan church establishment.

The wills from Cork therefore seem to confirm Nicholas Canny's suggestion that the Tudor Reformations could well have succeeded in Ireland.[95] Eamon Duffy has cautioned that testators often responded to official animosity towards Catholicism by writing wills that were prudently discreet about their true religious convictions.[96] Therefore, it would be wise to hesitate

---

91 *Gentleman's Magazine* (Nov. 1861), 505.   92 *Gentleman's Magazine* (Sept. 1861), 257.
93 *Gentleman's Magazine* (June 1862), 713–14.   94 Bolster, *Diocese of Cork*, 2, 80.
95 Nicholas Canny, 'Why the reformation failed in Ireland: *une question mal posée*?', *Journal of Ecclesiastical History*, 30 (1979), 423–50.   96 Eamon Duffy, *The stripping of the altars: traditional religion in England, c.1400–c.1580* (London, 1992), pp 513–14.

before citing the wills from Cork as a reflection of the phenomenon known in England as 'church papistry', whereby some individuals who were Catholic by conviction continued to quietly attend their parish church though services were conducted with the *Book of Common Prayer*.[97] Nonethless, England's experience shows that people's commitment to specific Catholic doctrines was eroded over the years by Protestant preaching and the passage of time. Given the age profile of the population of Cork in the 1580s, with life expectancy lower than today, there were very few indeed who could have remembered the old Latin liturgies being celebrated in their parish churches, and hardly anyone who would have been able to remember the days of the Catholic church before Henry VIII's schism. Yet, in a remarkably short space of time the Catholic Counter-Reformation swept all before it in Cork.

William Lyon was already bishop of Ross when, in May 1583, Elizabeth directed that he hold the diocese of Cork and Cloyne diocese *in commendam*.[98] Lyon administered his united dioceses with zeal. He re-built churches and furnished them with English bibles, New Testaments and service books. He devoted some attention to education, and made an annual inspection of the schools.[99] The bishop was highly praised by Lord Deputy Fitzwilliam for preaching the word of God, and for encouraging people to receive Holy Communion. During the thanksgiving service after the dispersal of the Spanish Armada in 1588 Lyon preached to a huge congregation in Cork city.[1]

Meanwhile, Dr Dermot Creagh, who had been trained as a Gaelic bard at Cahir before becoming a priest, was provided to Cork diocese by the pope in October 1580 and showed remarkable energy in his work to revive Catholicism in southern Ireland.[2] Creagh sought to win Ireland over to the Counter-Reformation through preaching, and the overthrow of English rule. Miler Magrath, the Elizabethan archbishop of Cashel, wrote in 1590 that Creagh,

> uses all manner of spiritual jurisdictions in the whole province, being the pope's legate; consecrating churches, making priests, confirming children, deciding matrimonial cases ... this Creagh draws the whole country in general to disloyalty and breaking of laws, his credit is so much.[3]

Creagh formed a network of Counter-Reformation priests in Munster with surnames representative of the propertied classes of the region, including men with Irish surnames as well as English.[4] Contrary to a popular misconception,

---

[97] Alexandra Walsham, *Church papists: Catholicism, conformity and confessional polemic in early modern England* (Woodbridge, 1993). [98] *Works of Ware*, 1, p. 565. [99] *CSPI, 1596–7*, p. 15. [1] *CSPI, 1596–7*, p. 14. [2] Bolster, *Diocese of Cork*, 2, pp 87–94, 98–104; Jefferies, *Irish church*, pp 198, 214, 239, 249–54, 260–3, 269, 270. [3] SP 63/156/12. [4] Jefferies, *Irish church*, pp 252–3.

the Counter-Reformation priesthood was not predominantly drawn from urban communities in Ireland.

By 1592 Bishop Creagh was demanding that priests and people take oaths disassociating themselves from the Elizabethan religious establishment. Archbishop Magrath reported,

> This Creagh uses all means to bring all sorts of people to the acknowledging of the pope's authority ... First, he has set down an order that all priests in Ireland, and especially in Munster, shall be denounced as heretics unless they be allowed by himself or such as like authority from the pope amongst them, and to those he allows he has given general instructions to receive none to any part of their seven sacraments but such as will swear, first to keep and obey the pope's laws and authority, and especially to give their help to the pope's army whensoever they shall land, to whom he affirms the whole government, spiritual and temporal, of right to appertain. By this means the most part of the inhabitants of Munster have professed to be subjects to the pope, for as many as communicate, are married, confirmed, absolved or dispensed with are driven to swear to that oath, yea when any infant is baptised the parents are sworn to the pope. Such as shall swear in this sort, their names are written presently in a book which is the register written by the said Dr Creagh's own hand and termed the 'Book of Life', and no Irishman can have life everlasting unless his name be written in the same book. The said doctor sends a copy to Rome and Spain once every year with other intelligences of the incidents and of the states of England and Ireland.[5]

Magrath lamented in 1593 that 'the general unbridled multitude there [in Munster are] notorious Papists and reconciled to the pope and king of Spain'.[6]

Lyon, the royally appointed bishop of Cork, Cloyne and Ross, found the clergy of his dioceses resigning their benefices *en masse*. In his visitation of 1592, he learned that he had only twenty-five clergymen to serve the seventy-five parishes in Cork diocese, thirty for the 125 parishes in Cloyne and thirteen for the twenty-six parishes in Ross.[7] In a letter of September 1595 he wrote of people being sworn against the Church of Ireland and of priests forsaking their benefices to become 'Massing priests'.[8] As Munster was swept by the Nine Years War (1594–1603) the Church of Ireland was swept away by it.[9] Before 1598, Bishop Lyon had lost all jurisdiction in his dioceses and was obliged to live as an ordinary man in Cork.[10]

5 SP 63/164/47. 6 SP 63/170/4. 7 Alan Ford, *The Protestant Reformation in Ireland, 1590–1641* (Dublin, 1997), p. 37. 8 SP 63/182/47. 9 SP 63/205/225. 10 SP 63/208,

In 1596, Lyon depicted the scale of the Counter-Reformation success in Cork in dramatic terms.[11] Women never attended Protestant services in the city, and only office-holding men were generally present. The *Book of Common Prayer* was denigrated as the 'devil's service' and people crossed themselves in the street 'after the popish manner' when passing a Protestant minister for fear of diabolical contamination. The children had abandoned the local grammar school when the teacher was required to take them to church for Protestant services. The frontispiece and endleaf of the school's textbooks, where the royal style was reproduced and the queen prayed for, were systematically ripped out. No fewer than ten 'seminary and seducing priests' were maintained in Cork. They provided not only Sunday Masses but a complete round of Catholic devotional liturgies and practices. The priests perambulated the city streets in the company of the social elites and their material needs were met by public subscription. While the Protestant churches were empty the people thronged to the Catholic services, the young merchants of Cork flaunting swords and pistols as they went to Mass, daring the English authorities to interfere. As Brendan Bradshaw observed, thenceforth the commitment to the Counter-Reformation in Cork, as in other Irish cities, 'was to be undeviating'.[12]

It is impossible to explain exactly why this transformation in the religious scene in Cork happened. It does not simply reflect any failings on the part of Bishop Lyon, an energetic prelate who warrants a study in his own right: the same pattern of dramatic collapse of the Church of Ireland can also be traced in Limerick and Galway.[13] It was not, as has been shown in the discussion of the wills, simply a reflection of an indomitable Catholic zeal that was immune to the Reformations. Rather, it seems to reflect a popular response to the Elizabethan government's policies of conquest, colonization and anglicization as well as Reformation in the final decades of the sixteenth century. The Munster plantation, the build-up of a Protestant English military and civil establishment in the south, and the intrusion of English Protestant clergymen into the church, seem to have alienated the local population, including the urban oligarchs who considered themselves English, though they may not always have been accepted as such by the Protestant 'New English'.[14] The extension of the Nine Years War to Munster in 1595 provided the opportunity for the citizens in Cork to openly demonstrate the depth of their alienation from the Church of Ireland.[15] Nonetheless, the very existence of the

pt 2/154. 11 *CSPI, 1596–7*, pp 13–20; Bradshaw, 'Reformation in the cities', pp 463–6. 12 Bradshaw, 'Reformation in the cities', p. 466. 13 Ibid. 14 Bradshaw, 'Reformation in the cities', pp 466–7. 15 For context see Hiram Morgan, *Tyrone's rebellion: the outbreak of the Nine Years War in Tudor Ireland* (Dublin, 1993). For a survey of the war, which suggests that it was more deliberate than Morgan argues, see Jefferies, 'Hugh O'Neill, earl of Tyrone, c.1550–1616' in Charles Dillon and Henry A. Jefferies (eds), *Tyrone: history and society* (Dublin, 2000).

seminary priests referred to by Bishop Lyon does show that there was sufficient enthusiasm for the Catholic faith in and around Cork for the Counter-Reformation in Cork to be successfully effected. Clearly, the dramatic shift in favour of the Catholic church in Cork did indeed have a religious basis, though it was not simply a religious phenomenon.

In 1600, Bishop Lyon wrote that 'The whole kingdom is of a conspiracy by means of the Romish priests which were and are the plotters of this general rebellion' among whom he singled out Dermot Creagh.[16] Sir George Carew, the president of Munster, commented in July 1601 that people in Cork were 'no less affectioned to the Spaniard than the rest of the cities in this kingdom'.[17] Captain Vaughan reported in May 1601 that the cities of Waterford, Cork and Limerick had 'bound themselves' to receive any Spanish force that might land in Munster.[18] The Ulster lords were certainly confident that the cities would join them once the Spanish arrived.[19] Bishop Lyon, in a letter of February 1600, was adamant that, 'The towns are the nurses of this rebellion, for they furnish the rebels with munition and victual, as wine, salt, *aqua vitae, et cetera*'. He explained how the trade in war material operated: 'the merchant of Cork buys his [gun] powder of the Frenchman, sells it to the rebel for a [cow] hide, and that hide he returns back to the Frenchman for a French crown'.[20] When the earl of Tyrone led a Confederate army to Kinsale in the Spring of 1600 and passed within a musket shot of Cork, the mayor of the city ordered that no one was to challenge the army of O'Neill and O'Donnell, neither to shoot at them nor sally outside the walls. Yet, significantly, there was a 'town Captain' willing to skirmish with the Ulster lords along with 100 volunteers from the city.[21] The evidence points to division and ambiguity within the city. John Meade, the city's recorder, and Edmund Tirry, an alderman, were condemned by Lyon as 'evil-minded men to the state and her majesty's government'.[22] However, the lords' defeat at the Battle of Kinsale (1601) changed everything. Carew remarked of the citizens at Cork that,

> While Tyrone with his army lay upon our backs the townsmen of Cork were proud and would not know those Englishmen with whom they were familiarly acquainted, no sooner was the victory ours but their faces changed, and ever since are tractable.[23]

The Nine Years War was over, but the struggle for souls simply entered a new phase.

Once rumours of Elizabeth's death reached Cork in March 1603, the citizens manned the city's gates and prevented the entry of any English soldiers,

16 SP 63/207, pt 1/108.   17 SP 63/208, pt 3/56.   18 SP 63/208, pt 2/73.   19 Jefferies, *Irish church*, pp 260–75.   20 SP 63/207, pt 1/108.   21 SP 63/207, pt 2/13.   22 SP 63/207, pt 1/108.   23 *CSPI 1601–3*, p. 276.

unless they were disarmed. They did not proclaim James Stuart as the new king when directed to do so, but instead sent a messenger (using a false name) to consult with the corporation in Waterford. They imprisoned the royal officers in charge of the English army's ordnance and victuals that were stored in Skiddy's Castle in the city, and they seized the ordnance and the victuals. They sent some men in boats to Hawlbowline to regain possession of the island from the English garrison there and demolished the fort that President Carew had obliged them to build immediately south of their city walls to 'bridle' them.[24] The citizens barricaded the two main streets of the city, mounted cannon on the walls and opened fire every day, either on Shandon Castle, the headquarters of Munster's presidency, or on the Protestant bishop's house.[25] When English soldiers approached the city the citizens trained the cannons on them.[26]

The revolt in Cork was, by any reckoning, an extraordinary affair. The 'greatest and chiefest stirrer up of all these broils' was Cork's recorder, William Meade, supported by the mayor of Cork and other members of the corporation.[27] He and the mayor, 'with many others', attended a sermon in the city in which a friar 'openly preached that the king's majesty is not a lawful king until the pope has confirmed him'.[28] Meade subsequently became one of Hugh O'Neill's principal agents after the 'flight of the earls'.

Sir Jeffery Fenton stated at the time that the revolt in Cork was really 'a quarrel of state' and that the citizens only proclaimed it as an affair of religion in the hope of winning Spanish support.[29] However, Fenton subsequently changed his mind and complained that Cork's corporation had been poisoned with a blind zeal towards the pope and his 'counterfeit' religion.[30] The evidence strongly points to religion as being the major motivation for the Corkonians' revolt. The citizens of Cork took solemn oaths on sacraments before priests to uphold the Catholic religion with their lives, lands and goods, and even declared they were content to be buried within the city's walls if they were denied it.[31] In the event, the men of Cork found that they were very vulnerable to English cannon mounted on the former religious buildings in the suburbs to the north and south of the city, and once the other cities and towns that had participated in the 'recusants' revolt' capitulated Cork's elites decided to submit, just before Deputy Mountjoy arrived at the city in person on 10 May.[32]

Anthony J. Sheehan highlighted the economic and constitutional grievances that formed the backdrop to the 'spontaneous popular displays of religious freedom for which the [recusants'] revolt is chiefly remembered'.[33]

24 *CSPI, James*, ed. C. W Russell and J.P. Prendergast (London, 1923), pp 51–3. 25 *CSPI, James*, pp 44, 48. 26 *CSPI, James*, p. 37. 27 *CSPI, James*, p. 55. 28 *CSPI, James*, p. 36. 29 *CSPI, James*, pp 46–7. 30 *CSPI, James*, p. 46. 31 *CSPI, James*, pp 44, 48. 32 *CSPI, James*, pp 43–5, 55–7. 33 Anthony J. Sheehan, 'The recusancy revolt

However, the evidence points very firmly to the centrality of religion in the revolt. Clearly in Cork resentment against the Munster presidency and the English garrisons was particularly acute, but everywhere else 'liberty of conscience' was the only demand made by the urban communities and even in Cork it was the central demand. Sheehan concluded that 'the townsfolk of Munster acted in a foolish and short-sighted manner'.[34] However, he failed to appreciate how religious passions can colour men's and women's calculations in politics.

Mountjoy did not exact retribution on the recusant citizens, apart from an unsuccessful attempt to prosecute the recorder of Cork and a few others who were most aggressively involved.[35] His philosophy was that,

> I am persuaded that a violent course therein will do little good to win men's consciences, but, howsoever, it is too soon to begin it; and it is most sure that it will breed a new war and, as I believe, make all the towns and nobility solicit Spanish aids. ... I am of the opinion that all religions do grow under persecution.[36]

Mountjoy was a lot more prescient than most English officials.

One could not have confidently predicted the ultimate failure of the Reformation in Cork. The loyalty of its elites to the English crown made it conceivable that they would embrace the English Reformation, despite their attachment to Catholic beliefs and practices. The wills from the time of Bishop Sheyne's episcopate hint at the possibility of Catholicism losing ground in Cork. However, when Richard Whyte visited Cork in 1590 he was accosted for religion (he being a Protestant) by Andrew Skydmore (one of the local mercantile oligarchs) and by Sir Warham St Leger (the English provincial governor!), 'with a great train following them, they arrogantly barking condemned the religion established [by law]' and put him 'in great fear' for his life.[37] All of the aldermen of Cork, he claimed, spoke out against the queen's religion. The veil of religious conformity was thrown off and it was to be a long time before the tensions exposed between the Catholic citizens of Cork and the Protestant state of which they were subjects were even tentatively resolved

---

of 1603: a re-interpretation' *Archivium Hibernicum*, 38 (1983), 10.   **34** Sheehan, 'Recusancy revolt', 12.   **35** Sheehan, 'Recusancy revolt', 3.   **36** *CSPI, 1601–3*, pp 556–7.   **37** SP 63/152/15.

The limits of Old English liberty: the case of Thomas Arthur, MD (1593–1675), in Limerick and Dublin

MARY ANN LYONS

The amount of my fees for this year past is £74 1s. 8d. for which and for other gifts conferred upon me, unworthy, I return boundless thanks to the Almighty God, Who has thus deigned to bless the beginning of my medical practice; and I beg Him to vouchsafe to direct, govern and sanctify the rest of my actions, to the praise and glory of His Name, through Christ our Lord, Amen.[1]

Thus wrote the Limerick physician, Thomas Arthur, in his feebook in March 1619, marking the end of the first year of his medical practice in that city. Having arrived fresh from completing his medical studies at the universities of Paris and Rheims, he had immediately commenced practice in Limerick. Signalling confidence for his future career, within two years he began constructing a large stone house in Irishtown, dominating the corner of Mungret Street, High Street and Broad Street, on the south side of the city. That confidence proved well founded as he was to become Ireland's leading physician, particularly during the 1620s and 30s. As this examination of his life and career will suggest, Arthur, in his relatively unique role among Old English professionals, deployed his means, position and contacts to test the limits of the liberties asserted and enjoyed by his class in the cities of Limerick and Dublin. His story, therefore, offers a rare and revealing perspective on the changing world in which he and his community negotiated their survival through decades of tolerance, 'thorough',[2] turbulence, transplantation and, finally, Restoration.

I

The son of an Old English Catholic Limerick merchant, William Arthur, and his wife, Anastace Rice, Thomas had a privileged upbringing during which he wholeheartedly embraced the fundamental values of his familial and

---

[1] Miscellaneous entry-book of Thomas Arthur, MD, of Limerick (BL, Add. MS 31,885, f. 116), hereafter Entry-book. [2] The nickname for Thomas Wentworth's policy aimed at restoring the interests of church and king in Ireland at the expense of Old English recalcitrance and New English corruption.

municipal heritage. The Arthurs were one of the city's four leading patrician families (the others being Sextons, Whites and Creaghs). Together with another eight mercantile families, including the Rices, they formed the ascendant elite who prided themselves on their families' long-standing civic service dating from the medieval era and their role in maintaining municipal stability and integrity in the face of escalating political, economic and religious change from the mid-sixteenth century onwards. Serving as cultural cynosures through their patronage of education, learning and piety, the Arthurs and other members of this elite laid the basis for Limerick's blossoming cultural and literary life, and for Catholic survivalism in the late sixteenth and seventeenth centuries.[3] A relative of Thomas, styled 'a popish Schoolemaster' by royal commissioners in 1615, taught 'a publique Schoole and had a great resort of Schollers' in the preceding years.[4] Thomas grew up in a milieu in which the socio-political harmony of this governing class rested upon a social cohesion achieved through careful ritualizing of the civic *cursus honorum*, assiduous stewardship of wealth and property by investment and partnership, induction of amenable newcomers, and the creation of close ties of affinity through intermarriage within the order – all of which he embraced in adulthood.[5] As a child, Thomas was not impervious to the religious tensions that prevailed in the greater north Munster region. He was born within a few years of the martyrdom of Bishop Patrick O'Healy of Mayo and his Franciscan companion, Conn O'Rourke, in Kilmallock, Co. Limerick, in 1579, and that of his own relative, Richard Creagh, Catholic archbishop of Armagh, who died in prison in 1585. Shortly before his birth, several priests, including a number of Jesuits, were rounded up in Munster and Connaught and sent as prisoners to Dublin where some were executed.[6] In 1604 the lord president of Munster, Sir Henry Brouncker, launched a vigorous campaign against Catholicism, ordering the expulsion of priests, the deposition of Catholic mayors, and the re-imposition of fines on all who refused to attend established church services. Tensions ran particularly high in Limerick where the mayor, Edmond Fox, refused, as a Catholic, to take the oath of supremacy and further declined to attend Protestant services. Fox was dismissed and from then until 1616 a succession of Catholic mayors were deposed and replaced by conformists: throughout the following decade, Limerick had an unbroken line of Protestant mayors.[7] Thus, around the time that Thomas 'as a beardless boy' joined dozens of the city's Catholic boys and

---

3 Colm Lennon, *The urban patriciates of early modern Ireland: a case-study of Limerick* (Dublin, 1999), pp 6, 7, 14.   4 Quoted in T. Corcoran (ed.), *Selected texts on education systems in Ireland from the close of the Middle Ages* (Dublin, 1928), p. 16.   5 Lennon, *Urban patriciates*, p. 6.   6 Maurice Lenihan, *Limerick: its history and antiquities* (Dublin, 1866), pp 103–21; Colm Lennon, *An Irish prisoner of conscience of the Tudor era: Archbishop Richard Creagh of Armagh, 1523–86* (Dublin, 2000).   7 Liam Irwin, 'Seventeenth-century Limerick' in David Lee (ed.), *Remembering Limerick* (Limerick, 1997), pp 115–16; Lennon,

men travelling to Bordeaux to pursue their education, their families were being forced into a defensive position. They claimed credit for having secured full borough status for the city in 1609, and were determined to resist incursions on their authority and liberties. Although fractured along denominational lines they were resolute in their shared conviction that through continued conciliar solidarity, civic progress towards independence could be maintained. For essentially political and economic reasons, their unity held firm until the 1640s; the few Protestant or newly arrived families subscribed to the prevailing municipal if not religious ethos.[8]

Thomas Arthur was one of a new breed of Old English Catholic professionals who emerged during the 1610s. With no option but to pursue their medical studies abroad (Trinity College did not offer medical degrees at that time),[9] Arthur and another Old English Catholic, Christopher Talbot, were among the first Irish students to graduate from the Faculty of Medicine at Rheims University and return to Ireland to embark upon careers as physicians. Unlike his contemporaries seeking admission to public office or admission to the Bar, Arthur enjoyed the advantage of working within an unregulated milieu of medical pluralism in which there was, at worst, no *de jure* and at best, no *de facto* bar against a Catholic (or indeed anyone) practising as a physician.[10]

Thomas carried a regard for the fundamental values of his Old English urban Catholic upbringing into adulthood. His going to Bordeaux *may* intimate that he began his university career as a clerical student since, at that time, Bordeaux was a popular choice for clerical students from Limerick diocese.[11] His opportunity to study at three major Catholic universities (Bordeaux, Paris and Rheims), each of which embraced the rigorous discipline of Counter-Reformation Catholicism during and after the Religious Wars (1562–98), clearly left its mark in his personal piety, his loyalty to the Catholic tra-

---

Richard Creagh.   8 Entry-book, f. 190r.; Lennon, *Urban patriciates*, pp 8, 13; idem, 'Religious and social change in early modern Limerick: the testimony of the Sexton family papers' in Liam Irwin et al. (eds), *Limerick: history & society* (Dublin, 2009), p. 118.   9 J.D.H. Widdess, *A history of the Royal College of Physicians of Ireland, 1654–1963* (Edinburgh & London, 1963), pp 5, 13; John F. Fleetwood, *The history of medicine in Ireland* (Dublin, 1983), pp 32–3; James Kelly, 'The emergence of scientific and institutional medical practice in Ireland, 1650–1800' in Greta Jones and Elizabeth Malcolm (eds), *Medicine, disease and the state in Ireland, 1650–1940* (Cork, 1999), pp 22–3.   10 See Mary Ann Lyons, 'The role of graduate physicians in professionalizing medical practice in Ireland, c.1619–54' in James Kelly and Fiona Clark (eds), *Ireland and medicine in the seventeenth and eighteenth centuries* (Farnham, 2010), pp 17–38.   11 Entry-book, f. 190r. Between 1603 and 1617, thirteen students from Limerick diocese were recorded as resident in the Irish College, Bordeaux. See '*Catalogue de quelques clerics ecclesiastiques Hibernois*' (Bordeaux, 1619), in Charles Russell and John P. Prendergast (eds), *CSPI James I, 1615–1625* (London, 1880), pp 318–22. Arthur's name is not included: evidently he found lodgings elsewhere.

dition, and his life-long scholarly interest in the history of Catholicism in Ireland. The latter was inspired by his relative Archbishop Richard Creagh and shaped by the new historiography moulded within Irish émigré circles on the Continent during the 1620s and 30s.[12] Arthur's commitment to Catholicism on all three levels is reflected in his library collection, which included copies of several standard texts read by the Old English Catholics of his day.[13] Among these were Alfonso Villagas' *Lives of the saints* (incorporating lives of Saints Patrick, Brigid and Columba), and a panegyric by the bishop of Cork, William Tirry. He also owned copies of David Rothe's *Brigida Thaumaturga* (Paris, 1620) and his *Analecta sacra et mira*. First published in Paris in 1616, the *Analecta* was of particular interest for its lengthy accounts of the aforementioned mistreatment afforded Catholics in Limerick and Munster during the late 1500s when, according to Arthur's own account, his grand-uncle, Fr Edmund, was among those priests, abbots and laypeople who experienced great hardship.[14] That he owned a copy of T. Alfield's *True report on the death and martyrdom of ... Edmund Campion, Ralph Sherwin and Alexander Briant, Jesuit priests at Tyburn in December 1581* (London, 1581) is also unsurprising given Campion's personal associations with the Old English during the early 1570s, the strength of the Jesuit tradition in Limerick city, and Arthur's preoccupation with researching the treatment of Catholics during that era. His special interest in the history of Limerick diocese is likewise reflected in the inclusion of a section on the see, commencing with the first bishop, Gilbert (*c*.1106–40), in his manuscript lives of Irish saints (1627).[15]

Arthur's intense pride in his Old English lineage found expression in his many Latin verse compositions, notably a 'Genealogical idyll', composed for his descendants. It hailed his ancestors as 'Noble from great-great-great grandparents and made sound by a distinguished descent, surpassing all families of the city in official dignity' and celebrated their adherence to the Catholic faith and espousal of the values that defined their class.[16] He praised his grand-uncle Edmund, 'a priest of the sacred mysteries, a very learned girder of his age ... who bore undiminished and unshaken contests and hardships for the teachings of Christ.'[17] Highlighting his grandfather Thomas' (d.1581) distinguished civic service, he recounted how 'a civil honour embraces this man and he is chosen as the first sheriff'. He commended his uncle Thomas for being 'hard-working and wealthy', and his two aunts,

12 See Simonne Guenée, *Bibliographie de l'histoire des universities françaises des origines à la Revolution* (2 vols, Paris, 1978), ii, 70–1; André Tuilier, *Histoire de l'Université de Paris et de la Sorbonne. Vol 1, Des origines à Richelieu* (Paris, 1994), p. 442; Robert Benoit, *Vivre et mourir à Reims au Grand Siècle, 1580–1720* (Arras, 1999), p. 58.   13 Entry-book, ff 12r., 13r.   14 Ibid., f. 183v.   15 Thomas Arthur, 'MS Vitae Sanctor', 1627, Russell Library, St Patrick's College, Maynooth, MS 3 G 1 (R.B. Case 201), ff 227–30. This substantial Latin text, written in small hand, runs to 260 pages.   16 Entry-book, f. 183v.   17 Ibid., f. 183v.

Helena and Joanna, as ladies 'who submit to authority and to grace'. He reserved particularly warm praise for his father, William, especially for his civic service (he was 'chosen as the first sheriff' in 1576 and 1597) and for being 'upright', 'generous, lenient and kind-hearted', 'a promoter of faith and of God' whose 'kindly hospitable house lies open to wandering strangers and the righteous priests of thundering Jupiter'.[18] Among his mother Anastase Rice's many virtues, he cited her practice of sending 'gifts to the destitute through the streets of the city and through the homes', and her 'long fasting' which 'wears that lady out'.[19] In good Old English humanist tradition, Thomas' brother, Edmund, was an accomplished Latinist: Thomas acclaimed him for his 'extraordinary uprightness and a paternal openness of mind, love and honesty'.[20]

Furthermore, determined to ensure that his antecedents' service as civic dignitaries and senior ecclesiastics was recorded for posterity, and that accurate legal records of their stake in the physical and aesthetic development of the city were kept in order to protect familial interests in future generations, Arthur, like Archbishop Richard Creagh and Edmund Sexton, assembled a collection of cartularies, annals, civil chronicles, family business and genealogical records, and scholarly tracts.[21] The Arthurs in particular had much to be proud of, having supplied no fewer than twenty-one mayors of the city across the fifteenth, sixteenth and early seventeenth centuries,[22] and the papal bull of consecration of Archbishop Creagh was among Thomas' most prized documents.[23]

II

From the start of his career, Arthur recognized the limits associated with trying to establish his reputation and realize his potential as a continentally trained physician in a small provincial city: he therefore set his sights on Dublin. Despite Donagh O'Brien, the Protestant fourth earl of Thomond's unpopularity with Limerick's patrician families after his attempted imposition of his authority on them in 1599–1600,[24] Arthur was willing to take full advantage of the earl's patronage (especially after O'Brien was appointed lord president of Munster in 1615) to establish his practice, initially in Munster and, more consequentially, in Dublin.[25] As a physician, Thomas Arthur was the consummate pragmatist. An ambitious man with a great fondness for money, from the outset he consciously assumed a non-partisan stance in his

---

18 Ibid., f. 188v.; Lenihan, *History*, pp 699, 700. 19 Entry-book, f. 189r. 20 Ibid., f. 189v. 21 Lennon, *Urban patriciates*, pp 6, 11–12. 22 Lenihan, *History*, pp 695–702. 23 Ibid., p. 118. 24 Clodagh Tait, 'Broken heads and trampled hats: rioting in Limerick in 1599' in Irwin et al. (eds), *Limerick*, pp 91–111. 25 Entry-book, f. 190r.

professional dealings with all clients, regardless of their political outlook, denominational affiliation, ethnic origin, or socio-economic status, provided they or a sponsor could pay their fee. That he adhered to that stance throughout his career is evidenced by the comprehensive and eclectic list of patients recorded in his entry-book (1619–66). During his early years in practice, while based mainly in Limerick, he saw approximately seventy clients per year and earned just over £74 in 1619, £75 in 1620, £46 in 1621, £58 in 1622 and £61 in 1623. Although his clients did include a handful of Gaelic men, aristocrats and Protestant prelates in the greater Munster area, these were very much the exception. The majority were Catholic men from Limerick, many of them members of the city's Old English families (Creaghs, Sextons, Arthurs, Roches, Whites, Wolfes and Stritches among others). They were variously employed as merchants, craftsmen, bakers, students and fishermen; several were members of Limerick Corporation and some were beggars. Typically each paid 10$d.$ or less per visit.[26] There were, however, promising signs for his future: in May 1620 he was summoned to Co. Antrim where he attended the wife of Sir Arthur Chichester, treasurer of Ireland, and Sir Randal mac Sorley MacDonnell, Viscount Dunluce, and in return he received the tidy sum of £6.[27] Mindful that he needed to establish a practice in the metropolitan marketplace if he was to become as successful as he expected, from April 1624 he began spending more time in Dublin.[28] But while his reputation as a physician was certainly spreading throughout Ireland (evidenced by his extended geographical catchment and increasing instances of complex medical conditions including paralysis), his client list was as yet unremarkable.[29] That, however, was about to change dramatically.

III

Arthur's timing in establishing his Dublin practice in the mid-1620s was fortuitous, coinciding as it did with the succession of Charles Stuart as king in 1625. As Aidan Clarke has highlighted, in one semi-public respect, the position of Catholics in Ireland improved during Charles I's reign (1625–49): after 1628, they were allowed to practice as barristers and solicitors on condition that they took the oath of allegiance.[30] Two years before, as Charles held out the prospect of official toleration for Catholicism, there were already encouraging signs of a growing acceptance of Catholic physicians among senior-ranking members of the Dublin Castle administration. In that year three Irish

---

26 Ibid., ff 15r.–22r.   27 Ibid., f. 17v.; for a profile of MacDonnell see Terry Clavin, 'MacDonnell, Sir Randal mac Sorley, 1st earl of Antrim', *DIB*.   28 Entry-book, ff 20r.–20v.   29 Ibid., ff 20r.–24r.   30 Aidan Clarke, *The Old English in Ireland, 1625–42* (repr. Dublin, 2000), p. 121.

Catholic physicians (Dermot O'Meara, Christopher Talbot and John Verdon), joined by two physicians attached to Dublin Castle (James Metcalfe and Paul Delaune), petitioned Charles I to take steps to professionalize medical practice in Ireland by founding a college of physicians in Dublin, based on the London college model.[31] Charles was positively disposed to the proposal and in August 1626 he went so far as to instruct Lord Deputy Henry Cary, Viscount Falkland, and the Irish privy council to establish in Dublin 'a college, society, and corporation of physicians, according to the rule and form of the charter ... granted to the physicians in our city of London, for the incorporating of them'.[32] That the physicians' campaign ended in failure was not entirely disadvantageous to Old English Catholic practitioners such as Arthur as it left the Irish medical marketplace in a highly unregulated state, with physicians free to establish and run their practices without legal impediment for several decades.

Thomas Arthur also contributed to that growing acceptance of Irish Catholic physicians within the top échelons of government in Dublin through his successful treatment of the Church of Ireland Primate James Ussher who was suffering from a disease that royal physicians in England had been unable to diagnose or cure.[33] In June 1626, having completed a three-month course of treatment on Lambay Island, Arthur and Ussher presented themselves before Lord Deputy Falkland. According to Arthur, after he explained the nature of the disease 'so scientifically', Falkland 'admitted candidly that he was quite satisfied [with the explanation], and so he put away ... the possibility of any pretext for the old envy and malice', meaning the physician's Catholicism. Crucially for Arthur, in a public expression of his approval, Falkland immediately appointed him physician 'to both himself and all his nearest and dearest'.[34] Arthur appreciated that this was a vital turning point in his career, making him 'renowned and popular among Englishmen, to whom I have been hateful on account of the Catholic religion'.[35] Prior to 1626 he had treated several prominent English Protestant clerics and laymen, including Bernard Adams '*pseudo-episcopus*' of Limerick, John Ryder, '*psudo-episcopus*' of Killaloe,[36] and even Sir Christopher Sibthorpe, an English judge and religious writer who published three theological polemics against Catholicism.[37] Yet, in summer 1626 he was acutely conscious of the opportunities and rewards that would attend this acceptance that he had gained from a new clientele – the top-ranking figures within the government and ecclesiastical establishment in Dublin. The difference in his

---

[31] Lyons, 'Professionalisation', p. 25. [32] James Morrin (ed.), *Calendar of the patent and close rolls of chancery in Ireland of the reign of Charles the first* (Dublin, 1863), p. 277; Lyons, 'Professionalisation', pp 25–8. [33] Repeated bouts of what contemporaries termed '*quartan ague*' immobilised the archbishop for long spells during 1625 and early 1626. See John McCafferty, 'Ussher, James', *DIB*. [34] Entry-book, f. 24r. [35] Ibid., f. 24r. [36] Ibid., ff 20r., 20v. [37] Ibid., f. 24v.; Terry Clavin, 'Sibthorpe, Sir Christopher', *DIB*.

The limits of Old English liberty

attitude towards his two highest-paying clients, Sir Randal mac Sorley MacDonnell, earl of Antrim, and Archbishop Ussher, is revealing. Despite the fact that MacDonnell was among Arthur's earliest, most generous and constant patients, the earl's deep attachment to his Catholic Gaelic heritage, combined with his physical and ideological isolation from the centre of government in Dublin, made him less useful to Arthur than Ussher whose approval could open doors to the homes of the most senior figures within political and ecclesiastical circles and metropolitan society for the ambitious physician.

IV

The impact on Arthur's practice of his successful treatment of Ussher was both immediate and profound in terms of his client profile, social circle and income. Within a year of Falkland's declaration of confidence, true to his word, both he and his eldest son were attending the physician.[38] The knock-on effect of the lord deputy's readiness to cross the confessional divide was evident when the virulently anti-Catholic Sir Charles Coote senior followed Falkland's lead and began attending Arthur for insomnia on 18 November 1627.[39] Arthur also saw a growing number of Protestant clergymen who were doubtless influenced by Ussher's tolerance of a Catholic physician.[40]

As a by-product of bridging the confessional divide in his medical practice, Arthur gained access to Dublin's elite scholarly circle through his exchanges with Ussher, then widely recognized as Ireland's leading polymath, and through his acquaintance with the work of other prominent figures in that circle, including Sir James Ware, a protégé of Ussher. In this way, Arthur was afforded the opportunity to contribute to the grand enterprise in which manuscripts and information were exchanged between Ussher, Ware and leading Irish Catholic scholars at home and on the Continent, all of whom were engaged in fundamental research on Ireland's history. The professional relationship between Arthur and Ussher quickly evolved into a personal one, with Ussher granting Arthur access to his collections of lives of Irish saints which Arthur used in the collation of his own edition in 1627.[41]

---

38 Entry-book, ff 26v., 27r., 29r. 39 Ibid., f. 27v.; Robert Armstrong, 'Coote, Sir Charles', *DIB*. 40 Among the first of these to attend was the Welsh-born Lewis Jones, dean of Cashel, whose brother-in-law, James Ussher, recommended him for the archbishopric of Cashel. He was not appointed but in 1632 he was nominated to the diocese of Killaloe: see Entry-book, f. 24v.; Aidan Clarke, 'Jones, Lewis', *DIB*. 41 In researching this work, Arthur's interest was animated by the current dispute which erupted when Scottish writer, Thomas Dempster, appropriated several Irish men and women to the pantheon of Scottish saints. Undoubtedly it was through his connection with Archbishop Usher that Arthur acquired copies of Dempster's *Scotia illustrior* and David Rothe's vig-

Yet, in spite of their shared Old English lineage, their passion for scholarly research, and their genial professional and personal relationship, Arthur remained as firmly entrenched on his side of the confessional divide as did Ussher. Indeed, his insistence upon using the prefix '*pseudo*' when referring to all Protestant clerics (Ussher included) in his private entry-book offers a revealing insight into the depth and rigidity of his commitment to Catholicism, and intimates that on a private, personal level, he was far from indifferent on the matter of religious persuasion.

In addition to his enhanced reputation as a physician and his admittance to Dublin's elite scholarly circle, Arthur's income from his medical practice received a significant boost after he began treating Ussher who paid him the exceptional sum of £51 for his services in 1626 alone.[42] By the end of March 1628 his practice had expanded to the point that his annual income reached just over £140.[43] Arthur was astute in maintaining a client base in Limerick, tending to patients during his occasional visits home: during one four-month sojourn (6 August–23 November 1629) he saw thirty-eight patients and earned £22 5s.[44] Nevertheless, by 1630, his Dublin practice was growing so significantly he recognized that he 'could not be absent without sustaining great loss of time and gain'.[45] In August he moved his wife and children to live with him in the capital – a telling indicator of his sense of confidence and security in running his practice within full view of the viceroy and the political and ecclesiastical establishment.

V

With Arthur mostly in full-time residence in Dublin, his practice blossomed during the 1630s. His reputation for impartiality and trustworthiness, reflected in the diversity of his clientele throughout the late 1620s and 30s,

---

orous counter-attack, *Hibernia resurgens*, published in 1620 and 1621 respectively, together with a copy of another less well-known text generated by this dispute, *In Dympsterum Vindiciae*, by John Roche, Catholic bishop of Ferns. Ussher almost certainly also presented Arthur with copies of his *Brief declaration of the universalitie of the church of Christ*, his *Answer to a challenge made by a Jesuite in Ireland*, his *Veterum epistolarum Hibernicarum*, and his *Immanuel* listed in the physician's library catalogue. Similarly, Arthur's ownership of Ware's *Archiepiscoporum Casseliensium* and his *De Scriptoribus Hiberniae* most likely came about as a result of his professional relationship with the family since he was physician to Ware's elderly parents during the early 1630s. As literary executor to Richard Creagh, archbishop of Armagh, Arthur held Creagh's writings, including his important catechism and incomplete history of the church, both of which would have been of interest to Ussher and Ware. See Entry-book, ff 12r., 13r.; Lennon, *Urban patriciates*, p. 15.   42 Entry-book, f. 24v.   43 Ibid., f. 29r.   44 Ibid., ff 32r.–32v.   45 Entry-book, f. 168r.; J.D.H. Widdess, 'A notable Irish physician', *Irish Journal of Medical Science*, 373 (1957), 25.

The limits of Old English liberty

is best illustrated by the fact that he treated Rory O'More in the same week (2–8 October 1633) as several figures closely associated with Wentworth's faction (namely Christopher Wandesford and Sir George Radcliffe) and members of his household.[46] As a result, Arthur enjoyed a substantial and largely stable annual income throughout the 1630s: £282 (1631–2), £233 (1632–3), £278 (1633–4), £328 (1634–5), £293 (1635–6), £210 (1636–7), £278 (1637–8), £302 (1638–9), and £253 (1639–40).[47] On the strength of this thriving practice, he and his family enjoyed a lifestyle appropriate to their rank as Old English patrician elite, unimpeded by anxiety arising from legislative restrictions on his professional activities. However, the position of that elite was becoming increasingly untenable during the 1630s. Despite their continued appeals to their English blood and historic loyalty, they were largely excluded from the more influential and lucrative offices of central and local government, and Catholic religious services were subject to sporadic repression.[48]

In the two years before the outbreak of the 1641 uprising, Arthur's client list remained as eclectic as ever, including Sir John Clotworthy, the Ulster Scots' leading spokesman, whose daughter attended; Lord Deputy Thomas Wentworth, earl of Strafford, whose eldest son paid several visits; Sir Maurice Eustace, speaker of the Irish House of Commons; Archbishop James Ussher and his brother, Robert Ussher, '*pseudo-episcopus*' of Kildare; the countess of Kildare; Sir Randal mac Sorley MacDonnell; and Lord Justice Sir William Parsons.[49] While he may have dealt with all of his patients in an impartial, professional manner, Arthur was discerning and at times acerbic in his character assessments. For instance, he despised Wentworth and his administration for having inflicted enormous damage on the country and on innocent subjects like him who were loyal to the king. With subversive amusement in the privacy of his study, later in life he penned 'A physiognomical anagram' based on 'Thomas Wentworth, a harsh Viceroy of Ireland and an abominable man' whom he styled a 'savage man, a Prince of Darkness'. In this, we overhear the candid thoughts of a provincial Old English Catholic royalist in Dublin who, although not in the vanguard of campaigning for the Graces, nonetheless in private bitterly resented the exploitative treatment that his class and the country in general endured at the hands of the Wentworth administration. Arthur was also scathing in relation to Sir George Radcliffe, Wentworth's chief adviser (1633–41), who attended

---

46 Entry-book, f. 46r. Furthermore, during his occasional tours beyond Dublin, he never missed an opportunity to treat all who approached him and most importantly could pay him. Thus, in summer 1634, while in Antrim attending his long-term patient, Sir Randal MacSorley MacDonnell, he treated two Puritan ministers, a priest and a Catholic bishop among several others: ibid., ff 48v., 49r., 50v.   47 Ibid., ff 40, 43v., 48r., 51r., 54r., 55v., 59v., 64v., 68v.   48 S.J. Connolly, *Divided kingdom: Ireland, 1630–1800* (Oxford, 2008), p. 7.   49 Entry-book, ff 65r.–72r.

his practice frequently throughout that period. In a series of anagrams he denounced Radcliffe as 'a wilde beast [who was] treacherie to the flock ... for he and the Lord Deputie by his advice hindered the subjects to make anie appeale or complainte to the King'. To amuse himself, Arthur also attributed confessional utterances to Radcliffe, among them 'I gave advice, shewed reasons and prompted to him [Wentworth] who was bringing great miserie, misfortune, loss, hurt, destruction and ruyne uppon the Kingdome' and 'I shall be reduced and brought againe to be of noe accompt, to be vile and base'.[50] Just as he privately mocked some of his clients, Arthur was quick to capitalize on his professional relationships with them to protect and enhance his very substantial investment portfolio throughout the 1630s and 40s.[51]

VI

Not satisfied with the income from his practice, Arthur was deeply involved in money-lending, speculation and investment to the point that during the 1630s typically his return from rents and mortgages greatly exceeded his physician fees, sometimes by a factor of three. Thus, while he earned £328 from his practice in the year ending March 1635, between 19 December 1634 and 6 January 1635 alone he made a profit of £617 7s. 8d. on his investment portfolio.[52] His extended family played a vital supporting role, augmenting and administering his expanding array of properties and investments, especially during his absences from Limerick. He relied heavily on one brother-in-law, James Mahon, to administer his properties, and on another, Patrick Woulfe, 'who had good insight into surveying lands', to advise him.[53] The scale and diversity of his interests is illustrated by the following transactions. On one day, 1 December 1631, he paid £220 for the fee simple of land and fishing weirs near Ballina, Co. Tipperary, and another £31 for purchase of two half-quarters of a ploughland (Mehannach and Droumnakearten).[54] He gave a mortgage of just over £1,000 to Lord Henry O'Brien, earl of Thomond, in 1635 on the strength of three-and-a-half ploughlands (which yielded until 1642 an annual rental of £1,000).[55] He also loaned £1,000 to James, earl of Ormond, in 1640, with £100 per annum interest to be repaid out of his estates in Co. Carlow.[56] An exceptionally litigious individual who

50 Ibid., f. 175r.   51 For example, the master of the Court of Wards and Irish privy councillor, Sir William Parsons, was attending Arthur in the mid-1630s when he granted the physician alienation of a property at Williamstown, Co. Limerick. See ibid., f. 92r.   52 Ibid., ff 36r., 48r. One exception was in the calendar year Nov. 1631–Nov. 1632 when he received some £587 from his Limerick properties and disbursed £483 to receive a net income of some £104 – ibid., ff 169r.–170r. His account for the period 19 Dec. 1634–6 Jan. 1635 indicates that he received £764 19s. 8d. and spent £147 12s. – ibid., ff 172r.–172v.   53 Ibid., ff 91v., 168r.–173r.   54 Ibid., f. 95r.   55 Ibid., ff 102r.–102v.   56 Ibid.,

was quick to resort to legal action against those who crossed him or who were slow in making payments,[57] he was well acquainted with the technicalities of land and property law. His meticulous record of all financial transactions also demonstrates that he was unrelenting in his money-lending activities, particularly his pursuit of surviving relatives of deceased bad debtors.[58] As his investment interests multiplied exponentially throughout the 1620s and 30s, so did the number of protracted and often costly law suits that he initiated against offending parties in these and subsequent decades.[59]

Thus, on the eve of the 1641 uprising, then in his late forties, Arthur had attained an exceptionally privileged position. He had personal access to the most influential figures in government and ecclesiastical circles, as well as to the Old English and Gaelic aristocracy and gentry. He had a highly successful medical practice in Dublin and an extensive, carefully administered, property and investment portfolio largely concentrated around Limerick. Both provided him with substantial and discrete incomes, and in summer 1641 he had no reason to suspect that either was in imminent jeopardy.

VII

That was to change dramatically after the uprising on 23 October 1641. In the ensuing panic, despite his popularity and standing with all factions, Arthur was uneasy in Dublin: by December, he and his family were back in Limerick.[60] The speed at which Arthur left the capital is indicative of the suddenly exposed vulnerability of his position as a Catholic physician treating leading figures on both sides of the conflict in the midst of mayhem. He left for personal reasons – to ensure his safety and that of his wife and daughters – but also out of concern for the preservation of his business interests in the Limerick region which required his urgent and personal attention. In abandoning his Dublin practice and returning to Limerick, a Catholic stronghold, Arthur very publicly assumed his position in the royalist Old English line of defense in his native city during the conflict of the next ten years.

Overnight, one of his incomes had collapsed. Although he was able to fall back on the small practice in Limerick that he had maintained during visits home throughout the 20s and 30s, it was very modest in comparison to Dublin. Furthermore, Arthur now had to contend with competition from another five or six 'doctors' who were practising in the city, several of them in close proximity to him.[61] That his life was thrown into chaos is evident

f. 124v.   **57** See, for example, ibid., ff 92r.–92v., 114v.–118r.   **58** Ibid., ff 100v.–101r.
59 In pursuing these cases, Arthur expected support from justices of the Limerick assizes, the court of common pleas, and even the lord deputy and lord lieutenant. See, for examples, ibid., ff 95v., 101r.–101v., 103r.–103v., 104r.   **60** Ibid., f. 100r.   **61** These were David Rice, William Field, Dominic White, Nicholas Power; John Hickey and Dr Creedan.

from his entry-book. From mid-June 1641 to the end of March 1646, for the first time since he commenced practice, Arthur no longer recorded the date of each client's visit, though he did keep an account of fees received. The scale of his financial losses is also striking: his fees for 1643 and 1644 combined were a mere £24 6s.[62] To add to his financial woes, even before the uprising, Arthur was encountering difficulties in extracting outstanding rents and other payments due on his properties;[63] later, during the Confederate and Cromwellian wars, he was obliged to suspend charging interest on several loans, and he had to pay onerous levies imposed on all citizens of Limerick following the siege of the city by the Parliamentarian forces (1651–3).[64]

In late October 1643, when Limerick became a flashpoint in the dispute within the ranks of the Confederates, for the first time Arthur publicly nailed his political colours to the mast. He declared support for the mayor and Corporation when they refused to allow the papal envoy, Fr Peter Francis Scarampi, to enter the city because they favoured compromise and suspected the motives of those trying to move the Supreme Council of the Confederation from Kilkenny to Limerick. On this occasion, after the incensed Catholic bishop of Limerick, Richard Arthur, placed the mayor and his supporters on the Corporation under interdict for their hostile treatment of Scarampi, Arthur was tasked with writing a letter of apology to the papal envoy; the mayor and his followers also requested the envoy's assistance in having the bishop's penalty removed. In a second letter composed by Thomas Arthur, the mayor and his followers dissuaded Scarampi from going to Limerick while the political situation remained so uncertain.[65] When the confederate divisions resulted in a major split, particularly on the terms of a peace concluded at Dublin in March 1646 between confederate delegates and the duke of Ormond, Thomas Arthur, like the majority of Limerick corporation, publicly sided with the Ormondist party. The latter favoured a religious compromise with King Charles I against the Clericalist party, inspired by Papal Nuncio Rinuccini, who insisted on firmer guarantees for the Catholic faith.

On 20 and 21 August 1646 the mayor, John Burke, together with the aldermen and several of the city's eminent citizens, among them Thomas Arthur, met to discuss the peace. During the morning of 21 August Fr Walter Lynch arrived in Limerick to publicize Rinuccini's excommunication order against supporters of the peace. He hastened to the mayor's house where, in the hall 'full of auditors and spectators', he spoke for more than an hour. Thomas Arthur and Dr Dominic White, an alderman and canon

---

62 Entry-book, f. 73r.   63 See, for example, ibid., ff 100v.–101r., 109r., 113v., 115v., 118r., 119v., 122v.   64 Lenihan, *History*, pp 185–6; Edward MacLysaght and John Ainsworth, 'The Arthur manuscript', *North Munster Antiquarian Journal*, 2 (1940), 47; 6 (1950–1), 29–49, 65–82; 7 (1953–7), 168–82, 4–10; 8 (1958–9), 2–19, 79–87; 9 (1962–5), 51–9, 113–16, 155–64.   65 Lenihan, *History*, pp 153–5, n. 2; Irwin, 'Seventeenth-century Limerick', p. 117.

lawyer, disputed with Lynch over the excommunication order. Advocating adoption of the peace,[66] Arthur's familiarity with points of law was evident in his assertion that '[al]though the words for the freedom of religion and his Majesty's graces weare *de futuro*, yet that was noe materiall exception; because surely they would be confirmed in Parliament, and acted *per verba presentia*; and, in the interim, could not otherwise be couched or declared then *de futuro*'.[67] Soon after Lynch left the meeting, heralds began proclaiming the peace at the High Cross in the presence and with the assent of Mayor Burke and the majority of the assembly, a crowd of 500 citizens, led by Limerick layman, Dominic Fanning, and a Dominican friar, Fr Wolfe, gathered at the scene. During the ensuing 'Stony Thursday' riot, supporters of the treaty were assaulted and forced to flee and the mayor was injured and taken to prison. Arthur, who had been taking cover in the mayor's house, tried (as Burke had done) to diffuse the crisis. He 'went downe amongst them [the crowd] to qualiyfie and appease their furye; but not prevayling with them, and being endaungered in his owne life, returned backe againe' to warn the king-at-arms and heralds, who had also been hiding in the house, to make good their escape.[68] While this was his most public show of support for the Ormond faction, Arthur continued to serve the duke behind the scenes (in return for a fee). In November 1650, six months after he reminded Ormond at Loughrea, Co. Galway, that he had received no recompense for his 'exertions' on the duke's behalf, he received £10 stg from the Treasury.[69]

During his leanest years (December 1641–March 1646) of the Confederate Wars, Arthur earned just over £58 from his medical practice.[70] However, from Spring 1646 his physician's income increased significantly so that in the year ending March 1647 he earned over £36.[71] That upward trend continued in the eighteen-month period between May 1648 and January 1650, when he earned in excess of £74.[72] Arthur used this and any income that he received from his property and loans to complete work on his family home on Mungret Street, to pay the substantial levies for which he was liable, and to defray his legal costs in a number of cases that he pursued. Notable among these was his protracted suit against Murtagh O'Brien of Annagh, Co. Tipperary, who was withholding land that Arthur had purchased at a high

---

66 'A list of the cheefe men that were for the peace in Lymerick' in John T. Gilbert (ed.), *History of the Irish Confederation and the war in Ireland* (7 vols, Dublin, 1882–91), 6, p. 131. 67 Letter to bishops of Waterford and Ferns, etc., from Walter Lynch, vicar capitular of Tuam, and warden of Galway College, 21 Aug. 1646 in John T. Gilbert (ed.), *A contemporary history of affairs in Ireland from 1641 to 1652* (3 vols, Dublin, 1879), 1, pt 2, p. 698; O. Ogle, W.H. Bliss et al. (eds), *Calendar of the Clarendon state papers preserved in the Bodleian Library* (5 vols, Oxford, 1869–1970), 1, p. 329. 68 Statement by William Kirkeby, pursuivant-at-armes [1646], in Gilbert (ed.), *History of the Irish Confederation*, 6, p. 130. 69 See Lenihan, *History*, p. 169. 70 Entry-book, ff 72v.–73v. 71 Ibid., f. 74r. 72 Ibid., ff 76r.–78v.

cost.⁷³ Reflecting the uncompromising milieu of the 1640s, and in contrast with the pre-1641 era, Arthur's clientele throughout the decade was remarkably homogenous, being almost exclusively local, Catholic, Old English and, to a much lesser extent, Old Irish.⁷⁴ When, in 1651, Limerick was besieged by the Parliamentary army commanded by Henry Ireton, although Arthur's clientele remained largely the same, his work as physician changed in certain fundamental respects. Now, in addition to continuing with his practice, he tended to local civilian casualties, among them Dominic FitzDavid Rice and Dr Creedon MD whose wounds necessitated limb amputations.⁷⁵ Following the outbreak of plague in the besieged city in autumn, he also tended to an unprecedented number of civilian plague victims.⁷⁶

VIII

When the siege ended in December 1651, Arthur faced a dilemma regarding his future. His colleague, Dr O'Higgins, had been executed for resisting the Parliamentary forces.⁷⁷ As a royalist, Arthur had land and property confiscated in advance of the Cromwellian land settlement (1652).⁷⁸ Immediately after the siege was lifted, notwithstanding his political and religious convictions, he treated several Parliamentarian army officers, soldiers and their family member for scurvy, *cholera morbus*, pestilence and war wounds.⁷⁹ Within months, his clientele was radically and irrevocably altered. At the beginning of March 1652 Arthur returned to Dublin where he stayed several months, trying to re-establish his medical practice, before attending Sir Charles Coote's army at the siege of Galway.⁸⁰ On his return to Dublin, Arthur found himself in an altogether new world. The outbreak of plague in 1650 had 'exceedingly depopulated' the city.⁸¹ His former client-base had almost entirely disappeared and, in a new departure, a significant number of his clients were army personnel, particularly officers, and government officials, notably Lord Deputy Charles Fleetwood who attended with migraine, and Oliver Cromwell's brother, Henry, whom Arthur treated for inflamed tonsils.⁸² By 1654 his coterie of Old English Limerick clients had disappeared, largely as a result of his relocation to Dublin, but also, no doubt, partly in reaction against his perceived support for the Cromwellian admin-

---

73 Ibid., ff 239r.–240v., 110r.–110v, 114r.–118r.; Lenihan, *History*, pp 185–6; *CSPI, 1647–1660*, p. 278.   74 Entry-book, ff 72v.–77v.   75 Ibid., ff 79v., 80r.–81r.   76 Ibid., ff 80v.–81r.   77 Widdess, 'A notable Irish physician', pp 26–7.   78 Robert C. Simington (ed.), *The Civil Survey, AD 1654–1656* (10 vols, Dublin: IMC, 1931–61), 6, pp 411, 413, 414, 428, 440.   79 Entry-book, f. 81r.ff; Lenihan, *History*, pp 182, n. 1, 183, n. 1.   80 Entry-book, f. 83r.; Widdess, 'A notable Irish physician', p. 26.   81 Tony Farmar, *Patients, potions and physicians: a social history of medicine in Ireland, 1654–2004* (Dublin, 2004), p. 29.   82 Entry-book, ff 85r., 146r.

istration. Conversely, from early 1652 the preponderance of Protestant names in his entry-book (Molesworth, Hopthon, Hughson, Challiner, Molyneaux, Jackson, Ormsby, Eivers, Jenkins, Crutchfield, Stopford and Thomlinson among others) testifies to Arthur's characteristic pragmatism as he rebuilt his professional practice in Dublin during this final phase of his career.[83] A review of his cases in the year ending March 1657, when he earned over £117, offers a revealing glimpse into the new milieu in which Arthur worked. Among his patients he treated a Dublin merchant named Travers for fever, Mr Willoughby for chest pains, Mr Chapell for diarrhoea and dysentery, Mr Cardwardin for a haemorrhage, George Ryder for hypochondria, Colonel John Cole's epileptic son, Henry Cromwell for inflamed tonsils, Mr Vincent's wife who suffered from dysentery, Mr John Lylle of Trim and Mr Arthur Chichester for gonorrhoea, Captain Eivers for fever, diarrhoea and melancholia, and Mr Joseph Travers for arthritis. As the cases of Lylle and Chichester indicate, Arthur also saw a significantly higher number of male and female clients with sexually transmitted diseases (mainly gonorrhoea or syphilis but sometimes both) in Dublin throughout the 1650s – the inevitable consequence of war and a reflection of the high proportion of military men who attended him.[84] Down to September 1666, when he retired, Arthur enjoyed a relatively constant income from his practice: in the years ending March 1659 and March 1662 he earned just over £185 and £151 respectively.[85] In the last six months of his practice, he saw in the region of forty patients, many of them on a repeat basis, and received just over £60 in fees. Even then, his clientele was mixed, including aristocrats (Arthur Viscount Ranelagh, Lady FitzGerald of Allen, the marchioness of Antrim, Sir Hans Hamilton, Sir Roebuck Lynch, Sir Robert Kennedy), Gaelic Irish (Callough Geoghegan), and the oriental scholar and jurist, Dr Dudley Loftus, who paid the £1 fee for his son, Arthur's last client, on 30 September 1666.[86] This was, however, a far cry from what he had earned during the 1630s.

There are many reasons for his failure to replicate his earlier success. On his return to Dublin, in addition to facing the challenge of building this new client base, Arthur had entered a new professional context. The Confederate and Cromwellian wars had brought an influx of English and continentally trained physicians, apothecaries and surgeons to Dublin, notably Abraham Yarner, a physician appointed officer in the lord lieutenant's horse troop, and Sir William Petty, a fellow of the Royal College of Physicians in London, who was appointed physician to the army in Ireland.[87] Consequently, for the first time, in the early 1650s Dublin had a critical mass of accomplished

---

83 Ibid., ff 83v.-86v., 144r.ff. 84 Ibid., f. 83ff. 85 Ibid., ff 155v., 162r. 86 Ibid., ff 141r.-141v.; Elizabethanne Boran, 'Loftus, Dudley', *DIB*. 87 Lyons, 'Professionalisation', p. 36.

physicians, some with connections to the Royal College of Physicians in London as well as to Oxford and Cambridge universities. Competition was, therefore, stiffer than it had been when Arthur had last practised in the capital and the move towards corporate regulation of medical qualifications and practice was rapidly gaining pace. In social and professional terms, this was a positive development for Arthur. In fostering an *esprit de corps* among the city's physicians, Yarner, who was elected president of the College of Physicians in Dublin in 1672, made a point of inviting Thomas Arthur and another eminent Catholic physician and colleague, Gerald Fennell, to informal social and philosophical gatherings during the early 1650s. Both Yarner's invitation to one of these events and Arthur's response demonstrate that bonds of professional affinity among physicians continued to transcend cleavages in religious, political and even cultural interests and identities, up to a point that is. In his reply, Arthur expressed regret at not being able to accept the invitation from 'the most loving and able Dr A. Yarner' and thanked him for his 'usual generosity' in inviting him. Arthur also thanked Yarner and 'the other medical worthies dining with him ... for the unparalleled kindness with which you, sirs, have aided me when tossed about with storms of war and with cares' and for having 'steadied me with your advice and succoured me with your patronage'.[88] However, while Arthur may well have been part of this informal circle that evolved into the Fraternity of Physicians in 1654, there were limits to that fraternalism. This new generation's acceptance of the grand old doctor was based upon their personal acquaintance with him and their regard for his long-standing and enduring reputation as Ireland's leading physician, in spite of his Catholicism, his advanced age, and his adherence to the increasingly outmoded Galenist approach to medicine.[89] By retiring in 1666, a year after negotiations to obtain a royal charter for a College of Physicians in Ireland began and a year before a royal charter conferring rights and privileges on a College was issued, Arthur removed himself from the profession at an opportune moment. As the exclusively Protestant composition of the College's first office-holders demonstrated, the medical profession in Ireland had entered a new era in which the enforcement of corporate regulation, with its attendant requirement for religious conformity, severely limited opportunities for Catholic physicians such as Arthur to practice. That Catholics were excluded by the College of Physicians is evidenced by their establishment of their own college in Kilkenny during the reign of James II.[90] Arthur's retirement therefore coincided with the termination of unregulated

---

88 Ibid., pp 36–7. 89 On the basis of his library, Arthur appears not to have kept abreast of current medical advances. The vast majority of his books date from the late sixteenth and early seventeenth centuries and he did not acquire copies of seminal works such as William Harvey's *Exercitatio anatomica de motu cordis et sanguinis in animalibus* (Frankfurt, 1628) and (perhaps more understandably, given its date) Thomas Willis' *Cerebri anatome* (London, 1664).   90 Farmar, *Patients*, p. 16.

access to the one profession that had for decades exceptionally remained open to Catholics and enabled him to amass a substantial estate.[91]

IX

Following the Restoration, Thomas Arthur had his confiscated land and property restored.[92] Like most Old English men of property who managed to recover from confiscation of their estates and titles, guaranteeing his succession by a male heir bearing the family name was a major priority with which he was preoccupied throughout his adult life. In his 'Genealogical idyll' he recounted in laconic terms how although he and his wife Christina had ten children, six died in infancy, three of them boys. His disappointment at having four surviving daughters was palpable ('Look! Four daughters merely draw life from death, Alas! Only just a weak progeny of the family line').[93] Transferring his hopes for a male heir to the next generation, he had three of his daughters marry sons of Limerick's Old English elite families. He arranged for his eldest daughter, Mary, to marry Bartholomew Stackpole. His second daughter, Dymphna, married her second cousin, John Arthur, resident in Galway ('for name's sake, in hope that God be graciously pleased to raise us a hopeful posterity in them'). In a further bid to secure the succession, Thomas arranged for his third daughter, Anastace, to marry another Arthur (Daniel). His contingencies proved necessary as both Anastace and Mary predeceased their father. Fortunately, Dymphna and John had two sons, William and Thomas. In accordance with Thomas' last will and testament, William became heir to the entire estate following his grandfather's death in January 1675.[94]

X

The fact that during the early phase of his adult life Thomas Arthur, an Old English continentally educated Catholic physician, managed to carve out a distinct professional niche for himself and his family, and enjoyed a comfortable living on two incomes from his medical practices and his money-lending and investment activities, demonstrates just how much scope existed for a certain cohort of enterprising Old English Catholic professionals to thrive, unimpeded by legislative bars on confessional grounds, in early seventeenth-century Ireland. Although convinced that the Protestant political and ecclesi-

[91] Widdess, *History of the Royal College of Physicians*, p. 14.   [92] Widdess, 'A notable Irish physician', p. 27.   [93] Entry-book, f. 189v.   [94] Widdess, 'A notable Irish physician', pp 30–1.

astical establishment in Ireland viewed Catholics in general with suspicion, by dint of his reputation as an exceptional physician, Arthur, in spite of his Catholicism, was allowed great liberty to conduct his practice as and where he deemed appropriate. However, the crisis of the 1640s changed that situation irrevocably. Because of his Catholicism, Arthur experienced the double blow of losing his lucrative Dublin practice and confiscation of property and land in which he had invested so much of his physician's income. Whereas up to the 1640s, he had made a point of remaining non-partisan on issues of politics or religion and reaped rewards by having a very mixed clientele, after his public declarations of support for the Ormondist party and its peace treaty in his native Limerick in 1646, his ideological and religious convictions became public knowledge and undoubtedly alienated some former and prospective clients. The same can be said of his pragmatic decision to embrace the Cromwellian military and civilian population in order to revive his Dublin practice and provide him with an income whilst he lobbied for restoration of his confiscated holdings. Arthur's profession gave him a lifeline that enabled him to recover from the wars and confiscations which undermined the privileged position of his Old English class in Ireland. Because of his relatively unique professional status and reputation, his exceptional business acumen and pragmatic character, Arthur successfully tested and negotiated the bounds of Old English liberty and, unlike many of that group, survived the crisis of the 1640s and 50s by both re-establishing his medical practice and securing the return of his land and property. Yet, by the end of his career in the mid-1660s, it was clear even to Ireland's leading physician that the days had passed when an Old English Catholic physician could carry on his practice in the capital independent of regulation and attendant demands for confessional conformity.

Henry Burnell and Richard Netterville: lawyers in civic life in the English Pale, 1562–1615

NESSA MALONE

In 1561, Henry Burnell and the brothers Richard and John Netterville organized twenty-five Irish-born students living at the Inns of Court in London, a substantial and growing minority group there,[1] to sign a petition against the levying of cess. At the centre of their objection was the 'poor subject' of the Pale: the husbandmen and carters in a region of Ireland 'as quiet and as answerable to laws as is any part of England'. The students declared that the five shires of the Pale, 'scarcely bigger' than their English equivalents, were suffering from 'impoverishment through war and cesses', calculated at £30,000 sterling. Soldiers were 'not answerable to the common law' or the 'Queen highness's lawes', but could only be tried by 'their martial law'.[2] They expressed a third important grievance: the restrictions on their freedom to travel between Ireland and England without the lord deputy's permission.

Led subsequently by Burnell and Richard Netterville, the commonwealthmen of late sixteenth-century Ireland presented a unique opposition to government policy and to the unchecked use of prerogative law in the Elizabethan kingdoms. Embedded through alliance and intermarriage in Pale society, their opposition to the imposition of cess was supported and abetted by the Irish and Pale nobility, particularly Viscount Gormanston, Lord Howth, and the earls of Ormond and Kildare. Their influence on the husbandmen and small farmers of the Pale came to be greatly feared by members of the Irish council. However, they were also motivated by a wavering mix of independent principle and self-interest. This chapter places moments of public demonstration by the commonwealthmen in the context of the biographies of these two individuals, who were clearly the leaders of the movement against cess from their earliest petition in 1562 to the parliament of 1614–16. The continuity of the strategies they employed, the language they used, and the unfolding of their protests is illustrated from their perspective, as much as the sources will allow.

---

[1] Donal F. Cregan, 'Irish Catholic admissions to the English Inns of Court, 1558–1625', *Irish Jurist*, 5 (1970), 99–113; Colum Kenny, *King's Inns and the kingdom of Ireland* (Dublin, 1994), p. 40; Valerie McGowan-Doyle, *The Book of Howth: Elizabethan conquest and the Old English* (Cork, 2011); *The black books of Lincoln's Inns, volume 1*, ed. W.P. Baildon (London, 1896), pp 8, 23, 169; *Calendar of inquisitions, County Dublin: formerly in the office of the chief remembrance of the exchequer prepared from the MSS of the Irish record commission*, ed. Margaret C. Griffith (Dublin, 1991), p. 159. [2] 'A book comprehending the miserable estate of the English Pale', 20 Mar. 1561, PRO, SP 63/5/51, f. 134r.

Due to the fragmentary nature of Irish medieval and early modern archives, the lives of Burnell and Netterville must be pieced together from references in the state papers and a small number of other manuscript and calendared sources. Much of what there is to know about them must be analysed through the prosopographical methods so effectively used by Colm Lennon to reconstruct the associations between members of the Dublin corporation and guilds.[3] The rest is found in the references in the state papers, in which they are consistently described in hostile terms. The marginal presence they seemed to hold in the mainstream of political affairs belied the extent of their influence in networks throughout Ireland and England, in the court, in the country, among the mercantile elite and the Irish nobility, and at the London Inns of Court. The current historiography of this group is significantly influenced by Ciaran Brady's extensive work on the cess, its politics and its administration, which has provided a definitive account of its administrative and economic context.[4] The lawyers emerge as part of an ethnic monolith of Old English reactionary 'conservative subversives', deeply attached to tradition, Catholicism and maintaining the status quo.[5] Canny, Bradshaw and Brady have all seen the revolt of the Pale against the cess as bringing about momentary unity within the Old English community, with the lawyers at its centre. It is argued here that the lawyers' interests differed from those of the nobles and merchants they represented. Burnell's biography is used to trace the development of Old English opposition politics through the cess controversies of 1577–8, the parliament of 1585, and up to the parliament of 1613. It illustrates how a small group of common lawyers were involved in all of these demonstrations against the state.

Burnell and Netterville's education at the Inns of Court provided a cosmopolitan environment in which to test ideas, a 'situated public sphere'[6] where they became lifetime members of a strongly independent institution within the Elizabethan kingdoms. They were outward looking, aware of the nuances of court politics, and politically pragmatic. However, their commitment to their principal employers, particularly the earl of Kildare, caused their counterparts in the

---

3 As in Colm Lennon, *The lords of Dublin in the age of Reformation* (Dublin, 1981).
4 See Ciaran Brady, *The chief governors, the rise and fall of reform government in Tudor Ireland, 1536–1588* (Cambridge, 1994) and 'Conservative subversives: the community of the Pale and the Dublin administration, 1556–86' in Patrick Corish et al. (eds), *Radicals, rebels and establishments: Historical Studies, 15* (Belfast, 1985), pp 11–32. This has been influential in the treatment of the subject in later works, including Steven G. Ellis, *Ireland in the age of the Tudors, 1447–1603: English expansion and the end of Gaelic rule* (London, 1998); Lennon, *Sixteenth-century Ireland* (Dublin, 1994), Natalie Mears, *Queenship and political discourse in the Elizabethan realms* (Cambridge, 2005), pp 190–1; S.J. Connolly, *Contested island: Ireland, 1460–1630* (Oxford, 2008), pp 124–5; Terry Clavin, Judy Barry, 'Burnell, Henry' in James McGuire and James Quinn (eds), *Dictionary of Irish biography* (Cambridge, 2009).   5 See Brady, 'Conservative subversives', pp 11–32.
6 Mears, *Queenship and political discourse*, p. 187.

administration to doubt the sincerity of their claims. Even if they expressed their commitment to the ideology of the common law in bad faith, they still were more effective and influential in securing rights from the crown than many of the rebel Gaelic lords, and stayed on the correct side of Elizabeth's favour to successive lord deputies. Their behaviour was a significant demonstration over crown prerogative that preceeded early constitutional struggles in England, such as Bates' case (1606) and the 1611 English parliament. The 'commonwealth' lawyers' constitutional politics had enduring impact within Ireland and particularly on their legal successors, William Talbot and Richard Hadsor,[7] who would influence in turn Patrick Darcy and the Catholic confederacy of 1641. They are key figures in reconstructing the Irish constitutionalist tradition.

Cess has been treated in the historiography of the period as a uniquely Irish administrative innovation separated from the broader history of responses to taxation across the British and Irish Isles. However, it was close to 'assessed' tax and purveyance in England and Wales, which was likewise problematic to levy until composition policies were introduced.[8] The eastern part of Ireland is thus as recognizable as a 'fiscal feudal state' as England, even if these systems were operating in a hybrid manner with Gaelic systems.[9] Throughout the Tudor period, the idea of national taxation emerged unevenly, geographically and socially. The enormous militarization of Ireland in the late sixteenth century and use of martial law made it a place where little-to-no consultation of the political nation happened at all.[10]

Acceptance of purveyance involved an intricate balance: it had to be condoned by the political nation, but could not be refused either.[11] The activities of Burnell and Netterville also reveal much about the workings of the commonwealth group in relation to their clients and their business interests, particularly in maintaining property within small kinship groups. For apparently marginal actors in the political sphere of early modern Ireland, they had a surprising level of importance in Ireland and influence at court in England.

I

Henry Burnell (*c*.1540–1614) was a member of a branch of the family living in the Dublin suburb of Castleknock. The Burnells claimed noble descent

---

7 See Victor Treadwell, 'New light on Richard Hadsor. I: Richard Hadsor and the authorship of "Advertisements for Ireland", 1622/3', *IHS*, 30 (1997), 305–36. 8 M.J. Braddick, *The nerves of state: taxation and the financing of the English state, 1558–1714* (Oxford, 1996), p. 94. 9 See Braddick, *The nerves of state*, pp 167–80; John Walter, 'Responsibility under the commonwealth' in J. Braddick and John Walter (eds), *Negotiating power in early modern society* (Cambridge, 2001), pp 127–8. 10 See David Edwards, 'The escalation of violence in sixteenth-century Ireland' in David Edwards, Pádraig Lenihan and Clodagh Tait (eds), *Age of atrocity: violence and political conflict in early modern Ireland* (Dublin, 2007), pp 34–8. 11 J.D. Alsop, 'The theory and practice of Tudor taxation', *EHR*, 97:382 (1982), 13.

from Orleans and the Norman invasion in 1179, detailed in the most significant surviving document directly relating to them, a commonplace book that appears to have been held by Henry's cousin Robert Burnell, mayor of Drogheda in 1569.[12] From the thirteenth to the early sixteenth centuries the Burnells were active in two elite institutions at the centre of municipal life – the corporation of Dublin and St Anne's guild in the church of St Audeon's – and resided at Burnell's Inns on Cook Street. By the early sixteenth century, they held the barony of Balgriffin near Howth. They had intermarried with successive generations of Old English gentry and nobility, particularly the Dillons of west Kilkenny, Barnewalls of Trimleston, Cusacks of Meath and Talbots of Carton. Burnell's mother, Katherine, was a daughter of the Barnewall family. His sister, Elizabeth, was married to a member of the Cusack family and another sister married a Talbot.[13]

Burnell's most significant client was Gerald FitzGerald, the eleventh earl of Kildare. John of Balgriffin, an uncle of Henry and the wealthiest of the Burnells in the early sixteenth century, had joined the Geraldine rebellion in 1534. Described as 'brother by the same mother' to FitzGerald, he was taken with Thomas FitzGerald's brothers to London and was the sole non-FitzGerald to be executed publicly at Tyburn.[14] On his attainder, Henry's father was granted the manor of Castleknock in 1541. Henry Burnell's background as a gentleman farmer can be seen in his will, which included a clause distributing seven cows to his servants.[15] Burnell entered Lincoln's Inn in 1560, where Robert Dillon, Nicholas Nugent, Patrick Bathe and John Talbot were also Irish students.[16] Described by Fitzwilliam and Sidney as a very brilliant lawyer, Burnell's knowledge of the legal texts was said to be unparalleled in Ireland. His connections with Gaelic Ireland were also significant: he was married to a daughter of the O'Reilly. As an attorney in the Court of Chancery, he had extensive knowledge of equity and Brehon laws.

The Irish students at the Inns of Court made political and social connections that persisted to the end of their lives. Burnell's closest associate and ally was Richard Netterville, who had chambers at Middle Temple. Richard's father, Luke Netterville, was himself a prominent lawyer, commissioned in 1558 to assist the restoration of the possessions of the late earl of Kildare,

---

12 'The Burnell book', Townley Hall MSS, NLI, MS 95, 96, f. 31.   13 NAI, Chancery Pleadings B64; NLI, Genealogical Office, MS 38. See McGowan-Doyle, *The Book of Howth*, p. 13, for comparison to the St Lawrence family.   14 Richard Stanihurst, 'History of Ireland' in *Holinshed's Irish Chronicle: the history of Ireland from the first habitation thereof, unto the yeares 1509 & continued till the yeare 1547*, ed. Liam Miller and Eileen Power (New Jersey, 1979); Lennon, *Sixteenth-century Ireland*, p. 111.   15 'Manuscripts of Francis Elrington-Ball's *History of Dublin*, vol. ix', RSAI, Elrington-Ball MSS, vol. xi, f. 34.   16 Donal F. Cregan, 'Irish Catholic admissions to the English Inns of Court, 1558–1625', *Irish Jurist*, n.s., 5 (1970), 99; *The black books of Lincoln's Inns*, ed. Baildon, pp 331–2.

Garret Óg FitzGerald, with Barnaby Scurlock, attorney general, and James Stanihurst, recorder of Dublin.[17] Rather than merely attending the Inns of Court to finish their education, the Irish students returned with significant expertise in English common law, driven by the desire to protect their estates and interests. They saw themselves as English within Ireland and were convinced that English common law was Irish common law too. Christopher St Lawrence, Lord Howth, cited in the Book of Howth the five standard texts for an Inns of Court student which he claimed showed cess to be illegal.[18]

The Old English graduates of the Inns of Court also included the Dublin merchants Patrick Gough and Walter Archer. Gough was already being watched by the council on suspicion of harbouring a Spanish spy.[19] Their objection to a 1571 letter by the Irish council claiming its rights to cess led to the formation of a group describing themselves as 'commonwealthmen'. Paul Slack describes the notion of commonwealth as a 'public transcript', available to all to draw upon,[20] and Burnell and Netterville capitalized on this either for principled political reasons or for personal gain. Their idea of commonwealth had subversive currency and impact in England and in Ireland.

Over the winter of 1574, the commonwealth group emerged in a public demonstration against the government. Richard Netterville, described by the exchequer official John Symcott as their 'chief captain', organized the signing of another petition from members of the Pale sent to Fitzwilliam in November 1574 and began to collect money to send agents to England to protest against the cess.[21] They spread their message in public: Symcott, who described himself as 'hated and foresaken' by the Irish-born lawyers, complained of their muttering 'in secret conventicles', and of 'lewd preaching in open pulpits by their appointed preachers for commonweal' to large audiences where they 'in outrageous manner spare not to enveigh against the state itself'.[22] The 1574 petition echoed the common law language of the petition of 1562, describing the petitioners as 'subjects of the English shires'.[23] The commonwealthmen declared that the lords, knights and gentlemen of the Pale claimed 'by the benefit of the law' relief from cess, demanding that commis-

---

17 Judy Barry, 'Netterville, Richard' in James McGuire and James Quinn (eds), *Dictionary of Irish biography* (Cambridge, 2009). 18 'The Book of Howth' (*Cal. Carew MSS, Book of Howth, Miscellaneous*, p. 62). The texts were Staunford, Brookes, Bracton, Brytton and Glandeville, many of which had been reprinted by the queen's printer, Richard Tottel, in the late 1550s and early 1560s. 19 Memoranda concerning Ireland, 1571, PRO, SP 63/34/172, f. 120. 20 Paul Slack, 'Public transcripts and popular agency' in John Walter (ed.), *Crowds and popular politics in early modern England* (Manchester, 2006), pp 197–8. 21 As this is mentioned from Fitzwilliam's perspective, it is hard to discern if Netterville intended to go himself. Fitzwilliam to the privy council, 17 Nov. 1574, PRO, SP 63/48/52, f. 111; Fitzwilliam to Burghley, 17 Nov. 1574, PRO, SP 63/48/53, f. 117r. 22 Symcott to Burghley, 3 Dec. 1574, PRO, SP 63/48/67 f. 202. 23 Gormanston, Netterville et al. to privy council, 17 Nov. 1574, PRO, SP 63/48/52i, f. 114r.

sioners be called in and that no further action should occur except 'according to the Queen's law'. Furthermore, in the absence of crown protection for their lands, they defended keeping kern, even if such Gaelic mercenaries were 'ancient enemies to the queen's English subjects'.[24]

The petition was signed by the young noble, Viscount Gormanston, the earl of Kildare's nephew, and three Kildare gentlemen and lawyers, John Alen, Robert Taaffe and George FitzGerald. On 2 January 1575, Fitzwilliam wrote to the privy council describing an imminent controversy over cess as going 'hotly forwardes', compelled by 'these young lords' and 'busy headed' others who were 'very resolute in it'. He noted their 'great unwillingness' to answer 'any issue otherwise than by composition', 'which it may grow to in time I leave to your lords to consider'.[25] Symcott regarded the group as subversive and Fitzwilliam considered imprisoning the petitioners, although he was overruled by the Irish council. This was curious in a period during which the Elizabethan government was highly paranoid, unstable and experimental in its administration of Ireland.[26] Prior to Henry Sidney's arrival in Ireland with composition, the young lawyers had helped to establish a commonwealth movement, financially prepared to demonstrate against the state.

II

Between 1562 and 1573 Burnell disappears from the records. He held the recordership of the Dublin Corporation from 1573. Burnell used the office to attempt to engineer a new taxation regime in favour of the Corporation members, most of whom were merchants. He tried to procure the green wax money, a set of fines demanded by an amercement bearing a seal of green wax to be delivered to the exchequer. This aroused the attention of John Symcott, who reported it to Lord Burghley as an attempt to prevent the Irish council's collection of the tax by £10 a year. The city's sheriffs had not paid dues to the exchequer in recent years, and he noted that 'the queen's council would have been well contented to allow their plea if they suspected not other men's forseeing thereof'.[27]

In July 1575, Burnell suddenly resigned his office as recorder and secretly departed for England without licence to support the earl of Kildare.[28] The eleventh earl had been granted martial powers in the 1570s, which he then

---

[24] Fitzwilliam to the privy council, 17 Nov. 1574, PRO, SP 63/48/52, f. 111r.; Fitzwilliam to Burghley, 17 Nov. 1574, PRO, SP 63/48/53, f. 117r.   [25] Fitzwilliam to the privy council, 2 Jan. 1575, PRO, SP 63/49/2, f. 3r.   [26] See Stephen Alford, *The watchers* (London, 2012), which illustrates the extent and activity of Walsingham and Burleigh's intelligence networks across Europe.   [27] John Symcott to Burghley, 10 Mar. 1575, *CSPI, 1571–5*, ed. M. O'Dowd (revised edition, London and Dublin, 2000), pp 765–7.   [28] Fitzwilliam to Burghley, 7 July 1575, *CSPI, 1571–5*, p. 883.

proceeded to abuse. Sir Robert Dillon and John Allen, other powerful Kildare landowners, collected depositions against the earl and, with Fitzwilliam, sought to indict him in February 1575. Kildare was brought to London for interrogation. The arrest was sought by his noble nephews and friends involved with the 'commonwealth group' including William Nugent, the baron of Delvin, Lord Louth and Viscount Gormanston.[29] It was rare for a city recorder – a prestigious position for a man of Burnell's age and experience – to resign. He bade the mayor, members of the Corporation, and his parents 'farewell by a letter'. Fitzwilliam wrote to Burghley, Walsingham and the Council to alert them to Burnell's 'especial affection' towards Kildare. He warned that Burnell was 'very wise ... well learned in the laws, one of the very best spoken of this whole land.' He told them how Burnell had sought to prevent the interrogations of those who might implicate Kildare in the O'Connor rebellion, 'partly with using plain speeches to some to remember flesh and blood and to forget all former unkindness and partly with finer practices to some others that he durst deal not so plainly with'.[30]

On Burnell's arrival in London, he was brought to the city recorder, William Fleetwood, who questioned him on the activities of Kildare's servants, and on the nature of his counsel with Kildare. Burnell was prudent not to implicate himself: describing Kildare's responses, the lawyer would 'not seem that they satisfied' him because, as he stated to Fleetwood, 'I would have him think upon the matters very well'. The earl had apparently 'burst into a great colour' at this, declaring 'Thou and all Ireland shall not make me a rebel' to which Burnell diplomatically responded 'That is the thing of all other things furthest from my thought.' Burnell was committed to the Fleet with Meyler Hussey, Kildare's chief steward, until after 13 January 1576.[31] He returned to Ireland, where he began petitioning and making public speeches with the commonwealth group.

III

When Fitzwilliam's replacement, Henry Sidney, arrived in Ireland seeking to implement the new, and extensive, composition tax, Burnell and Netterville had not as yet acted specifically as the legal agents of a wider Pale protest. However, Symcott had already been observing the commonwealth group for a number of years, concerned about the potentially blurred distinction between

---

29 Vincent Carey, *Surviving the Tudors: the 'wizard' earl of Kildare and English rule in Ireland, 1537–1586* (Dublin, 2002), pp 166–9.   **30** Fitzwilliam to Lord Burghley, Sir Thomas Radcliffe, earl of Sussex, and Robert Dudley, earl of Leicester, 7 July 1575, *CSPI, 1571–5*, p. 854.   **31** HMC, *Acts of the privy council, 1575–7*, ix, p. 12; HMC, *Acts of the privy council, 1575–7*, ix, p. 75; HMC, *Acts of the privy council, 1575–7*, ix, p. 12, 75; *Cal. Fiants Elizabeth*, iii, p. 386.

opposition to the cess and opposition to the state. In 1576 William Gerrard was sent by Burghley to find out whether Viscount Baltinglass and the barons of Delvin, Trimleston, and Howth opposed the state, and 'how loth they were to make any submission'. In October, Gerrard delivered a report to Burghley on the private lives, dwellings and characters of the lawyers and judges in Ireland. The connection between members of the commonwealth group and the Old English legal elite was clear. Barnaby Scurlock had married the daughter of Chief Justice Plunkett and John Netterville of Dowth was married to Plunkett's sister. Like Symcott, Gerrard argued that corruption was so rotten and deep – and so entwined with family connections – that the replacement of Irish-born lawyers with English ones should be immediate.[32]

Open conflict between the Palesmen and government, with Burnell and Netterville as agents, began in late 1576. Immediately on his arrival in Ireland Henry Sidney had started to negotiate his substantial new composition taxation with the Pale to replace irregular cessing. At the Meath assizes in October 1576, Christopher Barnewall of Ardstown, a lawyer, instructed the clerk to draw up an indictment of Sidney and the council against the cess, which referred to Trissilian's execution in the reign of Richard II for treasonous exactions.[33] Burnell and Netterville appeared in the court of castle chamber to defend those who refused to pay cess on the basis of private letters of exemption. In January 1577, a petition dated and signed by a group of Pale lords and gentlemen was sent to the queen and privy council. The lawyers entered into a series of negotiations with the lord deputy and chancellor over the following months. Gerrard informed the privy council of how Burnell, Netterville, St Lawrence and other lawyers made powerful speeches on the antiquity and legality of the cess, declaring against the government. The details of these speeches are not recorded, but they claimed consistently that the Magna Carta and English law would apply simultaneously and equally to Ireland. It was feared that this would 'breed trouble'.[34]

Using the transcripts of the common law and commonwealth, and coming from the Inns of Court, the lawyers understood the theatrical nature of court politics. Even at this stage, Burnell and Netterville claimed to have devised a scheme that would reduce the tax and bring it to a compromise without 'murmur and grudge'. To the evident frustration of the council, discussions ended when Netterville withdrew. The 'firmest of the three', he persuaded Burnell and Scurlock to prepare to leave without licence for England on 20 March 1577. After this, Sidney imprisoned Howth, Gormanston and their sponsors in Dublin Castle.[35]

---

32 Charles McNeill (ed.), 'Lord Chancellor Gerrard's notes of his report on Ireland', *Analecta Hibernica*, 2 (1931–2), 114–15.   33 Jon G. Crawford, *A star chamber court in Ireland: the court of castle chamber, 1571–1641* (Dublin, 2005), p. 220.   34 Sir William Drury to Walsingham, 24 Feb. 1577, PRO, SP 63/57/27, f. 103r.   35 Charles McNeill

The agents travelled to Westminster, aiming to get an audience with Elizabeth since, as they claimed, she alone could levy taxation on them as citizens. Extraordinarily, they were successful. The letters of introduction that gained them admission to court are not extant, but the involvement of the highest members of the nobility must have been apparent. The agents stated before Elizabeth that cess should be completely removed 'as a thing contrary to law'.[36] The audience did not go well: Elizabeth declared to the lord deputy and council that she was 'greatly offended with this presumptuous and undutiful manner of proceeding',[37] and Burnell and Netterville were imprisoned in the Fleet.

The country cause was briefly united, and the agents sent messengers to their counterparts imprisoned in Dublin Castle. On 1 June 1577, four of the lords and gentlemen captive there, including Scurlock, made their submission to the queen.[38] By July, they had apologized for their refusal to sign an agreement with Sidney in Dublin in March, and denied that they believed the agents could have been successful. Nicholas Nugent, Christopher Fleming, Sir Christopher Cheevers and George Plunkett made submissions, identifying Netterville as the chief cause of sedition and claiming they had not fully understood the queen's royal prerogative prior to that time.[39] The privy council then advised Sidney to release any imprisoned lords and gentlemen. This was the end of a coalesced unity between the lawyers and the rest of 'the country'. In the 1590s, the heirs of Sir Christopher Cheevers and Lord Howth were sued by Burnell and Netterville for debts owed in the court of chancery.[40]

Burnell and Netterville were transferred from the Fleet to separate cells in the Tower of London.[41] In October 1577, the lieutenant of the Tower wrote to Burghley that the lawyers sought 'pen and ink' and a servant, 'as they are desirous to write unto their Lordships'. He was instructed that 'in no case' should they be allowed to confer and write together 'either to their Lordships or any other person'.[42] Sidney declared to the queen that Burnell 'thirsts earnestly to see the English government withdrawn from hence'. The

---

(ed.), 'Gerrard papers', *Analecta Hibernica*, 2 (1931), 132–3.   36 'The privy council to the lord deputy', *Cal. Carew MSS* ii, p. 80; 'The Queen to the lord deputy and Council', *Cal. Carew MSS*, ii, p. 78.   37 Elizabeth to lord deputy and Irish council, 14 May 1577 *Cal. Carew MSS*, ii, pp 77–8.   38 Submission of Barnaby Scurlock and others, 1 June 1577, *Cal. Carew MSS*, ii, p. 83.   39 The declaration of Christopher Cheevers and George Plunkett, [July] 1577, *Cal. Carew MSS*, ii, p. 104.   40 Writs, NAI Dublin, CP Box J / 150; Box B / 237; Box I / 214.   41 Examinations of John Netterville and others, 1 July 1577, *CSPI*, *1574–85*, p. 118; 'A collection of the causes for which it has been thought necessary to commit Netterville and Burnell prisoners to the Tower of London', Dec. 1577, PRO, SP 63/59/28, f. 72; Examinations of John Netterville and others, 1 July 1577, *CSPI*, *1574–85*, p. 118.   42 Henry Burnell and Richard Netterville to Walsingham, 2 Dec. 1578, PRO, SP 63/63/35, ff 68–9; Meeting, privy council, 18 Dec. 1578, PRO, PC 2/12, f. 43.

agents had become 'pillars of their commonwealth', Sidney claimed, and to undermine their cause would 'procure such obedience in this country'.[43] Although the three legal agents submitted to the privy council, Burnell and Netterville were thought too dangerous and were again committed to the Tower in December 1577.

The Irish council suspected that Burnell and Netterville were working unilaterally. In May 1578, Netterville wrote to Lord Howth to request further funds.[44] In December, Burnell and Netterville wrote to Walsingham proclaiming their poverty, and said they had spent £500 of their own money. Burnell additionally requested that Walsingham would prefer his nephew, one Talbot, to an office held by the lawyer Robert Byce.[45] The Irish council recommended that the agents be made an example of in public (such as in the stocks) and fined heavily. Sidney was advised to meet with the nobility in order to separate them from the three lawyers and to 'demand of them whether they have authorized Burnell and Netterville to make in their behalf any composition touching the cess'. If this was denied, the agents were threatened with further imprisonment in Dublin Castle upon their return. As a placatory measure, it was suggested that open positions on the courts of queen's bench and common pleas be filled by well-known Old English lawyers who were opposed to the cess, such as Sir John Plunkett, Netterville's father-in-law, and James Dowdall. In December, Sidney wrote to Burghley that 'the Irish require to be as free from charge as her majesty's subjects in England'.[46]

While in the Tower, Burnell crafted an agreement that the Pale landowners pay £2000 a year prior to calling parliament. Negotiated between the agents, landowners, victuallers and administration, this became known as 'Burnell's device', and provided a temporary settlement to the conflict.[47] Burnell stated that the 'contribution shalbe without comparison lesse than the present cesse, and more easie to come bye with the free will and consent of the subject ... than anye contribution that I have yet h[e]ard of; a less supplye in which obtayned shall stand her Majestie in better stead than a greater gotten with murmur and grudge'.[48]

Burnell and Netterville were not passive actors in their representation of the commonwealth: they were acting as committed politicians outside of parliament. Brady has claimed that the sheer cost of the composition caused the commonwealth revolt in 1576–8.[49] However, the lawyers' behaviour and

---

[43] Lord Deputy Sidney to Elizabeth, 20 May 1577, *Cal. Carew MSS*, iv, p. 279. [44] Richard Netterville to Lord Howth, 18 May 1577, PRO SP 63/58/26, f. 81. [45] This was probably William Talbot, son of Robert Talbot of Carton. Henry Burnell and Richard Nettervyll to Walsingham, 2 Dec. 1578, PRO, SP 63/63/35, ff 68–9; Meeting, privy council, 18 Dec. 1578, PRO, PC 2/12, f. 43. [46] 'Sidney to Elizabeth', in *Letters and memorials of state*, Arthur Collins (ed.), vol. 1 (T. Osborne, London, 1746), p. 183. [47] See privy council to Irish council, PRO 63/60/24, f. 51; Clavin and Barry, 'Burnell, Henry', *DIB*. [48] McNeill (ed.), 'Gerrard papers', p. 157. [49] Lord deputy to Burghley, 12 Dec.1577,

manipulation of the position they occupied as plenipotentiaries suggests that they were both compelled by their beliefs and as representatives of the Irish nobility in court struggles. Their petition to Walsingham indicates that Burnell and Netterville may have been providing him with intelligence and that their network led to him. The involvement of the earl of Ormond, who sought to oust Sidney, adds another layer of intrigue to this settlement. Ormond had allied with Kildare in backing the country and in facilitating William Gerrard's report of 1578 that ended Sidney's composition.[50] The queen wrote to the earl of Kildare in July 1579 to commend him on 'his diligence in reducing those who were backward in the matter of cess to conformity'.[51] Burnell and Netterville simply could not have maintained their stance for as long as they did without the backing of the earl of Kildare. However, the letter to Walsingham shows that the lawyers had a political and intellectual agenda separate to that of their noble benefactors.

IV

In spite of the success of 'Burnell's device' in bringing a momentary conclusion to the crisis over cess, Burnell the lawyer had gained significant enemies by demonstrating against the lord deputy's prerogative. Moreover, the involvement of the earl of Kildare in the Nugent conspiracy gave Burnell's position a new precarity. When Kildare and his nephew, the baron of Delvin, were arrested at council for their apparent complicity in the Baltinglass rebellion in December 1580, Burnell was present as Kildare's attorney during his interrogation. James Fitzmaurice FitzGerald, the earl of Baltinglass, had little connection to the commonwealthmen, although he had been a legal student at the Inns of Court in the later 1560s. William Nugent, Delvin's brother, organized a revolt with other minor Pale gentry, supported eventually by Turlough Luineach O'Neill, O'Rourke and O'Reilly, that sought to free Delvin and Kildare. Their action became known as the 'Nugent conspiracy'. By November 1581, twenty-five men, including Richard Netterville's younger brother, had been arrested and tried under martial law.[52] The particularly vicious campaign by Robert Dillon against Sir Nicholas Nugent, the lord justice, in January 1582, resulted in Nugent's execution. Notably both Dillon and Nugent had been Burnell and Richard Netterville's contemporaries at Lincoln's Inn.[53] Nugent was married to Ellen

PRO, SP 63/59, f. 151r. **50** David Edwards, *The Ormond lordship in County Kilkenny, 1515–1642: the rise and fall of Butler power* (Dublin, 2003), p. 224. **51** The queen to the earl of Kildare, 28 July 1579, *CSPI, 1574–85*, p. 176. **52** Ellis, *Ireland in the age of the Tudors*, pp 315–16; Lennon, *Sixteenth-century Ireland*, pp 202–5; Helen Coburn-Walsh, 'The rebellion of William Nugent, 1581' in Comerford et al. (eds), *Religion, conflict and coexistence in Ireland* (Dublin, 1990), pp 26–52. **53** Crawford, *A star chamber court in*

Plunkett, the daughter of Sir John Plunkett of Dunsoghly, Co. Dublin, and the sister of Netterville's wife.

In January 1583, Burnell departed for London to pursue a suit seeking the restoration to the minor heir of William Wogan, who had been executed for his part in the conspiracy, of Rathcoffey, an area under the earl of Kildare's control. His client, Richard Wogan, would eventually marry Burnell's eldest daughter, Elizabeth. The administrator Ludowick Bryskett wanted the Wogan lands, and his pursuit of the claim was assisted by his particularly antagonistic and anti-Irish colleague Henry Wallop, who sought to discredit Burnell during these years.[54] Backing Ludowick Bryskett's claim, Wallop suggested that Burnell was not working in the interests of the feoffees of the deed. He told Walsingham that the value of the parcels of land could not 'be great' and that it would be better to grant them to Bryskett in order to prevent the 'cross dealing' of Burnell.[55] Wallop associated Burnell's suits with Ormond's attempts to influence government.[56]

However, it is possible that Burnell was also present in London to aid his old client, the earl of Kildare. Kildare's involvement in the rebellion of 1581 and the Nugent conspiracy in 1582 was suspected, but never confirmed. In 1581, Wallop sent a letter in cipher to Walsingham identifying Burnell and Lady Kildare as subjects for questioning, and warning Walsingham of Burnell's passage into England. He described Burnell as 'a ringleader of the opponents of Her Majesty's prerogative', 'not well affected in religion', deceitful and 'one that hateth all our nation'.[57] Burnell seems to have anticipated this, and arrived in London with a selection of letters of introduction from other members of the Irish council including Ormond, Sir Nicholas White, Sir Adam Loftus, the lord chancellor, Geoffrey Fenton, the secretary of state, Edmund Waterhouse, and his cousin, Sir Lucas Dillon, who described Burnell as his 'mere kinsman' whom he 'heartily' loved.[58] Kildare was pardoned of treason by June 1583 and banned from court.[59]

In 1582, three common lawyers – Patrick Bermingham, Gerald Aylmer and Roger Garland – revived the country cause in Meath without the direct involvement of Burnell or Netterville. Bermingham's father had been involved in opposing cess in the 1550s and 60s, while Aylmer and Garland had been lesser members of the commonwealth group. Bermingham gathered a collection and petition, and entered into the Irish council chamber, declaring that

---

Ireland, p. 238; Coburn-Walsh, 'The rebellion of William Nugent', pp 26–52. **54** Richard A. McCabe, 'Bryskett, Lodowick (c.1546–1609)', *ODNB*. **55** Wallop to Walsingham, 16 Mar. 1583, PRO, SP 63/100/19, f. 34r. **56** Wallop to Walsingham, *CSPI, 1574–84*, p. 432. **57** Henry Wallop to Walsingham, 6 Jan. 1581, *CSPI, 1574–85*, p. 279. **58** Nicholas White to Walsingham, 12 Mar. 1583, PRO, SP 63/108/64, f. 163; Lucas Dillon to Walsingham, 29 Mar. 1583, PRO, SP 63/108/66, f. 167; Adam Loftus to Walsingham, 29 Mar., 1583, PRO, SP 63/108/14, f. 37. **59** Carey, *Surviving the Tudors*, pp 201–2.

subjects should 'freely complain of their grief' without the threat of imprisonment, and should have 'free liberty' to seek out the Queen's 'most royall presence'.[60] In September 1582, he sought Aylmer to represent him at court, and requested that 'Mr Burnell shold be sent for' as Burnell would be wealthy enough to shoulder the costs.[61] Bermingham attended another assembly in Navan to publicly remonstrate against the cess of 'Sir Henry Harrington's horsemen': Harrington was a New English soldier who was engaged in a dispute with the earl of Kildare. Although warned his activities were seditious, Bermingham formulated a petition signed by himself and twenty-four other Meath nobles and gentry to be delivered to the queen by Aylmer. The lawyer was thrown into Dublin Castle in April and sought clemency from the queen.[62] Burnell does not seem to have come to his aid.

Burnell, Netterville and the commonwealthmen had always insisted that, besides the queen's prerogative, agreement in parliament was the only legitimate way to levy cess. On his appointment to the lord deputyship in 1584, John Perrot called the first parliament since 1571 to redistribute the attainted lands of Desmond. To deter potential subversive activity, the electoral boroughs were redrawn and Burnell and Netterville were invited as 'two of the cunningest' to meet Sir Lucas Dillon to arrange a reasonable cess for the deputy's household for three months to distract them from organizing further opposition.[63]

The crown's plan was not successful: the two men used their most intimate family connections to gather a small set of elected parliamentary allies. Their group were a mix of lawyers, including Roger Garland, lesser members of the Nugent and O'Reilly families, who were Burnell's brothers-in-law, and a 'poor burgess'.[64] One bill before the parliament intended the abolition of Poynings' Law,[65] In opposing this, the lawyers presented Poynings' Law as they had portrayed the Magna Carta: part of a constitutional basis for their entitlements as subjects. They formed a group in the Commons to oppose the abolition of Poynings' Law and obstructed legislation on composition, fraudulent enfeoffments and the act of impleading and jeofailies that had allowed Irish-born lawyers to go to the Inns of Court.[66]

When their obstruction proved too disruptive, the opposition were excluded from the Commons and punished by imprisonment. Perrot linked

60 Patrick Bermingham to the Queen, 4 Apr. 1582, PRO, SP 63/91/13, f. 25r. 61 Patrick Bermingham to Garret Aylmer, 6 Sept. 1582, PRO, SP 63/95/21, f. 44. 62 Patrick Bermingham et al. to the Queen, PRO, SP 63/100/61, f. 133. 63 Victor Treadwell, 'Sir John Perrot and the Irish Parliament of 1585-6', *PRIA*, 85C (1985), p. 270. 64 *Tracts relating to Ireland*, ed. Hardiman, p. 142; 'Abridgement of confessions taken against the disturbers of the parliament, June 1585', PRO, SP 63/117/62, ff 139-40. 65 'A bill for repealing Poynings' act', June 1585, *Cal. Carew MSS*, ii, p. 403. 66 'Acts of parliament', 1586, *Cal. Carew MSS*, ii, p. 425. For full treatment of the statute of jeofailies, see Kenny, *King's Inns*.

this to the lawyers 'working underhand ... to disturb all'.[67] As they were interrogated, the full involvement of Burnell and Netterville and their broader network of common lawyers was evident in the organization of the opposition. The lawyers had personally called to the houses of the MPs and encouraged them to resist.[68] Patrick Tyrell described how Netterville invited him 'to labour others to stand against those bills for that if they should pass be they were undone forever and their freedoms would come in question to the other coming both of private men and corporate towns.'[69] Edward Nugent had told MPs that the suspension of Poynings' act would mean the possibility that the 'lord deputy might quarter them, overthrow all laws and take away their lands from them and their children.'[70] Richard and John Netterville declared that they would not allow a suspension of Poynings' act until they knew of the composition arrangement.[71] Perrot described them as 'good country men as they would be gloriously termed, [who] have been ever of this same against all governors'.[72] The opposition claimed that their freedoms had been assaulted.

The composition agreement arranged during parliament resolved the problem of an uneven cess and normalized the taxation regime.[73] However, it is obvious that the lawyers' arguments were more significant than simply resolving the taxation problem around which their discontent coalesced: for Burnell and Netterville, there was a larger, ideological dimension attached to their commitment to ideas about common wealth and the common law.

V

During the Nine Years War and up to 1605, Burnell and Netterville remained in public life and were known recusants, but were not active as 'commonwealthmen'. Their rhetoric had always placed a heavy emphasis on loyalty to the crown and on freedoms for subjects. The challenge of Hugh O'Neill for the crown authorities and the ideas of militarily minded crown servants in Ireland may have overshadowed this. Cess continued to be a significant problem, particularly in the Pale around 1597 when it was speculated by English officials that Dublin would rebel during a period of intense pressure on food supplies and currency shortage.[74] The Old English community

---

67 Lord deputy to Walsingham, 18 June 1585, PRO, SP 63/117/36, f. 92. **68** Lord deputy to Walsingham, 18 June 1585, PRO, SP 63/117/36, f. 91. **69** 'Abridgement of confessions taken against the disturbers of the parliament, June 1585', PRO, SP 63/117/62, f. 91. **70** 'Abridgement of confessions taken against the disturbers of the parliament', f. 139; Lord deputy to Walsingham, 18 June 1585, PRO, SP 63/117/36, f. 91. **71** 'Abridgement of confessions taken against the disturbers of the parliament', f. 140. **72** Perrot to Walsingham, 18 June 1585, PRO, SP 63/117/36, f. 92r. **73** Bernadette Cunningham, 'The composition of Connacht in the lordships of Clanricard and Thomond, 1577–1641', *IHS*, 24:93 (1984), 1–14. **74** Lennon, *Sixteenth-century Ireland*, p. 295

had grown circumspect, and the former commonwealthmen were closely watched. For example, in 1593, the Irish council sent Burghley a copy of a letter by the lawyer Walter Scurlock, the queen's attorney for Connacht, to Henry Burnell. Scurlock wished that Hugh O'Neill, earl of Tyrone, would receive appropriate 'desert' for his recent violent activities, and that 'God may sort to the safety of our prince'.[75] Scurlock expected Burnell not to support O'Neill at this point. After 1599, O'Neill drew on the transcripts formed by commonwealth treatises about Ireland in attempting for the first time to unite Old English and Irish under Catholicism.[76] This put the former defenders of the freedoms of the Irish subject in a difficult position.

Burnell and Netterville still held significant power over opposition politics, but chose not to use it. Due to their education, they were two of the most trusted and employed counsel within the Pale and worked both for and against state interests. Burnell was appointed as a justice of the queen's bench for a single term on 15 October 1590.[77] How or why he received this office is unclear. In September 1591, Burnell was appointed with the queen's solicitor, Roger Wilbraham, on a commission to bring the rents of the tenants on McMahon's attainted lands to the crown.[78] In 1592, Burnell and Netterville were appointed by members of the Catholic confraternity of the Guild of St Anne, one of the most powerful landholding corporations, to defend the guild's property rights against the state.[79] Members of the Burnell and Scurlock families had been associated with the guild from the fourteenth century.[80] They were successful in defending it.

Throughout the 1590s Burnell and Netterville seemed significantly less closely tied to the houses of Kildare and Ormond. In 1597, an anonymous correspondent claimed that Burnell and Netterville had sought to defraud the queen and the earl of Kildare. Burnell had gained land at a discount when Henry Wallop had offered significantly more.[81] Ormond had an ancient patent for prize wines that had rarely netted the crown more than £20 per year until Burnell had discovered and reported this concealment (which appears to have been ignored by the authorities) in 1603.[82]

75 Walter Scurlock to Henry Burnell, c.May 1593, *CSPI, 1592–6*, p. 101. 76 Lennon, *Sixteenth-century Ireland*, p. 298. 77 *A chronological table of the law officers with the promotions, deaths and resignations from the reign of Queen Elizabeth to the present time, judges, salaries in 1690, and as fixed by the Second and Third William IV with an outline of the legal history of Ireland, and copious indexes*, ed. Constantine J. Smyth (London, 1839), p. 103. 78 *Calendar of fiants, Elizabeth*, Appendix to the thirteenth report of the deputy keeper, PROI (Dublin, 1875–90), no. 5582, p. 229. 79 Clavin and Barry, 'Burnell, Henry', *ODIB*. 80 RIA, 'Grant', 12 S 28, 26, 21 Sept. 1347; 12 S 31 395, 30 Oct. 1347; 'Grant' 12 S 27 (53), 288, 12 May 1348; 'Grant', 12 S 31, 51, 295, 27 Jan. 1428. 81 'Memorandum stating that Her Majesty was exceedingly wronged in a grant that she gave to the earl of Kildare', 10 Aug. 1597, PRO, SP 63/200/ 84, f. 234; 'Memorandum', 9 Aug. 1597, PRO, SP 63/200, ff 84–5). See 18 July 1567 in Ireland, PRO, SP 63/200/33, f. 106 also. 82 'Chichester to Salisbury', 24 Jan. 1608, PRO, SP/223/21, f. 21.

A schism created between Burnell and the FitzGeralds of Kildare ended their association in the period between 1603 and Burnell's death in 1614. Burnell had continued to work as a legal counsellor and remained part of the household following the death of the eleventh earl of Kildare[83] while the Kildare family were under close scrutiny. Mabel, dowager Lady Kildare, an open recusant who kept priests in her house at Maynooth, was seen as vulnerable to malign influences after her husband's death, and was interrogated in 1594. In 1595, William Cecil sent in a spy, William Udall, who married one of the 'base' FitzGeralds. Henry FitzGerald, the twelfth earl, wrote to Cecil of the 'ill angels that haunted him' in the Kildare household, to which Cecil responded that Udall was a dangerous Catholic.[84] Henry FitzGerald died in 1597, and in 1599, his successor as earl of Kildare, his youngest brother William, was drowned.

The prior death of Henry and William FitzGerald's elder brother, Gerald, Lord Offaly, gave his daughter (and the eleventh earl's granddaughter) Lady Lettice Digby, a lady in waiting to the queen, a strong claim to the Kildare estates. She and her courtier husband, Sir Robert Digby, settled at the Kildare manor at Portlester in 1600 and a suit at common law was initiated in 1602 in defence of her entitlements. It emerged that Burnell had forged enfeoffments on a deed, including names of dead men and his own nephew, the commonwealth lawyer, Christopher Barnewall,[85] allegedly with Lady Kildare's approval in order to enfranchise her sons and to disenfranchise Lady Digby.

Mabel, Lady Kildare, professed innocence of the laws under crown interrogation, stating that she entrusted legal matters to Burnell, 'whom shee supposed to be a man of some conscience and counsell'.[86] Without heirs and with her religious activities under increased scrutiny, the advantage for the dowager countess in an alliance with the Digby interest is obvious. The other dowager countess, Frances Howard, widow of Henry FitzGerald, also threw in her lot with the Digbys, commanding Burnell to declare that the deed was forged in 1602, and stating 'it becomes me to do right to all living creatures, especially where I may procure rest to the dead and blessing to the living, and free my conscience'.[87] The court of castle chamber found in favour of the

---

[83] Loose deeds, NLI MS 20, 265; *Salisbury MSS*, xii, p. 359. [84] Udall continued to inform on Tyrone, Lord Delvin, Lord Essex and the Kildares throughout the 1590s, and informed the queen of an attempt to create a new earl of Kildare and Baltinglass in 1599: Udall, PRO, SP 63/180/40, f. 123; 63/180/58, f. 181; draft letter, Sir Robert Cecil to the earl of Kildare, PRO, SP 63/185/7, f. 12; PRO, SP 63/181/36, f. 75; SP 63/180/58, f. 181. The queen told Mabel that she meant to have Udall tried: observing the Kildare family to see how far their loyalty stretched. [85] Victor Treadwell, *Buckingham and Ireland, 1616–1628: a study in Anglo-Irish politics* (Dublin, 1998), pp 116–17. [86] Decree of sentence in court of castle chamber, 3 Feb. 1608, PRO, SP 63/226/19, f. 59. [87] *Cal. Salisbury MSS*, vol. xii, p. 359.

Digbys' claim on 3 February 1609. Burnell was fined £500 sterling, sentenced to imprisonment, and had his privileges as a counsellor-at-law removed. The fourteenth earl, Garret FitzGerald, petitioned for Burnell's release from the fine, 'his estate being but poore', and asked the lord deputy to 'give him leave to go home ... as a prisoner to attend the next term.'[88]

Burnell had only recently been released from another period of detention. The commonwealth lawyers had remained quiet as the crown passed from Elizabeth to James VI & I, until 1605, when Lord Deputy Arthur Chichester used prerogative powers to issue legal mandates to attend church service to prominent members of the Dublin Corporation.[89] Six wealthy and influential Dublin merchants, all close allies of the commonwealth, had been singled out to lead by example. For the first time, the conflict between the commonwealthmen led by Burnell and the crown was predominantly religious. Fitzwilliam had described as Burnell a 'perverse papist' in 1574.[90] The Counter-Reformation had limited impact in Ireland – the campaigns against cess were based on ideological and material opposition – but the Nine Years War had re-ordered the political and constitutional landscape. Burnell, Aylmer and Netterville organized a petition of public protest in 1605 against the attempt to use prerogative law to enforce religious conformity. At the same time, the Meath lawyer Patrick Barnewall – brother-in-law to Hugh O'Neill – emerged as a significant young leader, who warned of the potential for violent revolt.[91] The bishops of Dublin and Meath described unrest within the Pale, stirred up by 'priests and discontented gentry'.[92] An order to expel secular priests and Jesuits was made after the discovery of the Powder Plot in November 1605. 'Old' Burnell 'the lawyer' and Netterville drafted a petition to be presented to the king signed by 5,000 people within the Pale, along with Viscount Gormanston, Sir James Dillon, the lord of Finglas, Lord Louth, and Christopher Flattisbury, a chancery attorney who had protested against the cess.[93] The council described most ordinary Dublin citizens as 'indifferent' to the new laws.[94] By 10 November 1605, the government had received the submission of most of the protesters and Chichester negotiated an agreement between Aylmer, Barnewall and Burnell. Due to the use of prerogative

---

88 Garret Kildare on behalf of Henry Burnell, PRO, SP 63/226/72, f. 194.   89 John McCavitt, *Arthur Chichester: lord deputy of Ireland, 1605–16* (Belfast, 1998), pp 111–12.   90 Acts of the privy council, PRO, PC 2/12, ff 195, 455.   91 Gormanston and others to the earl of Salisbury, 8 Dec. 1605, *CSPI, 1603–6*, p 365; Patrick Barnewall to Salisbury, 16 Dec. 1605, PRO, SP 63/217/96, f. 267; Lord deputy and council to the king, 10 Nov. 1605, PRO, SP 63/218/39, f. 56.   92 Bishops of Dublin and Meath to the king, 4 June 1603, *CSPI, 1603–6*, pp 58–9; certificate of the diocese of Dublin, May 1604, *CSPI, 1603–6*, p. 175.   93 Patrick Barnewall to Salisbury, 16 Dec. 1605, PRO, SP 63/217/96, f. 246. Dillon was the son of Sir Lucas, and therefore a cousin of Burnell. Lord deputy and council to the king, 10 Nov. 1605, PRO, SP 63/218/39, f. 57.   94 Lord deputy and council to privy council, PRO, SP 63/218/28i.

law to impel them to conform the lawyers continued to resist.[95] Thomas Luttrell refused to 'make any acknowledgement of a fault' and remained imprisoned as Burnell, Netterville and Edward Nugent were called before the court of castle chamber. Nugent and Netterville were imprisoned in the castle, while Burnell, then described as 'sickly', was brought to the serjeant-at-arms' house and kept there.[96]

VI

As martial law was increasingly used in place of other legal systems in Ireland, the commonwealthmen found that constitutionalist solutions were increasingly difficult to agitate for. Over the course of the 1590s, the legal profession was affected by the increasingly hard Protestant streak in the Irish state. The King's Inns, founded and dominated by Old English lawyers since 1567, closed its chambers in Dublin's Blackfriars in 1584.[97] In 1607, it was refounded. After 1608, any recusant barrister wishing to join the Inns would have to take the oath of supremacy.[98] Catholic lawyers continued to be a thorn in the side of the government, however. During the 1612 elections for the parliament, Sir Robert Jacob described how leading Pale nobles and gentry including Burnell's nephew William Talbot, as well as 'Sir William Bourke, Sir John Everard, Sir Chrisopher Nugent, Sir James Goghe, Sir Christopher Plunkett, Sutton called the Baron of Galtrim, Thomas Luttrell, and William Talbot, Robert Barnewell, Richard Wadding and Verdon the lawyers' were 'often ... [in] meetings and consultations' with 'Sir Patrick Barnewall and old Burnell'. Robert Barnewall and William Talbot had been consulted by the 'corrupted' sheriffs of Dublin, to assist the election of 'two of the most Spanish and seditious schismatiques in all the city', without the mayor's assent or knowledge. In the first session of parliament, the opposition targeted the lord deputy with a protest against cess, making eleven points against it, before the opposition withdrew.[99] Talbot and Luttrell then made their way to London with a petition on behalf of the parliamentary opposition to protest in person to James I, as advised by Burnell. They were imprisoned in the Tower. A few days after the opening of parliament on 5 April,

---

[95] Sir Patrick Barnewall made statements against the use of prerogative law. Interrogatories administered to Sir Patrick Barnewall, 1608, *CSPI, 1603–6*, p. 449. [96] Agreement of lord deputy and council with gentry of the Pale, 16 June 1605, *CSPI, 1603–6*, p. 289; Lord deputy and council to the king, 10 Nov. 1605, PRO, SP 63/118/39, f. 57. [97] Crawford, *A star chamber court in Ireland*, p. 130; Kenny, *Kings Inns*, pp 52–3. [98] *King's Inns admission papers, 1607–1867*, ed. Edward Keane, P. Beryl Phair, Thomas U. Sadleir (IMC, Dublin, 1984), pp 21, 156, 288, 490, 492. [99] Transcription of William Farmer by J.T. Gilbert, Dublin City Archive, MS 145, Gilbert Collection, f. 56.

1614, Philip Gawdy wrote to his cousin that Talbot was fined £10,000 and 'imprisoned during the King's pleasure and acknowledgment of his fault at the next parliaments both in England and Ireland: he is an Irish man worthily punished for his wild and erroneous speeches in saying the Pope had power to depose kings.'[1]

Netterville died in 1607. Burnell was said to have been residing at Castlerickard in Co. Meath in 1603,[2] and died in 1614. A copy of his will, made when he was 'very sicke but of perfect understanding and memory', details his close relationships with the servants on his estate to whom he bequeathed livestock and gifts.[3] He had two daughters, Elizabeth and Joann, one of whom was married to Nicholas Wogan of Rathcoffey in Kildare,[4] and a son, Christopher, who was his surviving heir at Castleknock. Aspects of Burnell's political legacy were found in his grandson's play *Landgartha* (1639), performed on St Patrick's Day 1640 at the opening of the Irish parliament.[5] Burnell and Netterville's methods of publicly demonstrating opposition in and outside parliament were radical in going as far as possible without veering from constitutional methods, yet espousing views that in other contexts would have been treason. They never denied Elizabeth's position as monarch, yet posed frequent challenges to it using the emerging language of commonwealth. Their methods became an established way to express opposition, and their influence was notable in England and in Ireland.

---

1 HMC, *Frere MSS* (London, 1879), p. 527. 2 'Notes on the Fitzgeralds, Eustaces, etc. Addenda : Undated papers, 651', *CSPI, 1601–3 (with addenda 1565–1654)*, p. 651. 3 RSAI, Elrington Ball MSS, vol. ix, f. 34. For instance, he bequeathed a broadcloath gown to a servant, Margaret Feakin. 4 Funeral Entries, GO MS 64, NLI, f. 70. 5 Deana Rankin, *Between Spenser and Swift: English writing in seventeenth-century Ireland* (Cambridge, 2005), p. 105.
The author would like to thank Matthew Symonds for his comments on early drafts of this chapter.

Goliath and the boy David: Henry Fitzsimon, James Ussher and the birth of Irish religious debate

ALAN FORD

On 27 June 1600, an Irish Jesuit, Henry Fitzsimon, met with a Trinity student, James Ussher, to debate the theological differences between Catholics and Protestants. It was a strange occasion. Fitzsimon was a 34-year-old Counter-Reformation missionary at the height of his powers; Ussher was a 19-year-old student at the recently founded Trinity College, Dublin. Unsurprisingly, Ussher likened Fitzsimon to the giant Goliath and himself to David, 'the least boye of the adverse campe'.[1] They met in Dublin Castle, where Fitzsimon was held prisoner, and ambitiously set out to cover all the key theological issues in dispute between the two sides in a series of debates. But Fitzsimon, unhappy, according to Ussher, at having to deal with a mere 'boy', called off the meetings.[2] Though abortive, the meeting is more than just an historical footnote. It was in fact a richly symbolic encounter, embodying, in its timing, the participants, its format and content, and in the way it was subsequently recorded by historians, the division of Ireland into two rival religious camps. The purpose of this chapter is to investigate its significance, and to edit two previously unpublished manuscripts which throw additional light onto what actually happened.

TIMING

Religious historians have long laboured over the chronology of the Reformation and Counter-Reformation in Ireland. The simple assumption that the Reformation began in the reign of Henry VIII and was immediately rejected by the Irish people who subsequently remained loyal to Catholicism, was challenged by late twentieth-century historians, who pointed to the confused state of both the Irish polity and Irish religious allegiance throughout the sixteenth century. Without a single central authority, riven by rebellions and ethnic, linguistic and cultural divisions, Ireland lacked any of the essential requirements that enabled a religious Reformation – Catholic or Protestant – to get off the ground: universities, humanist-educated clergy and ruling elites, a printing press, or fora for public intellectual debate.[3]

---

1 Bodleian Library, Oxford, MS Barlow 13, fol. 83v. 2 Richard Parr, *The life of ... James Usher* (London, 1686), p. 6. 3 For a judicious resolution of the debate, see K.S.

The contrast is particularly striking in relation to religious debate. In Germany and Switzerland formal religious disputations covering the points controverted by Protestants and Catholics were a common feature of the early Reformation – they were a key way of winning over the populace and, much more importantly, civic rulers, to the new religious ideas. Thus Luther had debated with Eck in Leipzig in a twenty-three-day marathon in 1519, and Zwingli with his Catholic and Anabaptist opponents in Zürich in the early 1520s, encounters that were transmitted to a wider audience through print.[4] But in Ireland it was hard to find trained protagonists or the means of dissemination. It was not until 1551 that the first book was printed in Ireland. It was not until 1594 that the first university opened. And it was only with the arrival in the 1570s and 80s of Counter-Reformation-trained priests from Europe, and Oxford- and Cambridge-educated clergy from England, that a cadre of trained controversialists was provided. Even then, Fitzsimon complained vociferously about the difficulty in finding Protestant opponents, a claim confirmed by Ussher's age. The clash between Ussher and Fitzsimon was therefore the first formal disputation between Protestant and Catholic in Ireland, and marked the theological coming-of-age of the Irish Reformation and Counter Reformation. And, of course, not only did it inaugurate a period of intense religious debate in print and in person over the next forty years, but it also laid down the basic template for public theological controversy which lasted for over 350 years, only brought to a close by the slow growth of ecumenical awareness from the middle of the twentieth century.[5]

Bottigheimer, 'The Reformation in Ireland revisited' in *Journal of British Studies*, 15 (1976), 140–9.   4 Martin Brecht, *Martin Luther: his road to Reformation, 1483–1521* (Minneapolis, 1995), pp 299–348; for an example of a Reformation disputation, see S.M. Jackson (ed.), *Ulrich Zwingli, 1484–1531: selected works* (Philadelphia, 1972), pp 81ff.   5 See, for example, the series of debates in the 1820s and 1830s, a product of the second Reformation, covering many of the topics which Ussher and Fitzsimon had intended to cover: P.D. Hardy, *Full and impartial report of the speeches ... and the arguments ... by the Roman Catholic and Protestant gentlemen ... at Carrick on-Shannon* (Dublin, 1824); *Authenticated report of the discussion ... at Londonderry, between six roman catholic priests and six clergymen of the established church in the diocese of Derry* (Dublin, 1828); W.B. Stoney and J.R.C. Hughes, *Authentic report of an important discussion held in Castlebar, between the Rev. W.B. Stoney ... and the Rev. James Hughes ... from Friday January 6, to Friday January 13, 1837* (Dublin, 1837); B. McAuley and R. Stewart, *Authenticated report of the controversial discussion upon the supremacy of St Peter* (Belfast, 1827); R.T.P. Pope and Thomas Maguire, *Authenticated report of the discussion ... between the Rev. R.T.P. Pope and the Rev. T. Maguire* (Dublin, 1827); T.D. Gregg, *Authenticated report of the discussion which took place between the Rev. T.D. Gregg, and the Rev. Thomas Maguire in the round room of the Rotundo on the 29th May, 1838, 30th, 31st, June 1st, 2nd, 4th, 5th, 6th, 7th* (Dublin, 1838).

PARTICIPANTS

The two participants were themselves very much part of this process of religious differentiation in Ireland, with their personal histories bearing witness to the complex way in which confessional allegiance was being decided in Dublin in the later sixteenth and early seventeenth centuries. Both were members of the Anglo-Irish (Old English) community, those descendants of the Norman settlers who had traditionally supplied the state with its officials and the city with its merchants and civic leaders. Already politically alienated from the government by the imposition of cess, this community came under increasing pressure to abandon the state church from the seminary priests returning to Ireland.[6] Fitzsimon represented this new style of Counter-Reformation cleric, continentally trained, dedicated to the creation of a separate, doctrinally-aware Catholic church. He had been born into the Dublin patriciate, his father, Sir Nicholas Fitzsimon, was an alderman, his mother, Anna Sedgrave, came from another distinguished family. Educated at Hart Hall, Oxford, he had converted to Protestantism, but while studying at Paris University he had returned to Catholicism. He studied philosophy at the Jesuit University of Pont à Mousson before entering the Society in 1592. He went on to study theology at Louvain, and taught philosophy at Douai before returning to Ireland in 1597 to serve on the Jesuit mission.[7]

Fitzsimon's mission in Dublin was both flamboyant and successful. He was clearly an extrovert – his superiors were concerned that his high profile might draw too much attention to their activities, and sought to restrain his exuberance.[8] He travelled round with three or four gentlemen as companions, never dining without six or eight guests. He was determined to establish a fully functioning separate Catholic church, preaching on feast days and Sundays, hearing confessions, setting up a sodality of the Virgin Mary, rais-

---

[6] For a discussion of the process of secular alienation, see Ciaran Brady, *The chief governors: the rise and fall of reform government in Tudor Ireland, 1536–1588* (Cambridge, 1994); for an analysis of the religious differentiation of the Dublin community see Colm Lennon, *The lords of Dublin in the age of Reformation* (Dublin, 1989). [7] For the most recent biographical treatment of Fitzsimon, see C.E. O'Neill and J.M. Dominguez (eds), *Diccionario historico de la Compania de Jesus* (Madrid, 2001), 2, pp 1468–9; the standard account remains that of Edmund Hogan, *Words of comfort to persecuted Catholics ... by Father Henry Fitzsimon ... with a sketch of his life* (Dublin, 1881), pp 200–83; reprinted in Edmund Hogan, *Distinguished Irishmen of the sixteenth century* (London, 1894), pp 96–310; see also James Corboy, 'Father Henry Fitzsimon, SJ 1566–1643', *Studies*, 32:126 (1943), 260–6. [8] Oliver Mannaerts (Manareus) to the Jesuit General, Claudio Aquaviva, 22 Aug. 1598, Irish Jesuit Archives, IE/Mace/Trans/1598; Aquaviva to Fitzsimon, 26 Sept. 1598, ibid.; Richard Field to Aquaviva, 1 Sept. 1599, ibid.; T.J. Morrissey, '"Archdevil" and Jesuit. The background, life, and times of James Archer from 1550–1604' (MA, UCD, 1968), p. 263. [9] Adam Loftus and Henry Jones to Archbishop John Whitgift, 7 Apr. 1600, *CSPI, 1600–1*, ed. E.G. Atkinson (London, 1905), pp 76–80.

ing money to send Irish students to study abroad, and celebrating the first High Mass in Dublin for forty years. According to Archbishop Loftus of Dublin and Bishop Jones of Meath, Fitzsimon won over large numbers of Dubliners to Catholicism, attracting four or five hundred of the 'best sort' of citizens to Mass.[9] Torn between the desire not to alienate the Old English in the middle of the Nine Years War, and the fear of Jesuit subversion, the authorities finally acted in 1599, arresting and imprisoning Fitzsimon in Dublin Castle. There he repeatedly sought to debate with Protestant clergy, but struggled to find a worthy opponent, portraying himself as being like 'a bear tied to a stake' wanting someone to bate him. After the abortive encounter with James Ussher, he was challenged by John Rider, the Oxford-educated dean of St Patrick's Cathedral, who engaged in a lengthy controversy in person and in print, replete with generous insults on both sides. He was finally released in 1604 and went on to serve in Bohemia as an army chaplain. Despite his requests his superiors were reluctant allow him to come back to Ireland, and it was not until 1631 that he returned, dying in 1643.[10]

Ussher came from precisely the same class as Fitzsimon – indeed, they were cousins – and his family demonstrates the way in which religious identities split in the later sixteenth century. An uncle, John Ussher, an alderman, was one of the earliest native Dublin lay Protestants, the driving force behind the establishment of a university in the city. Another uncle, also closely involved in the foundation of Trinity, was Henry Ussher, educated at Cambridge and Oxford, who went on to become the Protestant archbishop of Armagh. But Ussher's mother, Margaret, a sister of Richard Stanyhurst, was converted to Catholicism, much to Ussher's chagrin, and remained loyal to the faith until her death. Ussher was one of the first and most precocious students of the newly founded Trinity, immersed in Calvinist theology and the writings of the church fathers, and chosen to perform before the earl of Essex in a public disputation in 1599.[11] He went on to serve as professor of theological controversies, bishop of Meath and, from 1625, archbishop of Armagh, dying in England in 1656 as one of the most famous scholars in Europe.[12]

---

10 Bernadette Cunningham, 'FitzSimon, Henry (1566–1643)', *ODNB*; David Murphy, 'Fitzsimon, Henry', *DIB*; Brian Jackson, 'The construction of argument: Henry Fitzsimon, John Rider and religious controversy in Dublin, 1599–1614' in C.F. Brady and Jane Ohlmeyer (eds), *British interventions in early-modern Ireland* (Cambridge, 2005), pp 97–115. 11 Nicholas Bernard, *The life and death of James Usher* (Dublin, 1656), pp 33ff. 12 The most recent biographical treatments of Ussher are: Alan Ford, 'Ussher, James (1581–1656)', *ODNB*; John McCafferty, 'Ussher, James', *DIB*; Alan Ford, *James Ussher: theology, history, and politics in early-modern Ireland and England* (Oxford, 2007).

FORMAT AND CONTENT

The formal academic disputation lay at the core of the medieval scholastic system, and remained a key part of university education across Europe right through the early modern period. In essence it performed a similar purpose to an exam in the modern education system – a means of testing the knowledge of students. But it was much more than a means of assessment – it also served more broadly as a way of teaching and enquiry, as academics and students engaged jointly in disputation over difficult or contentious issues. The format was based upon the rules of Aristotelian logic, proceeding by a series of linked steps from an initial question to a final determination by way of syllogisms and answers, all based on strict rules. In the academic arena the confrontation had the benefit of a moderator who would ensure that correct syllogistic procedure was followed and often sum up the arguments at the end. It was, in short, a process designed to test and generate truth.[13]

With the advent of the Reformation, the disputation was transformed from a university exercise, arguing about often quite arcane issues, to a public debate, tackling the major theological controversies that were tearing apart western Christendom. The transition from university to the public forum was hardly surprising – both Protestant and Catholic leaders had been trained in this method and naturally turned to it as a means of settling differences. But resolution proved tantalizing. Much depended in disputation upon an agreed assumption, yet Protestants and Catholics started from fundamentally opposed premises. Equally, the judicious resolution provided by the president or moderator was difficult to translate into the public sphere – no one was neutral in an age of religious polarization. As a result, few of the debates provided the apodictic certainty that logic seemed to promise: many were less genuine intellectual arguments than staged confrontations, carefully managed by the civil authorities to secure the right result.[14]

In this case, however, while the authorities presumably sanctioned the debate in allowing Ussher access to the prisoner, the choice of topics was left up to the participants and the participants did seek to follow the rules of disputation. It thus provides a rare verbatim record of a genuine syllogistic debate between a Protestant and a Catholic. Ussher had suggested that they

---

[13] For university disputations in early modern England, see W.T. Costello, *The scholastic curriculum at seventeenth-century Cambridge* (Cambridge, MA, 1958).   [14] S.E. Ozment, *The Reformation in the cities* (New Haven, 1980), p. 125; on religious disputations in England, see Josh Rodda, ' "Dayes of gall and wormwood": public religious disputation in England, 1558–1626' (PhD, University of Nottingham, 2012); Bernard Capp, 'The religious marketplace: public disputations in civil war and interregnum England', *EHR*, 128 (2013), 47–78; for a seventeenth-century English listing of post-Reformation religious disputations, see John Ley, *A discourse of disputations chiefly concerning matters of religion* (London, 1658), pp 40ff.

'conferre syllogisticallye on the whole body of the controversyes as in order they lay in Bellarmine.' This was a potentially vast enterprise. Building on the systematic formulation of Catholic theology at the Council of Trent (1545–1563), the Jesuit scholar, Robert Bellarmine (1542–1621), provided in his *magnum opus*, *Disputations about the controversies of the Christian faith against contemporary heretics*, the standard Catholic reply to the works of Luther, Zwingli and Calvin.[15] Bellarmine's confident tone and comprehensive scope provoked myriad Protestant replies across Europe, not least in Ireland, where, of course, the publication of his work coincided neatly with the intellectual coming-of-age of the Catholic and Protestant churches. As a result, from the turn of the century, much of the scholarly effort of the Protestant clergy and of Trinity College, Dublin, was expended on refuting Bellarmine. Henry Ussher, according to Fitzsimon, had made refuting Bellarmine his life's work. James Ussher's first major research project when appointed to the staff of Trinity was to respond to Bellarmine's arguments on scripture, and later in his career he returned to the fray, to attack Bellarmine's ecclesiology. His successor as professor of theology spent eighteen years preparing a lengthy reply to Bellarmine's views on the real presence, while his brother Ambrose, before his early death, wrote extensively against Bellarmine.[16]

Ussher's choice of topic for the first disputation – 'Whether the pope be antichrist?' – may seem to modern eyes somewhat tangential, but to a contemporary Protestant it was a fundamental question on which everything, from the possibility of salvation for Catholics, the legitimacy of their church, to government policy towards them, all depended. Luther's conviction that the pope was antichrist had been developed by his successors into an elaborate apocalyptic worldview that encompassed the whole of Christian history. The obscure imagery of the Book of Revelation – the seven trumpets and seven vials etc. – was applied to specific events in history. In particular, the thousand-year binding of Satan, from Revelation ch. 20, was dated from the time of Christ, and its expiry, around AD 1000, was marked by the rise of antichrist in the person of Gregory VII and his successors. The Reformation marked the beginning of the final battle as the forces of righteousness confonted the papal antichrist. For Protestant clergy and politicians who took this presentist apocalyptic hermeneutic seriously, it had significant practical implications: since the Roman Catholic church was under the rule of Satan, all who remained within it were at risk of damnation; and toleration for Catholics was not just impolitic, it was a sin. Ussher himself was one of the first Irish

---

15 Robert Bellarmine, *Disputationes de controversiis Christianae fidei adversus hujus temporis haereticos* (3 vols, Ingolstadt, 1586–1593). 16 Pierre Bayle, *Dictionnaire historique et critique*, 4 vols (5th ed., Amsterdam, Leiden, The Hague, Utrecht, 1740), iv, p. 480; R.B. Knox, *James Ussher archbishop of Armagh* (Cardiff, 1967), pp 161ff; Vivienne Larminie, 'Hoyle, Joshua (bap. 1588, d. 1654)', *ODNB*; TCD Library, MSS 285–6, 291.

Protestants to apply this logic to the history of religion and the conduct of religious policy in Ireland. He argued strongly against toleration for Catholicism – an apostatical religion, as his fellow bishops put it – and went further than the Thirty-Nine Articles by including the statement that the pope was that man of sin – antichrist – in the 1615 Irish Articles.[17] Bellarmine, aware of the potential damage of such an identification, had devoted a whole chapter in the third section of his first volume of the *Disputationes* to explaining why antichrist had nothing to do with the papacy, arguing instead that he would be a particular person still safely in the future, who would return just before the end of the world and would be crowned by the Jews in the temple in Jerusalem.[18]

This, then, sets the scene for the encounter in Dublin Castle. Ussher began as opponent by stating that he intended to prove that Rome, not Jerusalem, was the seat of antichrist, and set out syllogistically to prove it. Fitzsimon soon tired of the logical exercise, abandoning the exchange of syllogisms, and lamenting that he had decided to take part: 'whether antichrists seat shalbe at Rome or at Jerusalem it maketh nothing to prove that this present Pope is antichrist ... If I had thought you would have brought such trifles, I would never have entered into communication with you. And indeed I must condempe myselfe of great imprudencie, that ever I admitted your conference, having more waightie matters to deale in'. Ussher, still convinced that he could prove his point syllogistically, was disappointed that Fitzsimon had refused to respond to his logical argument, and lamented the lack of a moderator.[19] Fitzsimon, though, proved willing to continue to the disputation, and Ussher sought to exploit some classic apocalyptic texts, such as 2 Thessalonians 2:4 – he that sits in the temple of God shows himself to be antichrist. This led to a detailed dispute over whether or not the pope usurps the role of God.

Ussher and Fitzsimon then switch sides, with the latter opposing the thesis. He opens by arguing: 'Antichrist shall raigne 3 yeares and an halfe onlie; The Pope hath raigned farr longer: Therfore the Pope is not Antichrist', leading into a discussion of the apocalyptic significance of the days and months referred to in apocalyptic passages of Daniel and the New Testament, whether they should be taken literally, or metaphorically as representing years.[20] After further debate over the identification of the pope with God, the disputation breaks down with an argument over the correct use of syllogisms, which is followed by Fitzsimon again losing his patience. 'I have

---

17 Alan Ford, '"Force and fear of punishment": Protestants and religious coercion in Ireland, 1603–33' in Elizabethanne Boran and Crawford Gribben (eds), *Enforcing Reformation in Ireland and Scotland, 1550–1700* (Aldershot, 2006), pp 91–130; Ford, *James Ussher*, pp 59–66, 94, 145–7; Alan Ford, 'Apocalyptic Ireland: 1580–1641', *Irish Theological Quarterly*, 78:2 (2013), 123–48. 18 Bellarmine, *Disputationes*, i, ch. 3. 19 Bodelian Library, Oxford, MS Barlow 13, f. 80. 20 Ibid., f. 82r.

spent longer time with you, then I could well afforde; for I assure you before your comming I had matters that greatly concerned my reputation'. Ussher attempted to refer the issues to their next conference, but Fitzsimon again indicated his lack of interest: 'Trulie I am so busie that I cann have no leesure to meddle with these matters; And in the controversyes I have taken noe great paines for I came into this land for exhortation, not for disputation.' After agreeing to exchange letters, the disputation ended with a conciliatory comment from Fitzsimon: 'God grant that we may al see the truth, you praie not this for you only, but for my selfe also.'[21]

HISTORIOGRAPHY

Subsequent interpretation of this debate was, almost inevitably, a product of the divisions that it helped create. What happened in the disputation – indeed, whether it even happened – for a long time depended upon which religious tradition you happened to be reading. The basic sources which later historians relied on were threefold. First there was Fitzsimon's own account, in his 1614 work, *Britannomachia Ministrorum*, where he recalled meeting a precocious youth of eighteen, who sought to dispute with him about the most abstruse aspects of theology, even though he had not finished studying philosophy. Fitzsimon does not explicitly refer to a disputation taking place – the key sentences are the concluding ones:

> Prodiit quidem semel in summa vocis vultusque trepidatione, octodenarius precocis sapientiae non tamen malae, ut videbatur indolis iuvenis, nescio an aurae popularis cupidior, saltem de abstrusissimus rebus theologicis cum adhuc philosophica studia non esset emensus, nec ephebus egressus, disputandi avidus. Hunc autem iussi suorum calculos adferre, quibus pugil seu agonista idoneus renunciaretur, et vel cum ipso disputationem me initurum. Sed sicut ipsi eum minime tanto honore dignati sunt, ita me vicissim sua deinceps praesentia dignatus ipse non fuit.[22]

---

21 Ibid., f. 82v. 22 Henry Fitzsimon, *Britannomachia ministrorum, in plerisque et fidei fundamentis, et fidei articulis dissidentium* (Douai, 1614), p. 14: 'Once, indeed, a youth of eighteen came forward with the greatest trepidation of face and voice. He was a precocious boy, but not of a bad disposition and talent as it seemed. Perhaps he was rather greedy of applause. Anyhow he was desirous of disputing about most abstruse points of divinity, although he had not yet finished the study of philosophy. I bid the youth bring me some proof that he was considered a fit champion by the Protestants, and I said that I would then enter into a discussion even with him. But as they did not at all think him a fit and proper person to defend them, he never again honoured me with his presence.' [Tr. by Hogan, *Words of comfort*, p. 224.]

There followed two Protestant accounts by Nicholas Bernard and Richard Parr, Ussher's chaplains and first biographers. Bernard's 1656 *Life of Ussher* claimed that Ussher offered to debate with Fitzsimon on the controversies of Bellarmine, once a week. The first topic was whether the pope was antichrist. 'Twice or thrice they disputed this, though the Jesuit acknowledges but once.'[23] Parr, in his *Life*, published in 1686, claims that Ussher accepted a general challenge issued by Fitzsimon and that they agreed to meet once a week to 'argue the chief points in controversie'. But, after the second debate, Fitzsimon broke it off. Ussher then wrote a letter, reproduced by Parr, in which he explained that he wanted the debates to resume but was concerned by reports that Fitzsimon had decided not to continue:

> I was not purposed (Mr Fitz-Symonds) to write unto you, before you had first written to me, concerning some chief points of your Religion (as at our last meeting you promised) but seeing you have deferred the same (for reasons best known to your self) I thought it not amiss to enquire further of your mind, concerning the continuation of the Conference began betwixt us. And to this I am the rather moved, because I am credibly informed of certain reports, which I could hardly be perswaded, should proceed from him, who in my presence pretended so great love and affection unto me. If I am a boy (as it hath pleased you very contemptuously to name me) I give thanks to the Lord, that my carriage toward you hath been such, as could minister unto you no just occasion to despise my Youth; your Spear belike is in your own conceit a Weavers Beam, and your abilities such, that you desire to encounter with the stoutest Champion in the Host of Israel, and therefore (like the Philistine) you contemn me as being a boy; yet this I would fain have you know, that I neither came then, nor now do come unto you in any confidence of any learning that is in me (in which respect, notwithstanding, I thank God I am what I am) but I come in the Name of the Lord of Hosts (whose Companies you have reproached, being certainly perswaded, that even out of the mouths of Babes and Sucklings he was able to shew forth his own Praises; for the further manifestation whereof, I do again earnestly request you, that (setting aside all vain comparisons of Persons) we may go plainly forward, in examining the matters that rest in controversie between us; otherwise I hope you will not be displeased, if as for your part you have begun; so I also for my own part may be bold, for the clearing of my self, and the truth which I profess, freely to make known, what hath already passed concerning this matter: Thus intreating you in a few lines, to make known unto me your purpose in this behalf, I end,

23 N. Barnard, *Life of Ussher* (London, 1656), p. 38.

praying the Lord, that both this, and all other enterprises that we take in hand, may be so ordered, as may most make for the advancement of his own Glory, and the Kingdom of his Son, Jesus Christ.[24]

Parr firmly established the Protestant interpretation of the debate: two or three meetings, with Fitzsimon withdrawing bruised. Subsequent Protestant biographers took up the theme. William Dillingham, in his *Life of Ussher*, quoted Fitzsimon's account of his encounter with Ussher, though he left out the final two sentences. Anthony a Wood, in his biography of Fitzsimon, recorded how 'Mr Jam. Usher, then 19 years of age ... did dispute with him once, or twice, or more concerning Antichrist, and was ready to proceed further', but Fitzsimon 'was, as 'tis said, weary of it and him.'[25] In the same vein, Thomas Smith, in 1707, gave an account of Ussher's meeting with Fitzsimon, using Ussher's letter to Fitzsimon, printed by Parr, as proof that the debate took place.[26]

That independent-minded French Protestant philosopher, Pierre Bayle, on the other hand, in his *Dictionnaire historique et critique*, one of the most widely-read books of the eighteenth century, focused upon Ussher's youth and preferred Fitzsimon's account of the disputation not going ahead because Ussher was not authorized – the very sentences omitted by Dillingham. Indeed, Bayle went on to question the good faith of such accounts, claiming that the sentences had been suppressed because they contradicted the claim that Ussher had triumphed in the debates. Bayle offered a choice: 'it is averred in the life of Ussher ... that he frequently and triumphantly disputed with the Jesuit ... Either the Jesuit's relation or that of the authors of Ussher's life must of necessity contain some falsities.'[27]

By the end of the nineteenth century, Bayle's Protestant scepticism about Ussher's ability to confront Fitzsimon, indeed about whether the debate took place at all, had been adopted by Catholic historians. The most thorough

---

24 Parr, *Life of Usher*, pp 6f.; I am not aware of a MS source for this letter.   25 William Dillingham, *Vita Laurentii Chadertoni ... una cum vita Jacobi Usserii* (Cambridge, 1700), p. 58; Anthony a Wood, *Athenae Oxonienses* (London, 1692), p. 24.   26 Thomas Smith, *Vitae quorundam eruditissimorum et illustrium virorum* (London, 1707), pp 18–21.   27 Bayle, *Dictionnaire*, iv, p. 482; *An historical and critical dictionary by Monsieur Bayle translated into English* (4 vols, London, 1710), iv, p. 3009; the expanded English edition of Bayle, *A general dictionary, historical and critical* (10 vols, London, 1734), x, p. 55, rejected Bayle's argument, citing the letter printed by Parr and Thomas Smith as authorities; for this edition, see J.M. Osborn, 'Thomas Birch and the "General Dictionary" (1734–41)', *Modern Philology*, 36 (1938), 25–46; by the time of the 1798 edition, *A new and general biographical dictionary; containing an historical and critical account of the lives and writings of the most eminent persons* (15 vols, London, 1798), xv, pp 146f., the account clearly stated that the debate took place and that Ussher was the 'winner': 'the Jesuit despised him at first, as but a boy; yet, after a conference or two, was so very sensible of the quickness of his wit ... as to decline any further contest with him.'

examination of the issue was provided by the Jesuit Edmund Hogan, a pioneer of his order's history.[28] In his biography of Fitzsimon, Hogan tells how Ussher went to Dublin Castle and 'had some conversation with his kinsman'. Protestant biographers, Hogan explained, give an 'an absurd account of this affair and they prop up their version of it by a real or forged letter of young Ussher.' Based on this, they 'claim for Ussher a victory which I think must be relegated to the realms of myths; and I suspect that the letter was never written, or, if written, was never sent.' Hogan detailed Ussher's youthful studies, but felt that while 'this desultory reading, writing, and arithmetic of a self-taught youth of eighteen was enough to make him very conceited and even very impertinent', such 'bolting and gluttonous study was poor training for an encounter with an old, a bold, and a practised disputant.' In conclusion, he hoped that 'this foolish story of Ussher's triumph over his cousin, Fitzsimon, will not be reproduced in subsequent lives of our illustrious countryman.'[29]

Nineteenth-century Protestant historians, on the other hand, had opted for Bernard's and Parr's account of the debate. Ussher's precocious scholarship was emphasized, the two debates took place, and Fitzsimon retired defeated. One example among many is the biography of Ussher by R.B. Hone, which records that he debated with Fitzsimon once or twice, after which the Jesuit 'retired from the field; and, not liking to own himself vanquished, gave out that he did not choose to waste his time in disputing with a boy.' In support of this, Hone quoted the letter published by Parr, and reproduced Fitzsimon's account of the affair, with, however, the final two sentences again omitted.[30] The most comprehensive modern biography of Ussher, written by the Trinity professor of divinity, Charles Elrington, and published in 1847, noted the difference between Fitzsimon's account and those of Bernard and Parr, and the doubts expressed by Bayle, but concluded that the letter from Parr, 'written at the time ... must give a more correct account of the transaction than the preface to the *Britannomachia*, published in a foreign country, and twenty years afterwards.'[31]

The difference of opinion continued into the twenty-first century, though the sectarian edge vanished. The *ODNB* entry for Fitzsimon assumes he debated with him; that for Ussher states that he did not.[32] *The dictionary of Irish biography*'s entry for Fitzsimon claims that he debated with Ussher, whereas the account of Ussher's life denies it: Ussher 'embarked on controversial theology by presenting himself as an opponent to his cousin, Henry Fitzsimon ... In the end Fitzsimon ... declined to debate with his relation

---

28 Eoghan Ó Raghallaigh, 'Hogan, Edmund Ignatius', *DIB*.   29 Hogan, *Words of comfort*, pp 221–4; cf. Hogan, *Distinguished Irishmen*, pp 226–33.   30 R.B. Hone, *Lives of eminent Christians* (London, 1833), pp 8f.   31 C.R. Elrington, *The whole works of ... James Ussher... with a life of the author* (Dublin, 1847), pp 11–14.   32 *ODNB*, 'Henry Fitzsimon', 'James Ussher'.

on grounds of his youth.'[33] Brian Jackson also denies that the debate ever occurred.[34]

CONCLUSION

The addition here of a second letter from Ussher to Fitzsimon, in Ussher's hand, together with a transcript of the disputation, would seem to confirm that the debate took place. The two letters can be fitted into a coherent sequence. The one cited by Parr came first, soon after the first and only debate. In this letter, Ussher complains that Fitzsimon had failed to fulfil his promise, made at the end of the disputation, to write to him about the principal heads of controversy. By the time of the second letter, Ussher had clearly received a response from Fitzsimon, indicating that he was breaking off the encounter. From Ussher's reply it can be inferred that Fitzsimon expressed concern that the state disapproved of the debate, that Ussher was 'to ignorant and slender a champion', and offered to continue the debate when Ussher was older.

The manuscript copy of the debate is a fascinating document, not only an account of the first formal theological encounter between the rival faiths in Ireland, but also a rare verbatim record of what took place in a disputation. What it reveals is a stark contrast in approach. Ussher is young and eager, with a naïve faith in the power of syllogistic argument, determined to use his considerable biblical and theological knowledge to prove that the pope is Antichrist. Fitzwilliam finds the basic premise absurd, and has, as a result, less faith in the ability of logic to resolve their fundamentally different starting positions. In fine, religious debate in Ireland had begun in the way in which it would continue for four hundred and fifty years, with mutual incomprehension.

NOTE

The transcription is taken from two different manuscripts, bound into one of Ussher's notebooks in the Bodelian Library, MS Barlow 13. Barlow 13 is 535-folio volume containing manuscript theological and antiquarian collections in the hand of Ussher and various contemporaries, written between 1600 and 1634.[35] Though I worked directly from the MS, I would like to thank Elizabethanne Boran for providing me with a digital version, which allowed

33 *DIB*, 'Henry Fitzsimon', 'James Ussher'.   34 Brian Jackson, 'The construction of argument', pp 99ff.   35 Falconer Madan (ed.), *A summary catalogue of western manuscripts in the Bodleian Library at Oxford* (7 vols in 8, Oxford, 1895–1953), 2, part 2, p. 1047.

me to check points of detail away from the Bodleian. The first manuscript is a transcription of the debate between Ussher and Fitzsimon, and consists of three folios, 80r.–82v., measuring approximately 27cm x 15cm, which are in an unidentified contemporary hand, presumably the note-taker who was present at the disputation.[36] There is a ruled margin on the left, indented between 2.5cm and 4cm, in which the speaker is indicated by the use of the terms Opponent and Answerer. Two notes are entered in Ussher's hand in this margin, linked to the text by an asterisk: in the transcription these notes, marked with an asterisk, are inserted in square brackets, underneath the text to which they are linked.

The first manuscript is immediately followed by two folios, 82 and 83, measuring 29cm x 20cm approximately. These are in the hand of Ussher, and consist of a letter to Henry Fitzsimon. The first folio contains the letter, the second the letter cover, endorsed 'To Mr Henry Fitz Simon at the castell', but otherwise blank.

The manuscripts are tightly bound, resulting in occasional loss of text on the versos; some text is also too faint to read. The second manuscript, the letter, has some small holes in a vertical line down the centre of the folio. These, together with the worn right edge of fol. 83r, and the tight binding on fol. 83v, result in further loss of text. At the base of some folios the manuscript is too faint to read. Where the manuscript is damaged or illegible, this is indicated by an ellipsis in square brackets. Contractions have been silently expanded.

Fol. 80r.

    The arguments of the conference betweene Mr Fitz Simons and Sr Uscher in the Queens Castle of Dublin the 27 of June 1600. Upon this quaestion: Whether the Pope be Antichrist?

    The arguments which were used for the affirmative parte.

Oppon; My first argument shall be drawn from the seate of Antichrist which Bellarmine would needes prove to be Jerusalem: But because you doe not all agree of this pointe, I would willingly understand your opinion of it; that I may know the better how to deale with you.

Answear I meane to give you noe advantage: and therfore directly disprove the Thesis or lett it alone.

---

36 See Fitzsimon's comment, f. 81r., 'I praie you note downe myne owne answeare'; and Ussher's request at the end of the debate, 'Repeat it distinctly, that it may be rightly noted downe': f. 82v.

Oppon.	I will then do so: and in their owne place take away your instances. Thus therfore I reason: Either the Pope or the Emperours are Antichrist: But not the emperors: therfore the Pope.
Answ.	I denie your Major.
Oppon.	I prove it. He onlie that maketh Rome his principall seate is Antichrist: But onlie the Pope and the Emperors maketh Rome their principall seate: Therfore the Pope or the Emperors are Antichrist.
Answ	I denie your Major.
Oppon.	I prove it. If Rome must be the principal seate of Antichrist then he onlie that maketh Rome his principal seate is Antichrist; But Rome must be the principal seate of Antichrist; therfore he onlie that maketh Rome his principal place is Antichrist.
Answ	I denie your Major.
Opp.	You do not wel way the force of the word onlie; which maketh this proposition most evident by the light of Nature.
Answ.	I admit your Major as impertinent.
Oppon.	Why? Do you not admit it as true?
Answ.	No: but as making nothing to the purpose.
Oppo.	Then you denie my minor.
Answ.	I admit it likewise, but as impertinent.
Oppon.	Belike you meane to graunt my conclusion.
Answ.	I wil also admit your conclusion, because it nothing hurteth the cause.
Oppon.	Is not the matter and fourme of this syllogisme good? And doth it not directly prove that which you denied?
Answ.	Whether Antichrists seat shalbe at Rome or at Jerusalem it maketh nothing to prove that this present Pope is Antichrist; If you thank me, I will admit any or both.
Oppon.	The course of disputation hath brought, the deciding of the first quaestion, to the triall of this last syllogisme: which if you cannot answear you fall from the principal; And as for thanks, my syllogismes meane to give you none; but are readie to extorte from you whither you wil or noe, that Rome must of necessity be the seat of Antichrist.
Fol. 8ov.	
Answ.	If I had thought you would have brought such trifles, I would never have entered into communication with you. And indeed I must condempe myselfe of great imprudencie, that ever I admitted your conference, having more waightie matters to deale in, and a great concourse of people resorting to me to be resolved in matters of Conscience.

Oppon.	This seemeth to argue a distrust of your cause; for when we came first unto you, you wuld have found leasure to talke with us when we would either in matters of divinity or philosophi. But to come to the matter in hand, I never heard before in a sollogistical disputation how an argument directly concluding that which was denied, could be shifted of without deniing or distinguishing some part. I would we had that which you the last tyme desired, I meane a Moderator, to judge of this dealing. But seeing I am forced to leave my first argument, which I purposed to prosecute with many
Arg. 2	syllogismes: I wil now urdge an other reason. Either the Pope is Antichrist or he whom you say shall raigne three yeares and an half; But not hee that shall raigne three yeares and an half: Therfore the Pope.
Answ.	I denie your Minor
Oppo:	Antichrists kingdom shall have an end when Christ commeth to judgment. But the kingdome of that man whom yee saie shal raigne three yeares and an half shall not then be ended. Therfore he is not Antichrist.
Answ.	I answear to your Major that Antichrists kingdom shall not just then have an end but before.
Oppon.	I will admitt 45 daies which your owne men saie shalbe betwixt Antichrists death and the daie of judgment, and yet myne argument shal stand.
Answ.	Prove that Antichrists kingdom shalbe ended just at Christ coming.
Oppon.	I wil prove it. If Christ shall abolish Antichrist by his coming, then Antichrists kingdom shalbe ended just with Christs coming. But Christ shall abolish Antichrist by his comming. Therfore Antichrists kingdome shalbe ended just with Christs coming.
Answ.	I denie your Minor.
Oppos.	I prove it by the expresse wordes of the Apostle Paul 2 Thess. 2.8 Then shall that wicked one be revealed whom the Lord shall confound with the spiritt of his mouth, and shall destroie with the brightness of his coming.
Answ.	Paul speaketh of Christ his coming in his saints, not of his coming to judgment.
Oppon	I will not seeke to press you further; seeing you are brought to invent such an exposition, as is contrarie both to the cleare wordes of the text and also
Arg. 3	to the opinion of your owne writers. I wil then use an other argument. He that in shew is like the lamb but speaketh as the dragon is Antichrist Apoc. 11. The Pope in outward shewe is like the lamb. For he calleth himself the vickar and the servant of the ser-

	vants of Christ but speaketh as the dragon. Therfore the Pope is Antichrist.
[...]	The Pope speaketh not like the dragon.
[...]	He that teacheth doctrine of deviles, speaketh as the dragon. Apoc. 12.10 The Pope teacheth doctrine of deviles, therfore the Pope speaketh as the dragon.
[...]	You must thinke that my eares do glowe at such speaches.
[...]	And you must thinke that we are touched with the tyrannie that the [...] hath exercised over the church of Christ.

Fol. 81r.

Answ:	Prove your Minor.
Oppon.	I prove it thus. He that after the full abolyshing of the use of the ceremoniall lawe, enjoyeth a religious abstinence from certaine meates teacheth doctrine of devills; But the Pope after the full abolishing of the use of the ceremoniall lawe, enjoyneth a religious abstinance from certaine meates; Therefore the Pope teacheth doctrine of divells.
Answ.	I denie the sequele of your major.
Oppon.	Then you denie my major itselfe.
Answ.	It followeth not; I praie you note downe myne owne answeare.
Oppon.	The sequele of my major is proved by the testimony of the Apostle Paul: 1 Tim. 4 v. 1 et 3. Now the spirit speaketh evidently, that in the latter times some shall depart from the faith, gyving heede to spirites of error, and doctrine of divells, comanding to abstaine from meates which God hath created to be receaved with gyving thankes etc..
Answ.	Paul speaketh of those that should forbid meates as uncleane in itselfe; But the Pope forbiddeth not the use of meates as uncleane by nature; for God in the beginning sawe that all things which he made wear exceeding good; but as uncleane by commaundment.
Oppon.	No Popes commaundement can make meates uncleane as I wil prove by Scripture. That which God hath made cleane, the *Popes commaundement cannot make uncleane; But after the use of the ceremoniall lawe God hath made all meates cleane: Therfore noe Popes commaundement cann make them uncleane. [*because Peter [...]ould not Act 11,9]
Answ.	Your argument would make the Queenc to be Antichrist.
Oppon.	If you had marked the Major of my 2nd syllogisme you would not have saide soe; for there I expressly made mention of a religious abstinance, not of a politicke which her Majestie only regardeth.
Answ.	Her Majestie commaundeth a religious abstinance from certaine meates.

Oppon.	Let that be noted; All the world may judge of the truth of it.
Arg. 4	I will now goe to an other argument. He that sitteth in the temple of God sheweing himself that he is God, is Antichrist: (2 Thess. 2.) The Pope sytteth in the Temple of God, shewing himself that he is God: Therfore he is Antichrist.
Answ.	The Pope doth not showe himself to be God.
Oppon.	I have noted a fewe places for the proofe of it. In the decrees the Pope
Distinct.	thus reasoneth: It is manifest that God cannot be judged by men. Nowe
96. cap. satis	certaine it is that by the godly Prince Constantine the Pope was called God; And therfore it is evident inough that the Pope cannot in
evidenter	anie wise be bounde or loosed by the secular power. Baldus, Papa est Deus in terris. De electione C. Fundamenta in 6to Assumptus est in consortium individuae trinitatis. Lib 1. Ceremoniar. sect 8. Papa in nocte nativitatis benedixit eiusem, quem postea donat alicui principi, in signum summa potentiae Pontifici collatae, juxta illud, data est mihi omnis potestas in coelo et in terra.[37]
Answ	The Pope is God in denomination, not in nature and power.
Oppon.	We know verie well that the Pope is not God in nature and power; but seeing he taketh on him, that denomination, as you confesse, it is enough to prove him to be Antichrist.
Answ.	Noe; for the holy ghost saith; I have said: that you are Gods.[38]
Fol. 81v. Oppon.	That denomination is far unlike to that which is here in question. For God himself giveth to the civil magistrate the name of Gods, but the Pope arrogateth unto himself a name above all other names; and intendeth himself into the societie of the blessed trinitie; yea, and advanceth himself above all those whom God doth call Gods, making them to be subject to his jurisdiction and hold their kingdomes from him.
Answ	The meaning of Pauls place is that Antichrist shall advaunce himself against Gods owne person.
Oppo:	Those wordes, against all that is called God, do shewe that this must be meant of the powers on earth to whom the Lord attributeth the name of God; But to take your owne exposition, I say that the Pope advaunceth himself against Gods other person,

---

[37] Cf. Georg Sohn, *Disputatio theologica quod papa Romanus sit antichristus ille, de quo prophetae et apostoli praedixerunt: quae VII. et XXI. Septemb. horis antemeridianis in auditorio theologico habebitur* (Heidelberg, 1588), p. 22.   [38] Jn 10:34.

	because he arrogateth to himself that which is [...] to God; and therfore must be that Antichrist.
Answ.	You speake too confidently; you should have saide in my opinion, and as far as I can [...]
Oppon.	I neaded no such speache; for I was certainly persuded of the truth of that which I said.
Answ.	Prove that the Pope doth arrogate to himselfe that which is proper to God.
Oppon.	I prove it. He that braggeth that he can translate kingdoms from one nation to an other people, arrogateth to himself that which is proper to God.* But the Pope braggeth that he can translate the kingdomes from one nation to another people: Therfore the Pope arrogateth that to himself which is proper to God. [* If you had suffered the last testimonie which was brought out of the Book of Ceremonies to be read you needed not to ask this ground anew.]
Answ.	God hath this potestate propria; but the Pope, potestate sibi credita.
Oppon.	Yea God giveth not his power to another, nor communicateth with anie creature that which is proper to himself; and therefore the Pope can not do this potestate sibi credita.
Answ.	God communicateth that which is proper to himself unto others; as for exampe God is only just and wise; and yet there are just and wise men also, and Christ is the foundation of the church and yet he communicateth the same to Peter.
Oppon.	Gods justice and wisedome being infinite cannot be communicated to anie creature. And as for the foundation of the Church we acknowledge only Jesus Christ: That the church was builded upon Peter I think you can hardly prove.
Answ.	Christ saith plainlie: Tu es Petra, et super hanc petram aedificabo ecclesiam. And the Apostle; we are built upon the foundation of the prophets and Apostles.
Oppon.	We are built upon the foundation of the doctrine and writings of the Prophets [...] Apostles proceeding from Christ; Our Saviours saying you have cited wronglie; for it is saide Τυ ἐς Πετρος thou art Peter; not Tu [...] petra, thou art a rocke.
Answ.	Petros or petra or petram they are all one.
Oppon.	He that hath but small skill in the Greeke tongue knoweth that Petros and petra are of diverse significations. I will propound another [...] He that teacheth doctrine directlie contrarie to the doctrine of Christ is Antichrist. The Pope teacheth doctrine directlie contrary to Christ [...] doctrine; therfore the Pope is Antichrist.
Answ.	I denie your minor.

Oppon.	I prove it. He that defendeth that a religious worshipp should be given to creatures teacheth a doctrine directlie contrarie to the doctrine of Christ; The Pope defendeth that a religious worship should be given to creatures: ergo.
Answ.	If you understand your Minor of such a religious worship as is proper to God, I denie it.
Oppon.	He that defendeth that with δουλεια creatures maie be honoured defendeth that religious worship proper to God maie be given to creatures: But the Pope defendeth that with δουλεια creatures maie be honored: Therfore the [...] defendeth that a religious worship proper to God may be given to creatures.

Fol 82r.

Answ.	I denie your major.
Oppon:	I prove it out of Matthew 4.10. Dominum Deum tuum adorabis, et illi soli servies.
Answ.	Dulia is not here appropriated to God.
Oppon:	Yes; for service is the same that is δουλευειν, saving that one is Greeke and the other Latin.
Answ.	There is great difference between the force of theis wordes; but I answear that we must not serve God alone as God: and this service the pope oweth to noe creature.
Oppon:	I prove that he doth: He that will have us serve the saintes as καρδιογνωσται will have us serve them as God; But the Pope will have us serve the saintes as καρδιογνωσται. Therfore the Pope will have us serve the saintes as God.
Answ.	What neede wee anie Greeke, or Latine, or French? I have already answeared you.
Opp;	But I have taken away your answear, by proving that you serve the saintes as God, because you serve them as serchers of the heart; which is proper onlie to God.
Answ;	God searcheth the heart only per se, but he may communicate the same also with others. I pray you let me now object 2 or 3 arguments against your Thesis.
Oppo	You shall verie willinglie.

Mr Fitz Simons arguments for the negative parte.

Oppo.	Antichrist shall raigne 3 yeares and an halfe onlie; The Pope hath raigned farr longer: Therfore the Pope is not Antichrist.
Answ	If you take years in the ordinarie and proper sence, I denie your major.
Oppon.	I will prove it owt of the 7 of Daniel, and 11 of the Apocalips.

Answ	Out of Daniel I answear you cannot prove it, for in sum nothing is properly spoaken of Antichrist.
Oppon.	You shall see it proved. In the 12 of the Apocalips the woman is said to have beene nouryshed in the wildernes for a time, times and halfe a time, which is for 3 yeares and an halfe, or 1260 dayes, or 42 monethes, as in the text it is expounded.
Answ	I denie that those yeares monethes or daies must be taken in there ordinary sence.
Oppon	I prove it: If there be noe cause why they should not be taken in their proper signification, then must they be taken in their proper signification; Therefore they must be understood in their usuall sence.
Answ.	I denie your minor.
Oppon.	What cause cann you bring?
Answ.	Looke you to that: It is noe reason I should give you advantage, when you refused to give me any.
Oppo;	This is against the order of disputation, and therfore if you cann [sic] shewe me cause my exposition must stand.
Answ;	I will give you then this reason; because in the writings of the Prophets it is not unusuall to have a day put for a yeare as may be seene in Daniels 70 weekes.
Oppo;	If you take the yeares soe, then you must take the monethes for the same.
Answ.	The same time is expressed by both theis dates; yet I say not that a whole year in this place is the same that a whole moneth [sic]; but that the partes of both, namely the daies of the yeares and moneths are taken in the same sence to witt, not ordinary, but prophetical daies.
Oppo;	Then you saie that Antichrists kingdome shall endure 1260 daies.
Answ.	I saie not that he shall all this time be in his full kingdome but that this […] his kingdom shall encrease by litle and little, till at last it come to his […] when it shall be made manifest to the worlde.

Fol. 82v.

Oppo.	But if Antichrist were come none should buie or sell throughowt the whole world, that should not have his marke in his forehead or […]
Answ	That followeth not; it is sufficient that they cannot buie or sell when Antichrists jurisdiction […]
Oppo:	I prove it out of the 13 of the Apocalips v. 16. 17. And he shall make all, small and great, rich and poor, freemen and servants, to have a marke in their right hand or foreheads, and that none maie

	buie or sell, but he that hath the character or the name of the beast, or the number of his name.
Answ:	This place maie be well understoode of all those that are subject to his dominion.
Oppo:	But the Pope doth not exclude all those from buying and selling within his dominions that have not his marke in their foreheads or right hand.
Answ:	Yes; for he suffereth none that professeth Christianitie to buie or sell within his kingdome, except he outwardlie professe himselfe to be a member of the Church of Rome, which open profession of the Popes doctrine is, as it were, a marke in the foreheade or right hand.
Oppo;	We professe not the Popes doctrine but the doctrine of Christ.
Answ.	I meane that all papists are constrained, to allow all doctrines which the Pope shall authorize by his decrees.
Oppo;	Antichrist shall denie Christ as Godhead: the pope denieth not Christs Godhead, therfore the Pope is not [...]
Answ.	I distinguish your proposition. Antichrist shall denie Christ his Godhead closely but not openly.
Oppon.	I prove that he shall denie it openly. He that shall open his mouth to blaspheme Gods name shall openly denie Christes deity; But Antichrist shall open his mouth to blaspheme Gods name; Therfore Antichrist shall openly denie Christes deitie.
Answ.	I denie your major for it followeth not, that everie one that blasphemeth doth openly denie?
Oppo;	He that usurpeth unto himself the name of God, openly denieth that Christ is God; Antichrist shall usurp unto himself the name of God; therfore he shall openly deny that Christ is God.
Answ.	I denie the major. For one may call himself God, and yet in word confess Christs deity.
Oppon.	Yea; but Antichrist shal so assume Gods name, that he shall take away openly Christs deity.
Answ.	Prove that.
Oppo;	He that commeth openly in his owne name shall openlie denie that Christ is God; But Antichrist shall openlie come in his owne name; therfore he shall openly deny that Christ is God.
Answ.	I denie your major.
Oppon.	I prove it; because to come in his owne name is openly contrarie to Christes name. But nothing is openlie contrarie to Christes name, but openlie to denie that Christ is God; Therfore he that shall come in his owne name, shall openlie denie that Christ is God.
Answ.	This is noe syllogisme.

Oppon:	What fault can you find in it?
Answ:	Repeat it distinctly, that it may be rightly noted downe and you shall see the fault.
Oppon:	Nomine suo venire est Christi nomini esse contrarius; at nihil Christi nomini est aperte contrarius, nisi aperte negare Christus esse Deus; Ergo qui nomine suo est venturus aperte negabit Christus […]
Answ.	What moode and figure is this in?
Oppon.	In Darii.[39]
Answ	First then the consequent of the conclusion should be the subject of the Major.
Oppon.	Syllogismes are not so exactly to be waged. For if you deale strictly there cann be no necessarie syllogismes made of Christ and Antichrist; because they are particular tearmes.
Answ.	Ther is difference betwixt particular and proper tearmes ; for though all particulars […]clude nothing, yet of proper termes a most sound syllogisme may be made.
Oppo;	Well, you meane to answeare this some other tyme.
Answ.	Nay, reduce your argument into a better fourme, and you shall be presently answeared. neither is this same syllogismes minor true.
Oppo;	I have spent longer time with you, then I could well afforde; for I assure you before your comming I had matters that greatly concerned my reputation:
Answ	Shall wee then propound theses for our next conference?
Oppon.	Trulie I am so busie that I cann have no leesure to meddle with these matters; And in the controversyes I have taken noe great paines for I came into this land for exhortation, not for disputation.
Answ.	We may yet agree upon some questions, and whensoever you are at leasure you maie send anie one for me.
Oppo;	I hope shortly to be at libertie, then you may have conference with me at any time on what questions sowever you will.
Answ.	Yet let me request you, that when your leasure shall serve, you will write me.
Oppon;	I will; and God grant that we may al see the truth, you praie not this for you only, but for my selfe also.
Finis.	

Fol. 83r.
Mr Fitzsimon, although I, being certified by your letter of your resolution to break of the course of our conference, was almost induced for my part also to

---

[39] A scholastic mnemonic used to remember one of the many different valid forms of a syllogism.

let the matter rest, as being not interrupted by any default of mine: yet now agayne, more deeply waying, how others, not acquaynted with my purpose might of ignorance misconstrue my intent, as though by reason of mine own insufficiencye or the weakness of the cause I had forgowen the defense of the same; I determined at last, once agayne to sollicite yow unto a farther triall and debating of these controversyes. If yow demaund what cause of any such suspicion hath been offred to go no farther, I suppose your writing had ministred unto me sufficient occasion to suspect what consequents might ensewe. For if to my face yow make no scruple to charge me with maynteyning such assertions, as to a Christian minde wear both offensive and odious: what maner of relation, trow yow, may I expect to be reported behinde my back? Surely he that had seen how busilye yow labour in objecting unto me, the defending of adinata[40] (as yo[...] like to write) impugning common principles of truthe, and I know not what newe wines of youthful conceyts, venting but froth and fumes: might not without cause have deemed, that of purpose yow had prepared an antidotum for m[...] least I should have surfetted with immoderat joye, hearing my selfe for forwardness and perfor[...]ance commended. Yet is not altogither unworthye of consideration to waye upon what sure ground yow builde so deep an accusation. I denied forsothe that Antichrist should openlye and in worde oppose himselfe to Christ; and therfore would not agree unto your conclusion, that the Pope was not Antichrist. Atque hinc illae lachrymae. Yow should also have added, that withall I affirmed, that Antichrist under the shaddowe of the name of Christ, did most notoriously oppugne the same; and howsoever in outward shewe he pretended the contrarye, yet indeed he blasphemed the name of God, and his tabernacle, and those that dwell in heaven. But this say yow, is contrarye to the prophet and common doctrine of all. And for the first, yow solemnlye quote in your margent the 7 and 11 chapters of Daniel. An easye matter it is to cite whole chapters, whear your answerer can not divine, what part maketh for your purpose. If yow had urged any particulars, I doubt not but with litle paynes, yow should receave a sufficient answear. Notwithstanding, if I be not deceaved, the edge [...] this argument was, before this, somewhat abated; when it was told yow, that out of Daniel no sure demonstration could be fetched in the question of Antichrist: but seeing yow scorne to be instructed by one of the meaner sort; I pray yow be not ashamed that Bellarmine should teach yow out of Cyprian and Jerom that Daniel in these places speaketh, ad literam, of Antiochus; and withal learne of your schoolmen that, Symbolica theologia non est argumentativa. Yea, but this is repugnant to the doctrine of [...] if we may beleeve yow on your worde. What (All) I pray yow? If

---

40 = adynata, a figure of speech, where hyperbole is taken to such lengths that it becomes an impossibility; from the Greek ἀδύνατά (my thanks to Professor John Rich for identifying this reference).

Popelings, yow have found out a compendious way to determine all doubtfull poyntes of your religion: if aswell theyr adversaryes as them [...] yow halfe perswade me, yow told me nothing but truthe, when yow affirmed that yow wear not greatly con[...]sant in matters of controversye; seing yow know not in what points of doctrine the protestants are at variance with yow. If yow will take but the paynes to turne to Rob. Bellarmine de Roman. Pontif. lib. 3 [...] 14 I will referre it even unto yow owne censure, to judge, whether your objection might not more justly be charged with petitio, then my answear with negatio principii. And seeing I am proceeded thus far [...] I thinke it not much impertinent, seing yow are so curious in espying moats in other mens eyes, whear [...] are; to serve yow with a messe of yowr ownc sauce, that yow may a litel look toward manticae quod in t[...] est.[41] Yow remember that being pressed with the argument drawen from the principall seat of Antichrist; yo[...] durst not (though provoked therunto) denye that it was Rome, knowing that yow should most evidently b[...] convicted by the manifest truthe of gods worde: but was constrayned to elude the argument brought against yow, by admitting the whole as impertinent, though playn contradictorye to that which your selfe formerly denied. Alas, Mr Fitzsimon, yow are brought to a very hard extremitye, when yow must admit that Rome must be throne of Antichrists kingdome. It litle avayleth the Jesuits to labour so much (agaynst the autho[...] of divine and humaine writers) in drawing Peter from his Apostleship to hold a bishoprick at Rome five [...] twentye yeares; if in the latter dayes Antichrist must thrust him out of his chayre: and no man may just[...] be blamed, if he suspect that doctrine which is broched out of the citye which God hath forwarned should make nations to drinke of the wine of the wrath of her fornication. Yow wear afrayde to confess that Antichrist should be killed 45 dayes before the ende of the world (though Bellarmine prove it, by comparing the 11 and 12 vers [...] of the last chapter of Daniel togither) and that place of the apostle 2 Thess. 2. 8 being urged yow affirmed very strangelye, that it was to be understood of Christ his coming in his saynts, not his comming unto judgm[...] Litle better was your exposition of Tobi. 14.16 at our first meeting, where when I offred to prove, that Toby lived above 99 yeares, contrary to your text in that apocryphall book; yow thought this σοφὸν φάρμακον[42] salved all, that he lived 99 years in timore Domini, but, it may be, longer in a more dissolute or less strict kinde of life: for proof wherof yow alledged a like phrase out of the gospell, whear it was sayd th[...] the body of our saviour should be three dayes in the grave : and the dissimilitude being objected, that in the words of the gospell was a manifest synecdoche integri pro membro, which in Toby possiblye could have no place; yow denied that the body of | Christ lay in the sepulchre

---

41 Presumably, manticae quod in tergo est: you don't see the load (knapsack) which is on your own back.   42 Clever medicine.

a part of three dayes, because it was written (said yow) that he rose from death before the sunne rising: which what other was it then to denye that Christ rose the third daye. The like might I say of your distorted syllogisme in Darii, with the assumption generall negative, pestered with more faults then sentences; and your excuse of the same, as if Christ and Antichrist being special termes, wear not capable of a sound forme of syllogisme: your rash affirmation of the intent of hir Ma[...]styes edict concerning abstinance from flesh on certayne dayes, with other assertions of like nature: wh[...] if they had slipt from my mouth, I know not what tragedyes yow would rayse therupon (though I mig[...] shrewdlye guesse by your to busye fault-finding, whear there is no cause) but for my selfe, I am sure I w[...] be halfe ashamed, as long as I lived. And these things (cosen) do I repeat, not because I take any delight in exprobrating ignorance in any man: but partly, that yow giving me occasion, Dum dicis quod vis, audias quod non vis; and partly also that yow may better consider your owne abilitye, before yow experience

Fol. 83v.
the chiefe. If dallying with the weaker, yow are driven to such exigences; beleeve me, it wear no poynt of good policye to encounter with the stronger: unless yow account it a greater glorye Achilles cecidisse manu; and (that I may use your owne saying) in putting me downe, yow vancquishe onely a batchelour of the colledge. Indeed I see now, yow are of the nature of Alexander that would strive with none but kings: where before by reason of your great challenges (in respect whereof I justlye resembled yow unto the Philistine; not simplye as yow seem to charge me) I had thought yow wear Goliath, that would not refuse to combat, unless Israel had sent out another giant to mate him, but be content to aunswear the least boye of the adverse campe. And that I may freelye open my minde unto yow as I have begonne, these proceedings of yours bewraye some spice of an ambitious humour, and argue that yow rather seek the glorye of man then of God if yow make not this pretence a covert to shrowde the weakness of your cause under; to which opinion I rather incline, because at my first coming I found yow so readye and desirous to conferre with me in divinitye or humanitye, but having profered to conferre syllogisticallye on the whole body of the controversyes as in order they lay in Bellarmine, and for a taste propounded but one argument, scarce could yow be intreated to suffer one dayes conference; and now what starting holes goe yow about to finde, wherby yow may avoyde further communication? Yow pretend that yow have had blame of the state.. It is not like yow had, for anything that [...]st privatlye betwixt us both, except by youre owne means yow procured it. And I remember at [...]ur first meeting, yow professed that yow weare readye to undergoe, not onely displeasure of the state, but bonds and death it selfe also; so you might do me good, or any other that sought to be resolved of any poynt at your hands. Now I perceave

eyther yowr minde is altered; or else yow utterlye despayre to do me good. But belike your purpose is to deferre this matter, untill by greater ripeness other perswasions may be more aptly ingendered, and after years move me to mislike my former conceyts (for thus, I take it, your wordes sound.) Indeed yow are to be commended for your forwardness and performance, in allotting such a time for perswasion when youre adversarye misliketh his cause; and assigning such a date for disputation, as in all liklyhood never will beginne: although yet methink's herin is litle reason, that yow should dispayre to winne your adversarye while he is young and weak, and hope to do great matters, when he is more ripe and strong. Lastly rejecting me, as to ignorant and slender a champion, yow desire to experience the chiefe. Touching the chiefe, it licth not in me to procure theyr conference with yow: and as for my abilitye I had rather others should judge therof then my selfe; onely thus much I say, that of all others yow had least cause to upbrayde me with ignorance; which if it wear admitted to be so great as yow would make it seem to be, yet wear it no sufficient reason why yow should break your promise. By the very first word yow spake to me, I had a promise of your willingness to conferr with me at any time; and by the very last, a promise that yow would deal with me in writing in some principall head of controversye: if after all this, upon some light surmises which yow fayne unto your selfe, yow refuse to go forward in that course which yourselfe have agreed unto, pardone me if I thinke, that yow eyther have small respect to your worde, or great diffidence in your cause.

As for the tearme of Boye, I count it not worth the standing upon: though (to cleer myselfe of giving any rash credence to misreports) some of your own profession affirmed that they hard yow utter such speeches in the heering of Mr Fitz-William of Miryon,[43] and others. But howsoever the matter is, I could well brook greater injuryes then this; so that through my sides profession of gods truthe be not thrust at. To conclude therfore, I would wish yow once more to advice of this matter, and in playne wordes signifye your determination: that we may eyther proceed furt[...] or else by that which hath already past, publikely make knowen, whither I cam unto yow in the name of the Lord of Hostes, or whither yow be against him.

James Usshers

---

[43] Merrion House in Co. Dublin was the seat of the Fitzwilliam family.

The dissolution of the monasteries and the parishes of the western liberty of Meath in the seventeenth century

RORY MASTERSON

One of the many functions performed by the religious houses of late medieval Ireland was that of rector of the parishes that were granted (impropriated) to them. This involved the obligation to maintain the chancel of the church and sometimes, though not always, to present a vicar to look after the parish. Much recent research has focused on the effects of the dissolution in relation to the distribution of the religious orders' lands and the social effects of this. Studies have also highlighted the role of the monasteries as hospitals and schools as well as the religious functions they performed within their communities.[1] This essay examines the role of the monasteries as rectors of the parishes they were endowed with, what was the extent of that endowment and how their dissolution affected those parishes. The western liberty of Meath corresponded with those areas of the medieval liberty of Meath granted to Hugh de Lacy where the initial Anglo-Norman conquest had failed to maintain itself by the early fifteenth and sixteenth centuries. Geographically it encompassed those areas of the de Lacy liberty represented by the modern counties of Westmeath and Longford and the parts of Offaly included in the dioceses of Meath and Clonmacnoise. Eighteen different religious houses held impropriations in this area, and each case will be examined to build a picture of the complex nature of ecclesiastical administration at parochial level prior to and after dissolution.

CISTERCIAN ABBEY OF ST MARY'S DUBLIN

The extent of lands and rectories of St Mary's Cistercian Abbey, Dublin, made at Skryne on 1 and 2 October 1540 lists the rectories of Mastrome (Mostrim) and Knockerath as part of its possessions. These, we are informed, were in O'Farrell's country (Longford) and were farmed by Fantasius McTege for four cows or 40s. Another extent of the abbey's possessions in Meath (Meath and Westmeath) was made at Fore on 6 October. The jurors

---

[1] B. Scott, 'The dissolution of the religious houses in the Tudor diocese of Meath', *Archivium Hibernicum*, 59 (2005), 260–76; Marian Lyons, *Church and society in County Kildare, c.1470–1547* (Dublin, 2000), pp 109–85.

were Oliver and Richard Nugent along with others. This extent lists the rectories of Castellostie, Porlanam, Poreshangen and Russhagh (Castlelost, Portloman, Portnashangan and Russagh). Castlelost was farmed by William, the late abbot, by an indenture dated 26 October 1537, for thirteen years at a rent of 'twenty-eight fat and proper cows'. Portloman, Portnashangan and Russagh were farmed by the abbot to Gerald Nugent for a term of years not yet expired for a rent of seventeen cows worth £8 10s.[2] All five parishes were leased for a total of £24 10s.

These parishes were of recent acquisition, unlike most that can be traced back to the initial Anglo-Norman settlement. In 1486 the prior of Little Malven sold the parishes of Clonsilla in Dublin, Portloman and its chapel at Weren, Castlelost and its chapel at Ballymolan in Fartullagh, along with Portshangan in Meath diocese and the churches of Knockrath and Mastrum (Mostrim) in Ardagh diocese for 450 marks (£350) to St Mary's, Dublin. They also purchased five carucates (*c.*600 acres of arable land) in Fartullagh from Little Malven but there is no reference to these lands in the extents. It can be assumed that St Mary's had subsequently alienated these lands. The five parishes were given by Hugh Tyrrell of Castleknock to Little Malven but it appears that he had retained the advowson (the right to appoint clergy to the living), as in 1486 Maurice Tyrrell of Fartullagh, Lord of Castlelost, granted the advowson of Castlelost, Portloman and Portnashangan to St Mary's. Richard Delamere, lord of Russagh, gave St Mary's the advowson of Russagh. There is no mention of the advowson of Mastrum. Evidently, Hugh Tyrrell of Castleknock owned the lands of all five parishes and had retained the right of advowson in all. Subsequently, he had alienated his lands in Russagh to the Delameres along with the right of advowson. In 1486 when the parishes were to be transferred to St Mary's, both Tyrrell and Delamere gave up their rights.[3]

Hugh Tyrrell's decision to give five parishes in Westmeath and Longford to the Benedictine priory of Little Malven in England was influenced by his English possessions. The Tyrrells owned lands at Little Marcle in Herefordshire and the priory of Little Malven was only about seven miles distant from there.[4]

As the first batch of Irish monastic dissolutions began in the summer of 1537 and Castlelost was leased in October 1537, it is likely that the leasing out of the tithes of these parishes was a recent policy in anticipation of the forthcoming dissolution. The absence of any reference to these parishes in the papal letters indicates that they were well run and administered.

2 N. White (ed.), *Extents of Irish monastic possessions, 1540–1541* (Dublin, 1943), pp 19, 22 [henceforth *Extents*].   3 J.T. Gilbert (ed.), *Chartularies of St Mary's Abbey, Dublin* (2 vols, London, 1884–6), 2, pp 17–18.   4 E. St John Brooks, 'The Tyrels of Castleknock', *JRSAI*, 76 (Dec. 1946), 151–4.

Subsequent references to these rectories are scanty. In 1552 the rectories of Castlelostle, Portloma, Portsangan, Rossaghe, Maystrome and Knockerathe were leased for twenty-one years to Walter Peppard from the termination of his lease.[5] However, in 1575 all six rectories were leased to Thomas, earl of Ormond, for sixty years.[6] As pointed out earlier it was the responsibility of the rector to maintain the chancel of the church and certainly the earl appears to have neglected his duties in this regard. In 1622, when Bishop Ussher conducted his survey of the parishes of the diocese of Meath he found that the churches and chancels were ruinous in Portnashangan, Portloman and Castlelost. Unfortunately the other three rectories were in Ardagh diocese and so are unrecorded but there is no reason to believe that their condition was any different.[7]

HOSPITALLERS OF KILMAINHAM

An extent of the properties of the Hospitallers was made at Athboy on 16 May 1541. One of the jurors was John McMahon of Dromkrey (Drumcree) and listed as part of the order's possessions is the rectory of Drumcre (Kilcummy, barony of Delvin). Three townlands, Drumcree, Robinstown and Johnstown were listed as paying tithes, while the alterages were valued at 10s. The tithes were leased to Sir Thomas Lutterell for 53s. 4d.[8] The gift of Drumcree/Kilcummy to the Hospitallers must originate from Gilbert Nugent who was granted the lands of Castletown – Delvin – by Hugh de Lacy. We know Gilbert Nugent granted some of his lands to the Llanthony canons and evidently granted this parish to the Hospitallers. In 1641 a James Nugent still owned all the lands of Kilcummy. Two of the 1641 townlands, Kilcummy and Ballinegall, are absent from the 1541 list.[9] It is likely that the tithes of these townlands constituted the vicars' share and so were not listed. In 1562 a patent was granted to Walter Hoppe (Hope) confirming a lease by the prior of St John of Jerusalem to him of the rectory of Drumcree.[10] In 1578 Hope (then 'of Mullingar') surrendered the rectory of Drumcree said to be formally in the tenure of W. Slattery of Dublin, butcher.[11] Evidently Walter Hope had purchased William Slattery's interest in the rectory. In the same year the rectory was re-leased to him for twenty-one years.[12] In 1622, both the church and chancel were repaired.[13]

---

5 *Fiants Ire. Edward*, no. 1083.   6 *Fiants Ire. Elizabeth*, no. 2660.   7 'A certificate of the state and revennewes of the bishoppricke of Meath and Clonemackenosh' in C.R. Elrington (ed.), *The whole works of the most Rev. James Ussher* (17 vols, Dublin, 1864), i, appendix v, pp cvii, cviii, cix.   8 *Extents*, p. 112.   9 J.C. Lyons (ed.), *The book of survey and distribution of the estates in the county of Westmeath* (Ledestown, 1852), p. 16.   10 James Morrin (ed.), *Calendar of the patent and close rolls rolls of chancery in Ireland* (3 vols, London, 1861–3), i, p. 473.   11 *Fiants Ire. Elizabeth*, no. 3318.   12 *Fiants Ire. Elizabeth*, no. 3323.   13 'Revennewes of the bishoppricke of Meath and Clonemackenosh', p. cxxi.

ST MARY'S ABBEY, KELLS

The extent for St Mary's Abbey, Kells, was made at Ardbraken on 3 October 1540 and amongst the rectories impropriate to the monastery was Kyllagh (Killagh, barony of Delvin). The rectory was valued at £8 and the alterages at £1 6s. 8d.[14] The parish was probably the gift of Gilbert Nugent. The rectory was granted to G. Fleming in tail mail and this would explain the absence of further references to it.[15] In 1622, the church and chancel were repaired.[16]

PRIORY OF CONNELL

In an extent made at Mullingar on the 10 April 1541 the jurors found that the rectory of Ballynorker (Ardnurcher) was part of the possessions of the priory of Connell. The rectory was 'in the district of McGeoghegan amongst the Irish' and so they were unable to value it. It was farmed by Edward, bishop of Meath, paying fifty cows (worth 6s. 8d. each) that were valued at £16 13s. 4d. He retained twelve cows for his procurations and synodals.[17]

The rectory of Ardnurcher originated in the grant of the cantred of Ardnurcher to Meiler FitzHenry. In 1202, he had also founded a monastery at Great Connell in Kildare and a confirmation of its possessions in 1205 lists Atornorohor. How extensive the original parish was is evidenced by a papal letter of 1400 requesting that the chapels of Rachayn (Rahin), Kylleacy (Killoughy), Ralyey (Rathleyne), Athalvy (Ballyboy), Drumcailynd (Drumcullen) and Eglays (Eglish) be detached from the mother church at Ardnurcher and created in a separate parish with the mother church at Lynally (then also a daughter church of Ardnurcher).[18] This separation took place in 1420. In 1622, Ussher's visitation of Meath lists Rathewe (Rahugh), Kilcomreagh (Kilcumreragh), Kilmanahen (Kilmanaghan) and Conrey (Conry) as chapels of ease of the mother church of St David's, Ardnurcher.[19] Kilmanaghan was not in the original parish as it is listed as one of the parishes in the possession of the Cistercian monastery of Granard.

Meiler died in 1220 and his cantred reverted to his lord, Walter de Lacy. Walter's grand-daughter Margery recovered the advowson from Great Connell. A subsequent papal letter informs us that the rector of the parish

---

14 *Extents*, p. 263.   15 *Fiants Ire. Henry*, no. 223.   16 'Revennewes of the bishoppricke of Meath and Clonemackenosh', p. xcviii.   17 *Extents*, p. 162.   18 G.H. Orpen (ed.), *Song of Dermot and the Earl* (Oxford, 1892), ll 3138–40; H.S. Sweetman (ed.), *Calendar of documents relating to Ireland* (5 vols, London, 1875–6), i, no. 273; *Cal. papal letters*, 5, p. 314.   19 *Cal. papal letters*, 7, p. 174; 'Revennewes of the bishoppricke of Meath and Clonemackenosh'; R. Masterson, 'Power, politics and parish formation in the medieval cantred of Ardnurcher: 1172–1690', *Offaly Heritage*, 6 (2011), 39–83.

was presented by her heirs, the Mortimers, and resided at Ardnurcher. Chaplains were appointed to each of the chapels of ease.[20] By 1400 the Mortimers had lost political control of the southern section of the cantred and hence the request to have the parish divided. By 1420 the Mortimer family had lost control of Ardnurcher as well and the separation of the parish was carried through. By 1540 the priory of Connell had recovered both the Lynally and Ardnurcher rectories via papal provision. The extent of 1540 only refers to Ardnurcher but from Ussher's records it is possible to determine that the rectory of Ardnurcher encompassed the civil parishes of Ardnurcher (the mother church), Rahugh, Kilcumreragh and Conry. The rectory of Fircill included the civil parishes of Lynally (the mother church), Eglish, Rathlihen, Ballyboy, Drumcullen, Killoughy and Kilbride (Kilcoursey).[21] Unfortunately no further grants of either rectory can be found in the *fiants*. In 1622 Ussher found the situation particularly bad. Within the two rectories only the mother church of Ardnurcher had the chancel repaired but the church (the nave) was ruined. In all other cases the churches and chancels were in ruins.[22]

BENEDICTINE PRIORY OF FORE

The extent of the property of the priory of Fore was made at Fore on 6 October 1540. Three of the jurors were Nugents. The priory was in possession of eight parishes in the region. The Blessed Mary in Fowre (St Mary's, Fore) was valued at £12 and St Fekin in Fowre (St Feighins, Fore) was valued at £12 13s. 4d. It had a chapel of ease at Arthideorum in Fore valued at £4; Fayron (Foyran) valued at £6; Faghley (Faughalstown) valued at £13; Mayne (Mayne) valued at £12; Lyghbaly (Lickbla) valued at £12; Dormysshkylle (Kilpatrick) valued at £8; and Ragarff (Rathgarve) valued at £10. The priory also owned the parish of Oldcastle (Co. Meath) valued at £6. The history of this Benedictine priory is well documented elsewhere and suffice to say that when dissolved the parishes in the region were well administered.[23] Each of the parishes had a stipendiary priest 'for celebrating therein' who received the alterages for his salary. The jurors also state that the priory owned 'divers other rectories in the Brenny in ORelis district where the King's writ does not run, the names of which are not known, the tithes and other profits of these, if they could be received, would be worth 106s. 8d.'[24]

The rectories in Breifne probably dated from the early thirteenth century. In 1212, a castle was under construction at Kilmore. Details of the parishes

---

20 *Cal. papal letters*, 5, pp 406–8. 21 'Revennewes of the bishoppricke of Meath and Clonemackenosh', p. cxvi. 22 Ibid., pp cxv, cxvi. 23 Rory Masterson, 'The alien priory of Fore, Co. Westmeath, in the Middle Ages', *Archivium Hibernicum* 53 (1999), pp 73–9; Rory Masterson, *The town of Fore and its priory* (Dublin, 2014). 24 *Extents*, p. 273.

are provided in a seventeenth-century survey of the see of Kilmore. Here the priory is listed as having possessed Kilmore, Urni (Urney), Laragh (Larah), Lauy (Lavey), Annaghgelliffe (Annegelliff), Drong (Drung), Denn (Denn), Ballitemple (Ballintemple), Kill/Killdrumfert (Crosserlough), Mollagh (Mullagh) and Killsardinny (Killdrumsherdan). By 1540, the priory had ceased to have any involvement in the administration of these parishes.

In 1540, Matthew Kyng of Kilmaynane received a lease for twenty-one years of the priory rectories including those in 'the Breny'.[25] The rectories were subsequently leased to William Sentlowe in 1551 when King's lease would expire in 1561.[26] Later the rectories were leased to Christopher Nugent for twenty-one years in 1567 but eleven years later were again leased to William Dodd for five years. In 1589 Nugent signed a thirty-year lease.[27]

In 1622, most of the churches of the former priory were in good repair. Mayne, Lickbla, Faughalstown, Rathgarve, St Feighins, Fore, and Kilpatrick's were each described as having their church and chancel repaired with only Foyran and St Mary's, Fore, described as ruined.[28] Perhaps the fact that the Nugent family were local, with large property interests in the area, encouraged them to take a more active interest in the fabric of the parish churches.

PRIORY OF TRISTERNAGH

The extent for this priory was made at Tristernagh on 8 October 1540. In total nine parishes were listed as impropriate to the priory. Trysternagh (Tristernagh) and Kylbyxy (Kilbixy) were listed as separate rectories in the extent, but by 1641 were treated as one parish. Treating the two rectories as a single unit, only seven townlands were listed for tithes whereas in 1641 thirteen townlands were enumerated. This suggests that the unlisted townlands paid their tithes to the vicarage. Kylluknewan (Kilmacnevan) and Impir (Empir) were also listed as separate rectories, but in 1641 were united into the parish of Kilmacnevan. Again only four townlands were listed for tithes in the extent, whereas in 1641 a total of eight townlands appeared. The other parishes listed were Sonnagh (Templeoran) valued at 217s. 6d.; Rysbak (Rathaspick) valued at 45s.; Leyn (Leny) valued at 150s.; Leken (Lacken) valued at 188s.; Staffarnan (Tyfarnham) valued at 22s. 6d.; Imper valued at 45s.; and Kilmacnevan at 50s. In addition, the priory owned the parish of Killoe in Co. Longford valued at 66s. 8d. As in the earlier cases, only some of the townlands were listed for tithes and we can assume that the remaining lands were tithed for the vicar.[29]

25 *Fiants Ire. Henry VIII*, no. 128.   26 *Fiants Ire. Edward*, no. 787.   27 *Fiants Ire. Elizabeth*, nos 1089, 1578, 1589; Scott, 'The dissolution of the religious houses in the Tudor diocese of Meath', 266–7.   28 'Revennewes of the bishoppricke of Meath and Clonemackenosh', pp cxix, cxx.   29 *Extents*, pp 277–8.

Thomas de Craville received the lands of Laragh and Shanonagh from Hugh de Lacy.[30] Shandonagh was listed as a townland in Sonnagh parish, while Laregh was listed as part of Kilmacnevan so we can take it that the lands granted to Thomas de Craville were the parishes of Sonnagh (Templeoran) and Kilmacnevan. A settlement charter of 1211 between Llanthony Prima and Secunda states that Secunda was to receive 'the churches in the land of Thomas de Craville'. It seems then that the priory of Tristernagh had come to some arrangement with the Llanthony canons relating to these two parishes. This would explain the deduction of 73s. 4d. 'to the farmer of the cell of Duleke' in the extents of Tristernagh.[31]

On dissolution, the rectories of the priory were first leased to Robert Delman of Dublin for twenty-one years. This lease was renewed in 1551, again for twenty-one years.[32] In 1562 William Pierce received a lease for twenty-one years to run from when the lease to Robert Delman expired. Pierce's lease was renewed in 1570 and again in 1580 for twenty-six years. Finally, in 1592 William Pierce received a lease of the rectories for another twenty-one years.[33] In 1622 Ussher found that both Kilmacnean and Kilbixy churches were ruined but their chancels were in repair, while both Templeoran's and Tyfarnham's chancels and churches were in ruins. Sonnagh and Shandonagh chapels were in ruins; Emper had no church at all; and the church and chancel of Leny were uncovered. Only Lacken church was repaired, albeit the chancel was uncovered.[34]

CISTERCIAN ABBEY OF GRANARD

This extent was made at Tristernagh on 8 October 1540 'because we did not venture to approach near for fear of the Irish'. The jurors were Richard O'Farrell, the late abbot, and Thady McGylleno, the late prior. The details provided are vague in the extreme. The jurors stated that when dissolved the convent had certain lands, holdings and spiritual possessions in Clyncolman, Bravun Obroyn, Calry and Delvyn McCoghlan, but that they could not certify exactly about these. They added, however, that they received from the Malaghlyn 66s. 8d. for the time being. They also confirmed that they were the parsons inpropriate (rectors) of all the parish churches 'in the said Clyncolman etc.', but that they were now 'ignorant of the amount of profit they received thence and so were unable to give a valuation'.[35]

30 Orpen, *Song of Dermot*, p. 3166. **31** *Extents*, pp 277–9; A. Hogan, *The priory of Llanthony Prima and Secunda in Ireland, 1172–1541* (Dublin, 2008), p. 63. **32** *Fiants Ire. Henry VIII*, no. 79; *Fiants Ire. Edward*, no. 858. **33** *Fiants Ire. Elizabeth*, nos 467, 1679, 3658, 5769. **34** 'Revennewes of the bishoppricke of Meath and Clonemackenosh', p. cix, cxii, cxiv. **35** *Extents*, pp 281–2.

The tithes of the parish church of Demor (Diamor), barony of Fore, Co. Meath, were farmed to Margaret FitzGerald for 53s. 4d. and the alterages were valued at 26s. 8d. and one cow worth 6s. 8d. The tithes of the parish church of Balloghere were farmed to Patrick Browne of Athboy for 53s. 4d. and the alterages to Thomas Plonket for 26s. 8d.[36] Balloghere is identified as Ballyloughloe, Co. Westmeath, in the index. This cannot be correct as Ballyloughloe was always known as Calree and has been referred to earlier as Calry, one of the possessions about which they cannot certify exactly.[37] Balloghere must refer to Loughcrew, explaining why the tithes were farmed to Patrick Browne of Athboy and the alterages to Thomas Plonket. In 1438 a papal letter confirming the parishes of the monastery refers to Dromare (Diamor) and Lochecrewe (Loughcrew) in the diocese of Meath, as part of their possessions of the gift of Richard Tuite.[38]

William Ologhlan paid 66s. 8d. for the tithes of six-quarters in Ballemanagh (Ballnamanagh, parish of Taghsheennod) as well as for the tithes of certain lands of the Lord McGennor (a district in Columbcille parish), Molaghlyn Duff. Brady paid 53s. 4d. for the tithes of certain lands in Mount Carbre (the district to the north-west of Co. Longford). Donagh O'herra paid 20s. for the tithes of certain lands held by the heirs of Morff O'Farrell, while Oliver Nugent and Gerald FytzGerald farmed the tithes of the whole of Maghyrt Granard (probably Abbeylara and Granard civil parishes) for £8. The monastery received the tithes of its five granges in Granard: Tonaghmore (Tonymore north and south, parish of Abbeylara), the grange of Ryncoll (Rincoolagh, parish of Granard), and the three granges called Cowldony (Cooldoney), Cloncrall (Coolcraff) and Deragh (Derragh) all in the parish of Abbeylara. The granges were worth £6.[39] It seems from the above description that most, though not all, of the civil parishes of Granard, Abbeylara and Columbcille were paying tithes to the monastery of Granard (Abbeylara). The extent tells us that the monastery also received the tithes of the parishes of Dromlonan (Dromlonan, Co. Cavan) worth 53s. 4d.; Balmak (Ballymachugh, Co. Cavan) worth 53s. 4d.; and Ballemakynlene (Scrabby, Co. Cavan) 'in McKiernan's country' which was valued at 13s. 4d. The monastery also possessed the parish of Strad (Streeet) with twenty acres of arable land valued at £8.[40]

Returning again to the districts of Clyncolman etc., we know that Calry was the parish of Ballyloughloe. Clyncolman refers to Clancolman, a territory approximately equal to the parish of Kilcleagh and corresponding to the lands of the O'Melaghlin family or Clan Colman after they lost the kingdom of Mide to the Anglo-Normans. Bravyn Obroyn or Brawny O'Bryne was the

36 *Extents*, p. 281.   37 Michael Herity (ed.), *Ordance Survey letters, Longford and Westmeath* (Dublin, 2011), pp 58–9.   38 *Cal. papal letters*, 9, pp 29–30.   39 *Extents*, pp 281–2.   40 *Extents*, p. 282.

territory of the O'Breens.⁴¹ It was co-extensive with the parish of St Mary's, Athlone. The district of Delvyn McCoghlan comprised the parishes in Co. Offaly that were in the diocese of Clonmacnoise and belonged to the MacCoghlans. A papal letter of 1438 confirming the possessions of St Mary's, Granard, states that they held 'for more than a hundred years or from time immemorial possession of the parish church of St Mary, *alias* St Patrick, Granard, with all its chapels ... all the churches and chapels of the tenement of Cyrecarboy (c. barony of Granard, i.e., parishes of Abbeylara, Columbcille and Clonbroney) or their rectories ..., and all the churches, land and chapels of the whole tenement of Delwenethie [Delbna Ethrae, the barony of Garrycastle, Co. Offaly] in the dioceses of Ardagh and Clonmacnoise ... to wit the parish churches of Lochlocha [Ballyloughloe], Lyach [Lemanaghan], Faygri [Fuygre or Wheery], Galingy [Gallen], Theachsaran [Tessaren].' The conditions were that Richard de Tuite and his heirs, who had given the patronage of these churches to the monastery, should have the right to present the vicars to them. The vicars were to receive half the tithes of each parish 'and pay therefrom episcopal and other dues etc., the other half to belong to the abbot and convent.'⁴²

The letter goes on to confirm the gift of St Mary, Maybracray (Street), to the monastery by the late Herbert de la Mare with the same conditions as those relating to Richard Tuite's gift. The final section deals with the gift of rectories of Dromare (Dimor) and Lochecrewe (Loughcrew) by Richard Tuite to the monastery, again with the same conditions attached.⁴³ This letter provides us with an insight not only as to what rectories were given to Granard, and who gave them, but also how they were to be administered. Both de la Mare and Tuite retained the right of presenting the vicars to the abbot, i.e., the vicarage was in lay patronage. St Mary's Granard was staffed by monks from St Mary's, Dublin, and was considered a colonial establishment. Its Anglo-Norman affiliations were such that it was singled out along with Inch in Co. Down in the Grand Remonstrance of 1317 for its virulent anti-Irish actions.⁴⁴ By 1405, the O'Farrells were building their castle at Granard and the monastery was forced to abandon its policy of excluding Gaelic monks.⁴⁵ When dissolved the monastery was totally gaelicized.

The parish of Ballyloughloe referred to in the papal confirmation was much larger than its subsequent civil parish successor. In 1452, another papal letter sanctioned the partition (which the bishop of Clonmacnoise had already carried out) of the rectory of Lochluacha into three vicarages, the mother church of Lochluacha, a second of Athluain (St Mary's, Athlone) 'and a third to be called Kyllomyleon' (Kilmanaghan).⁴⁶ Finally, a fiant leasing the recto-

---

41 Paul Walsh, *The placenames of Westmeath* (1957), pp xxxiii, 107.   42 *Cal. papal letters*, 9, pp 29–30.   43 Ibid.   44 E. Curtis and R.B. McDowell (eds), *Irish historical documents, 1172–1922* (London, 1943), p. 43.   45 *Cal. papal letters*, 5, pp 331, 346.   46 *Cal. papal letters*, 10,

ries of Granard refers to Renaghe (Reynagh, Co. Offaly) and Kilcliegh (Kilcliegh, Co. Westmeath) in O'Molaghlin's country as part of their possessions.[47] Evidently some further partitions had taken place.

What this rather exhaustive examination of the extent of the rectories owned by the monastery of Granard shows is that it was originally endowed with two rectories in Co. Meath, three in Co. Cavan, five in Co. Longford, and all the rectories of the diocese of Clonmacnoise in Westmeath and Offaly. By 1540, the monastery had evidently lost control of its rectories in Clonmacnoise. The how and why of this can be glimpsed from the papal letters. In 1432 the bishop of Clonmacnoise, the prior of Gallen, and a named canon of Clonmacnoise were mandated to enquire into the complaints of Maurice Macaedgain, also a canon of Clonmacnoise, regarding the alleged misdemeanours of the vicar of Ballyloughloe. If the rumours were found to be true they were to remove the vicar and institute Maurice in his place 'notwithstanding that Maurice holds a canony and preband of Clonmacnoise'. As the judges nominated to investigate the facts were normally chosen by the petitioner himself, the outcome was usually a foregone conclusion.[48] In 1451, when the parish of Ballyloughloe was partitioned, it was to Eugenius Omuleoyn, a canon of Clonmacnoise, that the vicarage of Kilmanaghan was conferred.[49] The most sweeping affront to the monastery's control of its parishes in Clonmacnoise diocese came in 1459. John, bishop of Clonmacnoise, along with the dean, archdeacon, sacrist and chapter had instituted a college of four priests canons over and above the existing canons. This, they explained, was because the existing canons were so impoverished that they could not reside together but wandered 'hither and thither'. As a result the church (presumably the cathedral church of Clonmacnoise) suffered in regard to divine services. The members of the new college were to reside continually and in person, again presumably at Clonmacnoise. For their maintenance the bishop had united to the college the rectory of Ballyloughloe, which he informed the pope was 'of the patronage of laymen, [though it wasn't; only the vicarage was] with the consent of the said laymen, [impossible as the Tuites were long gone] who gave the patronage of the said church to the dean and college for the purpose of such union in perpetuity'. The dean and college having obtained possession of the rectory then petitioned the pope to confirm their actions 'because the rectory was ruled for several years by monks of the Cistercian monastery of Granard'. The letter concluded with the usual directive to the prior of Gallen to investigate the facts and, if satisfied, to approve the union.[50] Other letters followed, requesting that the vicarage of St Mary's, Athlone, and, later, the vicarage of Kilmanaghan be united and made into a preband of the diocese.[51] But sufficient has been

p. 541.   47 *Fiants Ire. Elizabeth*, no. 3300.   48 *Cal. papal letters*, 8, pp 422–3.   49 *Cal. papal letters*, 10, pp 541–2.   50 *Cal. papal letters*, 12, pp 51–2.   51 *Cal. papal letters*, 14,

shown to demonstrate why the monastery of Granard knew little of, and received less from, its parishes in the diocese of Clonmacnoise.

In 1556, Richard Nugent was granted the tithes and properties of the monastery in Longford only.[52] In 1560, the three rectories in Cavan and Street in Westmeath were leased to Sir Thomas Cusack for twenty-one years. By 1569 this had changed and Thomas Cusack along with Jenet Sarsfield (his wife) received a lease of all the possessions of the monastery including its lands in Offaly. This was again for twenty-one years. By 1578 Jenet Sarsfield and John Plunkett (her new husband) surrendered the lease of 1569 only to have it renewed in the same year to Thomas Plunkett of Loughcrew, again for twenty-one years. Finally in 1590 William Bathe of Drumcondra was leasing the rectories, again for twenty-one years.[53] Unfortunately, because most of the rectories of the monastery were in the diocese of Ardagh, we have no information as to the condition of their churches in 1622. What we do have are details from Clonmacnoise and here we find that all the parish churches – except St Mary's, Athlone and Clonmacnoise – were entirely in ruins. The parish church of Athlone is described as being new.[54]

PRIORY OF LOUGHSEWDY (BALLYMORE)

This extent was taken at Tristernagh on the 8 October 1540 but the only juror was Thomas Tuite, the late prior, 'for reasons stated under Granard'.[55] Despite this the former prior gave a good clear factual list of the rectories impropriate to the monastery. The first rectory listed is Moyaghyr, valued at 66s. 8d. The index of the *Extents* stated that this was the parish of Agharra, Co. Longford. Subsequent references in the *fiants* show that Moyaghyr is Moyagher parish, Co. Meath.[56] The other rectories were:

> Srure and Kyllocamock (Shrule and Kilcommock), valued at 40s.
> Clongysse (Clongesh), valued at 66s. 8d.
> Kylsy (Killashee), valued at 36s. 8d.
> Balmacormyk (Ballymacormick), valued at 40s.
> Moygow (Moydow), valued at 40s.
> Tyssynert (Taghsheenod), valued at 26s. 8d.
> Tessynny (Taghshinny), valued at 26s. 8d.
> Kylglasse (Kilglass), valued at 20s.
> St Michael Babut (Templemichael), valued at 26s. 8d.
> St Patrick Moymore (Moyvore or Templepatrick), Co. Westmeath), valued at 53s. 8d.[57]

pp 9, 67. **52** Morrin, *Cal. pat. rolls Ire.*, i, p. 372. **53** *Fiants Ire. Elizabeth*, nos 326, 1401, 3248, 3300, 5516. **54** 'Revennewes of the bishoppricke of Meath and Clonemackenosh', pp cxxiii, cxxiv. **55** *Extents*, p. 284. **56** *Fiants Ire. Elizabeth*, no. 2806.

A subsequent inquisition identified the rectory of Rathreagh (Co. Longford) as also being appropriated to the priory.[58]

All the parishes listed, except Templepatrick, are in Co. Longford. There is some uncertainty as to who was the founder of the priory. Ware says it was founded in the twelfth century for Premonstrations by the de Lacys but this is corrected by Gwynn and Hadcock, who make it an Augustinian foundation.[59] They also suggest a date of *c.*1250, but given that Walter de Lacy had a demesne manor at Loughsewdy in 1211 an earlier date is more probable.[60] With a total of twelve parishes, mostly in Longford, the foundation represents the furthest extent of the Anglo-Norman thrust into Longford. One peculiar feature of the parishes impropriate to the priory is the absence of Loughsewdy parish itself. Evidently the founder retained the demesne parish in his own patronage. There is no suggestion in the extent that the tithes were farmed out but it may be that Thomas Tuyt failed to specify how the tithes were collected. Archdall suggests that an inquisition of 1593 listing the priory's appropriated rectories makes reference to the curate's stipend but I can find no evidence of this. Probably the curate received the alterages. Archdall also claims that an inquisition of the same year found that Agharra rectory in Co. Longford was a concealed rectory belonging to the priory. Again a *fiant* of that year, presumably based on the inquisition he was quoting from, does refer to Agherie (Agharra) as a concealed rectory but of the abbey of Shrule not Loughsewdy.[61] A list of the possessions of Loughsewdy follows in the *fiant* and that may explain his error.

In 1542, the rectories of Loughsewdy, or at least those they were aware of, were leased to Walter Tirrell of Dublin, merchant, for twenty-one years.[62] In 1566, the rectories were granted to Thomas le Strange, again for twenty-one years.[63] Thomas evidently did not trust that he would be left in possession of them as ten years later he got a renewal of his lease for a further twenty-one years to run from the original expiration date, and a third lease for thirty-one years was acquired four years later which would only come into force in 1608.[64] Strange's fears were well justified as in 1593, despite all the leases to the contrary, the rectories were leased to Francis Shane for forty-five years from the end of the interest that was then in force. Francis Shane was equally insecure, as in 1597 he surrendered his lease only to have it re-granted.[65] The insecurity arose because Edmond Barrett was claiming that the rectories and

---

57 *Extents*, p. 285. 58 *Irish patent rolls of James I; facsimile of the Irish Record Commission calendar prepared prior to 1830*. Foreword by M.C. Griffith (Dublin, 1966), p. 2. 59 A. Gwynn and R.N. Hadcock, *Medieval religious houses: Ireland* (repr. Dublin, 1988), p. 160. 60 Oliver Davies and D.B. Quinn (eds), 'The Irish pipe roll of 14 John, 1211–1212', *UJA*, 3rd ser., 4 (1941), supplement, 20–1. 61 M. Archdall, *Monasticum Hibernicum* (Dublin, 1786), p. 707; *Fiants Ire. Elizabeth*, no. 5832. 62 *Fiants Ire. Henry VIII*, no. 326. 63 *Fiants Ire. Elizabeth*, no. 882. 64 *Fiants Ire. Elizabeth*, nos 2154, 2806. 65 *Fiants Ire. Elizabeth*, nos 5832, 6130, 6131.

lands of Loughsewdy were concealed lands and therefore should be granted to him.[66] In the meantime the rectory of Rathreagh was 'discovered' and in 1594 granted to John Lye for 60 years.[67] The only detail as to the condition of the churches in 1622 is for Templepatrick where Ussher found that the church and chancel were ruined.[68]

AUGUSTINIAN PRIORY OF MULLINGAR

Continuing their itinerary through Westmeath the commissioners made their next extent at Mullingar on 10 October 1540. Here they found that the priory was possessed of the rectory of Vastina (Castletownkindalen) with the chapel of Churchhouse (Churchtown; in the taxation of 1302–6 it is referred to as Taghboyn) annexed to it.[69] Both were valued at £8. The rectory and its chapel were held for life by the late prior John Petyt by the king's letter patent. This patent of 7 May 1540 granted the prior and two others the lands of Slewyn and le Grainge along with the church and rectory of Vastina for twenty-one years in full satisfaction of £14 of an annual pension payable to the three individuals. John Petyt was to continue to hold the rectory of Vastina until 1561 unless he was promoted to a benefice of greater value.[70] A portion of the alterages was allocated as part of the vicar's portion, indicating that a vicarage was provided for.[71]

The priory was founded in c.1227 by Ralph Petit, bishop of Meath (1227–30), and Archdall says that Walter, earl of Ulster (d.1271), was also a patron of this priory.[72] As always Archdall's information must be treated with caution and in this case he may be only partially correct. Walter, earl of Ulster, was succeeded by his son Richard (d.1326). In 1333, an inquisition touching his lands outside of Ulster and Connacht refer to the lands of Le Wastyn or Castletownkindalen, which he had acquired in 1304. The extent was taken at Killeen in Castletownkindalen and lists lands in both Castletownkindalen and Churchtown. It is more likely, then, that it was Richard, second earl of Ulster, who endowed the priory with the two rectories rather than his father Walter.[73]

John Petyt did not retain the rectories for the full term of the lease as in 1552 they were again leased to Thomas Casie of Athboy and his wife Ismay Nugent for twenty-one years.[74] In 1564 custody of the parishes was granted to Thomas Gorie until direction should come from the queen as to whom

---

66 Morrin, *Cal. pat. rolls Ire.*, 2, p. 442.   67 *Fiants Ire. Elizabeth*, no. 5878.   68 'Revennewes of the bishoppricke of Meath and Clonemackenosh', p. cxiii.   69 *Extents*, pp 286, 288; Walsh, *The placenames of Westmeath* p. 336.   70 *Extents*, pp 287, 289.   71 *Extents*, p. 289.   72 Gwynn and Hadcock, *Medieval religious houses: Ireland*, p. 189; Archdall, *Monasticum Hibernicum*, p. 723.   73 G.H. Orpen, 'Earl of Ulster. Pt. V. Inquisition touching Le Wastyn', *JRSAI*, 6th series, 10 (1920), 167–77.   74 *Fiants Ire. Edward*, no. 1079.

they were to be leased to. In 1566, the rectories of Vastina and Churchetowne were granted to Walter Hope 'for ever'. The grant specified that he was to maintain curates in the churches.[75] In 1622, the church and chancel of Castletownkindalen were repaired and those of Churchtown were in ruins.[76]

PRIORY OF ST PETER, NEWTOWN BY TRIM

This extent was made at Trim on 12 October 1540 and two rectories in Westmeath were appropriated to it. Enneskoe (Enniscoffey) was valued at £9 6s. 8d. The tithes were leased to Sir Gerralde FitzGerald for 40s., so clearly he got them at a knockdown price. The mansion and alterages were assigned for the curate's stipend. Kylfare (Killare) was held by John Browne and Edward Bek for £4. Baskyn (Baskin – High and Low) is now two townlands in the parish of Drumraney. It is listed in the taxation of 1302–6 as Baskeny and by Ussher as Baskney, a chapel of ease belonging to the vicarage of Drumraney. In 1540 it is described as totally waste but valued when occupied at 13s. 4d.[77]

In 1561, the rectory of Enescoe was leased to William FitzWilliam for twenty-one years and this lease was renewed in 1563.[78] In 1570 a new twenty-one-year lease to Denis Kevan of Dublin, merchant, was issued. In 1583 his widow received a lease for twenty-one years on the same property.[79] In 1559 Henry Draycott was granted the rectory of Killare by knight's service with a proviso that he was to repair and maintain the chancel and provide curates to minister to the people.[80] In 1622, however, the church and chancel of both Enniscoffey and Killare were ruined.[81] Evidently, the proviso had fallen on deaf ears.

PRIORY OF BALLYBOGGAN

The extent for the priory of Ballyboggan was made at Carbury on 24 November 1540 and among its rectories was Kylbryde (Kilbride). The rectory was held by Sir William Byrmyngham (at will) for 40s. The advowson of the parish also belonged to the priory.[82] In 1575 the rectory was leased to Peter Bowder for the standard twenty-one years but by 1587 it was leased to Henry Duke. Finally, in 1596, the rectory was leased to Edward Loftus of Rathfarnham and Capt. Gifford of Roscommon for twenty-one years. It is

---

75 Morrin, *Cal. pat. rolls Ire.*, 1, p. 491; *Fiants Ire. Elizabeth*, no. 932.   76 'Revennewes of the bishoppricke of Meath and Clonemackenosh', p. cxiii.   77 *Extents*, p. 295.   78 *Fiants Ire. Elizabeth*, nos 399, 539.   79 *Fiants Ire. Elizabeth*, nos 1717, 4228.   80 Morrin, *Cal. pat. rolls Ire.*, 1, pp 427–8.   81 'Revennewes of the bishoppricke of Meath and Clonemackenosh', p. cviii.   82 *Extents*, pp 311–12.

noteworthy that none of their predecessors had retained their leases for the full term.[83] In 1622 the church and chancel were ruined.[84]

THE PRIORIES OF LLATHONY PRIMA AND SECUNDA

In 1482 Llanthony Secunda and Prima were reunited, thus their possessions – Mullingar, Rathconnell, Killulagh, Killua, Castletown-Delvin and Drumraney – are listed together here.[85]

In a charter dated 1174–84, Eugene, bishop of Clonard, confirmed the grant of Adam de Feypo of the parish of Rathconnel to the canons. Later, in c.1202–10, Walter de Lacy confirmed the gift of William Petit of the church of Rathconnel to the canons. This is confusing as the *Song* clearly states that de Lacy granted these lands to William Petit. Whatever the reason, the crown survey (1540–41) recorded that this rectory was worth £24 9s. 6d. and that the vicar held a manse of the rectory for which he paid 2s.[86] Mullingar had likewise been given to the canons by William Petit. The crown survey recorded the parish as being worth £19 3s. 4d. and that the vicar received certain tithes and the alterages.[87] Killulagh had been granted to the canons by the Nugent family. In 1541 it was valued at £6 13s. 4d.[88] Killua was valued at £10 13s. 4d.[89] and Castletown-Delvin was valued at £32 13s. 4d. in the crown survey. The latter parish was granted by Gilbert de Nugent to the canons c.1180.[90] Drumraney was the gift of Henry Dillon, c.1202–3.[91] However, like Richard Tuite in relation to Granard, Henry Dillon retained the right of presentation to the vicarage. In the crown survey no returns are listed for the rectory.

In 1569 the rectories of Mullingar, Killolaugh, Killovan (Killua), Rathconnell and Castletown-Delvin were leased to Francis Agarde for twenty-one years. By 1575 the rectory of Mullingar on its own was leased to Edward Brabazon for thirty years, but by 1579 all five were leased again to Edward Moore for forty-one years on the expiration of the lease of 1569. In 1578 the rectory of Dromrath (Drumraney) was leased to Edward Bewehier for ever.[92] By 1622 the church in Mullingar was described as reasonable but the chancel was ruined. At Rathconnell and Drumraney the church and chancel were repaired and Castletown-Delvin and Killulagh are both described as reasonably repaired. At Killagh (Killua) the church and chancel were ruined.[93]

---

83 *Fiants Ire. Elizabeth*, nos 2671, 5157, 6031.   84 'Revennewes of the bishoppricke of Meath and Clonemackenosh', p. civ.   85 Hogan, *Priory of Llanthony*, p. 179.   86 Hogan, *Priory of Llanthony*, pp 233, 252, 195; G. Mac Niochaill, *Crown surveys of lands, 1540–41* (Dublin, 1992), pp 42–3.   87 Hogan, *Priory of Llanthony*, pp 252, 194.   88 Mac Niochaill, *Crown surveys of lands*, p. 47.   89 Ibid., p. 43.   90 Hogan, *Priory of Llanthony*, pp 235–6; Mac Niochaill, *Crown surveys of lands*, p. 43.   91 Hogan, *Priory of Llanthony*, p. 250.   92 *Fiants Ire. Elizabeth*, nos 1460, 2698, 3564, 3322.   93 'Revennewes of the

ABBEY SHRULE (CISTERCIAN)

Called the abbey of Sroue in the Annale in the extents, no details were taken and evidently the only thing the commissioners were relying on was hearsay as to the existence of a Cistercian monastery at Shrule. No receipts were recorded but the rents were said to be worth 13s. 4d.[94] Founded by the O'Farrells with monks from Mellifont in 1200, it was not finally suppressed until 1592.[95] In an inquisition in 1567 the abbey was found to have owned the rectory of Shrowlle (Abbeyshrule) alias Urre, with three coples of corn and the alterages for the vicar excepted. A later grant stated that the rectory and tithes of Agherie were parcel of the estate of Shroill alias Shroyr. The lease of 1567 was to Thomas Bryan for twenty-one years and seems to have run full term though Bryan may have sold his interests in the property as a new lease of 1588 stated it was in the possession of William Collier. This new lease was to Robert Nangle for forty years. In 1593 the rectory of Agherie was declared concealed property of the crown and leased to John Lye for sixty years. But within four years it was leased again to Edward FitzGerald for thirty-one years.[96]

PRIORY OF MONASTERICK (ABBEYDERG)

Few details are provided in the extents except the name itself, the fact that the farm was worth 20s., and that John O'Farrell was the last abbot. It was also referred to as the monastery of Rabio.[97] In 1551–2, the lands and tithes of the monastery were leased to Shane O'Farrell (presumably the former abbot) for twenty-one years.[98] Abbeyderg itself is in Taghsheenod parish and a subsequent fiant of 1567 grants 'the rectory of Renike, two coples of corn and the alterages due to the vicar excepted' to Thomas Byram.[99] It seems from this that the monastery enjoyed the tithes of its lands in Taghsheenod that constituted a separate parish. A vicar must also have been in place as provision for his income is noted. Renike did not survive as a separate parish and was incorporated into Taghsheenod.

AUGHRIM, CO. GALWAY

The priory of St Catherine is said to have been founded by Theobald Walter (died 1206).[1] A seventeenth-century patent says that the rectory of

bishoppricke of Meath and Clonemackenosh', pp civ, cvi, cxi.   **94** *Extents*, p. 319.   **95** Gwynn and Hadcock, *Medieval religious houses: Ireland*, p. 125.   **96** *Fiants Ire. Elizabeth*, nos 1033, 5160, 5811, 6132; *Irish patent rolls of James I*, p. 54.   **97** *Extents*, p. 284; *Irish patent rolls of James I*, p. 420.   **98** *Fiants Ire. Edward*, no. 932.   **99** *Fiants Ire. Elizabeth*, no. 1033.   **1** Gwynn and Hadcock, *Medieval religious houses: Ireland*, p. 158.

Clonmacnoise in O'Melaghlin's country was parcel of the estate of the monastery of Aghrim. It also owned some lands in this area. In 1570, a grant of the churches of the monastery to the earl of Clanrickard included the vicarage of Clonmacnoise.[2] In 1622, its church and chancel were repaired.[3]

SAINTS ISLAND (ALL SAINTS IN LOUGH REE)

The priory of All Saints was founded for the Augustinian canons by a descendant of Sir Henry Dillon of Drumraney. In 1410, the valuation of the priory was given as up to 100 marks but by 1425 this had dropped to fifty marks.[4] A grant of the monastic property in the seventeenth century shows that it had formerly owned both the rectories and the vicarages of the parishes of Rathline (Rathcline) and Cashel.[5] This suggests that the canons ministered to these parishes themselves rather than employing vicars. In 1567, Christopher Nugent received both rectories for twenty-one years.[6]

PRIORY OF CRUTCHED FRIARS OF ST JOHN BAPTIST, KILKENNY WEST

The existence of this priory was noted by the commissioners and its farm was valued at £17 6s. but no further details are provided.[7] It was said to have been founded by the Tyrrells, but Lodge suggests that its benefactor was one of the Dillons.[8] Whoever the founder, a fiant of Elizabeth's time lists nine townlands whose tithes were attached to the priory. All appear to be in the parish of Kilkenny West and so we can take it that the parish was their only spiritual possession. The Elizabethan lease of the parish was for twenty-one years.[9]

CISTERCIAN ABBEY OF KILBEGGAN

Founded c.1150 by monks from Mellifont, this monastery, like Kilkenny, received only a two-line mention in the extents, telling us that the rents were valued at £6 13s. 4d.[10] However, a fiant of 1566 lists as part of its possessions the rectory of Kilbeggan 'and two coples of corn and the alterages reserved for the curate.' This shows that an established curate was in receipt of a fixed

---

2 *Irish patent rolls of James I*, pp 48, 180; *Fiants Ire. Elizabeth*, no. 1581.   **3** 'Revennewes of the bishoppricke of Meath and Clonemackenosh', p. cxxiii.   **4** Gwynn and Hadcock, *Medieval religious houses: Ireland*, p. 194.   **5** *Irish patent rolls of James I*, p. 74.   **6** *Fiants Ire. Elizabeth*, no. 1170.   **7** *Extents*, p. 320.   **8** Gwynn and Hadcock, *Medieval religious houses: Ireland*, p. 213.   **9** *Fiants Ire. Elizabeth*, no. 1355.   **10** Masterson, 'Power, politics and parish formation', 24–30; *Extents*, p. 320.

amount of the tithes and the alterages for his income and that the monks did not minister in the parish themselves.[11] In 1551, Francis Digby was granted the tithes of the monastery of Kilbeggan for twenty-one years.[12] The subsequent lease was to Ross MacGeoghagan and was also for twenty-one years. This was renewed in 1578 again for twenty-one years.[13] In 1622, Ussher recorded no church or chancel at Kilbeggan.[14]

PRIORY OF DURROW

The monastery of Durrow may have been founded by Murchad O'Malaghlin at the insistance of St Malachy.[15] In 1540–41 the abbey of Deevo, Co. Westmeath, is mentioned as worth 66s. 8d. In 1546, Con O'Molloy, late prior of Durrow, received a lease of the rectories of Kilbride and Durrow for twenty-one years.[16] A grant of the possessions of the monastery in 1562 informs us that it owned the rectories of Darrn (Durrow) and Kilbride.[17] Unlike the Cistercian abbey of Kilbeggan there are no references to tithes or alterages reserved for curates and so we can assume that the canons ministered to the parishes themselves. A papal letter of 1497 describes the abbey as having 'cure of souls'.[18] Kilbride (Ballycowan) is first mentioned in 1493 when a canon of Durrow is listed for the rectory of Mayleimach. Mayleimach is a variation of Moylena, which Dopping informs us was another name for Kilbride (Ballycowan).[19] In 1561, a direction was issued to grant a lease to Nicholas Harbert of Durrow of its possessions and in 1574 the rectories of Durrow and Kilbride were granted to Nicholas Harbert for ever.[20] In 1622, Ussher records that both churches and chancels were ruined.[21]

PARISHES IN LAY PATRONAGE

While it is evident that the vast majority of the parishes of the western liberty of Meath were appropriated to various monastic institutions, not all were. Some Anglo-Norman lords retained for themselves the right to nominate the rector. We have already seen how this operated at Ardnurcher up to 1420 with a rector resident at Ardnurcher and chaplains in the chapel of ease. Other examples follow here.

11 *Fiants Ire. Elizabeth*, no. 965.   12 *Fiants Ire. Edward*, no. 817.   13 *Fiants Ire. Elizabeth*, no. 3234.   14 'Revennewes of the bishoppricke of Meath and Clonemackenosh', p. cxvi.   15 Gwynn and Hadcock, *Medieval religious houses: Ireland*, p. 174.   16 *Fiants Ire. Henry VIII*, no. 518.   17 *Extents*, p. 322; *Fiants Ire. Elizabeth*, no. 448.   18 *Cal. papal letters*, 16, no. 699.   19 M.A. Costello (ed.), *De annatis Hiberniae*, p. 79; C.C. Ellison, 'Bishop Dopping's visitation book', *Ríocht na Mídhe*, 6 (1975), 4, 7.   20 *Cal. pat. rolls Ire.*, I, p. 471; *Fiants Ire. Elizabeth*, nos 448, 2522.   21 'Revennewes of the bishoppricke of Meath and Clonemackenosh', p. cxvi,

As discussed above, the absence of any reference to Ballymore Loughsewdy in the list of parishes appropriated to the monastery there is unusual. Whatever the reason, the de Lacys or the de Verdons decided to retain the parish in lay patronage. In 1414, the parish was described as the rectory of St Mary's, Loughsewdy, in the diocese of Meath, while in 1432 Andrew Okassayth was the rector of the parish.[22] In all there are a total of nine papal letters relating to the rectory between 1390 and 1490.[23] All mandated or appointed as adjudicators Gaelic clergymen from Ardagh, Kilmore or the Gaelic monastery of Kilbeggan. A letter of 1464 requested the dean and two canons of Kilmore to investigate the allegations made by Roger O'Farrell against the rector of Loughsewdy and, if they were found to be true, to remove him and appoint Roger instead. Roger claimed he could not have his case heard in Meath (diocese) for fear of Rory's (the rector's) power.[24] Rory was evidently the choice of the English/Anglo-Irish bishop of Meath who was about to be removed and replaced with a nominee of the Gaelic church via papal provision. This highlights one of the great problems for rectories or vicarages in lay patronage. The patrons no longer existed. The de Verdons had long since sold out their interest in Loughsewdy. Small wonder, therefore, that in 1534 one of those attainted for supporting the Kildare rebellion was Sir Richard Walsh, parson (rector) of Loghsendie.[25] In 1549 the lands of Richard, late parson of Loughsewdy, were granted to Richard Dillon. A final point to note is that Loughsewdy parish was much larger than its civil parish successor. In 1622, Bonowne, Monghwall (Noughwall) and Cloncall alias Forgney were listed as chapels of ease of Loughsewdy, explaining the absence of any record of them in previous records.[26] Loughsewdy parish was created into the cathedral church of the diocese in 1538 and so, not surprisingly, both its church and chancel were repaired in 1622.[27]

The rectory of Piercetown is mentioned twice in the papal letters. As in the case of Loughsewdy, both letters were addressed to officials of Ardagh diocese or the abbot of Abbeyshrule, i.e., Gaelic clerics. The rectory was referred to as the parish church of Ardgayce alias Ballepvaris and of lay patronage.[28] In 1641, the lands of the parish were in the possession of the Dalton, FitzGerald and Fox families, but evidently the Gaelic church, as with Loughsewdy, were installing their own personnel in the rectory.[29] In 1562, Edward Mastalle was presented to the rectory vacant by the death of Gerald Dalton. The rectory is described as being in the donation of the crown.[30] In 1622, both church and chancel were ruined.[31]

22 *Cal. papal letters*, 6, p. 481; 8, p. 420.   23 *Cal. papal letters*, 5, pp 108, 452; 6, p. 481; 8, p. 420; 9, pp 20, 96, 132; 12, p. 216; 13, p. 623.   24 *Cal. papal letters*, 12, pp 216–17.   25 *L&P Henry VIII*, 7, no. 1384.   26 'Revennewes of the bishoppricke of Meath and Clonemackenosh', p. cxiv.   27 *Cal. pat. rolls Ire.*, 1, p. 113; 'Revennewes of the bishoppricke of Meath and Clonemackenosh', p. cx.   28 *Cal. papal letters*, 5, p. 462; 14, p. 93.   29 Lyons, *The book of survey and distribution*, pp 61–2.   30 *Cal. pat. rolls Ire.*, 1, p. 475.   31 'Revennewes of the bishoppricke of Meath and Clonemackenosh', p. cxi.

The rectory of Multyfarnham was referred to as being of lay patronage, but a problem arose as to who was the patron.[32] The Delemares, lords of Multyfarnham, had by ancient right presented the rector. In 1500, however, they complained that during bishop Sherwood's time (1475–8) Richard Tuite, with the support of other nobles, had occupied and held the rectory until promoted to the priory of Tristernagh. After that the right of presenting was exercised by Andrew Nugent, the bishop of Meath having agreed to this in return for the gift of twelve cows out of the rectory. Now the situation changed, with the bishop of Meath appointing Andrew Dowgane as rector (presumably on the nomination of the Delemares) and Andrew Nugent appealing to Armagh.[33] Unfortunately, no final verdict is provided. It is likely, however, given the growing power of the Nugents in the area, that their seizure of the right to present to the rectory was successful. It is also noteworthy that, in areas retained by the Anglo-Normans, the authority of the bishop of Meath was still a reality. In areas further west, where Anglo-Norman lords no longer held authority, it was the bishops and officials of Ardagh and Kilmore, via papal provision, who selected the rectors. In 1622 both the church and chancel were described as reasonably repaired.[34]

In 1414, a papal letter appointed John Omiegaid to the parish church of Newtown the Feartulach (Newtown Fartullagh).[35] In 1542, Richard Whit, rector of Newtown-Fertullaght was witness to a deed of Christ Church.[36] Who the original lay patrons were is impossible to say. In 1232, Hugh Tyrell was granted a yearly fair at his manor of Newtown in Fartullagh, so it is possible he established the parish and retained the patronage.[37] By the sixteenth century all the parish lands were in the possession of the Gaelic McGeoghegans. In 1622, both the church and chancel were ruined.[38]

In 1414, John Omigaid was granted the rectory of Cluainfad in the diocese of Meath. Unfortunately, no further information can be found relating to this rectory.[39] In 1622, the church and chancel were described as ruined.[40]

Only a few references to the rectory of Lynn appear in the papal letters. In 1400 Ode Ocallan was assigned the church of Lynn when Thomas Carpentere resigned it because he did not understand the tongue of the parishioners. Ode states that he was presented by the lay patron but no details of who the patron was are provided.[41] By 1443 the bishop and dean of Clonmacnoise and a canon of Kildare were mandated to enquire about Philip Vallis, rector of Laynd in Meath, to remove him if they found the complaints made against him valid and

---

32 *Cal. papal letters*, 6, p. 262.   33 M.A. Sughi, *Registrum Octaviani* (Dublin, 1999), nos 63, 286   34 'Revennewes of the bishoppricke of Meath and Clonemackenosh', p. cv.   35 *Cal. papal letters*, 6, p. 481.   36 M.J. Mc Enery and R. Refaussé (eds), *Calendar to the Christ Church deeds, 1174–1684* (Dublin, 2004), no. 1184.   37 Sweetman, *Cal. documents Ire.*, 1, no. 1951.   38 'Revennewes of the bishoppricke of Meath and Clonemackenosh', p. cxv.   39 *Cal. papal letters*, 6, p. 478.   40 'Revennewes of the bishoppricke of Meath and Clonemackenosh'.   41 *Cal. papal letters*, 5, p. 284.

to replace him with the informant Odo Odunagayn. Again, there is a reference to Philip's power in the diocese of Meath preventing Odo getting justice there.[42] This shows that the rectory was now part of the power struggle between the Anglo-Norman and Gaelic churches.

In 1562, Edward Darcy was presented to the rectory of Lyn which, we are told, was in the donation of the crown.[43] The appointment of a resident rector may explain why in 1622 the chancel was reasonably repaired even though the church was said to be ruined.[44]

The rectory of Rathwire was co-terminous with the barony of Farbill granted to Robert de Lacy. This branch of the de Lacys sided with Edward Bruce and as a result they were declared felons and their lands confiscated. Evidently, Robert de Lacy, when he established his parish of Rathwire, had retained the patronage himself as both Rathwire and its patronage reverted to the Mortimers (heirs of Walter de Lacy through his grand-daughter). When Edward IV became king of England the Mortimer inheritance, including the patronage of Rathwire, reverted to the king. In 1484, a papal letter assigning the parish church of St Meygrieta the Virgin, Rhaghwyre (Rathwire) alias Kyllhukyn (Killucan), to Geoffrey Odaly says that the parish was of the patronage of the king of England. The letter informs us that Geoffrey alleged that he was presented by the late King Edward though John Wale alias Pupbulle had detained it for a long time. The abbots of St Peter, Clonard and Kilbeggan were to investigate the matter and to remove John Wale if necessary.[45] Even before the religious changes of the latter half of the 1530s the king was presenting the rector of Rathwire, and in 1533–4 William Colkes was so presented.[46] Unfortunately, no further references to the appointment of rectors can be found but in 1622 the church of Rathwire was described as reasonably repaired and the chancel as somewhat ruinous.[47]

In 1407, Nicholas Magnagh, parson (rector) of Dysart, and Richard King, vicar of Faghly, exchanged churches.[48] This shows that the rectory of Dysart was in lay patronage, but no information as to who the patron was is provided. In 1560–1 John Duffe was presented to the rectory of Dysart.[49] In 1622, the church and chancel were uncovered.[50]

Little information can be found on seven further parishes. There is nothing to throw light on the status of Carrick, Clonarney, Moylisker, Taghmon and Pass of Kilbride. In 1622 the church and chancel of Clonarney were reasonably repaired but both were ruined in the four others.[51] Meanwhile,

---

42 *Cal. papal letters*, 9, p. 373. 43 Morrin, *Cal. pat. rolls Ire.*, 1, p. 477. 44 'Revennewes of the bishoppricke of Meath and Clonemackenosh', p. ciii. 45 *Cal. papal letters*, 14, pp 68–9. 46 Morrin, *Cal. pat. rolls Ire.*, 1, p. 5. 47 *The whole works*, i, appendix v. 48 Peter Crooks (ed.), *A calendar of Irish chancery letters, c.1244–1509*, Patent Roll 8, Henry IV, § 50. 49 Morrin, *Cal. pat. rolls Ire.*, 1, p. 440. 50 'Revennewes of the bishoppricke of Meath and Clonemackenosh', p. cxi. 51 Ibid., pp cii, ciii, cv, cviii.

Ardagh probably belonged to the bishops of Ardagh while Mohill was very likely part of one of those Gaelic rural rectories identified by Nicholls as existing in the diocese of Ardagh.[52]

CONCLUSION

This examination of the status of the parishes of the western liberty of Meath shows the diversity of organization that existed. Most parishes were appropriated to the various monastic institutions but even within that system there were great variations. Many patrons such as Tuite and Dillon had retained the patronage of certain vicarages. Some monasteries, especially the Augustinians, performed the cure within some of their parishes themselves while most employed vicars or chaplains.

Lay patronage, whether of rectories or vicarages, proved to be extremely problematic. With the Gaelic revival lay patrons were no longer able, or in some cases did not exist, to perform the role they had designated for themselves and their heirs. Papal provision provided a means by which the new Gaelic rulers and the Gaelic church could gain control of these parishes, bypassing the technical difficulties of a non-existent lay patron.

At the time of the dissolution of the monasteries the vast majority of the parishes of the western liberty of Meath – later the counties of Westmeath, Longford and part of Offaly – were impropriated to the various monastic institutions. This was to have major implications for the success or otherwise of the new religious policy. The policy of treating the impropriated rectories as monastic property meant that most were vested in a succession of lay proprietors (many of them absentees) to whom the responsibility of maintaining the chancel and, in some cases, presenting the vicar devolved. Many evidently had little interest in this aspect of their grants and this was compounded by the leasing policy of the government. As can be seen above, most of the leases were for twenty-one years, followed by a grant to some other grantee. Such a policy was hardly designed to encourage long-term interest in, and expenditure on, the maintenance of either chancels or churches. The results of this policy can be seen in the condition of the churches and chapels of the dioceses of the region. By 1622, the clergy of the Church of Ireland faced the problem that before they could begin to persuade people to come to their churches they would have to start rebuilding them. This aspect of the dissolution of the monasteries was to have more lasting effects than the immediate closure of the cloisters or the redistribution of their lands.

---

52 K.W. Nicholls, 'Rectory, vicarage and parish in the western Irish dioceses', *JRSAI*, 101 (1971), 53–84.

Nuns and their networks in early modern Galway

BERNADETTE CUNNINGHAM

In the mid-seventeenth century, a large-scale pictorial map of Galway was produced, celebrating the 'city of the tribes'. The map's legend explained its contents, which included fourteen forts, fourteen towers, fourteen gates, fourteen principal streets, fourteen lanes, fourteen castles of the gentry, and fourteen religious houses (in addition to the collegiate church of Saint Nicholas). In the cartographer's scheme, there were seven convents for women, identified as the Poor Clares, the Rich Clares, the Sisters of the Third Order of Saint Francis, the Sisters of the Order of Saint Dominic, the Sisters of the Order of Saint Augustine, the Carmelite Sisters and, finally, 'various residences of Nuns (or pious ladies)'.[1] Of these, just two are reasonably well documented, and it is with those that the present essay is concerned.

The map dates from the 1660s but depicts the city c.1651, and John McErlean has argued that 'the people responsible for its production are quite evidently the older and the Roman Catholic inhabitants: fourteen ancient and illustrious Anglo-Irish families are their boast, and the fourteen convents in the town are mentioned with pride.'[2] While conceding that the map is schematic and may have had a propagandist purpose, the depiction of so many ecclesiastical buildings for women religious, and even a lane described as 'Poor Clare's Lane',[3] is evidence of the significance of these institutions in the minds of Galway's Catholic elite in the mid-seventeenth-century.

In broad terms, the foundation of several new convents of nuns in the town of Galway in the early 1640s reflected the growing confidence of the Roman Catholic church under the Confederate administration. At least three communities of women – the Poor Clares, Dominicans and Augustinians – were newly established in the city in that decade alone, each aligned with a corresponding religious house for men, from where their confessors were generally drawn. The Franciscan, Dominican and Augustinian orders of men had all experienced a significant revival of fortune by the 1630s, after an extended period of enforced exile.[4] Many of those who had been trained in the conti-

---

[1] J. McErlean, 'Notes on the pictorial map of Galway: the index to the map', *Journal of the Galway Archaeological and Historical Society [JGAHS]*, 4 (1905–6), 133–60, at 140–1. The map is now online: http://archives.library.nuigalway.ie/citymap (accessed 9 Dec. 2013). [2] McErlean, 'Notes on the pictorial map of Galway', 42–3. [3] 'Vicus Claristarum Pauperum', numbered 67 on the map; a laneway off New Tower Street, close to the town wall. [4] Raymond Gillespie, 'The Irish Franciscans, 1600–1700' in Edel Bhreathnach, Joseph MacMahon & John McCafferty (eds), *The Irish Franciscans, 1534–1990* (Dublin,

nental Irish colleges were now in a position to return to Ireland. The scant surviving evidence reveals that there were fewer convents of nuns than there were religious houses for men in early modern Ireland, but Galway proved one of the more vibrant, if sometimes troubled, locations for communities of women religious in the seventeenth and eighteenth centuries.

Galway was a compact walled town, of Anglo-Norman origin. Its population has been estimated as about 6,000 in the seventeenth century, and before the plague of the early 1650s it was a wealthy place, built by merchants who profited from trade with Spain and France.[5] The Galway laity sustained a recusant clergy in the decades following the dissolution of the monasteries in the 1530s.[6] Support for a Reformation church among Galway's elite in the sixteenth century proved short-lived. A tradition of lay support for Catholic clergy was even more in evidence in the early seventeenth century as clergy educated on the Continent, both secular and regular, returned to serve in a resurgent Irish church.

In the town and county of Galway, circumstances conducive to the development of Counter-Reformation Catholicism were supported by Richard Burke, fourth earl of Clanricard, who became president of Connacht in 1604. In November 1621, the Irish lord deputy, Sir Oliver St John, Viscount Grandison, who had known the earl from his days at the royal court,[7] complained to Clanricard about the proliferation of friars and friaries in his lordship.

> Noble Lord, I thought it needful to let your Lordship know the ill estate at this time of the government of the county and town of Galway, where priests and friars live with more boldness than in any part of the kingdom. Ross, an abbey of your L[ordship] is full of friars, and many of the town and that country are lately professed ... There are also friars in the Abbey of Kinelyhan, as also in Kilconnell and St Dominick's Abbey near Galway. I sent for John Donelan to undertake the ridding of the abbeys, but he would not meddle with it.[8]

2009), pp 45–57; Brian Mac Cuarta, *Catholic revival in the north of Ireland* (Dublin, 2007), pp 127–9; T.S. Flynn, *The Irish Dominicans, 1536–1641* (Dublin, 1993), pp 263–304; Paul Walsh, 'The foundation of the Augustinian friary at Galway: review of the sources', *JGAHS*, 40 (1985–6), 72–80; Hugh Fenning, 'The library of the Augustinians of Galway in 1731', *Collectanea Hibernica*, 31–2 (1990), 162–5. 5 M.D. O'Sullivan, *Old Galway: the history of a Norman colony in Ireland* (Cambridge, 1942), pp 38–9, 455. 6 Thomas Connors, 'Religion and the laity in early modern Galway' in Gerard Moran (ed.), *Galway history and society: interdisciplinary essays on the history of an Irish county* (Dublin, 1996), pp 131–48. 7 Sir Oliver St John had accompanied Richard Burke at the royal court in 1602. N.E. McClure (ed.), *The letters of John Chamberlain* (2 vols, Philadelphia, 1939), i, p. 146. 8 Bernadette Cunningham (ed.), 'Clanricard letters: letters and papers, 1605–1673, preserved in the National Library of Ireland, manuscript 3111', *JGAHS*, 48 (1996), 172.

The lord deputy further complained that the earl's brother, Sir William Burke, 'ran into a gross error to have 2 of his letters found in abetment and relieving of a popish vicar general'. William was being detained pending payment of a fine for the offence.[9] Clanricard, by this time, was normally resident in England, where his recusancy was tolerated by the authorities, and he had little sympathy with Sir Oliver St John's complaints.[10] Clanricard kept in touch with his Galway estates through his agent, Sir Henry Lynch of Galway, and his solicitor, John Donelan.[11] Sir Henry Lynch, like successive earls of Clanricard, profited from the acquisition of former monastic land[12] but, as is clear from the observations of Sir Oliver St John, the earl and the Galway townsmen continued to support the presence of religious orders in the locality. Thus, for example, in 1622 the town of Galway had the largest Dominican religious house for men in the country. By 1630 the number of friars had expanded from ten to thirteen and their confidence in the future was such that they contemplated establishing a seminary for diocesan and regular clergy.[13]

This atmosphere of increasingly confident Counter-Reformation Catholicism, with strong support from the local landed elite, formed the backdrop to the coming of new communities of nuns to Galway in the early 1640s. The history of these two orders, the Poor Clares and the Dominican nuns, in Ireland in the ensuing hundred years followed a remarkably similar pattern, and they functioned in very similar social and economic contexts. These convents, despite some discontinuities, have survived into modern times. An Augustinian convent of nuns was also established in Galway in the mid-seventeenth century, and may have continued until the mid-nineteenth century, but documentary evidence is slight.[14] A monastery of Carmelite nuns was also indicated on the 1651 map of Galway, but appears to have been short-lived. The Carmelites re-established themselves in Loughrea in the 1680s, a small town traditionally controlled by the Burkes, earls of Clanricard, which may have also supported a Poor Clare convent for a short time in the late 1640s.[15]

The annals of the Poor Clares, which survive in several variant manuscript versions derived from the chronicle of Mother Bonaventure Browne first

---

9 Cunningham (ed.), 'Clanricard letters', 173. **10** Timothy Wilks, 'Richard, fourth earl of Clanricard, and the English court' in Jane Fenlon (ed.), *Clanricard's Castle: Portumna House, Co. Galway* (Dublin, 2012). **11** Bernadette Cunningham, *Clanricard and Thomond, 1540–1640: provincial politics and society transformed* (Dublin, 2012). **12** *CSPI, 1625–32*, p. 548. **13** Hugh Fenning, 'The Dominicans of Galway, 1488–1988' in Eustás Ó Héideáin (ed.), *The Dominicans in Galway, 1241–1991* (Galway, 1991), pp 25–6. **14** Mrs Thomas [Helena] Concannon, *Irish nuns in penal days* (London, 1931), pp 91–4. **15** Concannon, *Irish nuns in penal days*, pp 86–7; Galway, Poor Clare convent, MS A6 [1647], agreement regarding the establishment of a convent at Loughrea; Celsus O'Brien (ed.), *Recollections of an Irish Poor Clare in the seventeenth century: Mother Mary Bonaventure Browne, third abbess of Galway, 1647–1650* (Galway, 1993), p. 11.

written in the 1670s, record the town's encouragement of the nuns' decision to relocate there from their previous residence at Bethlehem on the east shore of Lough Ree in Co. Westmeath:

> At length the people of Galway requested of the Provincial to send to the said town such of the nuns as were natives of it, with as many of the rest as he thought proper; both for the security of their persons & also to found there a Convent of the same first Rule of Saint Clare, with the Constitutions such as was observed at Bethlem.[16]

The Bethlehem convent, some 15 kilometres north of Athlone, was in an isolated location, on land owned by the Dillon family of Ballynacliffey. It had been newly built at the beginning of the 1630s to accommodate the community of Irish nuns who came together at a convent at Gravelines, in the Spanish Netherlands.[17] Returning to Ireland, they established themselves in Dublin in 1629, but moved to Westmeath as soon as the new convent was built there.[18] Two of the founding nuns were Dillon sisters from Ballinacliffey, daughters of Sir Theobald Dillon and Eleanor Tuite, and the support of that family had been key to their move to Co. Westmeath. The community expanded as new members joined, some of whom were from Galway families, including Catherine of St Francis Browne, the signed record of whose profession at the Bethlehem convent still survives.[19]

After the outbreak of war in 1641, the nuns experienced major disruption at Bethlehem and were forced to abandon the convent there. As Mother Cecily Dillon explained, 'we scarce know upon whom to turne our face for ye price of a habit in our need'.[20] They were afraid to return to Bethlehem because of its rural isolation and lack of a community that could support them.[21] Their experience seemed to justify the Tridentine decree that advocated that religious houses should relocate from rural to urban settings for the sake of the security of the nuns.[22] While some Poor Clares reassembled at

---

[16] 'An account of the establishment of the Poor Clares in Ireland', NLI microfilm P 3500, item 1, p. 13. Compiled by a member of the Poor Clares at Harold's Cross in the 1820s, drawing on Mother Bonaventure Browne's late seventeenth-century work. The manuscript from which the microfilm was made could not be traced in the Harold's Cross archives in 2011, and thus the microfilm copy is cited here. An older version of the Chronicle is preserved in the Poor Clare convent, Galway. [17] Bernadette Cunningham, 'The Poor Clare Order in Ireland' in Bhreathnach et al. (eds), *The Irish Franciscans*, pp 159–64. [18] Bernadette Cunningham 'Bethlehem: the Dillons and the Poor Clare convent at Ballinacliffey, Co. Westmeath', *Áitreabh: Group for the Study of Irish Historic Settlement Newsletter*, 17 (2012–13), 5–9. [19] Galway, Poor Clare convent, MS A1. Profession of Sr Catherine of St Francis [Browne], 29 Jan. 1631/2. She died at the Convent of St Clare in Bilbao in 1668. 'An account of the establishment of the Poor Clares in Ireland', p. 24. [20] Galway, Poor Clare convent, MS A3, 27 Sept. 1642 (copy). [21] 'An account of the establishment of the Poor Clares in Ireland', p. 18. [22] *The canons and decrees of the ... Council*

Athlone,[23] a significant number decided to move to Galway, and they rented a house in the town.

The choice of Galway doubtless was prompted by the presence there of family members who could be expected to support the cloistered nuns. The requirement that those women who chose the monastic life should observe strict enclosure effectively restricted access to an economic and social elite. Those who entered the convents came from families sufficiently wealthy to support them in a lifestyle in which they would not have to undertake menial tasks and would not have to seek alms. In the case of the Galway convents, daughters of merchants appear to have been particularly prominent. The surnames of some of the fourteen 'tribes of Galway' dominated in the late seventeenth century: several members of the Skerrett, Browne and Lynch families joined the Poor Clares, and more than one member of the Lynch, Browne, Blake, Darcy, Bodkin and French families joined the Dominican convent in the period up to 1712.[24] As elsewhere, the monastic communites of women that were supported in seventeenth-century Galway were rooted in a system of economic privilege.[25]

The best known of the Galway-born members of the original Poor Clare community in the town was Mother Mary Bonaventure Browne who later became the first historian of the order in Ireland. Having joined the community at Bethlehem in 1632, she was among the fourteen women who moved to Galway in 1642.[26] Mother Gabriel Martin, who had been the first woman from Galway to join the Bethlehem convent, became the first abbess of the new foundation in Galway.[27] When Mother Bonaventure Browne became abbess at Galway six years later she took the lead in ensuring the community would be more appropriately accommodated. In the summer of 1649, the nuns petitioned the Corporation of Galway for a grant of a site to build a convent just west of the town walls. They drew attention to hardships of the times, and their urgent need for accommodation.

> Shewing that your petitioners, members of this corporation, did some years sithence forsake the world for to serve the Almighty, and what through the distempers of the tyme and through God's holy will, have suffered great affliction these seaven years past, and in this necessity, as bound by nature, repaired to this towne. Shewing further that

of Trent, trans. J. Waterworth (London, 1848), pp 240–1. **23** *CSPI, 1633–47*, pp 662–3; Fergal Grannell, *The Franciscans in Athlone* (Athlone, 1978), pp 42–3. **24** Galway, Dominican convent, MS B/1, Original professions register; Galway, Poor Clare convent, MSS A4–A10. **25** Silvia Evangelisti, *Nuns: a history of convent life* (Oxford, 2007), p. 32. **26** O'Brien, *Recollections of an Irish Poor Clare*, p. [v]; Galway: Poor Clare convent, MS A2, Licence to found a convent at Galway, 30 Jan. 1642/3. **27** 'An account of the establishment of the Poor Clares in Ireland', p. 35. Mrs Thomas Concannon, *The Poor Clares in Ireland* (Dublin, 1929), p. xx.

> through necessity by reason of the tymes their parents and friends are unable to furnish their wants as in peacable tymes they have intended, and that your poore petitioners doe suffer much by the exorbitant rent they pay, and notwithstanding their due payment, are to be thrust out of their dwelling next May, their lease being then ended.[28]

The petition outlined the benefits that would accrue to the town into the future from the presence of a devout convent of nuns who would support the town through their prayers, and whose presence would be to honour it.

> The premises considered and taken to your consideracion the inconveniencie of religious women whoe want habitacion, the conveniencie of their residence [to] this place, the preferment of your children though poore shallbe releeved by God's assistance in our Convent, the everlasting prayers to be made for yow, the glory of God, the preservacion of the towne by your petitioners and their successors their intercessions, the honor of Galway to be founders of such a monasterie.[29]

In making their case for a site for a convent, with a garden and orchard adjoining, the nuns were aware of the potential concerns of the townsmen about the proposed convent building which was to be located outside the town walls. The petition asserted that the building and gardens on Oilean Altanagh and the adjoining island 'wilbe rather a strength than any annoyance, hinderance, or impeachment either to the highway leading to the other island or to the salfetie and preservacion of this Corporation.'[30]

At a meeting on 10 July 1649, the Corporation, under the leadership of Walter Blake as mayor, unanimously agreed to the request from the Poor Clares. This positive reception by the townsmen was recorded in the annals of the Order, as compiled in retrospect by Mother Bonaventure Browne for the edification of new members of the community.[31] A summary of the history of the property, provided by Dominic Deane in 1751, also recorded that 'Martin Blake of Cummer, the then sheriff, put them into the actual and peaceable possession of the said islands which they held and enjoyed till Cromwell's time'.[32] They established themselves on what – in time – became known as 'Nun's Island', although their occupation of that site was not continuous. In 1650, the nuns found it expedient to seek permission from the Franciscan provincial to leave the monastery whenever danger, disease or

---

28 J.T. Gilbert, 'Archives of the town of Galway, Queen's College Galway' in *Historical Manuscripts Commission, 10th report*, Appendix, part 5 (London, 1885), p. 498. 29 Gilbert, 'Archives of the town of Galway', p. 498. 30 Ibid., pp 498–9. 31 O'Brien, *Recollections of an Irish Poor Clare*, p. [v]. 32 Galway, Poor Clare convent, MS B7, 1751.

enemy approached the city.³³ Although they did not regain title to the land after the Restoration,³⁴ the Poor Clares were able to return to the same location in the early nineteenth century, having generally used premises on Market Street as an alternative in the intervening decades.³⁵

The same decade that saw the removal of the Poor Clares from Westmeath to Galway also saw the establishment of a convent of Dominican nuns in the town. Their first house, as marked on the 1660s pictorial map of Galway, was in New Tower Street, now St Augustine Street, in the centre of the old town.³⁶ The Irish Provincial Chapter of the Dominicans, meeting at Kilkenny in 1643, had approved the new convent for women at Galway, which took the title of the Convent of Jesus and Mary. The General Chapter of the order meeting at Rome in 1644 confirmed the foundation, while a visit from the papal nuncio, Cardinal Rinuccini, in 1647, further reaffirmed the status of the Galway convent. In a formal letter to the community, the papal nuncio outlined certain general guidelines for its functioning. He instructed them that they were to 'faithfully observe at all times the Constitutions and Ordinances of the nuns of St Dominick, who are under the care of Friar Preachers', and to adhere to the decrees of the Council of Trent and of the Sacred Congregations of cardinals regarding life in the cloister. The Tridentine decrees had emphasized the importance of enclosure for communities of nuns, and laid down that they required episcopal permission to go outside the convent 'except for some lawful cause'. Trent also controlled the numbers to be accepted into a convent.³⁷ In line with this, Rinuccini's letter further instructed that the number of nuns in the Dominican convent in Galway should not exceed twenty:

> judging from the usual dowry and the revenues hitherto acquired, that number only could be decently maintained according to the Decrees of the Sacred Congregation. Should anyone beyond this fixed number desire to enter, the dowry must be increased by one-third that is up to two hundred pounds, since the usual dowry should always be one hundred and fifty pounds.³⁸

33 Galway, Poor Clare convent, MS A7, 27 June 1650.   34 According to the evidence of Dominic Deane, they occupied the Nun's Island property in the mid-eighteenth century as tenants of Richard Martin and his heirs. Galway, Poor Clare convent, MS B7.   35 James Hardiman, *The history of the town and county of the town of Galway* (Dublin, 1820), p. 275; Marguerite Hayes McCoy (ed.), 'The Eyre documents in University College Galway [part 2]', *JGAHS*, 20 (1942–3), 151–79 at 178–9.   36 Rose O'Neill, *A rich inheritance: Galway Dominican nuns, 1644–1994* (Galway, 1994), pp 9–10.   37 *Canons and decrees of … the Council of Trent*, trans. Waterworth, p. 240.   38 English translation of Rinuccini's letter is printed in *Annals of the Dominican Convent of St Mary's, Cabra, with some account of its origin, 1647–1912* (Dublin, 1912), pp 5–7. A different translation, slightly abridged, is given in O'Neill, *A rich inheritance*, p. 198.

In a second letter, written at Galway on 26 October 1647, Cardinal Rinuccini directed the Dominican nuns to attend confession and receive communion monthly, and to recite the Rosary of the Blessed Virgin Mary. They were encouraged to pray for the eradication of heresy and for victory to the armies of the Catholics.[39] Such an exhortation would have helped ensure that the militarism of early modern Catholicism was part of the consciousness of the Dominican nuns in Galway. Even aside from Rinuccini's interventions, the nuns were not immune from the effects of the wars of the 1640s. Despite their cloistered lives, they would have maintained contact with their families. Indeed, in times of crisis or hardship, it was safer, and less expensive, to live with their own families, and there were times when the members of the Galway convents had no choice but to do so.

The Poor Clares were similarly well informed of political events, and acutely conscious of their implications for their own lives. In recalling the Cromwellian era, the historian of the Poor Clares noted that the inhabitants of Galway had held out, 'valiantly fighting for their faith & King an entire year. When the three kingdoms having yielded to the Parliament all Ecclesiastics & Religious etc were put to flight. And as our holy Order is a branch of our common Mother the Church ... it suffers when the Church suffers & when her rule extends it is enlarged'.[40]

Following a period of plague – which reached Galway in 1649 – and siege warfare, the town of Galway surrendered to Cromwellian forces in April 1652.[41] This had far-reaching consequences, and the various orders of nuns had little choice but to avail of the terms of the surrender, which allowed them to leave the country within six months. Under arrangements brokered by Revd Gregory O'Farrell, Irish Dominican nuns were accepted into convents in Spain, including Bilbao, Toledo and Valladollid, and most never returned to Ireland.[42] They do not appear to have sought to join the Irish Dominican convent of Bom Sucesso at Lisbon that had been in existence since 1639.[43] There are tantalizing hints in the Chapter Acts of the Dominicans in 1669 and 1672 that some Dominican nuns may have remained in Ireland.[44] The Poor Clares followed very similar paths to the Dominicans, with members of the community dispersing to Bilbao and nearby Orduña as well as the university towns of Madrid, Salamanca, Valladollid, and the southern port of Malaga.[45] Arrangements for their acceptance into Spanish

---

39 Thomas de Burgo, *Hibernia Dominicana* (Cologne, 1762), p. 351; English translation in *Annals of the Dominican Convent of St Mary's, Cabra, 1647–1912*, pp 7–8. **40** 'An account of the establishment of the Poor Clares in Ireland', p. 19. **41** E.P. Duffy, 'The siege and surrender of Galway, 1651–1652', *JGAHS*, 39 (1983–4), 115–42. **42** O'Neill, *A rich inheritance*, pp 12–14. **43** Honor McCabe, *A light undimmed: the story of the convent of Our Lady of Bom Sucesso, Lisbon, 1639–2006* (Dublin, 2007). **44** Hugh Fenning (ed.), *Acta capitulorum provinciae Hiberniae Sacri Ordinis Praedicatorum, 1669–1688* (Dublin, [1989]), pp 9, 16. I owe this reference to Raymond Gillespie. **45** O'Brien, *Recollections of an Irish*

convents appear to have been made by those who had ecclesiastical jurisdiction over them before they travelled. The annals of the Poor Clares reveal that those who left Galway were part of a wider evacuation that included some family members in the army and among the clergy.

> Having heard that such of their profession as would go to Spain would be graciously received, their ardent desire for conventual life pressed them so forceably, that having no other mode of crossing the sea than a vessel that was crowded with the army, amongst who however were several of their own relatives and some Ecclesiastics who were flying into banishment, almost destitute of necessities and wretchedly accommodated, these delicate creatures embarked in it.[46]

As the records of the Poor Clares reveal, 'all who had the means to do so', availed of the opportunity to leave.[47]

Trade routes with Spain used by Galway merchants offer the best explanation for the destinations chosen by the Galway nuns. Although the Poor Clares sailed first to Galicia, Bilbao proved a more appealing destination because of the significant Irish community already resident there.[48] Among the Dominican nuns from Galway who relocated to Bilbao were Mary Lynch and Julia Nolan, who had been professed in the Galway monastery in 1645 and 1647 respectively. They were received into the monastery of the Holy Cross at Bilbao on 14 September 1652. Initially, they relied on financial support from their Vicar, Revd Gregory French, who paid for their upkeep. They were incorporated into the community at Holy Cross after King Philip IV of Spain paid four thousand reales to the monastery for their dowries.[49] The Poor Clare nuns who moved to Spain received similar financial support on an annual basis from the Catholic Philip IV.[50]

Despite the official support that they enjoyed, the Irish nuns never fully integrated into the Spanish convents. Thus a story was told of Sr Julia Blake, of the Poor Clares, who had been accepted at the convent at Orduña. Miraculously on her deathbed she was able to speak Spanish, 'which until then she could not attempt'. She was thus enabled to confess her sins, 'not having at hand a clergyman that could hear her confession in her native language'.[51] Differences of language and culture would always have marked the

---

Poor Clare, p. 12. 46 'An account of the establishment of the Poor Clares in Ireland', p. 22. 47 O'Brien, *Recollections of an Irish Poor Clare*, p. 12. 48 'An account of the establishment of the Poor Clares in Ireland', p. 22. On the Irish merchant community in Bilbao in this period, see Anne P. Moran, 'The Irish merchant colony of Bilbao in the 17th and 18th centuries' (MA, UCD, 1960), pp 20–5; for the activities of Irish regular clergy in Bilbao, see ibid., pp 79–88. 49 Book of Foundations of Holy Cross monastery, Bilbao, cited in O'Neill, *A rich inheritance*, pp 12–13. 50 'An account of the establishment of the Poor Clares in Ireland', p. 21. 51 An account of the establishment of the Poor Clares in

Irish nuns. Few of those who had fled Ireland in the 1650s lived long enough to return in the late 1680s, though a small number did so.

Others of the Poor Clares, including Mother Mary Gabriel Martin, had opted to remain in Galway despite the prevailing political conditions, and she died in the town in 1672 and was buried in the Franciscan cemetery.[52] There is evidence that the Galway Poor Clares continued to function in the town during these years, however discreetly. In July 1683, Mother Elizabeth Skerrett, abbess of the Poor Clares, was authorized to admit new members to the community, 'on condition that they be kept and maintained perpetually within the cloister'.[53] That stipulation by the Franciscan provincial was in line with Tridentine norms, but its explicit restatement in 1683 suggests that claustration had not proved to be the norm in earlier decades. The religious orders were still functioning in secret, however, as indicated by the fact that the authorization issued by Revd Anthony Burke, OFM, was written 'in our place of refuge'.[54] A similar authorization was issued by Revd James Darcy, OFM, in 1684 to admit another two girls, 'privately, however, and without any great solemnity'.[55] He clearly judged it inappropriate that the kind of celebratory feasting for the girl's family that could accompany the acceptance of a new member into the convent community would be held in Galway at this time.[56]

With the accession of James II to the throne in 1685, a new optimism about Catholic toleration had prompted some exiled Dominicans to return to Ireland and attempt to re-establish their convent in Galway. The two surviving women from the original Dominican house in Galway, Mary Lynch and Julia Nolan, returned from Bilbao in 1686. Their journey took eight days to complete, in a favourable wind. Although they were arriving home, and according to their chaplain, John O'Heyne, were 'received by all with great joy',[57] they now faced the prospect of beginning again with the Galway convent. They received support from Sir John Kirwan, the Catholic mayor of the town, who allowed them the use of a house on Kirwan's Lane, a substantial stone town-house not far from the location of their previous convent.[58] Julia Nolan took on the office of prioress, and Mary Lynch served as mistress of novices. They were soon joined by others, with the first novice, Sr Agnes Browne, being professed on 7 May 1688.[59] Within ten years a total of fourteen novices had joined the community.[60]

Ireland', pp 28–9.   **52** Celsus O'Brien, *Poor Clares, Galway, 1642–1992* (Galway, 1992), p. 30.   **53** Galway, Poor Clare convent, MS A8.   **54** Galway, Poor Clare convent, MS A8.   **55** Galway, Poor Clare convent, MS A9.   **56** For comparable celebrations elsewhere, see Evangelisti, *Nuns: a history of convent life*, pp 13–14.   **57** John O'Heyne, *The Irish Dominicans of the seventeenth century*, ed. Ambrose Coleman (Dundalk, 1902), p. 163.   **58** O'Neill, *A rich inheritance*, p. 14, citing Hely Dutton, *A statistical and agricultural survey of the county of Galway* (Dublin, 1824), p. 504.   **59** *Annals of the Dominican Convent of St Mary's, Cabra, 1647–1912*, pp 12–14.   **60** O'Heyne, *The Irish Dominicans of the seventeenth*

By then, however, the Williamite war had taken a toll on the Galway monasteries. In summer 1690, the Poor Clares had again resorted to living with relatives and friends. Revd Edmund Delany, minister provincial of the Franciscans, reported that the women were 'reduced to such extremities that they cannot subsist together in cloister'.[61] The dowries of the nuns, on which convent finances relied, were generally linked to property in Galway and the surrounding districts, and the income from these sources had been disrupted by the war. The Poor Clare convent was virtually destroyed in the war, with the loss of altar fittings, altar plate and books, including the original manuscript of Mother Bonaventure Browne's history of the community, though a contemporary copy did survive. A medieval wooden statue of 'Our Lady of Bethlehem' also survived.[62]

In 1696, the Poor Clares were again admitting novices, but two years later new legislation obliged nuns to wear lay clothes, and they were not permitted to live in cloister. The minister provincial, Anthony O'Kelly, OFM, gave permission to the nuns in 1698 to go 'to some Catholic region, on the first available opportunity of travelling'. His formal letter commended the nuns 'to all the faithful, whether lay folk or clergy, to whom you turn, as poor exiled daughters, lovingly in the Lord'.[63] It seems that although almost all Franciscan clergy from Galway did depart, the Poor Clare nuns did not. The most senior remaining Franciscan in the province, Revd Anthony Burke, even gave permission to Sr Mary Gabriel [Skerrett] on 13 August 1698 to profess four new nuns.[64] In the following year, the community, including Sr Mary Gabriel, were living 'neere Mr Ambrose Ruisse ye Apothecary's house in Galway'.[65] The gift of a silver chalice in 1701, presented by John and Agnes Joyce, is tangible evidence that they continued to be regarded as a viable religious community in those years.[66]

The Dominicans, too, considered removing to the Continent again, but according to John O'Heyne, OP, who acted as their confessor for some months early in 1698, he advised them that this was unnecessary.[67] Nuns were not explicitly included in the banishment order for regular clergy and members of the hierarchy that came into effect in May of that year.[68] Most of the men who were part of the Galway Dominican community left Ireland about 20 March 1698.[69] The nuns opted merely to disperse either within the

century, p. 159.   61 Galway, Poor Clare convent, MS A12, 25 Aug. 1690.   62 Galway, Poor Clare convent, Chronicle, pp 16–19.   63 Galway, Poor Clare convent, MS A15 (1698).   64 Galway, Poor Clare convent, MS A17, 13 Aug. 1698.   65 Galway, Poor Clare convent, MS A18, 12 July 1699.   66 Galway, Poor Clare convent, Inventory of ecclesiastical silver plate, compiled by R.J. Lattimore, 1997.   67 *Annals of the Dominican Convent of St Mary's, Cabra, 1647–1912*, p. 16; Hugh Fenning, *The Irish Dominican Province, 1698–1797* (Dublin, 1990), p. 20.   68 *An Act for banishing all Papists exercising any Ecclesiastical Jurisdiction, and all Regulars of the Popish Clergy out of the Kingdom* (9 William III, c.1) [1697].   69 Fenning, *The Irish Dominican Province, 1698–1797*, p. 20.

town or surrounding area. They were able to return to their Kirwan's Lane house again in 1702, by which time the first of the regular clergy who had departed in 1698 were also beginning to return to Ireland. Sr Mary Lynch became prioress in the revived monastery, and at the end of 1702 there were thirteen women in the Galway house. At that time, the nuns in the Galway monastery comprised the largest Dominican community in Ireland.[70]

Thus in the closing years of the seventeenth century and the early years of the eighteenth century these communities of women rather than men were to the fore in fulfilling the social role of the religious orders as spiritual mediators for the lay community in the town. Their familial links to the townspeople had not lessened – the same 'Galway tribe' surnames persisted within the convents – but for the Catholic laity no less than the nuns the legal conditions under which they lived soon became increasingly restrictive. The celebration of Catholic liturgies and sacraments became an underground activity.

In the early eighteenth century, the political climate remained hostile for religious orders in Ireland, and the clergy of the Dominican Order found it expedient to confine themselves largely to Connacht, the most Catholic province.[71] 'An Act to prevent Popish Priests from coming into this kingdom' (2 Anne c. 3) passed into law in 1703, and was designed to reaffirm the 1697 banishment act. In addition, 'An Act to prevent the further Growth of Popery' (2 Anne c. 6), enacted in 1704, explicitly ordered that 'no person or persons that are or shall be papists ... shall come to dwell ... within the town of Galway or suburbs thereof'.[72]

A visitor to Galway in 1708 reported sympathetically on what he was told of the predicament of Catholics in the town. Don Giovanni Donato Mezzafalce noted that 'in order to hear Mass (which may not be celebrated in the city), men and women go outside on festal days not only to assist at Mass but also at vespers, which, because of the shortage of ecclesiastics, is sung by the laity. Within the city itself many persons have secret chapels where Mass is secretly celebrated'. Mezzafalce observed that 'they do not pay the slightest heed to the rigorous laws which have been passed by the parliament in Dublin against the Catholics, by which in recent years they have been deprived of every dignity, both civil and military, in such manner that they are not allowed even to keep or carry a sword.'[73] Indeed, it was claimed that people flocked to visit Mezzafalce's ship in the port of Galway when they heard there was a Catholic bishop aboard.[74]

70 O'Neill, *A rich inheritance*, p. 17; Fenning, *The Irish Dominican Province, 1698–1797*, pp 30–2.   71 Fenning, *The Irish Dominican Province, 1698–1797*, pp 29–32.   72 James Mitchell, 'The Catholics of Galway, 1708–13: a commentary on a report by Don Giovanni Donato Mezzafalce', *JGAHS*, 61 (2009), 84.   73 Mitchell, 'The Catholics of Galway, 1708–13', 90.   74 Ibid., 91.

Heightened political tension in 1708, prompted by fear that the French might land on the west coast of Ireland and receive help from the local Catholic population, resulted in official action against Catholics in the town of Galway. In March, the mayor of the city, Richard Wall, reported that he had complied with orders from the privy council and 'turned all the popish inhabitants out of the town and garrison, and have also committed the several popish priests to the gaol. I have also taken care to remove the market outside the walls, and have given orders to prevent Mass being said in town'. The Catholics were removed to the western suburbs, outside the town walls, and were forced to remain outside the town for four weeks, until the wider political crisis abated. Security was a concern to the mayor, who noted that the militia comprised just 250 poorly-armed men, and were greatly outnumbered by the popish inhabitants.[75] In the same year, 1708, the Dominican provincial, Revd Ambrose O'Connor, was actively exploring what lay patronage his order might attract. Among those he encountered in the city of Galway was 'A gentleman of the family of the Brownes [who] ... has assured me that with 500 well-disciplined men, he would undertake to make himself master of that place, as he knows it perfectly, both within and without'.[76] The claim reinforces the sense of political tension that pervaded the city in those years, and the challenges that faced the Catholic population. The nuns were not exempt from these constraints. In 1714, the mayor reported to the Dublin government:

> Pursuant to your commands, some time past I have made diligent search and dispersed the nuns that were in this town but now I am informed that they are gathering again, and that by the advice of several popish lawyers who tell them there is no law against their assembling and that if they be dispersed one day they may assemble again.[77]

The nuns survived by keeping a low profile. When Samuel Molyneux visited Galway in 1709, he noted that 'here are 2 nunneries, who, keeping somwhat private, are connived at by the governour and mayor'.[78] It seems that despite the mayor's outward show of obedience to government in 1708, and again in 1714, the nuns could normally rely on a degree of local support. As Maureen Wall explained, 'limited toleration, by connivance, of the Catholic religion', while maintaining Protestant supremacy, offered the best prospect of political stability.[79] The mayor and recorder of Galway took to print in 1717 to defend

---

75 Ibid., 84.   76 Nathaniel Hooke, *The secret history of Hooke's negotiations in Scotland* (Dublin, 1760), pp 105–11, cited in Fenning, *Irish Dominican Province, 1698–1797*, p. 53.   77 Cited in Desmond Forrestal, *The Siena story* (Drogheda, 1999), p. 13.   78 Peter Barry (ed.), 'The journeys of Samuel Molyneux in Ireland, 1708–1709', *Analecta Hibernica*, 46 (2015), 44.   79 Maureen Wall, *Catholic Ireland in the eighteenth century: collected essays*, ed. Gerard O'Brien (Dublin, 1989), p. 115.

themselves against accusations of favouring papists and in particular of assisting the concealment of two nunneries from the authorities.[80]

The very limited nature of toleration of Catholics made it difficult for the nuns to observe the rules of enclosure. Between 1712 and 1717 the nuns at Galway were considering removing their entire community of thirty-nine to the Continent. Attempts were made by Revd Edward Fitzgerald, OP, in 1712 to obtain support from the Spanish king, Philip V, to establish new houses in Spain for Irish Dominican clergy and nuns, to which those in Galway might relocate. The visitation by the provincial, Revd Hugh Callanan, OP, in 1714 found the Galway nuns had abandoned their convent and had been living with friends and relatives for some months.[81] A letter from Revd Thomas MacDermott, OP, to Revd Antoninus Cloche, OP, master general of the order, dated 30 December 1714, described their predicament. They had to wear secular clothes and their convent was regularly being searched by soldiers looking for priests and religious. Sometimes they had to disperse.[82] To live a cloistered life it appeared necessary to relocate, and by the mid-1710s some had already gone to Dublin. Others travelled to Madrid, hoping to be part of a new foundation at Seville. When that did not materialize they joined various Spanish convents, and spent the rest of their lives in Spain.[83]

Despite the difficulties, professions of new members grew significantly, with twenty-six nuns being professed in the Galway Dominican convent between 1711 and 1720, and a further thirty in the following decade. Such expansion was unsustainable for a single house, and transfers to other Irish urban centres ensued. When a group of Dominican nuns from Galway heeded the advice of Revd Hugh Callanan, OP, to move to Dublin in 1714, this marked the beginning of a new phase in the order's history.[84] Most of those who made the move had surnames associated with Pale families, such as Bellew, Keating, Plunkett, Rice and Weever, rather than the Galway 'tribes'.[85] By 1721, the new Dublin community was sufficiently well established to receive permission from the general chapter to elect their own superior.[86] The numbers in the community were then sufficient for them to found another convent at Drogheda, under the leadership of Catherine Plunkett who had professed at Galway in 1709, moved to Dublin and then to Brussels in 1717, before returning in 1721 to take charge of the Drogheda initiative. Her

---

80 *The Case of Robert Cotes, Esq., Mayor, and John Staunton, Esq., Recorder of Gallway, on behalf of themselves and the Majority of the Corporation of Gallway* ... (Dublin, 1717), pp 7–8. 81 Fenning, *Irish Dominican Province, 1698–1797*, p. 75. 82 Rome, General Archives of the Order of Preachers, XIII/157, cited in Fenning, *Irish Dominican Province, 1698–1797*, p. 77. 83 Fenning, *Irish Dominican Province, 1698–1797*, pp 78–9. 84 De Burgo, *Hibernia Dominicana*, pp 353–4; English translation in *Annals of the Dominican Convent of St Mary's, Cabra, 1647–1912*, pp 21–3. 85 The names are listed in De Burgo, *Hibernia Dominicana*, p. 353. 86 Fenning, *Irish Dominican Province, 1698–1797*, p. 97.

mother, Rose Plunkett, along with Hugh MacMahon, archbishop of Armagh, and Stephen MacEgan, then provincial of the Dominicans, were the key people behind this new venture.[87] A smaller convent was established at Waterford in the mid-1730s, though permission for it had been granted as early as 1725 at the general chapter held in Bologna, where it was also decided that those living in Dominican monasteries abroad should return to Ireland.[88] By the mid-1720s, conditions for Catholics had improved in Ireland, and those with jurisdiction over the nuns could turn their attention to the minutiae of how the convents were run. Revd Edmund Burke, OP, believed that stricter control of the convents at Galway and Dublin was necessary, and new restrictions were placed on nuns and their confessors in 1726.[89] The nuns at Galway, Dominican, Poor Clare and Augustinian, were again dispersed from their convents in 1732, and in 1734–7 Julia Browne, formerly of the Galway convent, attempted to purchase a house in Brussels that might serve as a refuge if required. Her plan was abandoned because the Dublin convent would not agree to finance it.[90]

In a story that closely paralleled that of the Dominican nuns, the Poor Clares in Galway also saw a marked rise in professions in the second decade of the eighteenth century.[91] They, too, opened a new convent in Dublin in those years. Indeed, they preceded the Dominicans in occupying the former Benedictine convent at Channel Row, taking up residence there in 1712. The Poor Clares soon relocated to less conspicuous premises in nearby North King Street where they remained until 1826, supporting themselves by taking in women boarders, and expanding to form a second convent in 1751.[92]

Despite all the disruptions and upheavals, which perhaps by their nature are the episodes that dominate the written records, it is clear that the Galway convents continued to be viable. One indication of this is found in the altar plate that survives to the present time. In the same year, 1714, during which dispersal was being considered once more, an ornate silver chalice, ten inches high, made in Galway by Mark Fallon for George Martin and Elizabeth Bodkin, was presented to the Dominican convent. In 1723, they received a silver reliquary made by Richard Joyce to enclose a relic of Sr Ursula which had been procured from Rome. Another silver chalice, heavily ornamented, presented in 1725, was also the work of Mark Fallon. A pair of silver candlesticks was presented in 1729 by John Lynch of Bordeaux, brother of Bridget and Ann Lynch, and the same benefactor presented two further pairs of silver candlesticks in 1732 and 1733, along with a silver host

---

87 Forrestal, *The Siena story*, pp 15–19; Fenning, *Irish Dominican Province, 1698–1797*, p. 98.   88 Fenning, *Irish Dominican Province, 1698–1797*, pp 110, 152–4.   89 Ibid., pp 117–20.   90 Ibid., pp 159–79.   91 Cunningham, 'The Poor Clare order in Ireland', p. 167. 92 Bernadette Cunningham, 'An account of the Poor Clare Order in eighteenth-century Dublin', *Archivum Franciscanum Historicum*, 105 (2012), 277–310.

box, engraved with the crest of the order, which he donated in 1733.[93] This John Lynch of Bordeaux can probably be identified with the Catholic supporter of James II who departed with the defeated king in 1691 and subsequently married into elite French society in Bordeaux. He acquired French citizenship in 1710, but retained close links with the Galway merchant community, as did his second son, John Arthur Lynch.[94] The Lynch sisters had been professed together on 11 December 1691, a move that may well have been linked to the enforced departure of their brother with the 'Wild Geese'. The breakup of the Lynch family was one of many among the Catholic elite precipitated by the political crisis of the 1690s. Despite the girls' entry into the convent and their brother's departure, family contacts were maintained, or re-established later, and even continued after John's death, when his widow presented further gifts to the Galway Dominicans. That this was possible is an indication both of the wealth of John Lynch, which allowed him the luxury of being a benefactor, but also reveals something of the networks of the Galway Dominicans that, through their families, could extend to distant mercantile centres in western Europe. In contrast to their brother, the Lynch sisters lived enclosed lives in Galway: Bridget Lynch died in the convent in 1744 while Ann lived until 1750.[95] In 1739 the Dominicans received a silver sanctuary lamp, the work of William Wilson of Dublin, as a gift from Lady Laetitia Burke, while in 1742 they received a solid silver chandelier that hung in the nuns' choir, a gift from the widow of John Lynch.[96] While some of the earlier gifts were easily portable, gifts such as a chandelier are certainly an indication of confidence in the permanence of the chapel for which it was intended.

The Poor Clares in Galway were also the recipients of gifts of altar plate in the early eighteenth century, including the silver chalice already mentioned, gifted by John and Agnes Joyce in 1701, and another silver chalice donated in 1712 by Marguerite Bodkin. Like their Dominican neighbours, the Poor Clares received gifts from Laetitia Burke, in their case a silver thurable and incense case, made in Dublin in the 1740s. From Dorothea Netterville they received a silver sanctuary lamp, made by Samuel Walker of Dublin in 1745.[97] A pattern of female patronage is evident here.

---

[93] Kurt Ticher, 'Galway silver in a Dominican convent', *The Antique Dealer and Collectors Guide* (Oct. 1977) [1–4] (National Library of Ireland, IR 700 P 62); Gordon St George Mark, 'A silver chandelier from Galway', *Irish Georgian Society* [Bulletin] (1982), 19–23; Galway, Dominican Convent archives, Typescript inventory of chalices and other silver.
[94] Bernadette Ní Loinsigh, 'Loinsigh Bhordeaux', *Galvia*, 7 (1960), 4–19, at pp 4–8.
[95] Galway, Dominican convent archives, MS B1, Professions register (unpaginated).
[96] St George Mark, 'A silver chandelier from Galway', 19–23; Galway, Dominican Convent archives, Typescript inventory of chalices and other silver.   [97] Galway, Poor Clare convent, Inventory of ecclesiastical silver plate, 1997; Kurt Ticher, 'The silver in the St Clare's monastery, Galway', *JGAHS*, 37 (1979–80), 62–77.

Gradually, by the mid-eighteenth century, the broader political environment became less hostile to Catholic communities of nuns, and their presence was tolerated by the secular authorities in several urban centres. A report on the state of popery in Galway in 1731 contained evidence of three nunneries in the town, two of which kept women boarders. An Augustinian house in Middle Street had 10 beds; a Franciscan nunnery in Lombard Street had 26 beds; while the Dominican house in Cross Street had 27 beds. Some boarders and servants were encountered, but the nuns themselves evaded detection.[98] Thomas de Burgo's history of the Dominicans recorded the names and ages of the thirty-one nuns in the Galway Dominican convent in 1756; the youngest, Maria Joyce was aged 41 and had been professed for twenty-five years, suggesting an era of stagnation by mid-century.[99] In 1750, Canon John Murphy, representing the Irish bishops, reported to the papacy that there were thirty Dominican nuns in Galway, the same number in Dublin, twelve or thirteen in Drogheda, and two or three in Waterford. In an attempt to bring them under the jurisdiction of the bishops rather than the provincial of the order, Murphy complained that the nuns did not observe a formal cloister, wore lay clothes, went out in public too often, and were insufficiently responsible to the superior general. Rome did not intervene, however, and the nuns remained under the jurisdiction of the Dominican provincial.[1] The Dominican monastery at Waterford proved unviable and dispersed in 1758, but the establishments at Galway, Dublin and Drogheda survived into modern times.[2] In these urban centres, as at Galway, religious women from similar elite social backgrounds could rely on support among the Catholic population.

In some instances, the women's entry to the convent may have been a convenient solution to the economic challenges facing upwardly-mobile merchant families who could not afford high-status marriages for all their daughters or sisters. But their enclosure did not distance the women from their relatives; their family connections helped ensure that they had the support of the Corporation as required, and family assistance in times of crisis, either for accommodation and sustenance or in extreme cases to arrange for their departure overseas. They continued to benefit from the benefactions of their relatives, particularly those who had prospered in trade. And through all of the upheavals of early modern life the nuns were a presence in Galway society, interceding for their communities through their life of prayer. The traces of their story in the broader historical record are not always easy to discern, but their experience is integral to the story of urban religion in early modern Ireland.

[98] *A Report from the Lords Committees appointed to enquire into the present state of Popery in this kingdom in relation to the state of Popery within the Counties of Mayo and Galway* ... (Dublin, 1731), p. 8. [99] De Burgo, *Hibernia Dominicana*, p. 354; for the similar dip in professions in the Poor Clares between 1730 and 1750, see Cunningham, 'The Poor Clare order in Ireland', p. 167. [1] Hugh Fenning, *The undoing of the friars in Ireland* (Louvain, 1972), pp 198–9. [2] Máire M. Kealy, *From Channel Row to Cabra* (Dublin, 2010), p. 20.

Religion and politics in a provincial town: Belfast, 1660–1720

RAYMOND GILLESPIE

One of the most important results of the interconnected political, economic, social and cultural revolutions that occurred in early modern Ireland was the establishment of an urban network across the country. The older medieval towns of Dublin, Waterford, Kilkenny, Cork, Limerick and Galway all saw significant expansion in the seventeenth century. In such towns the confessional position was mixed, with older Catholic inhabitants and newer Protestant settlers jostling for economic and political power in the first half of the seventeenth century, a process well atomized in Colm Lennon's work. On the other hand there were new towns that were established in the early seventeenth century, many as a result of plantation schemes, and they grew dramatically over the course of that century. In Ulster, Armagh, Belfast, Coleraine and Derry are good examples of this phenomenon. Such towns were confessionally distinct. They had no older populations and new, mostly Protestant, settlers dominated. Here the issue of confessional relations was not played out between Protestants and Catholics but among various Protestant groupings, creating problems not just for government but for the governing elite within the towns themselves. The solutions to such challenges in an age of rapid urban growth were as complex as the tensions resulting from Catholic–Protestant cohabitation on which most historians have focused.

Urban growth in seventeenth-century Ireland can be understood in a number of ways. It might be thought of as the expansion of particular types of spaces in the landscape. Most obvious was the growth of a physical space, marked out from the surrounding area by a much denser concentration of buildings and people. In the case of Belfast that physical space was demarcated, in part, by a rampart cast up around the town in 1642 and 1643 when its inhabitants felt threatened by the Irish insurrection, although no such attack came.[1] Second, Belfast was separated from the surrounding countryside because it was designated as a legal space, marked out by its charter. The charter, granted in 1613, created a corporation under the control of the local landowners, the Chichester family, later earls of Donegall. The corporation was charged with the management of the town although in practice it was a fairly ineffectual body before the 1640s. The real importance of the charter

---

[1] Raymond Gillespie, *Early Belfast: the origins and growth of an Ulster town to 1750* (Belfast, 2007), pp 75–8.

was not the institutions it created but rather its formation of a political space, divorced from other concerns, where the various elements in the town could negotiate a way of organizing urban life. Thus in 1671 both Presbyterian and Church of Ireland members of Belfast Corporation could come together with the landlord, the earl of Donegall, to negotiate a new charter to provide a framework for co-existence within the town.[2] The proposed charter was never granted but the sense of corporatism that charters created helped shape corporate values and identities that could transcend sectional, often religious, interests.[3] The rather limited powers of Belfast Corporation were supplemented by other linked institutions. The grand jury of the Corporation of Belfast, probably modelled on that of the Chichester family's other town of Carrickfergus, had developed by the 1640s as a way of drawing the freemen of the town into its government, which had been limited to a sovereign and twelve burgesses in 1613. By 1671 the proposals for a new charter tried to regularize the position of the quasi-legal grand juries.[4] In addition, by the 1670s guilds of a sort appear to have developed in Belfast to institutionalize the economic life of the town.[5]

A third feature of urban growth was the evolution of Belfast as an economic space. From its origin the town had received grants of the right to hold markets and fairs. By 1700 it had become a major port that some believed was one of the largest in Ireland. It had also emerged as a significant food processing centre as well as having a range of other urban-based trades.[6] Finally, and perhaps most importantly, early modern Belfast was a cultural and intellectual space. The concentration of people in a relatively small area meant that new and innovative ways of living together, within the existing legal and economic constraints, had to be devised. That concentration of people in one place provided opportunities to meet, to discuss larger questions and sometimes to devise new perspectives on the world. The economic potential of a town created a market not only for goods but for ideas also. From 1694, a printer was at work in Belfast producing books for a local market and, as a port, book imports containing new ideas flowed through the town.[7] The proximity of individuals meant that they might borrow and lend each other books as well as exchanging ideas through discussion of printed works.

2 R.M. Young (ed.), *The town book of the corporation of Belfast* (Belfast, 1892), p. 118. 3 J.R. Hill, 'Corporatist ideology and practice in Ireland, 1660–1800' in Sean Connolly (ed.), *Political ideas in eighteenth-century Ireland* (Dublin, 2000), pp 64–82.   4 Young (ed.), *Town book*, p. 118. For the context see Paul Halliday, *Dismembering the body politic: partisan politics in England's towns, 1650–1730* (Cambridge, 1998), pp 170–4; Gillespie, *Early Belfast*, pp 110–11.   5 Gillespie, *Early Belfast*, p. 111.   6 For a survey of development of Belfast see Raymond Gillespie, 'Making Belfast, 1600–1700' in S.J. Connolly (ed.), *Belfast 400: people, place and history* (Liverpool, 2012), pp 123–60 and Gillespie, *Early Belfast*, passim.   7 For the sort of books available in Belfast in the 1730s see Robert Whan, *The Presbyterians of Ulster, 1680–1730* (Woodbridge, 2013), p. 51.

All of these developments contributed to the uniquely urban society that marked Belfast off from the surrounding countryside. In the early eighteenth century, the Scottish historian Robert Woodrow observed that the two non-subscribing ministers in Belfast, James Kirkpatrick and Samuel Haliday, were well established since they were based 'in a town and in a collegiate life', where there was a density of people, a willingness to explore new ideas sometimes at variance with strict orthodoxy and enough wealth to support ministers.[8] Kirkpatrick, the minister of Second Belfast Presbyterian congregation, was a good example of the sort of intellectual curiosity that living in a town could promote. As a Glasgow-trained Presbyterian minister he was certainly well versed in theological matters. Theology impinged on a wide range of other subjects and Kirkpatrick's interest in the political implications of particular theological positions is revealed in his study of history. His early eighteenth-century writing and wide reading on the subject shows this interest. Kirkpatrick was not unusual in having access to books and a number of the books owned by the minister of the First Belfast Presbyterian congregation have survived as do some owned by his successor Samuel Haliday.[9] However, Kirkpatrick was also interested in science. He was trained as a doctor and his scientific credentials were clearly on display in 1734 when he entered into a debate on the use of Mrs Stephens' medicines for gallstones. Using himself as a guinea pig, he kept a detailed diary of his self-medication in order to test the claims of the cure, which he dedicated to the president of the Royal College of Physicians in Dublin, and published at Belfast in 1739. He had other claims to a scientific approach, including the ownership of a microscope.[10] Kirkpatrick was not alone in his interest in this new learning. In his work on the effectiveness of Mrs Stephens' medicines he listed forty individuals who had helped him with his clinical trial among whom were several Belfast doctors and prominent Belfast merchants as well as clergy and MPs, including the MP for Belfast.[11] Neither was Kirkpatrick the only Belfast minister with an interest in medicine. John McBride, the minister of First Belfast, in his will of 1718 left his 'physic books' to his son and at least some of those books he had acquired from Hans Sloane, the distinguished London doctor and Fellow of the Royal Society.[12]

There were also professional doctors in the town. The funeral register of the First Belfast Presbyterian church names twelve medical doctors all practising in the town between 1713 and 1736.[13] What made these men's practices

---

8 Quoted in Ian McBride, *Scripture politics: Ulster Presbyterians and Irish radicalism in the late eighteenth century* (Oxford, 1998), p. 48.   9 Whan, *The Presbyterians of Ulster*, pp 43–4.   10 James Kirkpatrick, *An account of the success of Mrs Stephens's medicine for the stone in the case of James Kirkpatrick, doctor of divinity* (Belfast, 1739), p. 13.   11 Kirkpatrick, *An account*, p. 41.   12 George Benn, *A history of the town of Belfast* (Belfast, 1877), p. 405, n. 2; British Library Sloane MS 4038, f. 117.   13 Jean Agnew (ed.), *Funeral register of the First Presbyterian church of Belfast* (Belfast, 1995).

viable was simply the concentration of people in Belfast that provided them with an easily-accessible client base. Clearly the quality of the doctors varied but one, Victor Ferguson, was more than a provincial physician. As he pointed out, he had medical friends in Dublin to whom he wrote, and he also had an extensive correspondence with Hans Sloane, asking Sloane to send him the latest medical publications from London, enquiring about scientific apparatus and reporting details of cases he was treating.[14] Another Belfast doctor, Magnus Prince, was also carrying out experiments with inoculation for smallpox in 1728 and was communicating with Sloane on the subject. The result was what he described in 1732 as a method of treating the disease 'which I take to be something out of the common road'.[15] All of this suggests that Belfast was not a provincial backwater in the early eighteenth century but rather a place where the concentration of population and wealth gave rise to an engagement with contemporary issues whether in religion or in science. As such it was a marketplace not just of goods but of ideas and a place of debate, much of which focused on the question of confessional co-existence and the distribution of political power within the town.

I

Despite the potential that large towns presented for the generation of new ideas and for exploring old ones from new perspectives, religious ideas in early modern Belfast proved to be remarkably orthodox. Few of those who embraced radical alternatives to institutional Christianity can be found in Belfast although, as in any large town, there were always some exceptions. In the 1770s, for instance, Ralph Mathews in his survey of millenarians recorded that in Belfast there was 'William Forde, Hercules Lane, a poor man. He is not so solid as EP [a millenarian in Carrickfergus] but teachable, and lives on roots and water, there is another in that debauched town, but I wait to see if it will prove as the seed sown in good ground'.[16] Even the smaller religious institutions found it difficult to make any impact in early modern Belfast. Quakerism, for instance, made little progress in late seventeenth-century Belfast despite being well-established at the nearby towns of Lisburn and Lurgan. In the 1650s the Quaker preacher William Edmundson noted that 'at Belfast, that town of great profession there was but one of all the inns and public houses that would lodge any of our Friends which was one Widow

---

14 Whan, *The Presbyterians of Ulster*, pp 145, 149–50; British Library, Sloane MS 4075, ff 122, 124; Sloane MS 4038, f. 38.   15 British Library, Sloane MS 4052, f. 192; Sloane MS 4050, f. 194; Sloane MS 406B, ff 34–34v.   16 'Ralph Mathers account of spiritual persons to Henry Brooke, 1775' in Christopher Walton, *Notes and materials for an adequate biography of ... William Law* (London, 1854), p. 595.

Partridge'. However, the Quaker John Tiffin did preach there 'often endeavouring to get an entrance for truth in that town but they resisted shutting their ears, doors and hearts against it'. Tiffin returned to England and it was not until the late 1660s that Ralph Sharpley appeared in the town and established a meeting there, acquiring a meeting house. Sharpley evidently had little success in organizing a viable meeting and by 1686 the meeting house was annexed by Sharpley for his own use and the following year he was disowned for drunkenness. Any Quaker organization had collapsed by this date and was never re-established.[17]

Not only was Belfast orthodox in religious terms but it was also resolutely confessionally Protestant. In the years before 1640 a few Irish names do appear in the Corporation records and according to the poll tax of 1660 'Irish', probably meaning Catholics, made up about a third of the population. In 1708 it was claimed there were no more than seven Catholics in the town. By 1757 the number had grown to 550 but that was a modest 6.5 per cent of Belfast's inhabitants.[18] Even the more transient elements of the town's population, seamen and fishermen, were Protestant. In 1697, it was estimated that of 268 seamen, fishermen and boatmen in Belfast and Carrickfergus only two were Catholic – the lowest number for any Irish port.[19] Organization reflected numbers and there does not seem to have been a settled place of Catholic worship although there is an unsupported early nineteenth-century tradition that Mass was said at Friars Bush graveyard to the south of the main town.[20] In 1704, the parish priest of Belfast, Phelomy O'Hamill, lived at Derriaghy, a considerable distance to the west, and there is no evidence that he attempted to establish himself within the town, where his following was limited.[21]

When Belfast was created in 1613 it was clearly envisaged that it would be dominated by members of the established church. At the level of government, the charter of 1613 required the newly elected sovereign to take the oath of supremacy as well as the oath of the sovereign. The vicar of Belfast in 1712, William Tisdall, was certainly clear that this was necessary 'to secure corporations in the hands of conformists'.[22] Unlike Derry and Coleraine, where the oath of supremacy was required for burgesses, in Belfast only a simpler oath

---

17 Sandra King, *History of the Religious Society of Friends, Frederick Street, Belfast* (Belfast, 1999), pp 2–4. In contrast to the confessional diversity, and conflict, in contemporary English provincial towns, see John Miller, *Cities divided: politics and religion in English provincial towns, 1660–1722* (Oxford, 2007), pp 132–55. **18** Gillespie, *Early Belfast*, pp 132–3. **19** 'A list of all the names of the seamen, fishermen, water men ... of what kind soever in the kingdom of Ireland according to a return made in 1697', *Philosophical Transactions of the Royal Society*, 22 (1700–1), p. 519. **20** Eamon Phoenix, *Two acres of Irish history* (Belfast, 2001), pp 7–8, 25. **21** *List of the names of the popish parish priests throughout the several counties in the kingdom of Ireland* (Dublin, 1705); W.P. Burke, *Irish priests in the penal times* (Waterford, 1914), p. 281. **22** William Tisdall, *The conduct of the dissenters of Ireland, with respect both to church and state* (Dublin, 1712), p. 18.

to do one's duty was required. The Cromwellian administration and the Jacobite charter of 1687 modified these arrangements by prescribing oaths of loyalty to the state and the king respectively. How effective such requirements were is unclear, particularly in years after 1690 when Presbyterians dominated the list of sovereigns, but the Corporation did have the text of the oath of supremacy, as well as the usual oath of the sovereign, copied into the corporation book in the 1660s.[23] At a lower social level the Corporation declared in 1615 that all householders who were absent from church on Sunday were to be fined 5s., every woman 2s. 6d. and every servant 12d. Alehouses were to close at times of worship and the freemen were to accompany the sovereign to church in a formal procession.[24] Such fines for absence from church were well in excess of those provided for in the act of supremacy but probably were little enforced.

Despite this the Church of Ireland community within Belfast was relatively small. A list drawn up by the Presbyterian minister James Kirkpatrick in 1713 as part of a dispute with the Church of Ireland minister, William Tisdall, named seventy-eight Church of Ireland individuals in Belfast and if most of these represented heads of families then this might provide an order of magnitude for the small community. This estimate is broadly in line with that of Archdeacon Pococke in 1754 who guessed there were sixty Church of Ireland individuals, 'most of them of the lower rank', but his was probably an underestimate to judge from the baptisms in the parish register.[25] Whatever the exact numbers, the Church of Ireland community in Belfast was in a very clear minority. Insofar as it is possible to judge the tenor of the churchmanship of the Belfast congregation it was inclined to the godlier end of the theological spectrum. William Tisdall, the high church Tory vicar of the parish of Shankill, in which the town lay, complained in 1712 that his curate, Matthew French, had been

> followed by the boys of the town and in the public street whooled and called (as the utmost mark of infamy) Dr Sachaverall and this indignity highly approved of and laughed at by some leading persons of the town whose duty it was to have protected a clergyman of the established church (of which they were professed members) from such insult.[26]

The high church Sachaverall clearly had little following among members of the Church of Ireland in Belfast.

23 Young (ed.), *Town book*, pp 71, 174, 160, 219. 24 Young (ed.), *Town book*, pp 3–4, 5, 6. 25 James Kirkpatrick, *An historical essay on the loyalty of Presbyterians in Great Britain and Ireland* ([Belfast], 1713), pp 434–5; Raymond Gillespie and Alison O'Keeffe (eds), *Register of the parish of Shankill, Belfast, 1745–1761* (Dublin, 2006), pp 26–8. 26 Tisdall, *Conduct*, p. 20.

Despite its minority status, the Church of Ireland provided a focus for many aspects of town life. The parish of Shankill was a basic building block of the town, although occupying an area larger than it. Indeed so close was the connection at one point that in 1645 the Corporation took upon itself to appoint the sexton of the parish church.[27] The parish was also one of the main urban institutions of poor relief. Individuals often left money to the poor of the parish, suggesting identification with that institution. Lord Donegall left £200 to the poor of the parish of Belfast in 1674 and others followed suit; John Biggar, an inn holder, bequeathed in his 1721 will 'to the poor of the parish church of Belfast the sum of 20 shillings ster[ling] to be paid to such of them as Rev Mr Fletcher [the curate] shall think most fit'.[28] There are also a number of acknowledgments in the town book for money received by the sovereign from the churchwardens for the relief of the poor. The parish and the Corporation clearly operated together to provide some form of poor relief although what the confessional bias was in the distribution of relief was not clear.[29] Even those of a Presbyterian background saw merit in the established church. Many Presbyterians were buried in the parish graveyards and their burials recorded in the parish register. In 1705, Isaac McCartney, although a Presbyterian, owned a seat in the gallery of the parish church and worried that it might be taken from him.[30]

By 1700 religious life in Belfast was dominated not by the established church but by Presbyterians of Scottish origin. Belfast in the late seventeenth and early eighteenth centuries was predominantly a Presbyterian town and Presbyterian influence had been growing. By 1708, it was estimated that there were some 3,000 people in the Belfast Presbyterian congregation before its division into two congregations.[31] This dominance was, however, a relatively recent phenomenon. While Belfast had been seized by Scottish Covenanting forces in the 1640s their influence had not lasted and as Scottish Presbyterian organization spread over Ulster in the 1650s it did not stretch further south than Carnmoney. The Commonwealth minister in the town, Essex Digby, was both an episcopalian and a nephew of Lady Donegall. Donegall control over the town held fast and evidenced a determination to ensure that radical Scottish Presbyterianism did not infiltrate the area.[32] If anything, the Donegalls preferred the more moderate English style of Presbyterianism and it was only slowly that a Scottish Presbyterian community developed in the town, reflecting the increase in Scottish settlement in the late seventeenth century. A congregation was formed by the 1670s, possibly under Lady Donegall's influence, although it may not have been until the 1690s that a

---

27 Young (ed.), *Town book*, pp 38–9. 28 PRONI, D3095/B/2/5; NAI, Prerogative will book, 1664–84, ff 59, 293v. 29 Young (ed.), *Town book*, pp 49, 55, 60, 67, 72, 73–4, 78, 133–4, 168. 30 Gillespie, *Early Belfast*, p. 93. 31 *Records of the General Synod of Ulster from 1691 to 1820* (3 vols, Belfast, 1890), i, p. 146. 32 Gillespie, *Early Belfast*, pp 79–81.

church was built on a site at Rosemary Street. The church expanded rapidly after 1690. By 1708 it was said that the recently constructed meeting house was too small and it was claimed that 120 Presbyterian families in Belfast could not attend services because of the restricted space available.[33] The congregation was divided, and by 1722 there were three Presbyterian congregations, all on the Rosemary Street site. According to a list of 'catechisable persons' produced by the third Presbyterian congregation in 1726, there were some 1,313 individuals, not including children, in that congregation alone.[34] The most distinctive feature of these congregations was that, like the Church of Ireland parish, they were highly organized. Local kirk sessions exercised oversight over behaviour, administered poor relief and could, if necessary, be powerful forces for order or disruption within the town.[35]

Not only did Presbyterians dominate Belfast numerically, they also controlled much of its wealth. As the Presbyterian minister James Kirkpatrick put it in 1713 'there are indeed very few in Belfast of the communion of the established church who are considerable dealers'. There were a few 'of the best station in town' but most 'follow the handicraft trades of tobacco spinners, tailors, shoemakers, smiths, saddlers, glovers, butchers, carpenters etc'. As Kirkpatrick realized, this was a relatively recent development. Before the 1690s the Church of Ireland had been more powerful among the mercantile community but by 1713 some notable members were dead, others had moved to estates outside the town and the children of others had entered the professions.[36] Unusually, the Presbyterian merchant community had been able to translate its economic power into political influence. Between 1689 and 1704 three-quarters of the burgesses elected in Belfast were Presbyterians compared with less than a third between 1660 and 1688.[37] This reflected both the growing power of the Presbyterian mercantile community after 1690 and the accommodating attitude of the earl of Donegall, who was required to approve such elections. While Donegall was certainly irenical in his outlook he may also have had an eye towards developments in Scotland, particularly Glasgow, with which many Belfast merchants had strong trading connections. There in the 1690s the control of the landlord, the archbishop of Glasgow, had been broken by the Presbyterian burgesses of the town. While it was unlikely that those events could be re-enacted in Belfast, it was prudent that Donegall engage in some form of power sharing.[38] Perhaps inevitably this combination of economic and political power in a confessional state placed the Presbyterians in a position that was difficult to maintain.

33 *Records of the General Synod of Ulster*, i, p. 146.   34 PRONI, MIC 1P/7/2.   35 Gillespie, 'Making Belfast', pp 141–2.   36 Kirkpatrick, *Historical essay*, pp 435, 436. For the merchant community see Jean Agnew, *Belfast merchant families in the seventeenth century* (Dublin, 1996).   37 Agnew, *Belfast merchant families*, pp 80, 92.   38 T.M. Devine and Gordon Jackson, *Glasgow: volume 1, beginnings to 1830* (Manchester, 1995), pp 63–9.

II

While life in late seventeenth-century Belfast was marked by limited confessional diversity there was little in the way of confessional conflict either. In other late seventeenth-century Ulster towns, such as Derry, conflict between the Presbyterian population of the town and its landlord, the Irish Society, was common and this was manifest in the politics of the Corporation.[39] Part of the reason for that lack of conflict in Belfast lay with the Chichesters. While the family were members of the Church of Ireland they were at the godlier end of the spectrum. Letitia, the wife of the first earl of Donegall, for instance, was a Presbyterian and also attended the Independent church of Thomas Harrison in Dublin in the 1670s and had both Independent and Presbyterian chaplains. She had certainly influenced the appointment of Presbyterian ministers in Belfast and the first minister in the late 1670s, the English Presbyterian William Keyes, was her domestic chaplain and his ministry in Belfast was certainly financially underpinned by this position. It may also have been her influence that ensured the Limerick English Presbyterian minister from the 1650s, Claudius Gilbert, was appointed vicar of Belfast at the Restoration. In many ways Gilbert's views echoed those of the Donegalls: a strong sense of the need for order, and for the state to enforce that order, combined with a godly approach to religious duty.[40] Catherine, the countess of Donegall at the time of the 1707 disputes in the town, was also steeped in the godly tradition being the daughter of the Presbyterian royalist Arthur Forbes, first earl of Granard, who had been instrumental in securing a royal subsidy, the *regium donum*, for Irish Presbyterians in 1672. Her mother had also been a Presbyterian who had attended Capel Street meeting house in Dublin. One practical indication of how the Donegalls might protect Belfast from tensions came in 1704 when the passage of a test act threatened to exclude Dissenters from public life. In Belfast, presided over by a Presbyterian sovereign, David Butle, the act was ignored and although Butle did resign he was replaced by a conforming sovereign, George McCartney, elected with Presbyterian support.[41] Chichester clearly supported their actions, or at least did not intervene. Even in 1705 when the lord lieutenant, the duke of Ormond, visited Belfast he was met by the conformist sovereign but a largely Presbyterian Corporation who in their address described their loyalty to 'the crown of England and the succession by law established' and their 'dutiful affection' to the duke himself, despite the fact that most were in breach of the

39 David Hayton, 'Exclusion, conformity and parliamentary representation: the impact of the sacramental test on Irish dissenting politics' in Kevin Herlihy (ed.), *The politics of Irish dissent, 1650–1800* (Dublin, 1997), pp 60–3.   40 Phil Kilroy, *Protestant dissent and controversy in Ireland, 1660–1714* (Cork, 1994), pp 40, 42, 45, 55 note, 121; PRONI, D1759/A/2, pp 87, 123, 130, 134.   41 Hayton, 'Exclusion, conformity and parliamentary representation', pp 63–4.

1704 act.[42] Such a position could only have been possible with the active support of Donegall for the Corporation's position. In part this may have been based on good personal relationships. For example, John McBride, the minister of the Belfast Presbyterian church, and the earl of Donegall were on good terms despite McBride's trenchant views on Presbyterianism. They were certainly on book borrowing and lending terms and in 1704, when McBride refused to take the abjuration oath, James Kirkpatrick commented that 'that great and noble patriot my Lord Donegall offered to be bound for Mr McBride to the full value of his estate'.[43] Such accommodations were necessary in a world in which economic power needed to align with political influence to ensure that the polity of Belfast could function on a day-to-day basis.

During the second half of the first decade of the eighteenth century the accommodations that had produced confessional tolerance came under stress from a number of sources from without and within confessional communities. Tensions from without are best seen is a series of three intertwined, yet distinct, events that historians have tended to conflate into one narrative that culminated in parliamentary proceedings in 1707. The first of these three intertwined strands revolved around the problem of payment for the vicar of Belfast. Payment of clergy in urban areas, where the use of tithes was not viable, was a contentious subject. An act of 1665 had gone some way to solving the problem in some corporate towns by providing a property tax of 12*d*. in the £ payable annually on a valuation of houses approved by the privy council. The tax was collected by the churchwardens, who had powers of distress, and was paid to the incumbent quarterly. Churchwardens who neglected their duty could be fined and imprisoned for a month.[44] Belfast was not included in this act and the arrangements for paying the incumbent were clearly *ad hoc* but by 1702 the vicar, James Echlin, had succeeded in having a commission of valuation appointed to extend the provisions of the 1665 act to Belfast as a way of solving some of his financial problems.[45] This immediately produced a reaction as many in the town refused to pay the house money. Some attempt appears to have been made at a compromise in February 1703, at which time Echlin was offered £100 or £120, but this came to nothing.[46] The most immediate sign of opposition was the appearance in Belfast of a printed handbill in 1703 attacking the Corporation's stance on house money. While this is the only surviving printed sheet the matter gen-

---

42 Young (ed.), *Town book*, p. 199. The speech is dated 1707 in the town book but this cannot be correct since Lord Donegall, who was killed in April 1706, was said to be alive. It most likely dates to April 1705 when Ormond was on progress to Ulster, see *Cal. S.P. Dom., 1704–5*, pp 235, 242, 248, 260.   43 Kirkpatrick, *Historical essay*, pp 474, 526; Tisdall, *Conduct*, p. 68.   44 17&18 Chas II c.7.   45 Benn, *History*, pp 380–1.   46 PRONI, D1449/13/1, pp 65, 66. The yield under the 1666 act for Belfast was estimated to be £180; see Kirkpatrick, *Historical essay*, p. 484. McBride's stipend as Presbyterian minister was said to be £160 a year.

erated other handbills. James Kirkpatrick referred to a 'printed half sheet' and a formal printed 'State of the case' that were circulating at the time of a law case in 1707, suggesting that this was a dispute that generated some heat.[47] The 1703 printed broadsheet coupled trade with house money by alleging that the Corporation of Belfast had charged a 'ship money' tax or quayage of 2d. per ton of cargo landed on the quay as well as raising money to oppose the charging of house money by the Church of Ireland incumbent. Such money was raised on presentments that were not made available and those failing to contribute towards the fund for opposing the house money had their goods distrained. The Corporation duly copied the document into the town book.[48] However, they were far from happy and the Presbyterian sovereign, David Butle, dismissed the document as 'a false ridiculous paper', claiming that the quayage was voluntary and that no money had been raised to oppose the minister but there had been a voluntary contribution that was paid by both members of the established church and Dissenters.[49] In short, according to the Corporation, this was a non-sectarian debate over the workings of trade that had been drawn into the world of religion by the vicar.

In the midst of this debate Echlin died, probably in 1704, and was replaced as vicar of Belfast by William Tisdall. Tisdall's father had been mayor and sheriff of the Donegall's other power base at Carrickfergus and it is through this Donegall connection that he probably acquired the living of Belfast. However, he was ill-suited to the position. He was a high church Tory who had a hatred of Presbyterians. Part of this was certainly ideological but he had also seen something of the dangers of Presbyterian dominance. In 1689, for instance, his father had become involved (and possibly wounded) in an attempt to collect Lord Donegall's rent from a group of intransigent Presbyterians at Six Mile Water, near Templepatrick.[50] Tisdall took the matter to law on the grounds that the inhabitants 'resolutely refuse to pay' his house money. He appealed to Convocation in February of 1705 for financial support. He argued that this could be a test case for other corporations and that his own resources could not compete with a 'large and rich corporation [that] is united and positively resolved to carry on the said suit by a common purse'. The bishops in Convocation resolved to support him as best they could.[51] The case was heard at Michaelmas 1706. The Corporation of Belfast relied on the argument that the town of Belfast was not a parish of itself but

---

47 PRONI, DIO4/5/3/28; copy in Public Records Office of Northern Ireland, T 1075/6, pp 57–8; Kirkpatrick, *Historical essay*, p. 484.   48 Young (ed.), *Town book*, p. 197. The edition of the Corporation book suggests that the parliamentary resolutions of 1707, discussed below, were copied together with the 1703 handbill whereas they are on separate pages of the original book; see PRONI, MIC 556, p. 765. A levy of 1d. was agreed in 1696: Young (ed.), *Town book*, p. 189.   49 PRONI, D1449/13/1, p. 67.   50 Tisdall, *Conduct*, p. 16; Kirkpatrick, *Historical essay*, pp 416–18.   51 Gerald Bray (ed.), *Records of Convocation xvii: Ireland, 1690–1869, part 1* (Woodbridge, 2006), pp 119–20, 133, 213.

part of the larger parish of Shankill, which had tithes and glebe land, so that the act dealing only with corporate towns that were parishes without tithes or glebe land did not apply. This argument carried the day and Tisdall lost his case.[52] His defeat in the courts did not end the matter. In January 1707 he noted that the Belfast Corporation was 'very exalted' at the victory but Tisdall was still mulling over his legal opinions. He sent his opinions to Archbishop King and seems to have had advice from King (who was experienced in such matters) in February on the conduct of a law suit.[53] In December 1706 Tisdall had petitioned the privy council and had sought to have the judgment of the court overturned. The privy council duly referred the matter to a committee that seems to have done nothing. However, on 22 October the House of Commons demanded that all MPs who were privy councillors were to ask the lord lieutenant to direct that Tisdall's petition 'relating to the town of Belfast' should be sent to the Commons. This was duly done on 25 October but with dark rumblings that the meddling of the council in the matters of corporations was 'arbitrary, illegal and [of] dangerous consequence to the parliamentary constitution of this kingdom'. On 27 October, both the Lords and the Commons began to consider the petition but three days later parliament was prorogued and no further action was taken.[54]

The second strand of events that created problems in Belfast was the death of the town's MP, William Cairnes. An election ensued and Samuel Ogle was declared elected, taking his seat and swearing the required oaths on 22 September 1707. A week later the defeated candidate, Alexander Cairnes, petitioned parliament to overturn the election on the grounds that he had been elected but that the sovereign of Belfast, George MacCartney, had returned Ogle. On 11 October, the town clerk of Belfast was ordered to produce to parliament the charter of Belfast, the cess book, the by-laws, the presentments and other public documents produced since 1 May 1704 when the test act took effect. All this was duly considered and on 18 October 1707 parliament produced a report that confirmed Ogle in the seat and the documents were returned to Belfast on 30 October.[55] The problems at issue here were not straightforward and revolved around the numbers of people entitled to vote in Belfast.[56] The confessional allegiance of the candidates was not a significant variable. William Cairnes, the late MP for Belfast, had been a Presbyterian although he was an occasional conformist and may have taken the sacramental test. Of the two contenders for the seat, William's brother, Alexander, was also a deeply committed Presbyterian and Samuel Ogle, while

[52] Kirkpatrick, *Historical essay*, pp 484–5; Tisdall, *Conduct*, pp 42–5.   [53] TCD, MS 1995–2008 /1239; MS 750/3/2/86.   [54] *Journals of the house of commons in the kingdom of Ireland* (19 vols, Dublin, 1796–1800), 2, pt 1, pp 559, 561, 563; *Journal of the house of lords [of Ireland]* (8 vols, Dublin, 1779–1800), 2, p. 229.   [55] *Journals of the house of commons ... Ireland*, 2, pt 1, pp 535, 536, 544, 551–2, 567.   [56] Agnew, *Belfast merchant families*, pp 99–101, describes the issues.

a former MP for Berwick-upon-Tweed in the London parliament, a supporter of the Whig administration and an Irish revenue official, was also a Presbyterian and it was thought that he would support a repeal of the sacramental test.[57] At least one contemporary regarded the election petition as a personal attack by Lady Donegall on the MacCartney interest in Belfast Corporation since MacCartney had been Ogle's main supporter and the manager of his campaign. The arch-Tory Robert Johnson, one of the barons of the exchequer, interpreted the result of the election petition and the ongoing complaints by the countess of Donegall as the countess acting 'in her own right and her son's' to prevent MacCartney's 'great power over the Corporation to the prejudice of the countess dowager and the young earl'.[58] There is truth in this analysis. However, of the three parliamentary disputes that involved Belfast in 1707 this was probably the least significant and whatever animosity may have existed between MacCartney and the Donegalls over electoral politics seems to have dissipated quickly. The failure of the countess of Donegall's later parliamentary petition against MacCartney, together with the departure of the countess to England in 1708 after the burning of Belfast Castle, brought those tensions to an end.

The third strand of events that increased tensions in Belfast was a petition presented to parliament by the countess of Donegall, again acting on behalf of her infant son, against the sovereign of Belfast, George MacCartney, on 9 October 1707 accusing him of 'several unwarrantable and illegal practices'. Evidence was duly called on 11 October and MacCartney himself appeared on 24 October. According to the Presbyterian minister James Kirkpatrick, MacCartney was questioned for eight to ten hours and some thirty to forty witnesses were called, some from Belfast, but that he had 'fully acquitted himself in the matters alleged against him'. It seemed that the challenge was over and MacCartney had won. This was certainly the view of contemporaries. William Tisdall, commenting from the high church Tory perspective, noted 'that affair was drop'd and miscarried in [the] house I know not'. The Presbyterian Kirkpatrick was clear that MacCartney 'was cleared by vote of the house' and copied out the relevant extract from the Commons journals to prove it. However, despite this supposed resolution of the matter, another document seems to have been tabled and parliamentary debate on the subject continued on 27 October and on 28 October parliament gave judgment.[59]

---

[57] Edith Mary Johnston-Liik, *History of the Irish parliament* (6 vols, Belfast, 2002), 3, pp 357–8; 359, 5, pp 394–5; H.C. Lawlor, *A history of the family of Cairnes or Cairns* (London, 1906), pp 82–6. On Ogle's English background: Eveline Cruickshanks, Stuart Handley and D.W. Hayton, *History of parliament: the house of commons, 1690–1715* (5 vols, Cambridge, 2002), 5, pp 6–9. [58] HMC, *Report on the manuscripts of the marquess of Ormonde* (new series, 8 vols, London, 1902–20), 8, pp 312–13; Agnew, *Belfast merchant families*, pp 100–1. [59] *Journals of the house of commons ... Ireland*, 2, pt 1, pp 542, 544, 558, 560, 563, 564; *Lords, jn Ire.*, 2, p. 217; Tisdall, *Conduct*, p. 31; Kirkpatrick, *Historical essay*, p. 465.

What exactly parliament gave judgment on is not clear. Since the complaints of the countess of Donegall had been dismissed on 24 October it cannot have been those. It is possible to infer what may have transpired from the judgment of 28 October. There were three grounds that related to 'unwarranted and illegal practices'. The first was that the Belfast burgesses were obliged under the terms of the 1704 act to receive the sacrament to hold office. Unusually, this was put to a vote and passed by sixty-five votes to fifty-three. The second judgment was that the office held by a burgess who had not fulfilled the terms of the act was vacant, and the third was that the taking of 2*d*. per ton by the Corporation of Belfast from every ship coming to quay 'is arbitrary and illegal'. The Corporation took due note and entered the judgment in the Corporation book.[60]

If these judgments were not the result of the Countess of Donegall's petition against MacCartney, and he is nowhere mentioned in them, then the questions must have been introduced into parliament on the back of the failure of the election petition. One possibility is that they were agreed by the countess and others as a way to solve problems that both had in the town. The issue of charging ships for the use of the quay at Belfast was a problem that went back some time and had surfaced most recently in 1703 when it was intertwined with the debate over house money. However, this dispute had much deeper roots about the financing of the Corporation and the rights of the Donegalls to impose duties in their town. Under the 1613 charter the Corporation had not been provided with any source of finance, apart from limited income from the markets, to carry out their duties including the development of the port. In 1671, the proposals for a new charter included provision for the levying of quayage but this was never implemented. Perhaps in response to this Lord Donegall granted to the sovereign the post of water bailiff that could be farmed and hence produce an income to improve the port. The quay was enlarged in 1671 and a second was built by 1696.[61] Grants of such offices reduced the authority and income of the Donegalls and were rarely made. It is hardly surprising that it should be one of the issues that emerged when Belfast society came under pressure with disputes over the quayage linked to house money in 1703. The decision of 1707 clearly strengthened the Donegalls' hand in controlling the finances of the town and ensuring that the Corporation depended on them.

The parliamentary petition over the quayage in 1707 did not end the matter since the financial viability of the Corporation rested on this issue. In April 1709, the MP for Belfast, Samuel Ogle, and his patron, George MacCartney, together with two others from the town were appointed by the Corporation to apply to parliament for an act permitting them to charge a levy on ships landing at Belfast in order to fund the cleaning of the dock and

60 Young (ed.), *Town book*, p. 197. **61** Young (ed.), *Town book*, pp 119, 120–8.

repairs to the quay. In May 1709, leave was given to introduce the legislation into Commons and within a fortnight it was sent to the lord lieutenant but failed to pass the privy council. The privy council seems to have reworked the document, increasing the power of the Donegalls by allowing them to nominate and supervise the burgess who would collect and account for the money. The Corporation clearly did not like the changes and offered arguments against them. These failed to impress and the bill foundered, copper-fastening the Donegalls' rights over the port of Belfast and its income.[62]

If the dispute over quayage adjudicated on by parliament in 1707 originated with the countess of Donegall then the demand to enforce the 1704 test probably did not. The Donegalls were well disposed to Presbyterians and had no interest in excluding them from the Corporation on religious grounds alone, as the election of the Presbyterian Ogle with Donegall support in 1707 demonstrated. The test provision in the 1707 judgment, therefore, may have originated elsewhere. Since the terms of the 1704 act as it had been applied to Belfast had been clarified in the Cairnes election petition case, it is uncertain what this sort of judgment could have added to the matter. It is possible that those in the House of Commons who favoured a relaxation of the test act, such as Belfast's MP Ogle, may have been using the episode to see what support they had for this measure. Another source for the petition may have been a discontented William Tisdall who lobbied the countess but yet another may have been MacCartney himself. Certainly according to Tisdall it was MacCartney, rather than the countess, who hastened back to Belfast and on 29 November, a month after the judgment, summoned a meeting of the Corporation to remove the Presbyterian burgesses.[63] What MacCartney may have had to gain from a confirmation of the 1704 act is not immediately clear. MacCartney was a member of the Church of Ireland but was a strident Whig who had supported Presbyterian candidates for parliament and had been supported by Presbyterians as sovereign of Belfast. One possibility is that by using the 1704 act to control those who might be appointed burgesses the electorate would be easier to manage in future parliamentary elections in which he might well be a candidate, as was the case after 1715. However, this can be mere speculation.

Confessional tensions from within are more difficult to chart than the pressures applied to religious groups from without. In 1708, the conflicts within Belfast Presbyterianism became clear. In 1703, the Presbyterian minister of Belfast, John McBride, had refused to take the oath abjuring the Stuarts and in consequence had fled to Glasgow where that oath was not required. He visited Belfast briefly in 1704, but then returned to Glasgow until 1708. Despite his absence, a new minister was not appointed to the

---

62 Young (ed.), *Town book*, pp 200–10; *Journals of the house of commons ... Ireland*, 2, pt 1, pp 583, 587, 589, 592.   63 Tisdall, *Conduct*, p. 31; Young (ed.), *Town book*, p. 236.

Presbyterian congregation. By 1706, there was clearly discontent about this and the congregation petitioned the synod to have James Kirkpatrick, minister of Templepatrick, moved to Belfast. Nothing was done and temporary ministers continued to supply the church. Indeed, there seems to have been talk of a secession and the formation of a new congregation since in his will of 1706 the Presbyterian merchant James Anderson left £20 towards the building of a new meetinghouse.[64] Tempers frayed over McBride's behaviour and it was later reported that in 1707 Kirkpatrick was said to have told one of the elders that McBride was 'imperious, censorious, *usurpaverit, superbus, malim absenti, quam ambisse*'.[65] Again in a conversation between the Belfast doctor and one of the leaders of the eventual split within the Belfast congregation, Victor Ferguson, and the Anglican Westenra Waring, Ferguson was said to have blamed McBride for introducing splits into Presbyterianism over the oath.[66] By 1708 some of McBride's congregation were ready to split. What may have added fuel to the discussions was the calling out of militia in May 1708 in the wake of the failed Jacobite invasion. In Belfast ninety individuals mustered of whom twenty-six refused to take the required oaths.[67] Clearly this raised a series of questions about the place of Presbyterians in the world of Belfast since militia service was a key test of participation in the local political system. McBride's refusal to take the abjuration oath had certainly raised questions about such matters in the minds of the authorities and this may have provoked hostility towards him of the kind expressed by Ferguson. At the General Synod on 1 June a group of Belfast elders with a petition 'subscribed by many hands' asked to set up a new congregation in Belfast. McBride disputed the petition and quibbled about the practical arrangements concerning his stipend and accommodation. Despite all this, the synod agreed on 1 June that the congregation could be divided. The decision produced an explosive result. Since the early 1690s the General Synod had met annually in June and always at Antrim. However, on 8 September, following the decision to split the congregation, what was clearly an emergency synod met in Belfast. Two factions, the followers of McBride and those of Kirkpatrick, were at loggerheads and the synod needed to effect some form of peace that both groups professed to want. The synod received petition and counter petition and moved 'for healing those rents in the Belfast congregation'. Much of the debate was about practical matters such as transfer of rights to seats and the limitation to be placed on fund-raising by the new congregation as well as the problem of surplus stipends. In the end, by means of the stick of the

---

64 NAI, Prerogative Will Book, 1704–8, ff 24–5.   65 *Records of the General Synod of Ulster*, 1, pp 110, 116, 148–9.   66 Tisdall, *Conduct*, p. 80. Ferguson subsequently challenged Waring's account of events but not his disapproval of McBride; see Kirkpatrick, *Historical essay*, pp 529–30.   67 Tisdall, *Conduct*, pp 37–8; Kirkpatrick, *Historical essay*, pp 466–76.

synod's authority and the carrot of arbitration, an arrangement was reached with a tidying up of outstanding matters at the following year's synod.[68] McBride returned to the remains of his congregation in 1708. While the episode seems to have had relatively little long-term effect it demonstrates the violence and speed with which factional politics could erupt within Belfast Presbyterianism and, given the dominance of that confession in the town, it would clearly have had a destabilizing effect on the wider corporate community of Belfast.

By themselves each of these developments – electoral politics, house money for the Church of Ireland clergy, the economics of the port, and the attack on the sovereign by Lady Donegall, as well as the internal disputes within Presbyterianism – might not have been significant but together they placed significant strains on Belfast society. Each dispute reinforced the others and inevitably created problems for urban government. They also raised wider questions about loyalty both to the state as a whole and to the corporate sense of Belfast itself. If the first decade of the eighteenth century created a framework for confessional relations in Belfast, then the working out of those new relationships is revealed in a series of pamphlets in the second decade of the century. In 1709, William Tisdall, the vicar of Belfast, took up his pen to attack Presbyterians in his *A sample of true-blew Presbyterian loyalty* (Dublin, 1709). He followed this with *The conduct of the dissenters of Ireland, with respect both to church and state* (Dublin, 1712) and *A seasonable enquiry into that most dangerous political principle of the kirk in power* (Dublin, 1713). One pamphlet might have been ignored but three could not be. Not surprisingly Tisdall's accusations of disloyalty among Presbyterians drew replies from both John McBride, minister of First Belfast, in his *A sample of jet-black prelatick calumny* (Glasgow, 1713), which seems quickly to have gone through three editions, and the minister of Second Belfast, James Kirkpatrick, in his massive *An historical essay upon the loyalty of Presbyterians in Great Britain and Ireland* ([Belfast], 1713). This group of pamphlets had two important characteristics. First, the terms of the debate were very different to the previous major debate between Presbyterians and the Church of Ireland, that between William King, bishop of Derry, Joseph Boyse, Presbyterian minister in Dublin, and Robert Craghead, Presbyterian minister in Derry. That earlier debate had focused mainly on well-established controversial issues of worship, dealing with bodily gestures, such as kneeling at communion or the sign of the cross (in 1636 these were part of a dispute between the bishop of Down and the Presbyterian ministers when they met at Belfast),[69] as well as the use of the ring at marriage and the nature of singing in church.[70] Indeed,

---

68 *Records of the General Synod of Ulster*, 1, pp 143–4, 145–6, 150, 159–61, 164–6, 178–9.
69 J.S. Reid, *History of the Presbyterian church in Ireland* (3 vols, Belfast, 1867), 1, pp 523–42.   70 For a summary, see Kilroy, *Protestant dissent*, pp 175–87.

John McBride's pamphlet *A vindication of marriage* ([Dublin?], 1702) might well be seen as a coda to that debate. By the 1710s, McBride, Kirkpatrick and Tisdall were more concerned with questions of loyalty than statements of belonging through participation in liturgy. Questions of loyalty inevitably operated on a number of levels. While the primary debate was about national loyalty, framed in the light of attempts by Presbyterians to break out of their traditional Ulster enclave and establish new congregations at Drogheda, Co. Louth, and Belturbet, Co. Cavan, in 1708 and 1712, it also engaged with local loyalties and it is no coincidence that all three participants in this debate were Belfast clergy. This meant that their local experience of the debates in the first decade of eighteenth-century Belfast became part of a much wider discussion but also shaped that wider debate to reflect on local experiences. The examples of 'disloyalty' that Tisdall produced and Kirkpatrick tried to refute all reflected as much of the loyalty of the Presbyterians to the corporate sense of Belfast as to any national body. The debate over house money and quayage examined by both men, for instance, was held by Tisdall to be an example of the Presbyterian Corporation acting 'contrary to the law' but they also had no 'interest' in the town and hence lacked corporate loyalty. According to Tisdall the experience of the Jacobite Corporation with its Presbyterians was typical: 'no sooner had they obtained a majority that they acted like Tyrants with respect to the minority of conforming brethren'. The failure of the Belfast Presbyterians to take their oath at the array of the militia in 1708 likewise demonstrated their unwillingness to be part of the corporate sense of the town by participating in its defence.[71] By contrast, Kirkpatrick replied that Presbyterians were not tyrants and were part of the corporate life, or as he put it in another context 'civil society', of Belfast.[72] Freemen of Belfast were part of this world, he claimed, not because they were part of a Presbyterian cabal but because each of them was 'an inhabitant of the place and would comply with the rules and charter and laws of the Corporation' and because 'men [are] chosen to offices according to their fitness' and not by their confessional allegiance. Hence Presbyterians, counter to Tisdall's assertions, did not disrupt the economic good of the town in the light of sectional interests by monopolizing trade or apprenticeships.[73] These were all local issues about the good government of their own place and loyalty to that government as expressed in the charter. The broader argument about national loyalty was grounded in such local loyalties to the corporate sense of Belfast. That such an argument was on the minds of the Belfast clergy in the 1710s was the result of the sort of tensions in confessional and corporate loyalty that the first decade of the eighteenth century had generated.

---

71 Tisdall, *Conduct*, p. 23. 72 James Kirkpatrick, *God's dominions over kings and other magistrates: a thanksgiving sermon preached in Belfast, October 20 1714* (Belfast, 1714), pp 5,12. 73 Kirkpatrick, *Historical essay*, pp 422, 433, 439.

III

By the beginning of the 1720s much of the heat of the controversies in Belfast politics had abated. In part, the Toleration Act of 1719 had taken some of the impetus for debate out of the situation. Some of the main Belfast protagonists had died or lost interest. John McBride, the minister of First Belfast, died in 1718, and William Tisdall's enthusiasm for pamphleteering waned, his last contribution to the debate over the sacramental test being in 1715. James Kirkpatrick, however, remained in the town as minister of the Second Belfast Presbyterian church. In February 1724 Kirkpatrick, together with the minister of First Belfast, Samuel Haliday, wrote to the minister of the newly established and highly orthodox Third Belfast congregation, Charles Masterson, stating their intention to participate in the communion service being organized by Third Belfast. Masterson refused permission since this would be a 'matter of stumbling and offence' to other communicants.[74] The issue at stake was the requirement by the Synod of Ulster in 1720 that all ministers should subscribe the Westminster Confession. In part this was a political development made necessary by the need to define orthodoxy after the Toleration Act but it was also a question of conscience. Some saw subscription as a guarantor of orthodoxy in the light of accusations of Arianism against a Dublin minister, Thomas Emlyn, while others thought that it infringed on their liberty by forcing them to subscribe to a particular set of principles whether or not they agreed with them.[75] The resulting subscription controversy split Ulster Presbyterianism through the 1720s. The events of 1724 were not the first manifestation of the problem in Belfast since Haliday had refused to subscribe the Confession when he became minister of First Belfast in 1721 but the non-subscribers had enough influence to allow such a difference to be maintained. The events of 1724 moved the dispute to a new level by 'making arbitrary enclosures about the table of our common Lord and turning his instituted seal of our unity and peace into a woeful engine of division and discord'. The refusal of inter-communion was not simply a matter that could be contained but a breach that 'must effectually destroy the peace not only of this church only, but of all Christian churches'.[76] This was a debate of a different character to those that preceded them about the corporate sense of Belfast, the relationship of the inhabitants of Belfast to their structures of government and the loyalty of those who lived there to the town

---

[74] James Kirkpatrick, *A scripture plea against a fatal rupture and breach of Christian communion amongst Presbyterians in the north of Ireland* (Belfast, 1724), pp v–vii.   [75] McBride, *Scripture politics*, pp 43–52; A.W. Godfrey Brown, 'A theological interpretation of the first subscription controversy (1719–28)' in J.L.M. Haire et al. (eds), *Challenge and conflict: essays in Irish Presbyterian history and doctrine* (Belfast, 1981), pp 28–45.   [76] Kirkpatrick, *A scripture plea*, p. iv.

and the wider state. The debates among Presbyterians from the 1720s were much more wide-ranging and deep-seated: they were now about the very fabric of Presbyterian identity and, as Kirkpatrick put it, 'arbitrary enclosures about the table of our common Lord'.[77] Such complex questions of theological orthodoxy had implications far beyond the town of Belfast and would be much less easily solved than the local problems of the opening decades of the eighteenth century.

---

77 Kirkpatrick, *A scripture plea*, p. iv.

Oaths and oath-taking: the civic experience in Dublin, 1660–1774

JACQUELINE HILL

The seventeenth and eighteenth centuries in Britain and Ireland witnessed a considerable increase in the range of contexts in which oaths were required to be administered. Whereas in modern times oaths are associated chiefly with judicial proceedings, during the period in question they were also deemed appropriate in a variety of other fields, including on occasions of swearing dynastic allegiance; acknowledging the royal supremacy over the church; taking up office; and pledging fiscal probity. Along with collegiate bodies and a growing range of public service positions, corporate bodies were particularly affected by the phenomenon. Focusing primarily on civic life in Dublin, this essay will consider the proliferation of oath-taking in the period in question, the contexts in which this proliferation took place, and the significance of oath-taking for inter-denominational relations in the capital city. Two main periods will be considered: first the Restoration era, and then the Williamite, later Stuart and early-to-mid Hanoverian periods, when the penal laws were imposed and remained substantially intact. It will be argued that although by the end of the period oath-taking had never been so widespread, the phenomenon contained various internal contradictions, which would, many decades later, lead to the first legislative restrictions on the oath-taking culture.

Before beginning this discussion, it may be useful to note what distinguished an oath from other forms of solemn or formal engagement. Evidence for oath-taking can be found in England as early as Anglo-Saxon times, while Celtic peoples were also accustomed to swear oaths by their tribal gods.[1] The key feature was that oaths involved a declaration that called on God to witness the solemnity and truthfulness of what was being attested to, and any commitment entered into by oath was considered to be binding. The assumption (still generally prevalent during the period under consideration) was that the oath-taker believed in a supreme being who would punish – either immediately or at some later date – any violation of the oath.[2] In courts of justice, the prospect of divine punishment alone was not deemed to constitute a sufficient deterrent: cases of false swearing ('perjury') that came to light were punishable by law.

---

[1] F.W. Maitland, *The constitutional history of England* (Cambridge, 1908), pp 115–18: Marie-Louise Sjoestedt, *Gods and heroes of the Celts* (trans. Myles Dillon) (Berkeley, CA, 1982), p. 12. [2] For an insightful analysis of the theoretical basis of swearing oaths, see Jonathan Gray, *Oaths and the English Reformation* (Cambridge, 2013), ch. 1.

1660-90

It is striking that one of the earliest decisions taken by Dublin Corporation following the restoration of Charles II in 1660 was to revive a custom concerning the admission of new freemen, which had apparently fallen into disuse during the Cromwellian era. At its midsummer assembly in 1660 the Corporation drew attention to one of 'the aunciant and laudable customes of this cittie [whereby] freemen were to be sworne kneelinge before the Maior and Sheriffes of the said cittie'. It was thereupon agreed

> that everie person that shalbe sworne a freeman of this cittie doe and shall ... come with his armes fixed, and upon his takeinge the oath of a freeman, take the same kneelinge, and that the clarke of the Tholsell do give unto the partie so sworne a coppie of his oath, taking for the said coppie sixpence onelie.[3]

The presence of an air of ceremony and formality to surround the business of oath-taking was demonstrated the following year, when note was taken of the expenses incurred 'uppon Oxmanton greene in entertayning the lords justices and council on the day that the militia of this cittie marched out in order to the takeinge of the oaths of allegiance and supremacie'.[4] On the latter occasion, oaths were being taken in the presence of the king's immediate representatives. More commonly, oaths (of civic office, and also state oaths) were administered by the lord mayor. Formal authority for the lord mayor to administer such oaths was set out in Lord Berkeley's rules for Dublin Corporation in 1671.[5]

What sorts of oaths were administered in this period, and what kinds of people would have taken them? With the exception of quarter brothers (discussed below), freemen constituted the lowest tier in the hierarchy of members of the corporation. Yet as the quotation above indicates, even freemen were expected to be in a position to expend 6*d*. on obtaining a copy of their oath. Clearly, therefore, they were not drawn from the poorest section of society: typically they would be artisans who had served an apprenticeship (or were the offspring of a freeman) and were proceeding to the status of self-employed. Higher officials would more usually come from the ranks of the merchants and more substantial master craftsmen. As for the nature of oaths, some indication of the range of civic oaths is indicated by those recorded in the Dublin Chain Book. The earliest part of this book dates back to the fourteenth century, but certain oaths have clearly been added later, with reference

---

[3] John T. and R.M. Gilbert (eds), *Calendar of ancient records of Dublin* (19 vols, Dublin, 1889–1944) (hereafter *CARD*), 4, p. 188.   [4] *CARD*, 4, p. 208.   [5] Dublin City Archives (DCA), Monday Book, 1658–1712, MR/18, ff 57A–60A; *CARD*, 5, pp 548–54.

to those current in the reigns of the first two Stuarts in the early seventeenth century.[6] They include oaths for the mayor (the title 'lord mayor' was not authorised until 1665)[7] as well as those for a freeman, alderman, coroner, sword-bearer, member of the city commons, city gaoler, marshal, attorney of the city court, and scavenger. Such oaths typically obliged the new incumbent to swear to be faithful to the king, and diligently to fulfil the duties associated with the office. Oaths pertaining to certain civic offices required the incumbent to promise to be 'obedyente' to the mayor and other city officials. They typically ended with some variation on the formula 'Soe helpe you God, and the holie contents of this booke', indicating the presence of a bible to reinforce the solemn and Christian nature of the event.[8]

Not all the oaths that civic officials were required to take related strictly to civic matters. As already noted, state oaths could also be required, including the oaths of supremacy and allegiance. During the 1660s, such requirements depended simply on civic by-laws[9] – owing to the relatively small numbers of members of the established church in Ireland, there was no Irish equivalent of the English Corporation Act of 1661 that confined civic offices to members of the established church. In 1671, government regulation of Irish corporations required that such oaths be taken not only by civic officials but also by freemen in general, but (for a variety of reasons) Lord Berkeley's rules proved controversial, and they were replaced in 1672 by Lord Essex's 'Rules ... for the better regulating the Corporation of the City of Dublin'. The new rules required the oaths to be taken only by the civic officials and members of the two houses of the Corporation rather than by freemen in general, and in keeping with Charles II's policy of indulgence towards Catholics, viceroys were subsequently empowered, at least for a time, to dispense with the oath of supremacy even for the officials.[10] (It is worth noting here that lord lieutenants in the late 1660s and early 1670s were under instructions from the king to try to divide the Catholic body by encouraging those who were prepared to sign the 'Irish Remonstrance', submitted to Charles II in 1661, which went far towards accepting that the king was independent of 'all foreign power', 'papal or princely'.)[11]

It is apparent that during the Restoration period the oath of supremacy still took the form in which it had been enacted early in Elizabeth's reign (it had been imposed on, among other officials, mayors and sheriffs of corporations); and this was also the case in England.[12] That oath required the oath-

6 *CARD*, 1, pp x-xi, 254–62. 7 Ibid., 4, pp 350–1. 8 For instance, freeman's oath, scavenger's oath, *CARD*, 1, pp 261–2; see also ibid., 1, p. 257. 9 *CARD*, 4, pp 198, 400, 425. 10 *CARD*, 5, p. 550; 1, pp 56–67, at pp 59–60; 5, p. xii; Jacqueline Hill, *From patriots to unionists: Dublin civic politics and Irish Protestant patriotism* (Oxford, 1997), pp 50–3. 11 Ronald Hutton, *Charles II: king of England, Scotland and Ireland* (Oxford, 1991), pp 267–8. 12 2 Eliz., c. 1 [Ire.] (1560); 1 Will. & Mary, c. 8 [Eng.] (1689); Colm Lennon, *The lords of Dublin in the age of Reformation* (Dublin, 1989), p. 132.

taker to swear that 'the [monarch] is the onely supreame governour of this realme ... as well in all spirituall or ecclesiasticall thinges or causes as temporall', and to 'utterly renounce and forsake all forreine jurisdictions, powers, superiorities and authorities.'[13] In the early part of Elizabeth's reign, when it still seemed that the prospect of moderate religious reform under what has been called 'tactful vice-regal control' might be realised, some (Catholic) civic officials in Dublin had been prepared to embrace 'church-papistry' – to take the oath of supremacy, and to attend services of the established church. But subsequently, the twin impacts of the Counter-Reformation and state attempts to enforce conformity helped to create a more polarized climate, and by the end of the century the phenomenon of recusancy in Ireland had become more marked in civic circles. Prospective mayors were less willing to take the supremacy oath, and this extended into the reigns of the first Stuarts.[14] In the Cromwellian period, the government had ruled that Catholics be excluded from walled towns, with the result that Dublin became for the first time a predominantly Protestant city. But the extent of Catholic exclusion had depended considerably on the attitudes of local Protestants. Dublin Corporation acted as early as 1653 to exclude Catholics from freedom, and the Corporation reiterated this policy soon after the Restoration: marginal notes in the assembly roll for January 1661 (erased during James II's reign) record 'Papists not to bee admitted to councell of cittie'; 'Noe Papist to bee free of this citty'.[15]

Nevertheless, in the climate of uncertainty about the Restoration government's commitment to the exclusion of Catholics from civic life, some Catholic freemen continued to trade in the city and even to serve as guild representatives on the city commons. Given that significant numbers of Catholics (laity as well as clergy) had been prepared to subscribe the Irish Remonstrance, it cannot be ruled out that, like their early Elizabethan predecessors, some Catholics may have been prepared to go a step further and take the oath of supremacy, and thus continue to take some legitimate part in civic life. At the first quarterly meeting of 1667 the Corporation decided that any representative who had not taken the oath of supremacy by the time of the next meeting should be struck off the city commons, but by Michaelmas no steps towards this end had been taken, and it was agreed to petition the lord lieutenant to empower civic officials to administer the oath.[16] However, four years later in 1671, complaints were raised about Catholic freemen who took 'Papist servants and apprentices', and it was again resolved that neither such apprentices nor any other Catholics should be admitted to freedom. But the power given to viceroys in 1672 to dispense with the supremacy oath for

---

13 For text of the oath, see *CARD*, 2, p. 430, n. 1. 14 Lennon, *Lords of Dublin*, pp 139–41, and ch. 6. 15 T.C. Barnard, *Cromwellian Ireland* (Oxford, 2000), pp 68–9; *CARD*, 4, p. 198, n. 1. 16 *CARD*, 4, pp 400, 425.

civic officials made it unlikely that there would be any marked change. In 1676 another route whereby Catholics could become freemen – by marrying the daughter of a freeman – was the subject of a complaint in the Corporation, which resolved to put an end to the practice; but again it seems unlikely that anything very effective was done.[17]

Ambivalent sentiments on the subject were expressed in 1677, when a number of guild masters complained to the Corporation that a civic by-law of 1675 was adversely affecting guild income. That by-law prevented the guilds from admitting anyone to the privileges of trading in the city (either as sworn freemen or simply on the payment of a quarterly fee, known as quarterage) unless they had first been admitted (and thus sworn) as freemen of the city. The guild masters alleged that many were anxious to gain access to legitimate trade either as freemen or as quarter brothers, but were being prevented from doing so. It was agreed to repeal the by-law in question, though only insofar as it related to the payment of quarterage: it was still required that applicants for full guild freedom must first become freemen of the city.[18] Following revelations in England about the so-called 'popish plot' of 1678, the Corporation resolved to admit no-one to freedom who had not taken the oaths of allegiance and supremacy.[19] Even so, it is apparent from complaints made in the later 1670s that the practice of guilds swearing freemen who were not already free of the city continued, and Lord Essex himself acknowledged in 1675 not only that this was the case in many Irish corporations, but that it accorded with royal wishes.[20]

Catholics became free in greater numbers during James II's reign, despite some initial attempts by the Corporation to resist their admission. The king ordered the lord lieutenant to ensure that qualified Catholic merchants and traders be admitted to freedom, subject simply to their taking the oath of allegiance and the usual civic oaths.[21] After some further delaying tactics, in April 1687 the Corporation ordered the erasure of acts of assembly that required freemen to take the oath of supremacy as well as that of allegiance, and assured the king that Catholics would be dealt with on an equal basis with Protestants in the affairs of the city. Shortly afterwards, the city lost its charter through a writ of quo warranto, and under the new charter the Corporation (its members now nominated by the crown, rather than locally selected, as before) contained a majority of Catholics.[22] By the early months of 1688 the number of Catholics applying for freedom was so great that applications had to be processed weekly, rather than at quarterly meetings. Moreover, in the period between William of Orange's intervention in England in November 1688 and his restoration of Protestant government in the city in

17 CARD, 4, pp 527–8; 5, p. 103.   18 CARD, 5, pp 130–1.   19 CARD, 5, pp 164.
20 CARD, 5, pp 154–5, 158, 166; 10, pp 515–18.   21 CARD, 5, pp xlii–xlv, 389–95, 401–7.   22 Ibid., 5, pp 422–6; Hill, *From patriots to unionists*, pp 59–61.

the summer of 1690, poor attendance by several Protestant members of the Corporation at quarterly meetings led to them being replaced by Catholics.[23]

If some Catholics were able to evade the civic by-laws about the supremacy oath, what of other denominations in the city? Protestant Dissenters (except for Quakers, who will be discussed below) had no issue with the supremacy oath. However, some Dissenters were opposed to a new state oath that began to be required from 1671, when it was among the changes introduced by Lord Berkeley's rules, and subsequently reconfirmed by Lord Essex's rules in 1672. This was the so-called 'non-resistance oath', first introduced for English corporations in 1661 as part of the Corporation Act of that year.[24] Besides the lord mayor, the recorder, sheriffs, aldermen, and guild officers were all required to take it. The oath required the official to swear that he believed that it was not lawful 'to take up arms against the king'.[25] Whereas the Elizabethan supremacy oath had been formulated with Catholics in mind, this oath was particularly preoccupied with possible threats emanating from Protestant Dissenters. It was criticized for requiring 'passive obedience', and formed part of the objections to the new viceregal rules, which produced an unsettled period in civic politics for some time in the early and mid-1670s. However, controversy about the 'non-resistance' oath did not prevent some Dissenters from taking office as lords mayor, and the nominated Jacobite assembly of 1687 contained a number of them.[26]

The Corporation was well disposed towards 'Protestant strangers' – mostly Huguenots fleeing persecution in France. However, even though willing to assist some of those in financial difficulties, and (in accordance with legislation) to admit such as were artisans or merchants to freedom without the usual fines or fees, it was insisted that they should take the oaths of allegiance and supremacy, in addition to the usual freeman's oath.[27]

Quakers formed a special group. Considering that oaths amounted to undermining everyday commitments entered into orally, they refused to swear oaths, which drew on them much suspicion from establishment figures. In Dublin, signs of such resistance to oath taking are recorded as early as 1672, when several Quakers were permitted to continue trading but only on condition that they pay additional yearly fines until they should have taken the usual oaths.[28]

---

23 *CARD*, 5, pp 461, 495–6.   24 13 Chas. II, st. 2, c. 1 (Eng.).   25 *CARD*, 5, p. 550; 1, p. 59. A text of the oath can also be found in at least one surviving set of guild records: see 'The test or little oath', inside the front cover of 'A book generall from 1676 to 1702 for the Corporation of Weavers' (Royal Society of Antiquaries of Ireland, Dublin). 26 Hill, *From patriots to unionists*, pp 49–55, 61.   27 'An act for encouraging Protestant strangers and others to inhabit and plant in the kingdom of Ireland', 14 & 15 Chas II, c. 13 (1662); *CARD*, 5, pp 228–30.   28 *CARD*, 5, p. 12.

1691–1774

During this period, the significance of oaths to be taken by members of Dublin Corporation and the freemen body in general underwent some important changes. To begin with, there was the sheer proliferation of oaths, both state and civic. At civic level oaths were resorted to increasingly for the purpose of combating corruption (or temptations to corruption) among Corporation members, civic officials, and tradesmen who sought payment for work done for the Corporation. State oaths – which in certain cases had to be taken by members of the freemen body – grew more numerous and complex following the upheavals set in train by the Williamite revolution, and in some cases a new element (new, at least, in the Irish context) appeared. This was the introduction of formulae designed to counteract attempts by Counter-Reformation casuists to insist on the ultimate spiritual authority of the pope over all Christians. Such developments gave rise to a climate that could not but enhance Protestant distrust of Catholics, and produce new barriers between the two main denominations.

In respect of state oaths, one effect of the Williamite revolution was to create rival contenders for the legitimate title to the throne, and this led early on to the introduction of a new oath of allegiance to William and Mary, and an anti-Catholic declaration instead of the (Elizabethan) oath of supremacy. The new oaths had been introduced for England as part of the Bill of Rights of 1689, and were required to be taken by all English office-holders and MPs, as well as clergy of the Church of England and Dissenters.[29] The requirement to take the new oaths was extended to Ireland in 1691.[30] Although the oath of allegiance made no mention of the new monarchs being 'lawful and rightful' rulers, obstacles placed before Catholics who might be tempted to take it were increased by the requirement that state office-holders, clergy and members of the two houses of the Irish parliament should also subscribe the declaration 'against transubstantiation' (originally required to be taken by members of the English parliament under the terms of the Test Act of 1678).[31] As its description indicated, this was not, strictly speaking, an oath. Although explicitly intended to be repeated audibly 'in the Presence of God', the term 'swear' was missing from the declaration, and so too were the words 'So help me God' at the end. Formulating the statement in such a way may have been intended to enable it to be subscribed without scruples by those (such as Quakers) who had reservations about swearing oaths. The declaration required those subscribing it to disavow transubstantiation, and to affirm that

---

29 1 Will. & Mary, sess. 2, c. 2; 1 Will. & Mary, c. 8. For further context concerning the English acts, see E. Neville Williams (ed.), *The eighteenth-century constitution, 1688–1815* (Cambridge, 1965), pp 6–7, 29–30, 39–42. 30 3 Will. & Mary, c. 2. 31 30 Chas. II, st. 2, c. 1.

the invocation of the Virgin Mary, and the sacrifice of the Mass, as used in 'the Church of Rome' were 'Superstitious and Idolatrous'. However, this was only part of the declaration's novelty in the Irish context. Having required a disavowal of these (Catholic) doctrines, it continued:

> And I do Solemnly, in the Presence of God, Profess, Testify and Declare, That I do make this Declaration and every part thereof, in the plain and ordinary Sense of the Words Read unto me, as they are commonly understood by Protestants, without any Evasion, Equivocation, or Mental Reservation whatsoever, and without any Dispensation already Granted me for this purpose, by the Pope or any other Authority or Person whatsoever, or without any Dispensation from any Person or Authority whatsoever, or without believing that I am or can be Acquitted before God or Man, or absolved of this Declaration or any part thereof, although the Pope or any other Person or Persons or Power whatsoever should Dispence [sic] with or Annul the same, or Declare that it was Null and Void from the beginning.[32]

These convoluted disclaimers had their origins in Protestant reactions to Jesuit casuistry, or use of moral theology, which in the later sixteenth century had sought to undermine the English monarchy's claim to spiritual as well as temporal supremacy over its subjects. In effect, English officials compiled casuistic arguments of their own to defend their legal and ethical understanding of the nature of obligation and allegiance.[33] Such discourse had originally been deployed in English legislation in 1606, when, following the gunpowder plot, a new oath of allegiance had been introduced for English Catholics. This required Catholics to swear allegiance to James I, acknowledging that he was 'lawful and rightful' king, the pope having no power or authority to depose him. Catholics were further required to disavow the 'damnable doctrine' that rulers excommunicated by the pope 'may be deposed or murdered by their subjects'. Of particular significance was the casuistic section towards the end:

> And I do believe and in my conscience am resolved, that neither the Pope nor any person whatsoever hath power to absolve me of this oath or any part thereof, which I acknowledge by good and full authority to be lawfully ministered unto me, and do renounce all pardons and dispensations to the contrary. And all these things I do plainly and sin-

---

[32] G. Meriton (ed.), *An exact abridgment of all the public printed Irish statutes now in force ... together with ... such English statutes now in force to this present time ... relating to the kingdom of Ireland* (Dublin, 1724), p. 208.   [33] David Martin Jones, *Conscience and allegiance in seventeenth century England: the political significance of oaths and engagements* (Rochester, NY, 1999), pp 42–7, 58–9.

cerely acknowledge and swear, according to these express words by me spoken, and according to the plain and common sense and understanding of the same words, without any equivocation or mental evasion or secret reservation whatsoever.[34]

Although initially designed to be taken by Catholics, this was one of the oaths required to be taken by office-holders under the English Test Act of 1673, and it remained in force in England until the Williamite revolution.[35]

By comparison with the 1606 formula, the casuistic elements in the declaration required by the act of 1691 had become subject to what one historian, David Martin Jones, has described as 'a creeping literalism'.[36] As Jones points out, no matter what efforts had been made in the seventeenth century to construct a fully-binding loyalty oath, there would always be those who sought to evade the obligations such oaths contained, and their existence had notoriously failed to prevent the overthrow of two Stuart monarchs. Yet far from weakening the state's attachment to them, the political instability of the century had reinforced the recourse to such oaths,[37] as exemplified by their extension to Ireland in the case of the Williamite oaths. Nor was it simply a few eminent persons who were required to take them: they were obligatory for all office-holders, clergy, barristers and attorneys, as well as peers of the realm. Moreover, in 1692 Dublin Corporation decided to make the allegiance oath and declaration a requirement for all new freemen of the city, thus involving merchants, artisans, and shopkeepers.[38] And while of course the state's purpose in using oaths was to inculcate obedience, the point has been made that oaths acted on the individual's conscience, and empowered individuals to think for themselves about what was right.[39] Thus from this period on (quite apart from their possession of a parliamentary vote) several thousand Dublin Protestant freemen would be implicitly invited by their oaths to consider themselves as participating in the political process. Those Protestants would also be given to understand, in the most solemn of circumstances, not merely that only Protestants could be fully loyal, but that they alone could be relied upon to take an oath in all honesty. Such implications could not fail to further underline divisions between Protestants and Catholics in the age of the penal laws

In fact, the fallout from the Jacobite period in Dublin provided plenty of practical reasons for Protestant resentment and suspicion of their fellow Catholics. In the first place, there was a sense that certain Catholics had

---

34 'An act for the better discovering and repressing of Popish recusants', 3 James I, c. 4 [Eng.] (1606). See also J.P. Kenyon (ed.), *The Stuart constitution* (Cambridge, 1969), pp 456–60.   35 Kenyon, *Stuart constitution*, pp 448, 456–60, 461–2; Jones, *Conscience and allegiance*, pp 46–58.   36 Jones, *Conscience and allegiance*, p. 266.   37 Ibid., pp 266–7.   38 *CARD*, 6, pp 7–8. For examples of this requirement in operation, see pp 21, 25.   39 Gray, *Oaths and the English Reformation*, p. 214.

gained unduly from the challenge to and replacement of the city's historic charters, and it is noteworthy that in a petition to the Corporation of October 1690, calling for the disfranchising of such Catholics, members of the city commons framed their criticism with reference to oaths:

> [C]ertain of the commons did petition the said assembly, setting forth that by the favour of their predecessors there were severall Papists formerly admitted to the freedome of the cittie who, contrary to their oathes, combined together to take away the cittie charters and to turne the severall Protestant magistrates, officers and freemen of this city out of their places and freedomes, and to sett up a new charter and government for themselves, contrary to the lawes of this kingdome and the customes and constitutions of this cittie.[40]

Of course, this was to single out the role of Dublin Catholics, while overlooking the policy of James II's government in calling in charters of many towns and cities, not merely in Ireland but also in England. However, it does suggest an awareness of the importance of oaths, and an assumption that Catholics, even if they had taken the former oaths required of freemen, were not to be relied on when it came to fulfilling their obligations. Indeed, it was soon being implied that any Catholics holding city employments were unworthy of trust:

> [C]omplaint had been made that severall persons who were employed in collecting the toll corne of this cittie were Papists, and therefore not qualified to be imployed in any such place of trust, it is therefore ordered and agreed upon, by the authority of the said assembly, that for the future noe person whatsoever shall be imployed in collecting or receiveing the said toll corne but who shall first take an oath of trust in his said employment, and shall alsoe take the oathes and subscribe the declaration pursuant to a late act of parliament in England.[41]

Certain other civic office-holders were also required to take the new oaths and declaration.[42] However, despite such concerns, the fact that some notorious Catholic Jacobites were left to pursue their trades during the early 1690s – a period when the Nine Years War with France was underway – does, perhaps, suggest that distrust of Catholics had its limits: or, perhaps, that (in the absence of any offspring to William and Mary) it was prudent not to offend Jacobites too seriously. For instance, James Malone, a Dublin bookseller who had been printer to James II, and who continued to insist that as a freeman

---

40 *CARD*, 5, p. 509. 41 Assembly of 19 Dec. 1692 (*CARD*, 6, p. 26). 42 *CARD*, 6, pp 67, 224.

he could continue to trade 'in popish bookes' despite not having taken the new oaths, was not disfranchised until 1696.[43] Nevertheless, anxieties were periodically expressed. Early in 1696 a petition to the Corporation raised concerns about the cleaning of the Tholsell (or city hall, where meetings of the Corporation took place), which was in the hands of 'one Mary Seamer and Christian Lawler',

> who are ... persons of very ill fame and knowne Papists, and frequently harbour in the Tholsell people of their owne character, to the hazard not only of the place, but also of a great part of the city by fire, to the dishonour of this antient and loyall Protestant corporation ...[44]

The petition accordingly urged the Corporation 'to order the removall of the said persons, and to put in theire places some honest English Protestant'. Even so, no immediate action was taken: instead, the allegations concerning the cleaners were referred to a high-powered committee, consisting mostly of aldermen and including either the lord mayor or the sheriffs. It was not until 1699 that a decision was taken to require all city employees to take the 1691 oath and to subscribe the declaration.[45]

Shortly after dealing with the Malone case, the Corporation's Easter assembly (10 March 1696) was much preoccupied with the news from England of a plot (15 February) to assassinate William and, with French assistance, to restore James II to the throne. Julian Hoppit argues that revelation of the plot did much to consolidate William's authority in England (Queen Mary had died in December 1694). The most important outcome in respect of oaths was an initiative taken by the king's supporters in the English House of Commons to establish an 'association', which declared William to be 'rightful and lawful king', thus in effect also requiring, for the first time, the abjuration of James.[46] In April, a new oath incorporating this shift became a requirement for office-holders in England. No Irish parliament was sitting just then, but on news of the plot Dublin Corporation promptly decided to require everyone who might in future be admitted to the freedom of the city, 'to subscribe the ensuing association'. The association set out that 'his present majestic, king William, is the rightfull and lawfull king of these realms, and that neither the late king James nor the pretended prince of Wales, nor any other person, hath any right whatsoever to the same'. (Quakers being admitted to freedom were permitted to avoid taking the usual oaths, but obliged to sign the declaration required by the 1691 act, and to subscribe the association.)[47] It was further decided that deputy aldermen and parish church-

---

43 CARD, 6, pp 137–8.   44 CARD, 6, p. 132.   45 CARD, 6, pp 132–3, 224.   46 Julian Hoppit, *A land of liberty? England 1689–1727* (Oxford, 2002), pp 153–4.   47 CARD, 6, pp 139–40.

wardens should be authorized to go from house to house to collect signatures to the association, and to record the names of all who refused to subscribe. The results would be returned to the lord mayor and retained as evidence of the city's 'loyalty to his majestie, king William, and mutuall obligations to stand by and assist each other in the defence of his sacred majestie, his interest, and the Protestant religion'.[48] And at some point following this initiative, the Corporation began to employ a person with the specific task of inducing local Catholics to take the oaths appointed by parliament (for a time this role was filled by a Joseph Kennedy, probably a member of the Dublin convert family of that name).[49]

The death of James II in 1701 prompted the English parliament to pass a bill (1702) requiring the abjuration of his son, the 'Old Pretender': it was passed only weeks before the unexpected death of William III. As Hoppit notes, the measure represented, in effect, a rejection of hereditary succession, and (given Queen Anne's lack of living children) was an implicit endorsement of the Hanoverian succession as set out in the Act of Settlement of the previous year.[50] In 1703 a further act of the English parliament required office-holders, lawyers and schoolmasters in Ireland to take the oath of abjuration, declaring Queen Anne to be the rightful sovereign, and disclaiming the Pretender.[51] These developments in respect of oaths further accentuated the divisions between Protestants and Catholics in Ireland; and it may be significant that a new book of oaths to be taken by the various officials and members of Dublin Corporation began to be compiled in Queen Anne's reign.[52]

The new reign witnessed the rise of the Tories to royal favour, with an accompanying emphasis on the rights of the established church. One of the significant ways in which Ireland at this period differed from England was that the English Test Act of 1673 was not in force there. That act (which was still on the English statute book) required all English office-holders to take the oaths of supremacy and allegiance, as well as to take the sacrament according to the Church of England, with the latter requirement effectively requiring Dissenters either to abandon public office or at least to become occasional conformists.[53] Pressures for a similar measure to be introduced for Ireland were soon apparent, and an act of 1704 passed by the Irish parliament (along with a raft of new anti-Catholic restrictions) accordingly introduced a requirement that all public office-holders take a sacramental test.[54]

The Test Act of 1704, as it would become known, quickly had an impact in Dublin. A Presbyterian merchant, Thomas Bell, who in 1702–3 had served

---

[48] *CARD*, 6, pp 140–1.   [49] *CARD*, 6, p. 417. For the Kennedys, see also pp 411, 500.
[50] Hoppit, *A land of liberty?*, pp 163–4.   [51] 1 Anne, st. 2, c. 17 [Eng.].   [52] It was still being updated in the nineteenth century (DCA, Book of oaths, MR/32).   [53] Kenyon, *Stuart constitution*, pp 461–2.   [54] 'An Act to prevent the further Growth of Popery', 2 Anne, c. 6.

as lord mayor and subsequently as city treasurer, refused to take the test (the only member of the board to do so), and consequently lost his place both as treasurer and alderman.[55] However, with the passage of indemnity acts from 1719, the Dissenter presence on the aldermanic board resumed, and Alderman Joseph Kane (Presbyterian) was lord mayor in 1725–6.[56] The test seems to have had a more enduring impact in the military sphere. As part of Dublin's commitment to supporting the war of the Spanish succession (1702–13), local militia arrangements were stepped up under the supervision of the lord mayor and commissioners of array. In 1702 officers (all of whom had to be sworn in) were commissioned for two foot regiments in the city. However, these arrangements were called into question when the Test Act came into force, for many of the militia officers resigned their commissions. Presumably they were Dissenters, and no longer eligible to hold office: new officers had to be appointed.[57] It would take another four decades before a lord lieutenant (Lord Chesterfield) was prepared to permit individual Dissenters to hold commissions in the militia, and it was only in 1756 that an act (29 Geo. II, c. 24) was passed to authorize Dissenters in general to hold such commissions.[58] Special arrangements were made for Quakers: in 1716 'An act to make the militia of this kingdom more useful' permitted any Quakers who were reluctant to serve personally in the militia to be deemed liable only for the same fines as other Protestants, rather than those imposed on 'papists or non-jurors' who refused to take the oath of abjuration, provided they were willing to make a solemn declaration. This required them to declare that George I was the 'lawful and rightful' king of the realm of Great Britain and Ireland', to abjure the Pretender, and to disclaim a raft of Catholic doctrines, along with the pope's dispensing power. The declaration also contained some of the usual formulae designed to counter Catholic casuistry: the declaration was to be made 'without any equivocation, or mental reservation, according to the true plainness, simplicity, and usual signification of the words'.[59] Thus Quakers too were drawn into a culture in which Protestants alone could be regarded as capable of taking an oath honestly and sincerely, while Catholics were deemed inherently untrustworthy and deceitful. It was scarcely surprising that in reacting to news of the impending Jacobite invasion of Britain in 1715, and reaffirming its own loyalty, Dublin Corporation should have referred to 'the obligations we lie under by the oaths we have taken to support and defend your majesty and the succession in the Protestant line'.[60]

---

55 Jacqueline Hill, 'Dublin Corporation, Protestant dissent, and politics, 1660–1800' in Kevin Herlihy (ed.), *The politics of Irish dissent, 1650–1800* (Dublin, 1997), pp 28–39, at pp 31–2.   56 Hill, 'Dublin Corporation, Protestant dissent, and politics', p. 33.   57 *CARD*, 6, pp 275, 314.   58 Ian McBride, *Eighteenth-century Ireland* (Dublin, 2009), p. 289.   59 2 Geo. I, c. 9, in *The statutes at large, passed in the parliaments held in Ireland*, 4, pp 337–42, at pp 341–2.   60 *CARD*, 6, p. 545.

Throughout the period of a Jacobite claim to the throne, and periodic invasion scares, there was a strong emphasis on the need for Protestants in Ireland to maintain military readiness. According to the 1716 act all Protestants aged between sixteen and sixty were to be liable for array, unless they could find a substitute. In Dublin, new freemen were supposed to provide themselves 'with arms sufficient for a foot soldier': having been sworn in, they were required to enter into a bond to that effect.[61] However, by 1740, when prohibitions on Catholics keeping arms were reinforced by the Irish parliament (13 Geo. II, c. 6), it was being alleged that few freemen were provided 'with any kind of arms', and the Corporation agreed to strengthen the formal commitment by inserting a new section into the freeman's oath, to the effect that 'you shall always, whilst you are able and in your power, keep a good musket, carbine, or fusee in good, clean and sufficient order'.[62] As late as the Seven Years War (1756–63) the Corporation was still making arrangements for arraying and enrolling the Protestant inhabitants.[63] All this must have given Protestants from outside the landed class a further sense that they belonged to an elite whose probity, loyalty and martial obligations set them apart from Catholics of whatever background.

Turning to the place of oaths in the more strictly civic sphere during this period, by the 1730s, in the context of expanding civic employment, it was becoming increasingly common for aspiring city office-holders to emphasize that they were freemen of Dublin – thus in principle (in view of their oaths) guaranteeing that they were loyal and honest Protestants.[64] Accordingly, cases in which freemen failed to live up to standards of straight-dealing could be dealt with severely. In 1732 the officers of the tallow-chandlers' guild were accused of bending the rules for admission to freedom of the guild by accepting a certificate of apprenticeship for an aspiring freeman which they knew to be false. On the strength of the said certificate the artisan in question, Nicholas Swan, had subsequently been admitted to freedom of the city. The Corporation ruled that the master of the guild, Peter Barré, should be disfranchised, together with two of the guild's representatives on the city commons, who had allegedly been particularly complicit in the deception. The matter was investigated by a Corporation committee in some detail, and ultimately the disfranchising of the two guild representatives was upheld, though Barré was cleared (he subsequently went on to become an alderman).[65]

Meanwhile, in the 1740s, with oligarchic tendencies in the Corporation and civic indebtedness growing, a drive began to prevent civic magistrates enriching themselves at the city's expense. A Corporation committee recommended in 1740 that lord mayors and sheriffs be prevented in future from selling city

---

61 For examples of such bonds, see DCA, Freedom bonds, Fr/Bond/1674–1759. 62 *CARD*, 8, p. 362. 63 *CARD*, 10, pp 285, 408, 444. 64 See, for example, *CARD*, 8, pp 76, 173–4, 223–4. 65 *CARD*, 8, pp 66–8, 76–7, 80–1.

employments, and instead be compensated with a payment of £150 at the end of their terms of office. To this end, a new oath was introduced, requiring lord mayors and sheriffs (so as to be entitled to the terminal payment) to swear that during their year of office they had received no financial reward or gratuities for the disposal of any city offices (beyond the traditional hogshead of wine, or twenty guineas, to the lord mayor on the election of an alderman, or two hogsheads of wine on the excusing of any one to serve as sheriff or as lord mayor).[66] Throughout the 1740s, 1750s and 1760s the oath continued to be taken.[67] By the 1770s the principle that Corporation members should not profit from city employments was being extended beyond the leading magistrates to lesser officials. For instance, in 1770 a new assistant to the master of the city works, on a salary of £50 per year, was required to take an oath to the effect that he would receive no gratuity for or on account of the exercise of his office, and that any tradesmen seeking to have their bills certified by him should take an oath to the effect that they had not paid and would not pay him any gratuity for such a certificate.[68]

The committee of 1740 was also given the task of considering the disposal and value of the various city employments. Thus, for instance, in 1742 it was recommended that the position of sword-bearer should in future come up for renewal annually, at a salary of 40s. per year, and that the incumbent should retain only half of the usual expenses for appraising goods (part of his official duties), the remainder being accounted for 'upon oath' and going to the use of the city.[69] Certain city offices were regulated not by Corporation decisions but by act of parliament. The office of weighmaster came under the latter description, with the act in question requiring the taking of an oath of office.[70] Whether regulated by the Corporation or by parliament, from the 1740s it became common for city employees, when claiming reimbursement for expenses incurred in the course of their official duties, to present their bills 'upon oath':[71] where appropriate, an affirmation was permitted.[72] These tendencies towards greater probity in the conduct of the Corporation culminated in 1770, when the lower house, which had been the driving force behind the reforms, decided to introduce what was in effect a place act, barring any of its own members from being elected to any civic place of profit, or employed in any of the city works.[73] And from 1773 onwards, an affidavit (a written declaration on oath) was required to guarantee the authenticity of all tradesmen's bills.[74]

66 *CARD*, 8, pp 360–2, 371–3. See also Hill, *From patriots to unionists*, pp 82–3.
67 Names of lord mayors and sheriffs who took the oath between 1740 and 1760 are listed in *CARD*, 9, pp 468–70. The practice continued into the 1760s: see 11, p. 450.
68 *CARD*, 12, pp 67, 129. 69 *CARD*, 9, pp 88–9. 70 *CARD*, 9, pp 166–7; 11, p. 72.
71 See, e.g., *CARD*, 9, pp 86, 93, 110. 72 *CARD*, 11, p. 431. 73 The new regulation was to come into effect at the end of 1771 (*CARD*, 12, p. 84); see also Hill, *From patriots to unionists*, pp 131–2. 74 *CARD*, 12, p. 242.

In conclusion, it has been argued above that by virtue of its place within the Irish polity, the Corporation shared the oath-taking culture of the seventeenth and eighteenth centuries. By the 1770s the incidence of oath-taking potentially involving Dublin freemen had become more extensive than ever before. And yet this culture contained some paradoxical features. On the one hand, the sheer proliferation of oaths would soon be raising questions in the minds of contemporaries. If oaths were taken in a compliant spirit, they might be deemed unnecessary; if taken unwillingly, they were unlikely to provide much by way of security.[75] These questions were likely to arise increasingly in Ireland from the 1770s onwards. Following the death of 'James III' in 1766, Rome had failed to recognize the title of 'Charles III', and this had given hope to those who sought a relaxation of the penal laws. A crucial step was to devise an oath of allegiance that Catholics could conscientiously take. After much discussion, an act of 1774 permitted Catholics to swear allegiance to George III. The oath set out in the act not only required the abjuration of 'Charles III', but the denial of the pope's temporal power within the realm. A complex casuistic section was included, extending well beyond the minimal wording proposed in the draft drawn up by the Catholic Committee earlier that year (additions are in italics):

> and I do solemnly *in the presence of God, and of His only son Jesus Christ, my Redeemer*, profess, *testifie and declare*, that I do make this declaration *and every part thereof*, in the plain and ordinary sense of the words *of this oath*, without any evasion, equivocation, or mental reservation whatever, *and without any dispensation already granted by the Pope or any authority of the see of Rome, or any person whatsoever, and without thinking that I am or can be acquitted before God or man, or absolved of this declaration, or any part thereof, although the pope, or any other person or persons, or authority whatsoever shall dispense with or annul the same, or declare that it was null and void from the beginning.* So help me God.[76]

Such wording showed clearly that concerns about Catholic integrity and the overarching influence of papal power remained all too present in the minds of the authorities. The oath proved predictably controversial for the Catholic

---

[75] For the expression of such doubts, dating from 1797, see David W. Miller, 'Radicalism and ritual in east Ulster' in Thomas Bartlett, David Dickson, Dáire Keogh & Kevin Whelan (eds), *1798: a bicentenary perspective* (Dublin, 2003), pp 195–211, at p. 208. See also Jones, *Conscience and allegiance*, pp 61, 267.   [76] For the full text of the oath, distinguishing between the draft and the official versions, see Maureen Wall, 'Catholic loyalty to king and pope in eighteenth-century Ireland' in *Catholic Ireland in the eighteenth century: collected essays of Maureen Wall*, ed. Gerard O'Brien (Dublin, 1989), pp 107–14, at p. 112.

bishops and clergy, and in the early years there was a good deal of reluctance to take it, though since the benefits of the relief act of 1778 (allowing Catholics to take long leases, and to inherit land) required the taking of the oath, opposition soon fell away.[77] However, at civic level it would take until 1793 before Catholics were legally permitted to become members of guilds and corporations, and although the relief act of that year removed the requirement for new freemen to take the oaths and subscribe the anti-Catholic declaration, they still had to be nominated for membership by guilds that, by and large, remained fearful of the implications of Catholic admission.[78] Catholic freemen were also required to take the oath contained in the 1774 act, as well as a new oath and declaration, disavowing any belief in the pope's infallibility, and any intention of subverting the land settlement or established church in Ireland.[79]

There was a further difficulty. State oaths devised in the sixteenth and seventeenth centuries to shore up the royal supremacy rested on the assumption that allegiance was due to the supremacy of the monarch in church and state, which included important personal and hereditary dimensions.[80] With the accession of William and Mary, and subsequently of the Hanoverians, those qualities were bound to suffer some diminution. The role of parliament was enhanced, and parliamentary revision of state oaths became more frequent. This inevitably strengthened the idea that allegiance was owed primarily to the law and the constitution – and that these could, in certain circumstances, be altered. Indeed, so far had the idea of mutability extended by the end of our period that even at the level of Dublin Corporation's lower house, in 1780, there was discussion about altering the terms of the freeman's oath.[81] And given that oath-taking had become so very pervasive in its application, even for some quite humdrum matters, the solemn and sacrosanct character of an oath could not but in some degree be compromised. It would take another sixty years before parliament would begin to tackle some of these challenging issues (Excise Declarations Act, 1 & 2 William IV, c. 4 (1831)), but the internal contradictions of the oath-taking culture were already becoming apparent.

---

77 Wall, 'Catholic loyalty to king and pope', pp 112–14. 78 On guild attitudes to the admission of Catholics, see Hill, *From patriots to unionists*, pp 230–34. 79 Catholic relief act (33 Geo. III, c. 21), section 7. 80 Jones, *Conscience and allegiance*, p. 60. 81 DCA, Journals of sheriffs and commons, C1/JSC/4 (Oct. 1776–Dec. 1780), f. 144v.

Catholic and Protestant Dublin weavers before the Spanish Inquisition, 1745-54[1]

THOMAS O'CONNOR

On 7 December 1751, the 25-year-old Maria Nichols, a native of Dublin and newly arrived in Spain, appeared before the Madrid tribunal of the Spanish Inquisition.[2] Hers was not quite the clichéd inquisitorial experience.[3] She had been neither summoned nor arrested, but rather presented of her own free will. Without any ostensible prompting she declared her desire to abjure her Protestant faith and expressed her wish to be admitted to the Catholic church. She appears to have had friends in court. In charge of the entire interview was an Inquisition commissioner, one John Lacy, a native of Kilfenora. It transpired that he had been instructing her for some time and was also acting as her interpreter. After a formal interview her renunciation was accepted and she was admitted to the church.

Maria Nichols' experience was repeated by more than a dozen of her Dublin co-religionists in the later 1740s and early 1750s. Most of them were textile workers, like her, and many were accompanied by their families. They, too, presented spontaneously to the Holy Office, renouncing their Protestant beliefs and seeking admission to the Catholic church.[4] Together they formed part of a larger group of nearly 100 Irish textile workers contracted in Dublin, most of them in the first half of 1750, by Irish agents of the Spanish king, Ferdinando VI. They were intended to staff the integrated woollens factory at Guadalajara, outside Madrid, and subsidiary plants at San Fernando and nearby Vicálvaro.

---

1 For the larger context see Thomas O'Connor, *Irish voices from the Spanish Inquisition: migrants, converts and brokers in early modern Iberia* (London, 2016). 2 Delación espontanea de Maria Nicols, Madrid, 7 Dec. 1751, Archivo Histórico Nacional [AHN], Inquisición [INQ], Libro [Lib] 1156, ff 434r–437v. 3 For a modern introduction to the Inquisition see Francisco Bethencourt, *The Inquisition: a global history, 1478–1834* (Cambridge, 2009). 4 Self-denunciation was the classic means of initiating a process of regularisation before the Inquisition. See Henry Kamen, *La inquisición Española* (Barcelona, 1999), p. 172. Those denouncing themselves were: John Scott (Dec. 1745); Thomas Gibson (Jan. 1751); John Hall (Jan. 1751); William Sheercraft (July 1751); Maria Nichols (Dec. 1751); Margaret Sheercraft (Dec. 1751); Thomas Hoey (Dec. 1751); Samuel Slattery, John Slattery and John Slattery Jr (May 1752); Charles Murray (May 1752); William O'Dwyer (May 1752); Francis Lawlor (May 1752); William Harden (July 1752); Elizabeth Fling (Aug. 1752); Samuel Nessfield (Jan. 1753); Santiago Campbell (Feb. 1753). Hoey, a watchmaker, and Campbell, a surgeon, do not appear to have had a direct connection with the woollens manufactory but were processed by the Inquisition with the weavers.

INDUSTRIAL INNOVATION IN BOURBON SPAIN: THE IRISH CONNECTION

How did these largely Dublin weavers and their dependants come to be in Spain? From their accession in 1700, the Spanish Bourbons had been anxious to modernize Spain's industrial production, particularly in the area of textiles.[5] Part of their strategy was to entice artisans from Northern Europe to Spain with attractive contracts. Given Ireland's reputation for textiles in the mid-eighteenth century, its dense network of contacts with Spain, and the Catholic reputation of the majority of its inhabitants, it was perhaps natural that the Spanish would recruit in Dublin and elsewhere in Ireland.[6] However, for most of the first half of the eighteenth century, artisan and technology exchange between Ireland and Spain had been hampered by the sporadically tense relations existing between Britain and the Spanish Bourbons. The trade arrangements of the Treaty of Utrecht (1713) had granted the *asiento* to England, and British–Spanish trade, including its Irish arm, was important to both countries.[7] However, for dynastic and strategic reasons, both countries were frequently at war. A relatively prolonged peace came only in 1748 when the treaty of Aix-la-Chapelle ushered in several years of diplomatic stability. Trade benefited from a commercial treaty concluded in 1750.[8] Richard Wall (1694–1777), the Irish protégé and London agent of the Spanish royal minister Josef de Caravajal y Lancaster (1698–1754), played a key role in the negotiations culminating in the commercial treaty.[9]

Although Aix-la-Chapelle acted as the foundation for seven years of cooperative peace between Spain and Britain, enduring mercantilist attitudes ensured restricted practices and official discouragement of both artisan and

---

5 See Clayburn la Force, 'Technological diffusion in the eighteenth century: the Spanish textile industry', *Technology and Culture*, 5:3 (1964), 322–43 and 'Royal textile factories in Spain 1700–1800', *Journal of Economic History*, 24:3 (1964), 337–63.   6 For a useful overview of the Dublin textile industry see John Warburton, James Whitelaw, and Robert Walsh, *A history of the city of Dublin* (2 vols, 1818), 2, pp 971–84. For a more recent overview see Nuala Burke, 'Dublin 1600–1800' (PhD, TCD, 1972).   7 On commercial exchange see Óscar Recio Morales, '"Los Extranjeros del rey": la nueva posición de los extranjeros en el comercio y ejército borbónico de Felipe V 1700–1746', *Dieciocho*, 35:1 (2012), 49–73 and, for the second half of the century, 'Las reformas Carolinas y los comerciantes extranjeros en España: actitudes y respuestas de las "naciones" a la offensive regalista 1759–1793', *Hispania: Revista Española de Historia*, 72:240 (2012), 67–94.   8 For the classic account see Jean O. McLachlan, *Trade and peace with Old Spain, 1667–1750* (Cambridge, 1940), pp 122–45. For more recent overviews see Óscar Recio Morales, 'Conectores de imperios: la figura del comerciante Irlandés en España y en el mundo Atlántico del XVIII' in Ana Crespo Solana (ed.), *Comunidades transnacionales: colonias de mercaderes extranjeros en el mundo Atlántico (1500–1830)* (Madrid, 2010), pp 313–36.   9 On Wall's role see Diego Téllez Alarcia, *D. Ricardo Wall: aut Caesar aut nullus* (Madrid, 2008), pp 102ff.

technology exchange. Any transfers that did occur were clandestine and industrial espionage was the order of the day, especially for the Spanish who needed the skills and technology of the more technically advanced north.[10] Such activities were supported at the highest levels. In 1749 Zenón de Somodevilla, first marqués de la Ensenada (1702–81), the Spanish naval minister, sent the polymath and naval engineer Jorge Juan y Santacilia (1713–73) to London on a mission to scout for naval technology and shipwrights. He controversially enticed a number of London-based Irish artisans to Spain, including Matthew Mullan (d. 1767), who later distinguished himself as a naval architect in Spain and Cuba.[11] Richard Wall was also involved in recruitment, mostly of textile workers. In 1749, when a Spanish agent called Richard Metcalf was sent to England to acquire machinery and mechanics for the Royal Company of Granada, Wall managed the financial side of the scheme, advancing him money as recruitment progressed. He was understandably distressed when Metcalf and his newly contracted English mechanics were detained by the British authorities.[12] Luckily for Wall, no compromising testimonies were extracted from the men concerned but things turned out badly for Metcalf.[13]

Wall was not the only Irish connection in this complex affair, nor was he the first. Irish textile immigrants had not been entirely uncommon in early eighteenth-century Spain[14] and there was a long history of Irish workers at Guadalajara[15] and elsewhere in the Madrid region.[16] In 1745 the Dubliner Cristobal MacKenna was a foreman and master in the Guadalajara textile manufactory, of which San Fernando and Vicálvaro were subsidiaries.[17] However, it was only in the second half of the 1740s that a consistent recruitment campaign in Ireland was considered. One of the crucial figures here was Teodoro Valente Argumosa (1712/13–74), who was superintendent of the royal manufactory in Guadalajara from 1750 to 1757.[18]

---

10 Juan Helguera Quijada, 'The beginnings of industrial espionage in Spain (1748–1760)' in Ian Inkster (ed.), *History of Technology 30: European technologies in Spanish history* (London, 2010), pp 1–12.   11 J.L. Moralez Hernández, 'Jorge Juan en Londres', *Revista General de Marina*, 184 (1973), 663–70.   12 Wall to Caravajal, London, 11 Aug. 1749, AGS [Archivo General de Simancas], Estado, Inglaterra [Ing], Legajo [Leg] 6914, cited by McLachlan, *Trade and peace with Old Spain*, p. 215, n. 127. See Téllez Alarcia, *D. Ricardo Wall*, p. 127.   13 McLachlan, *Trade and peace with Old Spain*, pp 142–3.   14 See Eugenio Larruga y Boneta, *Memorias politicas y económicas sobre los frutos, comercio, fabricas y minas de España* (45 vols, Madrid, 1787–1800), passim.   15 There were Irish employed here from the 1720s. Among the 186 employees in 1727 were one Irish 'emborrador', one master dyer, and a number of stampers. See Larruga, *Memorias*, xiv, pp 210–13.   16 According to Larruga, *Memorias*, ix, p. 329, an Irishman was brought to the Toledo by one Diego Gonzalez, from Ajofrin. Irish craftsmen were active in the leather industry in Bilbao, from the seventeenth century. See Amaia Bilbao Acedos, *The Irish community in the Basque country c.1700–1800* (Dublin, 2003), pp 19–57.   17 Petition of Santiago Pettel and Cristobal MacKenna [June 1745], AGS, Secretaria y Superintendencia de Hacienda [SSH], Leg 763 (1).   18 He resumed the superintendency in 1767. On this

Argumosa had come to public attention in Spain in 1743, thanks to the publication of his *Erudicción política: despertador sobre el comercio, agricultura y manufacturas* (Madrid, 1743).[19] This work, one of a number of reforming texts in circulation on Spain at the time, drew heavily on the economic thought of the French mercantilist, Jean François Melon (1675–1738).[20] Following Melon, Argumosa insisted that state intervention in commercial regulation and industrial production was the key to progress and that this included state-sponsored technical innovation and the acquisition of skilled artisans. In June 1745 Ensenada, who would later send Juan Jorge to London, commissioned Argumosa to investigate textile technology in northern Europe in general and to look into hiring foreign contract operatives to work in the Guadalajara complex and to train Spanish apprentices.[21] Argumosa's commission brought him, in September 1745, to Holland and there he made contact with an unnamed Irish agent, whom he contracted to take him to England. Their plans fell foul of the Jacobite landing in Scotland, which threw the country into a panic and caused tightened security in the ports.[22] Despite this setback, by the end of the year Argumosa had established an extensive network of contacts. He had also signed contracts with a number of master craftsmen, mostly in France and Holland, and they began arriving in Guadalajara shortly afterwards, joining foreigners like MacKenna and native Spanish workers and apprentices. Argumosa had a clear idea of the sort of foreign worker he wanted. In an undated report, probably from 1747, he explained that he preferred to hire married men who tended to be more settled and reliable. They were, he continued, more likely to be qualified and, because they brought their wives and families with them, it would be dissuasively expensive for them to return home before the expiration of their contracts.[23]

With his appointment as superintendent of Guadalajara in 1750 Argumosa assumed a directive role in the factory and recruitment. The Spanish were already actively recruiting in London, where Richard Wall inveigled a number of artisans to take ship to Spain. However, it proved difficult to find recruits who were both suitably qualified and Catholic, as Wall informed his Madrid

plant and its subsidiaries in San Fernando and Vicálvaro, see Lourdes Sánchez Domínguez, *Un espacio en el tiempo: Vicálvaro. real fábrica de tejidos cuartel y Universidad* (Vicálvaro, 2009). **19** This text plagiarized the work of the French writers, Jean François Melon and Jacques Savary de Bruslons. See M. Delgado Barrado, 'La transmisión de escritos económicos en España: el ejemplo de la *Erudicción política* de Teodoro Ventura Argumosa Gándara (1743)', *Cromohs*, 9 (2004), 1–11. **20** One of Melon's works had already been published in Ireland, in a translation by David Bindon, with a list of subscribers as *A political essay upon Commerce* (Dublin, 1738). See Ian McBride, *Eighteenth-century Ireland: the isle of slaves* (Dublin, 2009), pp 89–94. **21** Marques de la Ensenada to Argumosa, Madrid, 1 June 1745, AGS SSH Leg 763 (1). **22** Marques de Gil to Marques de la Ensenada, The Hague, 23 Sept. 1745, AGS SSH Leg 763 (1). **23** Argumosa to the Marques de la Ensenada, San Fernando, undated [1747], AGS SSH Leg 764 (1).

superiors in 1749.²⁴ Dublin, with its proportionally larger Catholic population, offered better prospects, a fact that may have prompted Argumosa to recruit specifically in Ireland for the new production unit planned for San Fernando.²⁵ In April 1750 he wrote to Caravajal about his project to employ an intermediary to hire artisans for a new project. Ambrose Berry, whom MacKenna knew and trusted, was contracted to recruit fifty weavers, twenty-five cloth shearers and nappers and a number of specialized workers including master fullers, carders and engineers to make and maintain machine blades. With these workers and technicians, Argumosa planned to establish a 'world-class' facility.²⁶

IRISH WEAVERS IN GUADALAJARA, SAN FERNANDO AND VICÁLVARO

Berry set to work immediately and seems to have concentrated his recruiting efforts on Dublin. Shortly afterwards, the first Irish contract workers began to arrive, some by way of Bilbao, others through Cádiz. As Argumosa had intended, there were a number of engineers among them, including Enrique Doyle.²⁷ He was associated with another engineer, Juan Dowling, who with his nephew, Patricio Bolger, would design engines, mostly pumps, polishing machines and mechanical looms, in several royal sites, including Guadalajara, San Fernando and Vicálvaro.²⁸

Initially, the Irish were received in San Fernando, near Guadalajara, where the new plant was planned. Not all of them were happy. Specifically, they found the cost of living higher than they had expected, and accordingly demanded better wages. Argumosa took a firm line with the grumbling Irish. However, when MacKenna approached him concerning a recently arrived acquaintance from Dublin who was threatening to return home, Argumosa proved more flexible.²⁹ As the Irish joined other workers, notably already established Dutch operatives, new complaints arose over perceived wage discrepancies. These caused resentment that continued into the following year.

24 Wall to Caravajal, London, 11 Sept. 1749, AHN Estado Leg 4267. 25 Larruga, *Memorias*, xvii, p. 286. 26 Argumosa to Caravajal, San Fernando, 25 Apr. 1750, AGS SSH Leg 764 (1). '50 texedores, 25 tundidores y perchadores 12 emboradores, un maestro batanero, otro cardero y otro de hacer y esmotar tisseras que es quanto necesitamos para de un golpe asegurar y perfeccionar la major fabrica deel mundo'. 27 See 'Suplica Dn Enrique Doil', 3 Apr. 1756, AGS SSH Leg 766 (1). 28 See Javier Echávarri Otero et al., 'Royal manufactures promoted by the Spanish crown during the 18th and 19th centuries: an approach to European industrialization' in Teun Koetsier and Marco Ceccarelli (eds), *Explorations in the history of machines and mechanisms: proceedings of HMM2012* (Dordrecht, 2012), pp 55–68, especially pp 60–2. 29 Argumosa to Caravajal, San Fernando, 15 Dec. 1750, AGS SSH Leg 764 (2).

In December 1751 a number of the Irish workers were so disgruntled that they considered travelling to Madrid to petition Caravajal directly for better conditions and wages. Although Argumosa threatened them with arrest on that occasion, his firm negotiating line was tempered by a desire to retain his Irish workers, for at least long enough to train up the Spanish apprentices.[30]

Wages and the cost of living were not the only problems. The original site intended for the Irish workers at San Fernando proved unsuitable, due to the contaminated local water supply. This caused repeated outbreaks of disease. MacKenna himself fell seriously ill in May 1750, to Argumosa's consternation, and many of the Irish succumbed on arrival.[31] In October of the same year illness ensured that only 20 looms were operative, with 12 cloth shearers active. By 1751 it was decided to relocate the workers, some of them Irish, to more salubrious accommodation in nearby Vicálvaro.[32] Despite the improved sanitary conditions, ordinary mortality took its grim toll. When Andrew Coyle, one of the contracted workers, died shortly after arrival, the parish death register recorded

> Andrew Coyle, 38 years old, died suddenly in Vicálvaro on 2 August 1751. He was an employee of the Royal Cloth factory, husband of Eleanor Lucas, his parents were James Coyle and Margaret Hylan; he was a native of GreatConel, diocese of Raphoe [?], in Ireland. He left no will, the parish priest of Torrejón testified to his poverty and funeral expenses were paid by his comrades ... He leaves behind a daughter, Margaret, aged nine and a son, Thomas, aged seven (both born in Dublin) and daughter Maria Eleanor, aged four months, born here in the royal domain.[33]

The contracts signed by the Irish sometimes made provision for widows and children but ensuring the observance of all contractual conditions often required the sort of persistent petitioning that the newly arrived Irish were not equipped to undertake. However, better established operatives, like MacKenna, successfully sought pension rights for their immediate families.[34] Some widows also managed to extract pensions from the administration. In 1767, for instance, Margaret Sheercraft (née Howell), on the death of her husband William Sheercraft, successfully petitioned for a pension.[35]

30 Argumosa to Caravajal, San Fernando, 18 Dec. 1751, AGS SSH Leg 765 (2). 31 Argumosa to Caravajal, San Fernando, 31 May 1750; Argumosa to Caravajal, San Fernando, 8 June 1750, AGS SSH Leg 764 (2). 32 About eighteen Irish workers were installed in Vilcálvaro, forming the largest single group of foreigners there. See Lourdes Sanchez Domínguez, *Un espacio en el tiempo*, p. 33. 33 Archivo parroquial Santa Maria la Antigua (Vilcálvaro), Libro de Difuntos, número 8 (1721–54). The author owes this reference to Valentín González of the Asociación de Investigación Histórica de Vicálvaro. 34 Suplica de C MacKenna [undated, post 1756], AGS SSH Leg 766 (2). 35 Suplica Da

Relations with the locals do not appear to have been a problem and were managed largely by the plant's directors. There were, perhaps inevitably, some incidents, particularly when the Irish workers left the factory complex, where they lived. One of these occurred when a trio of Irish workers went socializing in a Vicálvaro hostelry. In the course of the evening they were approached by an invalided Spanish soldier, a member of a local Madrid detachment, who demanded that they stand him a drink. The Irish were reluctant to indulge him and he was asked to vacate the premises, duly complying. On their returning home later in the evening, however, the disgruntled soldier attacked one of the Irish with a bayonet, whereupon all three fell on him, with predicable consequences for the Spaniard. The incident merited the Irish a stay in the guardhouse in San Fernando.[36]

There were also practical difficulties within the small migrant community itself, some of a moral nature. These worried the paternalistic Argumosa. He was concerned, for instance, when he discovered that a pair of Irish workers was cohabiting without ecclesiastical sanction. Sharpening his moral concern was the fact that both were Protestants. The Catholic chaplain, however, appeared to have things in hand and Argumosa was happy to announce that a marriage was in the offing. Of more concern to him, perhaps, was a second case, involving a married couple, in this case both Catholics. This time it would appear that the trauma of migration had strained family relations to breaking point. The wife of one of the weavers, on arrival in San Fernando, immediately and violently regretted the move. She refused to speak to her husband. This resulted in her ostracisation, causing Argumosa to fret that, bereft of means of support, she might be tempted to turn to an immoral profession. His solution was to secure her a place in a religious house.[37]

As well as managing personnel issues, Argumosa also had to ensure that the factory ran efficiently and, if possible, profitably. In April 1752, he was happy to report that the Irish, who by this time had been moved to Vicálvaro, were working well, as were their Dutch counterparts. He was still experiencing problems with workers who remained in San Fernando, some of whom may have been Irish. They were unhappy with their wages, which were less than those paid in associated plants. Argumosa informed Caravajal that he could not raise their salaries, for fear of exciting wage claims in the other plants.[38] With more specialized workers, however, Argumosa was willing to negotiate. He was particularly concerned to retain his Irish foremen, like MacKenna. In 1752, MacKenna and Thomas Beaven, an Irish Quaker,

---

Cathalina Howell viuda de Guillermo Sheercraft maestro que fue de perchadores y tundidores en la real fabrica de San Fernando, 6 Sept. 1767, AGS SSH Leg 768 (1). 36 Lourdes Sanchez Domínguez, *Un espacio en el tiempo*, p. 37, citing AGS SSH Leg 765 (1). 37 Argumosa to Caravajal, 28 Apr. 1752, AGS SSH Leg 765 (1). 38 Argumosa to Caravajal, San Fernando, 28 Apr. 1752, AGS SSH Leg 765 (1).

sought improved pay and conditions.[39] Argumosa advised Caravajal against a public concession but, because he was anxious to retain them, suggested some informal compensation instead.

In 1754, Argumosa drew up a general account of the plant and its operations.[40] At this stage the operation consisted of an integrated production unit with one hundred looms, fifty-nine of which were in use, twenty-two cloth shearing benches, thirty-four deknotting tables, two cloth presses, storage and ancillary buildings and sixty-one accommodation units for employees. In charge were foremen Cristobal MacKenna and one Santiago Petel. There were seven masters under their management, including the Irishmen Gerardo Floyster, master napper, William Sheercraft, master cloth shearer, and Andrew Creswell, master fuller. The chaplains were Alipio Mooney OSA[41] and Gerard Plunkett.

By 1754, the first of the three-year contracts were starting to expire and a number of the Irish weavers made arrangements for renewal, although they had the option of returning to Dublin.[42] They stated that they were ready to extend their contracts but only on condition that they continued to receive the same salary. Otherwise they preferred to return to Dublin, reminding the management that payment of the fare home on expiration of contract was part of the original agreement. In a note to Caravajal, 4 October 1754, Argumosa advised that the five in question be allowed to return to Ireland, with their passage paid, as they were no longer needed. The apprenticed Spaniards, he explained, were by now sufficiently well trained to permit them to maintain production without their Irish masters.

DUBLIN PROTESTANT WEAVERS BEFORE THE INQUISITION

As might be expected, the religious welfare of the migrant workers was an important concern for the factory administration. Elaborate arrangements were in place to cater for the spiritual needs of the mostly Catholic Irish operatives. There was no shortage of Irish clerical candidates for chaplaincy roles, as a number of Irish ecclesiastics staffed the local Irish colleges in Madrid and Alcalá or acted as chaplains in city hospitals and institutions. In the original royal site in San Fernando, located in the parish of Torrejón real de la Rivera, Gerardo Plunkett was employed as an assistant priest to look

---

39 Petition of Thomas Beaven, Santiago Petel and Cristobal MacKenna to Caravajal [undated, probably early 1753], AGS SSH Leg 765 (1).   40 'Estado de la real fabrica establecida en el real sitio de San Fernando ... 30 Abril de 1754', AGS SSH Leg 765 (2). 41 'El promoter fiscal de la Inquisicion de Corte contra el Dr. Don Juan de Lacy', AHN INQ Leg 3733, exp 46, f. 9v.   42 'Supplicantes los maestros texedores irlandeses de paño fino en la real fabrica de San Fernando, Vicálvaro', [undated probably early 1754], AGS SSH Leg 765 (2).

after the Irish. He had been rector of the Irish college in Alcalá de Henares.[43] In 1746 he was appointed to the royal site of San Fernando, to act as chaplain there and in 1748 was named parish priest.[44]

When some of the Irish moved to Vicálvaro, it appears that Alipio Mooney OSA was appointed as their chaplain. For reasons not entirely clear, his was a contested nomination and a group of workers insisted that they found him obnoxious. In a memorial addressed to Caravajal, eight of them pleaded that Mooney be replaced by a more suitable minister, claiming that the current chaplain was negligent and had threatened them with the Inquisition for refusing to confess to him.[45] The fact that the document was countersigned by the Irish Quaker foreman, Thomas Beaven, gave Argumosa pause and may account for his reporting the incident to Caravajal. The background to this affair is murky but there is evidence that Mooney was then in public dispute with another Irish cleric associated with the plant, one Juan Lacy, over the latter's alleged improper treatment of the wife of one of the Protestant workers, and other incidents. Lacy, however, was a force to be reckoned with. As an army veteran, nephew of the bishop of Limerick, censor of books, commissioner of the Inquisition, chaplain to San Antonio and drinking companion to Argumosa he wielded influence. Moreover, he was a frequent visitor to Vicálvaro, and not only to fulfil pastoral duties. It appears that he socialized there, with inebriated consequences, his enemies claimed.[46] The fact that the workers refused to confess to Mooney suggests that Lacy may not have been entirely innocent of the alienation of their spiritual affections.

The same pastoral team was responsible for the spiritual welfare of the Protestants among the Irish recruits. Their situation was complex. There is no doubt that the Spanish preferred to recruit Catholic artisans. However, even in Dublin it was not always possible to source artisans who were both Catholic and suitably qualified. Of the eighty or so workers recruited by Berry, it appears that about fifteen were not Catholic, about twenty per cent of the entire group.[47]

There was an already established legal context for the treatment of Protestants in Spain. This had been regulated under article 21 of the Treaty of London (1604). According to this article, conceived in the white heat of religious controversy, English and Irish Protestants were permitted to engage in commerce in Spain, provided they gave no scandal to Catholics. They were not to be compelled to attend Catholic services but were expected to respect

---

43 In 1744, as rector of Alcalá he endorsed an application for viaticum for four Irish priests: AGS, SSH Leg 966. 44 Caravajal to Argumosa, Madrid 12 Apr. 1752, AGS SSH Leg 765 (1). 45 'Los Irlandeses fabricantes en las reales fabricas de San Fernando y Vicalbaro prostratos a las pies de Vuestra Excelencia', Vicálvaro, 9 Jan. 1753, AGS SSH Leg 765 (1). 46 Segunda acusación [contra Lacy], Madrid, 9 May 1753, AHN INQ Leg 3733, exp. 46, f. 30v. 47 This figure assumes that all Protestant recruits converted.

Catholic beliefs and practices. As might be expected, provision was made for Protestants wishing to convert to Catholicism. They were expected to purge their heresy with an appropriate penance. Because Protestant baptism was considered valid by the Catholic church, rebaptism was not required.

While the religious passions that provided the context to the Treaty of London had cooled by the middle of the eighteenth century, the treaty continued to provide the legal instrument according to which Protestants in Spain were treated. The Irish Protestants in Vicálvaro were nonetheless exceptional. The Treaty of London dealt with transient Protestant visitors to Spain, ships' crewmen, merchants, their agents and the like. Permanent residents were a different matter and in their case some form of naturalization was deemed necessary not only to satisfy the local Inquisition but also for customary reasons. In the case of the Irish, three- and four-year contracts seem to have been considered as equivalent to permanent residence and, for this reason, naturalization, understood as religious conversion, was considered appropriate. There is no evidence of physical or even psychological compulsion. The weavers concerned seem to have accepted it as a part of the arrangement and requested rather than submitted to instruction.

There is some evidence that Argumosa profited from the process to leverage government support for his scheme in Vicálvaro. In a report penned in 1752, describing yet another difficult wage negotiation at San Fernando, he expressed his concern that if he did not grant the Irish a raise, they might quit royal service. For the Protestant Irish there was the added risk, he explained, that their departure would entail their loss to the church as the work of converting them to Catholicism, already underway, was incomplete.[48] On these grounds he recommended a concession. One gets a hint of opportunism here, but later Argumosa proved genuinely supportive of the conversions and followed the religious instruction of the group in question with great interest. On 14 May 1752 he observed 'that without either hypocrisy or credulity I can say that they [the Irish Protestants under instruction] were a source of great consolation'.[49]

As already mentioned, baptism in the Church of Ireland was recognized as valid by the Catholic church but the defects in the heretics' religious instruction could only be made up by catechetical instruction imparted by a qualified individual. This invariably involved a catechist, usually a Catholic priest and more often than not, due to the language difficulty, an Irish, English or Scots cleric. Plunkett, Lacy and Magennis all performed this role, no doubt making initial contact with their future charges in the course of ministering to their Catholic countrymen. It is not impossible that the clerics, attracted by the prospect of having a convert to their credit, encouraged the expatriate

---

48 Argumosa to Caravajal, 28 Apr. 1752, AGS SSH Leg 765 (1).   49 Argumosa to Caravajal, 14 May 1752, AGS SSH Leg 765 (1).

Protestants to convert. The fact that many of them, as we shall see, came from religiously mixed backgrounds may have made their passage easier.

Once the catechist judged the repentant 'heretic' sufficiently instructed, an audience was arranged with the local tribunal of the Inquisition. The catechist frequently accompanied the convert to the interview with the Holy Office, where he usually doubled up as interpreter. This supposed a close relationship between the repentant heretic and his or her catechist, a situation that occasionally created problems, as in the notorious case involving Lacy and Margaret Sheercraft, where Lacy was accused of improper behaviour.[50]

The audience was a straightforward affair. It took place in the chambers of the Inquisition, unless the penitent was ill or in danger of death. In the cases of Elizabeth Fling and Peter Sherry, for instance, the audience was held in the wards of the Hospital of the Passion. The audience was presided by an inquisitor or his commissioner, with a notary in attendance. The commissioner was sometimes the catechist who, as we have seen, often also acted as interpreter. The notary drew up an exact account of the interview, which followed a set format. Following the hearing it was read to the convert, signed and deposited in the Inquisition's archives. In the case of the Irish Protestant operatives whose conversions are recorded in the period under examination, Juan Lacy was commissioner and/or interpreter in nine of the conversions. Gerardo Plunkett appeared in six and Arturo Magennis and Pedro O'Dwyer SJ in one each. As already mentioned, the audience followed an established format: the penitents gave their names, nationality, profession and reason for petitioning the audience. The interpreter was sworn in and the interrogation began with the penitents delivering a short account of their lives and their religious history. They were then questioned by the commissioner about their religious knowledge. If the commissioner was satisfied with their level of instruction, he granted permission for them to be absolved. In cases where instruction was incomplete or unsatisfactory, the subject was entrusted to the catechist for further catechesis. Absolution was granted in all of the Irish cases.

Between 1745 and 1753 seventeen Irish Protestants connected with the woollens manufactory were processed, the majority between January 1751 and February 1753. Of these fourteen were male, the three females being spouses of workers. They were processed in small groups, suggesting that they may have come together from Ireland and perhaps were already associated there. Thus Thomas Gibson and John Hall were both processed in January 1751; William Sheercraft on his own the following July; Maria Nichols (acquaintance of Margaret Howell), Margaret Howell (Sheercraft's wife) and Thomas

50 'El promoter fiscal de la Inquisicion de Corte contra el Dr Don Juan de Lacy natural de Fenevera en Irlanda de 40 anos pro capellán maior de San Antonio de los Portugueses comisario y calificador del Santo Oficio por solicitatión y otros delitos, Madrid, 1752–54', AHN INQ Leg 3733, exp. 46, passim.

Hoey in December 1751; William O'Dwyer and Francis Lawlor in May 1752, brothers Samuel and John Slattery, and Samuel's son, John Junior, in May-June 1752; William Harden the following July and Samuel Nessfield and James Campbell in early 1753.

Of the seventeen, seven were from Dublin, three from Clare, two from Cork, and one each from Yorkshire, Mountmellick, Tipperary, Kildare and Roscommon. Their religious backgrounds were complex. Five were from solidly Protestant backgrounds, in the sense that both their parents were of the Protestant religion. In William Sheercraft's case, his father was a Protestant but his mother was a life-long Catholic. It was obviously his father who decided his son's religious affiliation. In the case of Samuel Slattery, his mother was a Protestant. His father, born a Catholic, converted temporarily to Protestantism, apparently to impress his prospective Protestant in-laws. On contracting the marriage he promptly reverted to Catholicism. However, Samuel, on marrying Mary Maher, a Catholic, raised their son John in the Protestant religion. In Francis Lawlor's case, his parents were Protestants who converted to Catholicism but he was raised a Protestant until the age of 12. Despite the fact that his father placed him in the house of a priest in Dublin, Lawlor practised as an Anglican all his life. In the case of Charles Murray, his father had been born a Catholic. The father had converted to Protestantism but later reverted to Catholicism, in which religion he died. His wife was a life-long Protestant and Murray *fils* followed her example. William O'Dwyer's case was somewhat different. Although both his parents were life-long Catholics, he himself practised as a Protestant. William Harden's mother was a Catholic, his father was of the established religion and the son followed his father's religious example. In the case of Elizabeth Fling, her father, who died young, was a Catholic; her mother was an Anglican and the daughter practised with her, though Isabel's brother, who lived in Dublin, was a Catholic. Santiago Campbell's parents were Protestants but they apprenticed him to a Catholic surgeon in Dublin called Peter Bergin, though he did not, at that time, convert. In Peter Sherry's case, both his parents were Catholics but they died when he was young. He was taken in by Protestant neighbours and raised an Anglican.

The majority of the converting Protestants were, therefore, from families of mixed religious background. The apparent ease with which they converted in Madrid raises questions about the depth of their religious convictions and of religious convictions in mid-eighteenth-century Dublin in general. Most work on eighteenth-century conversion in Ireland has concentrated on conversion from Catholicism to Protestantism.[51] This data on conversion in the opposite direction is useful, particularly as it provides some indication of motivation, apart from the purely economic. The case of Thomas Gibson is

---

[51] For example, see Michael Brown et al. (eds), *Converts and conversion in Ireland, 1650–1850* (Dublin, 2005).

interesting in this regard. This Dublin native was contracted as a cloth shearer at San Fernando. He had been born and raised a Protestant. However, he claimed that in Dublin he had formed such a good impression of the Catholic clergy and their ministry that his reformed faith was shaken.[52] Also interesting in this regard was the 35-year-old Dublin native, John Hall. He had been raised an Anglican but had come to entertain doubts about his faith. On travelling abroad he had spoken of these matters to a Catholic priest but it was not until he arrived in Madrid that he had the opportunity to take his doubts seriously and present himself to the Inquisition.[53]

In several cases, conversion was linked to the influence of a Catholic clergyman. The Dublin-born Protestant, John Scott, a dyer by trade, had arrived in Madrid in 1745. Having taken up soldering, he later fell on hard times and was reduced to begging. He sought alms at San Antonio's hostel, where he met Juan Lacy. They struck up a friendship. Lacy subsequently offered to keep him at his own expense and undertook to instruct him in the faith.[54] Lacy was also a central figure in the conversion of Maria Nichols in late 1751. She had come to Madrid in July of 1751, in the wake of her husband, who had travelled there in mid-1750.[55] They had two children, Thomas, who was being reared as a Catholic, and an infant. In the case of the Dublin-born, 25-year-old Isabel Fling, Lacy was again instrumental in organizing her audience. She was the wife of Peter Sherry, a weaver at San Fernando. Her deceased father, John Fling, had been a Catholic but her mother, Catharina Norton, was Anglican.[56] She had been reared by a Protestant aunt but claimed in her testimony that during the recent Holy Year celebrations in Dublin in 1750 she had begun to entertain doubts about her faith. On leaving Ireland in July 1752, she had travelled to Bilbao, subsequently arriving in San Fernando, where she had remained until falling ill, at which point she was hospitalized in Madrid. Indisposed and hospitalized at the same time was her 42-year-old husband, Peter.[57] Both were visited by Lacy who subsequently managed their conversions.

Lacy also took credit for William Scheercraft's conversion. The latter was a native of Mountmellick and a master cloth shearer.[58] As an infant, Sheercraft had been baptized by a minister named John Pits and later confirmed by the Anglican bishop of Ossory. He had one brother, John, who was serving in the army of the king of England. Prior to coming to Spain some time after August 1750, Sheercraft had been in England to perfect his craft. There he met his future wife, Margaret Howell. He claimed to have come to Spain with the purpose of converting and had enjoyed the good fortune, he said, of meeting Lacy,

52 AHN INQ Lib 1156, ff 359r–362r (Madrid, 4 Jan. 1751). 53 AHN INQ Lib 1156, ff 354r–358r (Madrid, 3 Jan. 1751). 54 AHN INQ Lib 1156, ff 158r–164v (Madrid, 13 Dec. 1745). 55 AHN INQ Lib 1156, ff 434r–437v (Madrid, 16 Dec. 1751). 56 AHN INQ Lib 1157, ff 138r–142r (Madrid, 29 Aug. 1752). 57 AHN INQ Lib 1157, ff 143r–144v (Madrid, 30 Aug. 1752). 58 AHN INQ Lib 1156, ff 397r–401v (Madrid, 5 July 1751).

who instructed him in the faith. With the assistance of the Spanish ambassador in London, Sheercraft stated that he intended to bring his wife, son and daughter to Spain so that they too might convert. He was as good as his word. Later that year, Sheercraft's wife arrived in San Fernando, where Lacy oversaw her religious instruction.[59] However, having been accused of sexual impropriety with Mrs Sheercraft, Lacy was stood aside.

The other chaplains, including Gerard Plunkett, now assumed Lacy's role. Plunkett processed the case of Samuel Slattery, a native of Clare, whose Catholic father had converted on marrying his Protestant mother, Isabel William, 'for a few years to please her parents but thereafter returned to the Catholic fold'.[60] Slattery was then working in San Fernando as a weaver and declared himself to be a widower and a life-long Protestant. On meeting Plunkett, two months previously, the 41-year-old was apprised of his errors. With him were his son John and his brother, another John, both of whom also sought reconciliation.[61] Plunkett also assisted William Harden of Cork,[62] the Kildare-born Francisco Lawler,[63] Carlos Murray[64] and the Tipperary native, William O'Dwyer.[65] Of Catholic parents, the latter had practised as a Protestant since 1743. Four years prior to his conversion he had signed up as a sailor to an English corsair. After six months' service he travelled to London, staying just a month, then travelling successively to Cork, Kilkenny and Dublin, where he was recruited for San Fernando.

Plunkett received occasional assistance from other Irish clergy including Arthur McGuinness, who absolved the Dublin-born Samuel Nessfield, a tanner and single man.[66] Nessfield had come to Bilbao three years earlier and had a brother working in the English New World plantations. Later in 1753 Pedro O'Dwyer OFM processed the case of the Roscommon native James Campbell.[67] He had been apprenticed to Samuel Howesden, an apothecary, in Kildare and later to a Dublin surgeon of the Catholic persuasion, one Pedro Brogan, before travelling to London and then to Spain 'to improve his surgical knowledge'. He was practising in the General Hospital in Madrid, where a number of the Irish who had fallen ill in Vicálvaro were treated. From all this it would appear that

---

59 AHN INQ Lib 1156, ff 438r–440v (Madrid, 6 Dec. 1751). 60 'por unos tres u quatro años para complacer a los parientes de la citada su mujer, y que después de dicho tiempo se reconcilio con Nra. Madre la Santa Iglesia Catholica Apostolica Romana', AHN INQ Lib 1157, ff 67r–72v. 61 Juan Senior converted. See AHN INQ Lib 1157, ff 95r–100r (San Fernando, 5 June 1752). Juan Junior also converted. See AHN INQ Lib 1157, ff 90r–94v (San Fernando, 3 June 1752). 62 AHN INQ Lib 1157, ff 101r–106r (San Fernando, 4 June 1752). 63 AHN INQ Lib 1157, ff 78r–84r (San Fernando, 30 May 1752). 64 AHN INQ Lib 1157, ff 85r–89r (San Fernando, 31 May 1752). 65 AHN INQ Lib 1157, ff 78r–87r (San Fernando, 29 May 1752). 66 AHN INQ Lib 1157, ff 61r–63r, 68r (Madrid, 27 Jan. 1753). O'Dwyer presented a memorial to the Inquisition on Campbell's part, 12 Nov. 1752. See AHN INQ Lib 1157, ff 58r–59r. 67 AHN INQ Lib 1157, ff 164r–167r (Madrid, 28 Feb. 1753).

conversion was both an unspoken part of their Spanish contracts and an inquisitorial requirement. It was also part of the individual's integration into the Irish migrant community in Spain and, in some cases, the first step in their permanent assimilation into Spanish society.

CONCLUSION

The longer-term fate of most of these Dublin weavers and their dependants is unclear. Some returned to Ireland but a number remained permanently in Spain. We know that one of them, Margaret Sheercraft, obtained a pension in 1767.[68] Cristobal MacKenna continued on as foreman for many years. Enrique Doyle later made a name for himself as a recruiter and industrial spy. The plants themselves enjoyed mixed fortunes. Those at Guadalajara, which included the complexes at San Fernando and Vicálvaro, were significant in the history of the textile industry in the Iberian peninsula, particularly with regard to the degree of vertical integration they achieved, concentrating the whole production process on one site and obviating the need to outsource to third parties.[69] However, these plants depended overwhelmingly on royal funding and never managed to integrate successfully into the local or national economy.

In the context of Irish migration, the experience of these Dublin Protestant weavers and their Catholic countrymen in this Spanish government-sponsored industrial enterprise is revealing. The affair points, first of all, to heretofore unexplored links between Spanish industrial innovators and Irish textile operatives in the mid-eighteenth century. These were both extensive and complex, included artisan recruitment and technology exchange, and enjoyed a high level of Spanish government support. Second, the episode provides unusual insight into the workings of an artificially created migrant colony engaged in a specialized economic activity. Information on the detail of eighteenth-century industry in Ireland is rare and even more uncommon for the migrant Irish. Third, the conversion narratives episode reveals the intriguing role of the Spanish Inquisition in what might be called the 'naturalization' of foreign workers. Its processing of the Irish demonstrates the range of its functions and illustrates how flexibly and opportunistically this behemoth of the Spanish old regime adapted to assume new functions. More generally, this episode complicates received views of migration from mid-eighteenth-century Ireland and offers new evidence of the intricacy of migrant motivation and of the role of religious conversion in social and economic assimilation.

68 'Suplica Da Cathalina Howell viuda de Guillermo Sheercraft maestro que fue de perchadores y tundidores en la real fabrica de San Fernando', 6 Sept. 1767, AGS SSH Leg 768 (1).   69 Clayburn la Force, 'Royal textiles factories in Spain', 346.

A saint for eighteenth-century Dublin? Father John Murphy

TOBY BARNARD

I

Few priests in eighteenth-century Ireland take on any strong personality unless a bishop or caught up in politics, like Father Sheehy in Co. Tipperary or Father Murphy of Wexford.[1] For most, bare biographical detail has to suffice. An exception is another John Murphy, a priest in Dublin, who died in 1753. As Fr Hugh Fenning has observed, more is known about the Dublin Murphy's career than about that of his contemporary, Michael O'Reilly, the archbishop of Armagh.[2] The reasons for this are in themselves worth exploring; so, too, are the wider implications of the way in which the Catholic church represented itself and its personnel. There are suggestive contrasts between Catholic strategies and those of the other confessional groups in eighteenth-century Ireland, especially in the uses of print. There are also striking divergences between the prevailing situation in Ireland and that in other European countries where Catholics formed the majority of the population.

Behind features which may have been special to Ireland – most obviously the legal disabilities under which both regular and secular clergy operated intermittently from the 1580s and then from the 1690s – are questions about the supposed differences in approach between Catholics and Protestants. In particular, Protestants contended that Catholics denied laypeople ready access to Holy Writ, and accordingly were reluctant to provide printed helps in the form of digests, commentaries and guides to the Scriptures. Instead, partisans alleged, the Word of God was mediated through clerics – often ignorant or negligent – or replaced by dependence on images and artefacts. There seems little doubt that among some Protestant churches in Ireland, as among their English, Scottish, Welsh and colonial American counterparts, there was concern to create a literate laity and to furnish it with printed helps as a pre-requisite for godly communities.[3] Among zealous Presbyterians in Ulster, reading was justified as 'a plain apostolic canon'.[4] Protestant activists frequently contrasted their own

[1] N. Furlong, *Fr John Murphy of Boolavogue, 1753–1798* (Dublin, 1991); T.P. Power, *Land, politics and society in eighteenth-century Tipperary* (Oxford, 1993), pp 260–70. [2] H. Fenning, *The undoing of the friars of Ireland: a study of the novitiate question in the eighteenth century* (Louvain, 1972), p. 161. [3] D.D. Hall, 'Introduction' in H. Amory and D.D. Hall (eds), *A history of the book in America: 1. The colonial book in the Atlantic world* (Chapel Hill, 2007), p. 2. [4] J. Duchal, *A sermon on occasion of the much lamented death of the late*

energy with the indifference or outright hostility of their Catholic rivals.⁵ Bit by bit, the Protestant contentions, if not a total caricature, have been revealed as a serious – and often deliberate – distortion. The Catholic church in its discussions at the Council of Trent appreciated how print could assist in renewal and expansion.⁶ Even so, the obstacles to a widespread embracing of print in Ireland were formidable ones. Factors which retarded the production and circulation of print throughout Ireland included remoteness, relative poverty and consequent low levels of literacy. In addition, official hostility inhibited and indeed penalized the practice, let alone the promotion, of Popery. These factors combined to stunt the printing of Catholic materials within Ireland. Such material as was available had to be imported from Britain or continental Europe. Dependence on imports meant that the print had originated elsewhere and was seldom aimed at the specific conditions of Irish Catholics.

Paradoxically, a characteristic of Catholic worship derided (and exaggerated) by Protestant opponents – a heavy reliance on visual, aural and sensory prompts to faith – was not pronounced in Ireland. Poverty, coupled with the circumspection about attracting unfriendly attention, prevented the architectural, sculptural and graphic display favoured by Counter-Reformation and baroque Catholicism elsewhere.⁷ Occasional donations from the faithful introduced traces of the ornamentation that was commonplace in continental European churches.⁸ However, a symptom of how little Catholic Irish laypeople could share in the aesthetic effusiveness of their counterparts overseas was the absence of any tradition of commissioning painted *ex-voto* thank-offerings for prayers answered and miraculous deliverances, which abounded in Mediterranean Europe.⁹ In Ireland, places and natural objects – springs, stones, trees – were preferred to the fabricated as the focus of cults.

Reverend Mr John Abernethy (Belfast and Dublin, 1741), p. 40.   5 C.N[ary], *The New Testament of our Lord and Saviour Jesus Christ* (n.p., 1719), sig. [a6]–[a6v]; P. Fagan, *Dublin's turbulent priest: Cornelius Nary, 1658–1738* (Dublin, 1991), pp 79–98; C.N[ary], *The New Testament of our Lord and Saviour Jesus Christ* (n.p., 1719), sig. [a6]–[a6v]; *Poor Robin's advice to the unwary, unthinking and unguarded Protestants of the city of Dublin* (n.p., n.d.); W. Sellon, *An abridgement of the Holy Scriptures* (Dublin, 1790), p. 203; *A serious and friendly address to the Roman Catholicks of Ireland to read the scriptures in a language they understand* (Dublin, 1721); *A short refutation of the principal errors of the Church of Rome* (Dublin, 1719); E. Welchman, *A dialogue betwixt a Protestant minister and a Romishpriest* (Dublin, 1719).   6 A.F. Allison and D.M. Rogers (eds), *The contemporary printed literature of the English Counter-Reformation between 1558 and 1640*, 2 vols (Aldershot, 1989–94); M.E. Ducreux, 'Reading unto death: books and readers in eighteenth-century Bohemia' in R. Chartier (ed.), *The culture of print* (Oxford, 1989), pp 191–229; H. Louthan, *Converting Bohemia: force and persuasion in the Catholic Reformation* (Cambridge, 2009), pp 211–44.   7 For one example: G. Kazerouni (ed.), *Les couleurs du ciel: peintures des églises de Paris au xviie siècle* (Paris, 2012).   8 T.C. Barnard, 'Fabrics of faith: the material worlds of Catholic Ireland and Protestant Ireland, 1500–1800' in Raghnall Ó Floinn (ed.), *Franciscan faith* (Dublin, 2011), pp 31–41; J. McDonnell, *Maynooth College bicentenary art exhibitions: ecclesiastical art of the penal era* (Maynooth, 1995).   9 F. Faranda,

The Revd John Murphy D.D., Catholic priest, 1710–53,
Dublin: Edward Lyons, Essex Bridge (d.s.), reproduced courtesy of the National
Library of Ireland.

Only slowly in the eighteenth century did matters change. Gradually the Catholic hierarchy shook off a defensive reticence which had amounted, so far as utilizing print was concerned, to near inertia. More importantly, entrepreneurs in the print trades realized the potential of a market among Irish Catholics that, until the 1720s, was virtually untapped by local operators. Faint stirrings of activity to cater for this readership can be detected during the 1720s; stronger ones by the 1740s. Moreover, the attitudes of the authorities were relaxing (although capable of sudden, usually localized, drives to enforce discriminatory laws). Also, more Catholics were prospering from trade and farming and buying education. In these conditions, a noticeable increase from the 1740s in the number of publications aimed specifically at Catholics is readily explained. Moreover, there emerged publishers and booksellers specializing in such material, sometimes with shadowy links to their Catholic colleagues in London. Yet, notwithstanding the growing vitality of printing for Irish Catholics, some of the earlier traits – of caution and reliance on what had originated outside Ireland – persisted.[10] The *Life* of Father Murphy, in avoiding these characteristics, stands out from the pack. Because it was unusual, it merits a closer examination both to try to establish the intentions behind its composition and publication, and to compare it with other examples of clerical biography (or hagiography), both Catholic and Protestant.

Murphy was not the first Dublin priest to be celebrated posthumously in print. However, in several respects – length and detail – the Murphy *Life* marks a notable advance on predecessors. It differs, too, from the near-contemporary memorialization of prominent Catholics, including two provincial clerics. To make clear the differences – and their implications – it is necessary to start with a fuller description of the *Life* itself.

II

Murphy's death in Dublin in 1753 occasioned a printed funeral oration and then (in the same year) the longer *Life*.[11] The latter, its author identified only

---

Fides tua te salvum fecit: i dipinti votivi nel Santuario di Santa Maria del Monte a Cesena (Modena, 1997); F. Faranda, *Per grazia ricevuta. Dipinti votivi in diocese di Imola* (Imola, 1993); F. Faranda, *P.G.R. Testimonianze dipinte dalle Chiese di Lugo di Romagna* (Rimini, 1992); J. Garnett and G. Rosser, *Spectacular miracles: transforming images in Italy from the Renaissance to the present* (London, 2013). 10 C.S. Begadon, 'Laity and clergy in the Catholic renewal of Dublin, c.1750–1830' (PhD, National University of Ireland, Maynooth, 2009); T. O'Connor, 'Religious change, 1550–1800' in R. Gillespie and A. Hadfield (eds), *The Oxford history of the Irish book; III. The Irish book in English, 1550–1800* (Oxford, 2006), pp 169–93. For the essential background: C. Lennon, 'The print trade, 1700–1800', ibid., pp 74–87. 11 Father [ ], *A funeral oration preach'd on the death of the Rev. John Murphy, DD* (Dublin, [1753]); J.K., *An account of the life and character of the late Rev. John Murphy, D.D. taken from authentic memoirs, and original papers* (Dublin, 1753). The name

with the initials J.K. (Father Fenning has suggested that they belong to Joseph Kelly, a fellow priest), was published by James Hoey.[12] Although not exclusively concerned with titles for Catholics, they formed an important component in Hoey's business.[13] The *Life* runs to almost 100 duodecimo pages, and survives in one known copy. It is not the sole source of information about Murphy. Thanks to the researches of Father Fenning, Murphy, while a priest in Dublin, is revealed as one of the *zelanti*. Owing to his support of reform, particularly of the friars, Murphy was sent to Rome in 1750 to press for action. Furthermore, his fame as a preacher and leader made some talk of him as a future archbishop of Dublin.[14] Inevitably, Murphy, as a partisan of a particular and controversial policy, incurred hostility.[15] The controversies around him may help to explain why he should become the subject of a printed account. The priest responsible for the text acted as an editor or compiler, bringing together recollections from Murphy's colleagues.[16] But it is probable that the stronger motive for the publication was conventional: Murphy as exemplar. The text promoted him explicitly as 'a model, well deserving the imitation of all men'.[17]

Accordingly, his virtues were spelt out: temperance, charity, gentle manners and a love of peace. At the same time, both his physical appearance and demeanour were described. Six foot tall and, as the hagiographer expressed it, 'elegantly put together', Murphy had a commanding presence. He charmed with 'his blithe conversation, and jocund air'. Tellingly, it was said that he could 'pass very well for a person of the highest rank or station'.[18] This was a theme that (as will be seen) had been introduced elsewhere in the *Life*.

Much in the account of his life sets out the steps leading towards his almost saintly status as a pastor in mid-eighteenth-century Dublin. In tracing his personal history there is greater emphasis on steadfastness in devotion than to loyalty. Born in 1710 and brought up in Dublin, Murphy had been educated at a school kept by the O'Reillys near St Audeon's Arch. Not unexpectedly Murphy excelled as a scholar. Marked out for the priesthood, he embarked for further study in Spain in 1727. Again he excelled: first at St Jago and then Salamanca.[19] All this then might appear unremarkable. But a

of the author of the *Funeral oration* is blacked out in the one known copy and is presently illegible. This slighter work was printed, perhaps opportunistically, by Thomas Hutchinson, an evanescent figure in the Dublin print trades: M. Pollard, *Dictionary of members of the Dublin book trade, 1550–1800* (London, 2000), p. 304.   12 Fenning, *The undoing of the friars*, p. 185.   13 Pollard, *Dictionary*, pp 291–3.   14 H. Fenning, 'Letters from a Jesuit in Dublin on the Confraternity of the Holy Name, 1747–1748', *Archivium Hibernicum*, 29 (1970), 136.   15 H. Fenning, *The Irish Dominican province, 1698–1797* (Dublin, 1990), pp 223–6; Fenning, *The undoing of the friars*, pp 161–7, 188–210.   16 Another priest, identified with the initials 'S.B.', was credited with revising the work.   17 J.K., *Life*, pp 78–9.   18 J.K., *Life*, pp 13, 80–1.   19 G. Nogol, V. Bray and D.J. O'Doherty, 'Students of the Irish College, Salamanca', *Archivium Hibernicum*, 6 (1915), 6; P. O'Connell, *The Irish College at Santiago de Compostella, 1605–1769* (Dublin,

couple of elements seem to speak of preoccupations on the part at least of the biographer – probably another Catholic priest in Dublin. Murphy's lineage was firmly native Irish and Catholic. A grandfather had fought in James II's army and had then served as an officer in an Irish regiment on the Continent where he died. Murphy's father, himself left fatherless, had been taken on as an apprentice to a chandler in central Dublin. This master was a Protestant dissenter and took the youthful Murphy with him to the meeting house. As a result, it seems that the future priest's father became a Protestant. However, Murphy's mother, also of distinguished Irish Catholic stock, remained a Catholic and ensured that the son was brought up as one.

The biographer indicates that Murphy was later derided for his lowly origins, with his father categorized as 'a mechanic'.[20] The detractors are answered in two ways. One argument was that ancient lineage counted for nothing if the beneficiary was a libertine and irreligious. True nobility and gentility arose not from heraldry and heredity. Instead, it was remembered that John Murphy's parents kept 'the genteelest house' in their neighbourhood and practised hospitality. Moreover, the young Murphy quickly acquired, at home and at school, polite accomplishments. As well as ancient and modern European languages, Murphy was taught music and dancing 'and other polite branches'.[21] It was recalled that the priest could always take 'second fiddle', although it was not to this talent that his later popularity was attributed.[22] These personable traits were enlarged and refined in the Iberian peninsula. It was said that with his politeness and natural ease he would have passed muster at the courts of Versailles and Madrid.[23]

Such emphasis on the social graces might seem almost gratuitous in the commemoration of a godly pastor. Their inclusion suggests a sensitivity of Catholic apologists to allegations by the Church of Ireland elite that Catholic priests were ignorant, uncouth and unfitted for polite society. Similar anxieties were expressed and refuted by Protestant dissenters, also anxious to conform to the demanding codes of the respectable.[24] Of the Revd William Taylor of Carncastle, it was remembered that his entire demeanour was 'smoothed and polished by good breeding'. Revd Samuel Haliday, well-travelled in continental Europe and conversant with books, mingled easily with 'men of the higher rank'.[25]

In Murphy's case, his mien, as well as his learning, earned him admiration. One or two other features of the characterization suggest an attempt to

2007), p. 112. **20** J.K., *Life*, pp 18–19. **21** J.K., *Life*, pp 35–6. **22** J.K., *Life*, p. 36. **23** J.K., *Life*, p. 39. **24** J. Seed, 'Gentlemen dissenters: the social and political meanings of rational dissent in the 1770s and 1780s', *Historical Journal*, 28 (1985), 299–325; R. Whan, 'Presbyterians in Ulster, c.1680–1730: a social and political study' (PhD, Queen's University Belfast, 2009). **25** Duchal, *A sermon on ... the late Reverend Mr John Abernethy*, pp 22, 23–4, 28–9, 30–1.

widen Murphy's appeal beyond an audience of devout Catholics. Once he had returned from Spain to Dublin, he is shown to have been active in charitable works, notably during the famine of 1740–1, and regularly thereafter. In addition, his popularity as a preacher brought listeners from outside the Catholic community. This notion that sermon-tasting blurred rigid confessional boundaries in the capital is an unfamiliar one. It has been assumed generally that, while inevitably there was regular commercial and utilitarian contact between Catholics and Protestants, what happened within their separate churches was unknown (and often suspect) to outsiders. If Murphy's eloquence was so renowned that it attracted non-Catholic strangers, then a more fluid state of inter-confessional relations is suggested, at least in the capital with its unique variety of worship. Maybe it was easier for the sermon-samplers to preserve anonymity in these crowded congregations.

Murphy's ministry had a strong social dimension. His charity and hospitality were particularly celebrated and instances were detailed. He was known too for his concern to educate the poor of the city.[26] Indeed, his mission to Rome in 1750 had been partly precipitated by growing disquiet about the impact of the Protestant charter schools and the need for Catholics to counter them more effectively.[27] Like the zealous clergy of other denominations, he sought to reform manners.[28] One target was profane swearing. Murphy was active in attempts – in the end unsuccessful – to establish in Dublin a confraternity of the Holy Name of Jesus.[29] Prostitutes, adulterers, drunkards and debtors all came within his remit.[30] More unusual were his attempts to eradicate trickery and frauds among tradespeople. It was said, too, that he intervened when riots disturbed Dublin. The dates are not specified, but disturbances occurred regularly throughout the 1740s and early 1750s.[31] Such was Murphy's standing and familiarity with the poorer Dubliners that he was appealed to by justices of the peace to use his influence to defuse potential dangers. Murphy, it would appear, was happy to do so. This attitude – socially conservative and supportive of the civil authorities – is hardly surprising but not much documented among eighteenth-century Irish priests before the 1790s. Murphy's stance shows that he shared the worry of Protestant clerics about immorality, irreligious behaviour and ignorance. If Murphy laboured against these perceived evils, it is unlikely that he was unique among his *confrères*, although he may have been unusually energetic.

26 Fenning, *The undoing of the friars*, pp 164, n. 3, 215.   27 Fenning, *The undoing of the friars*, pp 196–7, 208; *A funeral oration*, p. 5.   28 T.C. Barnard, 'Reforming Irish manners: the religious societies in Dublin during the 1690s', *Historical Journal*, 35 (1992), 805–38, reprinted in Barnard, *Irish Protestant ascents and descents* (Dublin, 2004), pp 143–78. 29 Fenning, 'Letters from a Jesuit in Dublin on the Confraternity of the Holy Name', pp 153–4.   30 *A funeral oration*, pp 12–13.   31 P. Fagan, 'The Dublin Catholic mob (1700–1750)', *Eighteenth-Century Ireland*, 4 (1989), 133–42; J. Kelly, *The Liberty and Ormond Boys: factional riot in eighteenth-century Ireland* (Dublin, 2005).

Suggestive, too, are the biographer's statements that the authorities acknowledged the power enjoyed by a priest of Murphy's calibre and were prepared to enlist it. Moreover, Murphy appeared willing to help to harden 'the social cement, which builds up the mighty fabric of society' and preserved a precarious order in mid-eighteenth-century Dublin.[32] It does not follow – and nothing is said of this in the biography – that Murphy was also happy to defend uncritically the political order of the time. However, had he been openly hostile to the prevailing system, it is improbable that the authorities would have turned to him for aid.

The public and secular dimensions to Murphy's ministry are a noteworthy element in the *Life*. However, the bulk of the account is concerned with more predictable aspects, as a comparison with the handful of similar printed memorials will show. Already the mixed but proudly Irish and Catholic lineage of Murphy has been mentioned. Schooling with the Reillys hints at what was available in Dublin for promising Catholic youths. It was not geared specifically towards those aiming at ordination; indeed, it hardly differed in its content and its ambitions from avowedly Protestant establishments. Not until Murphy departed for the Iberian peninsula and preparation for the priesthood did his education diverge sharply from that offered to Dubliners of the middling sorts. The *Life* noted that the Murphys, despite their modest circumstances, maintained 'the genteelest house' in their parish. It was to this milieu that Murphy would return after his training in Spain. Murphy's education with the Reillys and additional lessons in music and dancing showed that there was money to educate him. Nothing at present has been retrieved of the Reillys' establishment by St Audoen's Arch, but its ability to equip Murphy for the rigorous regime in Spain indicates the availability of advanced educational opportunities for some Irish Catholics within the capital.[33] It is also worth noting that the Reillys were later prominent in literary and linguistic endeavours on behalf of Irish Catholicism. They were, for example, generous subscribers to the publications of Charles O'Conor of Belanagare in the 1750s, and were the movers behind an Irish-language club planned in Dublin during that same decade.[34] Other episodes transcended narrow confession and spoke rather of conventions in biographical writing, especially that intended to fortify faith. Murphy (like Saint Paul) had narrowly escaped from a shipwreck. He ignored the commands of the captain and the panic of the other passengers. Heedless of the danger, he strove to

---

32 J.K., *Life*, p. 73. 33 R.E. Ward, J.F. Wrynn and C.C. Ward (eds), *Letters of Charles O'Conor of Belanagare* (Washington DC, 1988), pp 4, 360, 497. 34 D. Bouhours, *Life of St Francis Xavier* (Dublin, 1743), subscribers; J. Carney (ed.), *Poems of the O'Reillys* (Dublin, 1950), pp 21–2; J. Leerssen, *Mere Irish and Fíor-Ghael: studies in the ideas of Irish nationality, its development and literary expression prior to the nineteenth century* (Cork, 1996), pp 330–1; C. O'Conor, *Dissertations on the antient history of Ireland* (Dublin, 1753); Ward, Wrynn and Ward (eds), *Letters of Charles O'Conor*, pp 106, 107.

convert a Jew at this critical juncture.[35] Some scenes have a predictability that speaks of well-established biographical tropes. At the college in Salamanca, a preacher on St Patrick's day dropped dead and Murphy extemporized, brilliantly. The appropriateness of the festival is not laboured, but it is present.[36] While in Spain, his eulogy (in Latin) on the consecration of the bishop of Astorgs had been published.[37] Returning to Ireland after his prolonged studies in Spain, he arrived – fortuitously – as his mother was dying, so could minister to her both physically and spiritually. When, in turn, his father died, the obdurate Presbyterian refused to see his son, only to relent at the last. However, no death-bed conversion is recorded.[38]

Murphy's manner of preaching was praised. Notwithstanding his linguistic and intellectual accomplishments, he simplified his homilies, 'lest it should appear too pompous for the lower class of hearers'. He rejected older fashions: 'instead of teasing his audience or vexing their patience with speculative matter, endless quotations from idle and impertinent authorities, terrible denunciations of hell and damnation, tedious distinctions of faith', he constructed his own body of moral divinity.[39] If not literally true, the way in which Murphy's preaching is described caught the temper of the 1750s: 'his word, like electricity, permeated through the hearts of thousands who were his hearers and gave the shock to ten thousand who confessed its force and energy'.[40]

The effectiveness of preachers was a matter that concerned all denominations. Vocal power mattered; so, too, did the style of address. In all churches, there was criticism of clergy who either adopted a florid manner or handled abstruse questions. The General Synod cautioned Presbyterian preachers against over-elaboration lest it pass above the heads of auditors. Ministers were instructed to abstain 'from all romantick expressions and hard words, which the vulgar do not understand'.[41] The leading Presbyterian minister in Dublin between the 1730s and 1750s, John Leland, was praised for adapting his discourses to the differing capacities of his congregation. Milk was offered to babes, and meat to the stronger. Leland's style was invariably 'plain, correct and useful'.[42] Yet, exhortations to simplicity and clarity were impossible to enforce. Preachers were ruled more by temperament and vocal capacities than by injunctions from superiors. Those who appeared to extemporize, holding forth without reference to notes, were admired. Of one respected Presbyterian

35 J.K., *Life*, pp 27–8.   36 J.K., *Life*, p. 46.   37 J.K., *Life*, p. 35.   38 J.K., *Life*, pp 55–6.   39 J.K., *Life*, pp 66–7.   40 Annals of the Poor Clare nuns, s.d. 1753, formerly at Harold's Cross, Dublin, NLI, microfilm, P3500; Fenning, *The undoing of the friars*, pp 165–6; J.K., *Life*, p. 7.   41 *Records of the General Synod of Ulster from 1691 to 1820*, 3 vols (Belfast, 1897–8), i, p. 25. More generally: A. R. Holmes, *The shaping of Ulster Presbyterian belief and practice, 1770–1840* (Oxford, 2006), pp 126–62.   42 J. Leland to Astley, 27 Oct. 1758, Bodleian Library, Oxford, MS Eng. Lett. C. 352, f. 8v.; J. Leland, *Discourses on various subjects*, 4 vols (London, 1769), i, pp x–xi, xxi–xxii.

it was admitted that his sermons, 'tho' just and natural, and plain too, yet were not obvious to persons of no more than common invention'. This preacher, John Abernethy, was helped by 'a clear fine, strong voice' and was capable of entertaining his congregation. But he could be monotonous. To engage the emotions, he used pathos and introduced 'a tincture of rational enthusiasm'. Abernethy was begged to simplify his discourses for 'the understanding of all'. 'He descended as low as he could; yet he never could, as low as many desired'.[43] Similar concern was expressed over the obscurities and ornamentation in the sermons delivered by Catholics and Church of Ireland incumbents, and chimed with Quaker injunctions on verbal simplicity.[44]

Directness and simplicity were said to have been the hallmarks of Murphy's oratory. What is not made clear is the language in which he usually preached. Knowledge of Irish is not listed among his notable linguistic skills.[45] With no explicit statement it has to be inferred that English was his preferred medium. Such was his fame that his church attracted auditors 'of all sects and opinions'.[46] Murphy's funeral in 1753 was said to have attracted 7,000 or 8,000 mourners.[47]

Murphy's attributes and popularity did not necessarily endear him to colleagues. His conduct rebuked the low standards that he (and others) bemoaned among the friars in Ireland. If, as Murphy believed, lack of education disabled them from performing many of their duties satisfactorily, their modes of living further rendered them unfit for polite society. Murphy had hoped to enter the Society of Jesus and his continuing devotion to Francis Xavier and Ignatius Loyola was remarked on.[48] He appreciated the importance of the growing constituency of prosperous and respectable Catholics, particularly in and around the capital.[49] And, indeed, the publication of his lengthy life, running to almost a hundred duodecimo pages, must have been

---

43 Duchal, *A sermon on ... the late Reverend Mr John Abernethy*, pp 15–16.   44 Bp W. King to J. Bonnell, 28 May 1695, King MSS, TCD MSS 1995–2008/433; P. Delany, *Sixteen discourses upon doctrines and duties, more peculiarly Christian* (London, 1754), pp xii-xiv; [P. Delany], *The present state of learning, religion and infidelity in Great Britain* (London, 1732), pp 6–8, 11–15, 27–33; J.K., *Life*, pp 14–13, 63, 66–7, 78–9; E. Wettenhall, *Six sermons preached in Ireland, in difficult times* (London, 1695), sig. [A3v]–[A4v]. Cf. T.C. Barnard, 'Almoners of Providence: the clergy, 1647–1780' in T.C. Barnard and W.G. Neely, *The clergy of the Church of Ireland, 1000–2000: messengers, watchmen and stewards* (Dublin, 2006), pp 88–91; R. Gillespie, 'The reformed preacher: Irish Protestant preaching, 1660–1700' in A.J. Fletcher and R. Gillespie (eds), *Irish preaching, 700–1700* (Dublin, 2001), pp 127–43; A. Hunt, *The art of hearing: English preachers and their audiences, 1590–1640* (Cambridge, 2010), pp 89, 93–4, 185–6, 394, 397, 399–400; M. Morrissey, 'Scripture, style and persuasion in seventeenth-century theories of preaching', *Journal of Ecclesiastical History*, 53 (2002), 686–706.   45 J.K., *Life*, p. 35.   46 J.K., *Life*, pp 14–13, 63, 67, 78–9.   47 J.K., *Life*, p. 80.   48 J.K., *Life*, pp 57, 79. A 'John Murphy' subscribed to the Dublin edition of D. Bouhours, *Life of St Francis Xavier* (Dublin, 1743).   49 Fenning, *The undoing of the friars*, pp 202–3.

aimed principally at such readers. Although Murphy sought to stop it, something of a cult developed around him. Unusually, the oration at his funeral was published, and engravings were also printed and sold.[50] The images were taken from his death mask. During his life, Murphy had suppressed a portrait engraving. It was said, too, that panegyrics and eulogies were sold in the streets immediately after his death. Something of his teaching was preserved in a slim tract issued at this juncture.[51] Such was the demand that pirated editions of the biography and engraving were anticipated.[52] The verses appended to a print of Murphy showed his renown:

> By Patrick's wonders, pagan worship dies
> Through Murphy's labours sacred altars rise.
> Each saint deserves an everlasting crown,
> And Murphy shares with Patrick in renown.[53]

The commemoration of Murphy suggests the vigour of urban Catholicism and its ability by the 1750s to utilize print. Indeed, it seems that the eloquent and dynamic Murphy himself employed print for his campaigning. *The impartial examiner*, a defence of the Catholics and a plea for the moderation of the penalties under which they lived, published in 1746, is thought to have been written by Murphy under the pseudonym of John Jones.[54] Yet, the veneration of Murphy, if intense, did not endure.[55] The funeral oration and longer life are each now known only through one copy.[56] Again, the issue recurs of whether the chance survival of the *Life*, outside Ireland, should be interpreted as evidence of the popularity of the hagiographies which simply disintegrated. The *Funeral oration* sold for 1½d. and numbered sixteen pages. Similarly with the engraved portraits: with five different versions and mechanisms for their sale in the provinces, a well-developed network of Catholic print culture is hinted at.[57] Father Murphy himself recommended a devo-

---

50 *Funeral oration preach'd on the death of Rev. John Murphy, DD* (Dublin, 1753); H. Fenning, 'Dublin imprints of Catholic interest, 1740–59', *Collectanea Hibernica*, 41 (1999), 99; Pollard, *Dictionary*, p. 304.   51 *Two divine revelations, as related to St Augustine, St Bridget, and St Anne, by our Lord and Saviour, Jesus Christ ... Together with some salutary acts by the late Rev. Father John Murphy, DD* (?Dublin, 1753); Fenning, 'Dublin imprints of Catholic interest, 1740–59', p. 102.   52 J. Brady, *Catholics and Catholicism in the eighteenth-century press* (Maynooth, 1965), pp 82–3; J.K., *Life*, pp 15, 82, 86; Pollard, *Dictionary*, p. 374.   53 *Faulkner's Dublin Journal*, 11 Aug. 1753; Begadon, 'Laity and clergy in the Catholic renewal of Dublin, c.1750–1830', p. 316.   54 Fenning, *The undoing of the friars*, pp 167–8, 213; Fenning, 'Dublin imprints of Catholic interest, 1740–59', 81.   55 N. Donnelly, *Short histories of Dublin parishes IX* (Blackrock, n.d.), pp 222–3; M. Wall, *Catholic Ireland in the eighteenth century*, ed. G. O'Brien (Dublin, 1989), p. 55.   56 H. Fenning, 'Dublin imprints of Catholic interest, 1740–59', *Collectanea Hibernica*, 41 (1999), 98, 99.   57 Brady, *Catholics and Catholicism*, p. 86; J.C. Smith, *British mezzotinto portraits* (London, 1878–84), p. 1740; W.G. Strickland, *A dictionary of Irish artists*, 2 vols (Dublin, 1913), ii, p. 36.

tional work, *The burning Lamp*, said to be by a Jesuit. The printer of Murphy's life took the opportunity to advertise the second work, which he sold at 6*d*. Again, no copy of this edition is known to survive. Only a copy of the third edition of 1769 is recorded.[58] Here, too, the argument that this publication was so well-used that it perished is plausible.

III

Murphy was not the first Dublin priest to be the subject of a posthumous printed memoir. A few featured in the series of broadside elegies published in Dublin during the 1720s – fortunately collected and preserved.[59] Joining the company of prominent lawyers, merchants and Protestant clerics, the priests' inclusion indicates their local celebrity. More substantial than the single-sheet elegies is a printed funeral oration for a Dublin priest from 1726. It identifies neither the priest being eulogized nor the parish in which he had served. The purpose of the tract is explicitly instructional: to encourage the living in the pursuit of virtue 'from examples of a good life', and to fix the survivors' eyes 'as upon so many bright lamps hung out by the hand of providence to shine before us in the dark and intricate ways of his miserably deluded world'.[60] The author reminded readers of the veneration accorded to the recently dead by the Jews and early Christians, and regretted the neglect of the practice among contemporaries. The unnamed pastor was represented as the embodiment of Pauline injunctions for a good priest, but with some Irish twists: 'irreprehensible, sober, wise, comely, chaste, a man of hospitality, a teacher, not given to wine, no fighter but modest, no quarreller, not covetous, well-ruling his own house'. His preaching was praised for its simplicity: 'he preached Jesus Christ, not himself'. The qualities found in the priest were a mixture of the classical Roman and the primitive Christian: charity, joy, peace, patience, benignity, goodness, longanimity, mildness, faith, modesty and continence. Appended to the address was a poem, 'Menalcas', an accomplished pastoral in Virgilian mode, more redolent of the secular than the sacred.[61] Nothing was said of the dead man's background or training, so that he remained a type recognizable as an individual only to those who had known him.

58 J.W., *The burning lamp*, 3rd ed. (Dublin, 1769). Less surprising is the disappearance of his verses that were printed in Spain. J.K., *Life*, p. 35. 59 Oliver Dalton, *An elegy on the much lamented death of the Reverend Father James Fitzsimons a Romish priest* (Dublin, 1726); *An elegy on the much lamented death of Father Nicholas Dalton* (Dublin, 1725); *An elegy on the much lamented death of Dr Dennis Mc.Carthy priest of Corke* (Dublin, 1726); *An elegy on the much-lamented death of ... Dr Thaddeus Mc. Dermot, priest of St Francis's Chappel* (Dublin, 1725). 60 F.L., *A funeral oration upon the death of a Roman Catholick clergy-man of distinction* ([Dublin], 1726), pp 5, 9–10. 61 Ibid., pp 11–21.

To the veiled tribute of 1726 can be added three further publications closer in time to the account of Father Murphy and retailing lives of the faithful. All originate south of Dublin. Timothy (or Thady) O'Brien, parish priest at Castlelyons, Co. Cork, Archbishop Christopher Butler of Cashel, and Lady Margaret Burke, widow of Colonel Thomas Butler of Kilcash, each received printed encomia. Two were certainly printed in Waterford and the eulogist was named as Richard Hogan; the third, the account of Dr O'Brien, probably had similar origins. All were held up to readers as models, exhibiting scriptural if not apostolic virtues. Piety, both private and practical, was personified by these subjects. Attributes such as hospitality and charity exemplified obedience to Biblical injunctions, but might also be seen as the survival of habits of *noblesse oblige* which were felt to have declined, if not vanished, as the older Catholic elite was displaced by Protestant interlopers.

A degree of nostalgia permeates the lives. Not only did the subjects hold fast to their hereditary faith, they stayed faithful to the traditions of their dynasties. Not the least of Archbishop Butler's merits was his place in the venerable and extensive Butler clan, one of 'the most noble, ancient, and powerful families, of the rank of subjects, in all Europe'.[62] Lady Margaret, daughter of Lord Clanricarde, had married into the Butler family. Christopher Butler benefited too from forbears who included the Plantagenets and King Ferdinand of Castile: a prelate 'in whose veins did circulate a select collection of the most ancient, and noble blood of more than five kingdoms.'[63]

Hogan struck an elegiac note when he evoked the 'melancholy, tho' magnificent ruins, of so many stately monasteries, convents, hospitals, etc in England and Ireland'.[64] It paralleled the poetic laments over vanished or vanishing conventions uttered a few years earlier by Laurence Whyte.[65] Butler's behaviour was governed by the 'laws of civility, and good breeding'.[66] So, too, was Lady Margaret Burke's. It was remembered that her house at Kilcash was 'open to all ranks, degrees, and stations of people', with 'none excluded'. Kilcash was famed as a refuge of 'poor gentry of both sexes'. She saw to the education of the young in the rudiments of the faith and relieved the aged.[67] The sorrow at her passing – and with it the hospitable ambience which she had fostered – prefigured that of the Irish poet who lamented the felling of the fine woods of Kilcash.[68] Father O'Brien was promoted and favoured by

---

62 R. Hogan, *A funeral sermon on the most illustrious Christopher Butler, A.B. of Casshel* (Waterford, 1759), p. 9. 63 Hogan, *A funeral sermon on Christopher Butler*, pp 14–16. 64 Ibid., p. 18. 65 L. Whyte, *Poems on various subjects, serious and diverting* (Dublin, 1740), pp vii–viii, 68–99. 66 Hogan, *A funeral sermon on Christopher Butler*, p. 55. 67 R. Hogan, *A funeral sermon, on the right honourable, Lady Margaret Burk, of Clanrickard, Viscountess Iveagh* (Waterford, ?1750), pp 11–12, 18–20. 68 S. Ó Tuama and T. Kinsella (eds), *An Duanaire 1600–1900: poems of the dispossessed* (Mountrath, 1981), pp 328–31. Hogan revealed that he had delivered an obsequy for Colonel Butler of Kilcash, but whether or not it had been published is not made clear. Hogan, *A funeral sermon, on Lady*

Archbishop Butler, whose qualities occupied a substantial, even disproportionate, share of the text ostensibly devoted to O'Brien. The biographer's circuitous approach allowed a long disquisition on Butler's predecessor at Cashel, Cormac MacCullitan. The learning of Cormac was emphasized as was the belief that he was both a martyr and a saint.[69] The learning of the author was likewise paraded: sesquipedalian footnotes carry the exposition of points culled from Keating and Ware over several pages.

O'Brien on his own account had a lineage deserving of respect. Descent from the O'Briens, latterly earls, was traced to Brian Boru. Moreover, his mother's line was of the Barrys. (Given that the Barry, earls of Barrymore, had their main Irish seat at Castlelyons, O'Brien's nomination to that cure may be better explained.) Concern with ancestry is also displayed in the eulogy on Murphy. On the paternal side, Murphy was descended from the MacMahons of Armagh. Through his mother, he could claim descent from the Louth branch of the MacMahons, and thereby kinship with Lords Louth and Bellew.[70]

It was an asset to enjoy an ancient lineage but to parade it was a defect. Lady Margaret Burke was commended for never being known 'to throw her pedigree as a subject of discourse among her company'. Indeed, discreet conversation was another of her merits. She avoided the 'licentious chat, whispers, and the like dissolute behaviour common to the insolent, low-bred part of mankind'.[71] She eschewed grandeur and practised 'discreet moderation'. Lady Margaret personified a strand of seigneurial Catholicism that might be associated with the other values which have been characterized as distinctively 'Old English'. The preacher at her funeral did not completely avoid at least oblique political comment. Both her father and brother had been plunged into 'the universal calamity and ruin of their country', and sacrificed their lives 'to loyalty and religion'.[72] Moreover, her sister was married to the duke of Berwick, who had succeeded Tyrconnell as commander of the Jacobite forces in 1691. The duchess of Berwick, established in France, was 'admired, honoured, and esteemed in the most splendid, magnificent and polite court in the universe'.[73]

Nor were Jacobite associations altogether suppressed in recounting Archbishop Butler's history. His school in England was visited by James II, who was then praised for his 'heroic patience and magnanimous resignation to the will of heaven'.[74] Butler's subsequent encounters with an unsympathetic regime in Ireland are not mentioned. O'Brien, it was acknowledged, returned to Ireland at a critical juncture in 1715, but (it was asserted) peace quickly reasserted itself.[75] In 1745, when the uprising in Scotland called into

Margaret Burk, p. 3.   69 For a succinct summary of the present state of knowledge, P. Ó Riain, *A dictionary of Irish saints* (Dublin, 2011), pp 223–4.   70 J.K., *Life*, pp 16–18.   71 Hogan, *A funeral sermon, on Lady Margaret Burk*, pp 32–3, 40.   72 Ibid., pp 42–3.   73 Ibid., p. 42.   74 Hogan, *A funeral sermon on Christopher Butler*, p. 34.   75 *An essay*

question the loyalties of Catholics in Ireland, O'Brien insisted in print on the duty of Catholic obedience to a Protestant government.[76] Yet earlier, O'Brien had sought confrontation with Dean Davies of Cork.

O'Brien was admired as much as a worthy offshoot of two ancient and aristocratic Irish families. His clerical career – and the education that preceded it – are much more summarily covered than Murphy's would be. Two other aspects of O'Brien's life received greater attention. His training had been largely in France where he rose to be rector of the college in Toulouse. But even this episode is covered more cursorily than Murphy's time in Spain. O'Brien had returned to Ireland in the apparently unpropitious year of 1715. However, his biographer was at pains to stress that he suffered no serious harassment. In 1721, he had prepared instructions to observe a papal jubilee, but was persuaded to postpone their printing. He aimed to explain to the local authorities why there should be unexpected confluences of Catholics.[77] Compliance with the prevailing legal and political systems is further suggested by the notice of O'Brien's death published in the Dublin newspapers. 'Good behaviour and inoffensive deportment' were rewarded with interment in the chancel of the parish church at Castlelyons.[78] Stress on O'Brien's kinship with the Barrys, as with the Butler blood running in the archbishop's veins and Lady Margaret's Butler marriage, might have raised doubts about loyalties. Shortly before Dr O'Brien died, the Barrymores had fallen under suspicion of Jacobite sympathies and the mansion at Castleyons was searched.[79] Similarly, the exiled duke of Ormonde, head of the Butlers, died in 1745, reminding of his sensational defection to the Jacobites. Guilt was not automatically incurred by association. Nevertheless, the unswerving fidelity to Catholicism, which is a theme of all the eulogies, might pose questions about ultimate political allegiances.

More assertive was O'Brien's eagerness to engage in public contestation with prominent local Protestant clergymen. Through pamphlets he combated the doctrinal views of Rowland Davies, powerful within the lay and clerical society of Cork city.[80] More distant from the sectarian politics of early eighteenth-century Cork was O'Brien's attack on the doctrines of the Waldensians, especially as expounded by Pierre Boyer.[81] O'Brien's several forays into print gave him greater public visibility than most of his clerical colleagues. One aim was to provide sustenance to 'our poor Catholics' in his

towards the character of the late Rev. Doctor Thady O'Brien (Waterford, 1751), pp 12–13; H. Fenning, 'Cork imprints of Catholic historical interest, 1723–1804: a provisional checklist', *JCHAS*, 100 (1995), 132.   76 T[imothy]. [O']B[rien]., *Truth triumphant: in the defeat of a book, intitled, A replication to the rejoinder, &c.* (Cork, 1745).   77 *An essay towards the character of Doctor Thady O'Brien*.   78 Brady, *Catholics and Catholicism in the eighteenth-century press*, pp 74–5.   79 É. Ó Ciardha, *Ireland and the Jacobite cause, 1685–1766* (Dublin, 2002), pp 303–4.   80 Barnard, 'Almoners of Providence: the clergy, 1647–1780', pp 98–100 and plate 2.   81 T.B., *Truth triumphant*.

locality. He contrasted their needs, largely unrecognized, with those of 'gentlemen of a high education and a nice taste', able to 'purchase better books, and spare time for reading the same'.[82] By virtue of his publications he found a place in Walter Harris' enlarged and updated version of James Ware's *Writers of Ireland*.[83] In fact, O'Brien had written more – for example, to vindicate the Catholics of Ireland and impugn the Treaty of Limerick – but, owing to a lack of subscribers, had been unable to publish all of his output. Access to the press was uneven, and often impossible for those remote in the countryside, with only exiguous finances or without helpful links in the Dublin or London print trades.[84]

O'Brien's writings allowed his biographer to bulk out his otherwise bald and conventional account.[85] From the memoir, prefaced with an effusive dedication to Archbishop Butler (rather tangentially connected with the ostensible subject of O'Brien), less of a personality emerges than would with Murphy. Moreover, the ancestry of the two priests affords suggestive differences. An attempt is made, particularly through his mother, to connect Murphy with the Old Irish nobility, but it is sketchier than the vivid details of his confessionally hybrid upbringing in Dublin. Subsequently, there are inevitable contrasts between O'Brien's cure in the rural hinterland and Murphy's in the populous capital. No claims are advanced for O'Brien's sanctity. It is noted that he had had admirers keen to promote his claims to the bishopric of Cloyne, but that O'Brien had stopped any campaign on his behalf. Similarly, when in Rome Butler refused prestigious preferment, nor did he encourage those who wished to secure a red hat for him.[86]

Archbishop Butler, O'Brien and Murphy are portrayed as rejecting the debilitating fashions of their ages. Butler, sent to school in England among 'the flower of the young nobility of three nations', had to resist 'youthful libertines and voluptuous sensualists'. 'Modern bravos and modish men of fashion' threatened to corrupt him.[87] Regret at changed values threaded through Hogan's addresses. Similarly, O'Brien's eulogist inveighed against literary fashions, which preferred novels and romances and 'frivolous plays that often deprave and corrupt the reader's mind'. He lamented that *Pamela* and *Tom Jones* were more popular than devout tracts and, indeed, had gone into more editions than the Bible. The popularity of biographies was also recognized and reprobated. The author wished by offering his account of O'Brien to correct the passion for stories of daring in war. Too often, in the adulation of commanders and their victories, the issues of justice and piety were ignored.

82 Ibid., p. xi. 83 J. Ware, *The history of the writers of Ireland, in two books*, ed. W. Harris (Dublin, 1764), i, p. 273. 84 P. Ó Súilleabháin, 'Catholic books printed in Ireland, 1740–1820, containing lists of subscribers', *Collectanea Hibernica*, 6 & 7 (1963–4), 231–3. 85 Few of those listed are now known through surviving copies. Fenning, 'Cork imprints of Catholic historical interest', pp 131–2. 86 Hogan, *A funeral sermon on Christopher Butler*, pp 42, 65. 87 Ibid., pp 19, 32.

Indeed, the lionizing of martial heroes was proving 'very pernicious to religion'. As a corrective, the example of Dr O'Brien would display 'religion, goodness and virtue' and curb libertinism.[88]

The Catholic exemplars shared an anxiety over perceived moral decay. Through their own lives and exhortations they sought to win others to better ways. Only Father Murphy was recorded as taking more ambitious initiatives to attempt moral reformation among the laity. The city offered a more promising setting for institutions, notably confraternities, dedicated to combating the evils. Neither Butler nor O'Brien, or indeed Lady Margaret Burke, could be taxed with quietism. But it is Murphy, faced with a metropolis, who is noted as the greatest activist. Father Murphy, as has been stressed, exuded gentility, some of which was inherited, but more of it learnt. His *Life*, if it embeds him in the Ireland of his ancestors, offers the greatest detail as to how he then adapted his inheritance to contemporary conditions. In comparison, the other lives are unspecific about how exactly their subjects practised their piety. Nevertheless, Dr O'Brien is placed in a long and honoured tradition. Not only is context supplied with details relating to Cormac and Archbishop Butler, but the final section of the memoir consists of epitaphs from the tombs of earlier prelates and notables: Richard FitzRalph and Hugh McMahon, archbishops of Armagh; George Dowdall and Eugene Matthews of Dublin; Michael O'Gara and Florence Conry of Tuam; Daly, bishop-elect of Coimbra; and the scholars Luke Wadding, John Colgan and Cornelius Nary. Thereby, a powerful sense of a learned continuum was conveyed.[89]

The veneration of Lady Margaret Burke also seems to look backwards. Women, especially of high status, were important in preserving Catholicism. Some remained Catholic while husbands and sons converted, at least nominally, to Protestantism. For the moment, Lady Margaret was an isolated instance in Ireland of a woman whose fortitude was celebrated through print. As with their male contemporaries, female martyrs since the sixteenth-century reformations in Ireland were not held up for public admiration. Recent examples came from elsewhere: Teresa of Avila, Mary, Queen of Scots, and the English recusant, Lady Warner.[90] The life of the last, originating in England, was reprinted in Dublin in 1769.[91] Not until late in the eighteenth century did locals like Nano Nagle attract the wider fame offered by print.[92]

---

88 *An essay towards the character of the late Rev. Doctor Thady O'Brien*, sig. B2–B[3], p. 3. 89 *An essay towards the character of the late Rev. Doctor Thady O'Brien*, pp 21–2, 27–37. 90 *The life of the holy mother St Teresa* (Dublin, 1791 and 1794). 91 B. Higgons, *The history of the life and reign of Mary Queen of Scots* (Dublin, 1753); E. Scarisbrike, *The holy life of Lady Warner, Sister Clare of Jesus* (Dublin, 1769). Cf. G. Glickman, *The English Catholic community, 1688–1745: politics, culture and ideology* (Woodbridge, 2009), pp 50–1. 92 W. Coppinger, *The life of Miss Nano Nagle, as sketched by the Right Rev. Dr. Coppinger in a funeral sermon preached by him in Cork, on the anniversary of her death* (Cork, 1794).

The use of a funeral sermon simultaneously to praise an exemplary life, to comfort mourners and to expatiate on wider applications was well-established. However, giving such addresses larger circulation depended on access to printing presses and on the strategies of the various confessions. The Church of Ireland, enjoying its privileges as the established church and, until the 1690s, effectively monopolizing the Dublin press, used the device. In the main, it was its bishops who received this particular accolade.[93] Voluminous lives of prelates like James Ussher and John Bramhall, appended to collections of their writings, were intended for members of the clerical and official elites.[94] If, occasionally, a devout layman was treated in this manner, there were usually particular reasons. In the case of James Bonnell, a pious and well-connected government administrator, his widow organized an instructive and uplifting biography. It appeared in 1703.[95] By the eighteenth century, the fashion for such printed tributes within the Church of Ireland seems to have declined, though this was not obviously the result of any dramatic decline in the calibre of its bishops. Grieving relations and friends would sometimes ensure that eulogies were published.[96] Among Protestant dissenters, the genre survived longer.[97] It could be that the practice of reading and profiting from sermons persisted more strongly in such circles. Also, dissenters had gained easy access to printing within Ireland only in the 1690s.

---

[93] A. Dopping, *A sermon preached in Christ's-Church, Dublin November 18. 1693. At the funeral of his Grace Francis, Lord Archbishop of Dublin* (Dublin, 1694); H. Jones, *A sermon at the funeral of James Margetson, D.D. late Arch-Bishop of Armagh, and Primate of all Ireland. Preached at Christ Church Dublin, Aug. 30. 1678* (London, 1679); D. Loftus, *Oratio funebris habita post exuvias nuperi reverendissimi in Christo Patris Johannis Archiepiscopi Armachiani* (Dublin, 1663); J. Taylor, *A sermon preached in Chrisis-Church Dublin, July 16. 1663. at the funeral of the most reverend father in God, John, late Lord Archbishop of Armagh, and primate of all Ireland* (Dublin, 1663). [94] R. Parr, *The life of the most reverend father in God, James Usher, late Lord Arch-Bishop of Armagh, primate and metropolitan of all Ireland* (London, 1686); *The works of the Most Reverend Father in God, John Bramhall D.D. Late Lord Archbishop of Ardmagh, primate and metropolitane of all Ireland* (Dublin, 1676). [95] W. Hamilton, *The life and character of James Bonnell, Esq.* [96] Anon, *A sermon preached at the funeral of the Right Honourable Lady Ann Dawson, at Ematress in the county of Monaghan. March 8th, 1769. And published at the desire of Thomas Dawson, Esq* (Dublin, 1769); A. Montgomery, *A funeral sermon, on the death of Mark Ker of Granard M.D. preached in the church of Granard, on Sunday 21st. August 1791* (Dublin, 1792). [97] W. Boulton, *The blessedness of those who die in the Lord* (Dublin, 1764); A. Colvill, *A sermon occasioned by the death of the late reverend Mr Thomas Nevin* (Belfast, 1745); J. Duchal, *A sermon occasioned by the death of the Reverend Mr. Hugh Scot* (Belfast, 1736); J. Duchal, *A sermon on ... the late Reverend Mr. John Abernethy*; J. Duchal, *A sermon on occasion of the death of Dr Arbuckle, preached at Wood-Street, January 4th, 1746-7* (Dublin, 1747); S. Haliday, *A sermon occasioned by the death of the Reverend Mr Michael Bruce* (Belfast, 1735); W. Livingston, *The blessings of a long life well spent and happily concluded* (Belfast, 1721); J. Stouppe, *The uncertainty of human life* (Belfast, 1779).

IV

In *The life and character of the late Rev. John Murphy*, it is stated, 'if he had spent his days abroad, it is more presumable, [he] would have been canonized'.⁹⁸ This aside or wistful regret is worth a pause. In itself, the wistfulness tells of the limited influence which the post-Tridentine papacy exercised in Ireland. In terms of new saints, Italy and Spain did best. Of the fifty-five canonized between 1588 and 1767, twenty-six were Italian and seventeen Spanish. Ireland did not feature in the list.⁹⁹ The speed and effectiveness of the campaigns for the canonization of Carlo Borromeo and Philip Neri are in striking contrast to the muted (and unsuccessful) efforts on behalf of Murphy.¹ Advancing Murphy's claims to sanctity may also have been designed as a pre-emptive strike. The friars, identifying him as the villain responsible for their undoing, tried to besmirch his reputation. Partisans within the Catholic church were therefore likely to squabble over how Murphy was most accurately to be represented.

Before 1753 what is notable is the dearth of publications about the personnel of the Irish Catholic church since the reformations of the sixteenth century. Given the sufferings and martyrdoms it might have been expected that the faithful would be fortified with tales of clerical heroism and steadfastness. Yet, it would seem that only one – Oliver Plunkett – was commemorated in detail throughout the century after his execution in 1681. Plunkett wished his last words to be circulated. Accordingly, a copy had been prepared of his speech on the scaffold. This was certified as accurate and quickly printed.² Even then, although accounts of his trial and death were published in London and Dublin immediately after the event, their perpetuation occurred more surreptitiously. Hugh Reilly's *Ireland's case briefly stated*, appearing first on the Continent (either at Paris or Louvain) in 1695 and frequently reissued thereafter as an *Impartial history of Ireland*, included as an appendix the dying speech of Plunkett at Tyburn. Salutary as this reminder of sacrifice was and popular though Reilly's *Impartial history* might be, it does not seem to have inspired any vibrant cult of Plunkett in eighteenth-century Ireland.³

In the absence of sustained or successful campaigns to create more (and more recent) Irish saints, the attention devoted, albeit briefly, to Murphy is striking. Reasons for promoting Murphy in print have been advanced: he was a memorable exemplar for all and a partisan in the struggles between regulars

---

98 J.K., *Life*, p. vi.   99 P. Burke, 'How to be a Counter-Reformation saint' in K. von Greyerz (ed.), *Religion and society in early-modern Europe* (London, 1984), p. 49.   1 C. Bonino, *La vita e i miracoli di San Carlo Borromeo* (1610); *La regola e la fama. San Filippo Neri e l'arte* (Milan, 1995).   2 J. Hanly (ed.), *The letters of Saint Oliver Plunkett, 1625–1681* (Dublin, 1979), pp 584–7.   3 C. Tait, paper delivered in Oxford, 28 Jan. 2009.

and seculars. What remains for comment is the rarity of printed biographies of devout Irish Catholics of a recent vintage. The dearth reflects the sluggishness in producing Catholic print (whether through writing or publishing) within Ireland. Discretion under the threat of persecution, actual or possible, undoubtedly inhibited the leaders of the Irish church from the 1690s into the middle of the eighteenth century. The same factor which has been used to explain the failure within England to memorialize Catholics executed in the reign of Elizabeth I may have been at work in eighteenth-century Ireland. There were disagreements about the tactics to be adopted: disagreements which coincided with long-standing rivalries between different religious orders, and between regular and secular clergy.[4]

By the 1740s, however, a more relaxed atmosphere in Ireland, while liable to rapid alteration, encouraged greater boldness in asserting the claims of Catholicism. For a church under legal disabilities, it remained difficult – and indeed unwise – to adopt the full panoply of post-Tridentine worship. The visible and provocative, such as processions through the streets during patronal festivals, were avoided. The physical combat over the possession of church buildings and ancient places of sepulchre that had occurred during the seventeenth century, particularly in the 1640s and between 1688 and 1691, weakened.[5] Public spaces had been confessionalized in eighteenth-century Ireland: in Dublin they were virtually monopolized by the adherents of the Church of Ireland and Hanoverian state.[6] Nevertheless, it was becoming easier to introduce some of the methods of instruction and regeneration urged by the Council of Trent. The visibility of confraternities and sodalities (retrieved thanks to Colm Lennon's researches) is one sign.[7] Another is the more frequent use of printed helps to instruct, admonish and inspire, and to combat adversaries. From the 1740s, it seems, publishers and booksellers in Dublin (and later in the provinces) felt it both worth their while and safe to

---

4 T.M. McCoog, 'Constructing martyrdom in the English Catholic community 1582–1602' in E. Shagan (ed.), *Catholics and the Protestant nation* (Manchester, 2005), pp 95–127.   5 T.C. Barnard, 'Ireland, 1688–91' in T. Harris and S. Taylor (eds), *The final crisis of the Stuart monarchy* (Woodbridge, 2013), pp 157–87.   6 For the trouble that they might cause: D. Freist, 'Representation and appropriation of religious difference in a bi-confessional territory in 17th- and 18th-century Germany' in A. Höfele, S. Lagué, E. Ruge and G. Schmidt (eds), *Representing religious pluralization in early modern Europe* (Berlin, 2007), pp 144–8. Also, R. Usher, *Protestant Dublin, 1660–1760: architecture and iconography* (Basingstoke, 2012).   7 H.F. Berry, 'History of the religious guild of St Anne ... 1430–1740', *PRIA*, 25 (1904–5), 21–106; C. Lennon, 'The chantries and the Irish Reformation: the case of St Anne's Guild, Dublin, 1550–1630' in R.V. Comerford, M. Cullen, J.R. Hill and C. Lennon (eds), *Religion, conflict and coexistence in Ireland: essays presented to Mgr. Patrick Corish* (Dublin, 1992), pp 6–25, 293–7; C. Lennon, 'The confraternities and cultural duality in Ireland, 1450–1550' in C.F. Black and P. Graveslock (eds), *Early-modern confraternities in Europe and the Americas* (Aldershot, 2006), pp 35–52; also Begadon, 'Laity and clergy in the Catholic renewal of Dublin', pp 112–62.

cater for the increasing readership for Catholic works.[8] Frequently they worked in conjunction with counterparts in London; gradually they published and sold material that had originated outside Ireland.

In 1688, William Weston, a Catholic bookseller in Dublin, taking advantage of a permissive atmosphere, advertised seventeen devotional books. None had been written in Ireland and all were probably published elsewhere.[9] By 1740, Ignatius Kelly, another Catholic publisher and bookseller in Dublin, listed over eighty individual titles as well as generic school-books. Three-quarters of the offerings were clearly for Catholics. Moreover, Kelly stocked 'all other sorts of Catholic and controversy books', including 'large, middling and small mass books'. A further lure for devout customers was 'a great variety of beautiful pictures fit for prayer books'. The practice of supplying engravings of scenes from Christ's life and of saints was well-established. The single-sheet illustrations could be bought individually, either to be displayed on walls or for insertion into missals.[10] The appeal of imagery in order to implant religious rudiments, as approved by the Council of Trent, was exploited by the cheapest of Kelly's prints. This was 'an eye catechism'. It distilled 'the sum of Christian doctrine, beautifully printed in a broadside and on fine paper'. It was intended for children and 'unlearned Catholicks', and was designed 'to be framed or pasted up in Catholick houses'.[11] A similar intention lay behind the printed images of Father Murphy.

Kelly did not totally ignore the locally-produced and oriented. He stocked Luke Wadding's 'Garland of godly and divine songs', which cost a mere 4*d*. He could also offer Hugh MacCurtin's Irish Dictionary, yet at a price – 14*s*. – which put it beyond the reach of most.[12] He had an edition of Bishop Gallagher's *Sixteen Irish sermons*, but these (it has been argued) were designed primarily for the use of priests.[13] Indigenous Irish exemplars are notable through their absence. Instead, a life of St John Fisher, the martyred bishop of Rochester, was available.[14]

---

8 H. Fenning, 'The Catholic press in Munster in the eighteenth century' in G. Long (ed.), *Books beyond the Pale: aspects of the provincial book trade in Ireland before 1850* (Dublin, 1996), pp 19–27; Fenning, 'Cork imprints of Catholic historical interest', 129–48; Fenning, 'Dublin imprints of Catholic interest'. 9 R. Hudlestone, *Short and plain way to the faith of the church* (Dublin, 1688). 10 F.L., *A new year's gift*, pp [189–92]; Fenning, 'The Catholic press in Munster', p. 22. 11 F.L., *A new year's gift*, p. [192]. 12 By 1752 it was advertised for only 7*s*. 6*d*.: F.L., *A new year's gift* (Dublin, 1752), pp 189–92. 13 C. Mac Murchaidh, 'Dr James Gallagher, alumnus Kilmorensis: Bishop of Raphoe (1725–37) and Kildare and Leighlin (1737–51)', *Breifne*, 10 (2004), 219–35, C. Mac Murchaidh, '"My repeated troubles": Dr James Gallagher (bishop of Raphoe, 1725–37) and the impact of the penal laws' in J. Bergin et al. (eds), *New perspectives on the penal laws*, Eighteenth-Century Ireland special issue 1 (2011), 149–72. 14 Lewis of Granada, *The sinners guide* (Dublin, 1740), advertisement; F. Walsh, *Funiculus Triplex* (London, 1745), pp [157–60]. A 'John Murphy' subscribed for six copies of a Dublin reprint of Thomas Bailey, *The life and death of the renowned John Fisher* (Dublin, 1740).

If Catholic publications originating from England were most easily procured and read, too slavish a dependence on them was deprecated. This was chiefly because the calendar of saints celebrated by the two churches diverged. To avoid mistakes through the Irish following the English calendar, Philip Bowes offered 'The Roman Catholic calendar for the kingdom of Ireland, containing the feasts and fasts of the said kingdom; the Irish saints, the patrons of each diocese'. Rather than catering to popular lay devotions, this publication may have aimed to tighten episcopal and clerical control by confining celebrations to those saints 'universally granted [by the papacy] to this year 1750'. The calendar, costing only 1*d*., is another flimsy tract that has not apparently survived. Its disappearance may attest to the realization of Bowes' hope that 'all Catholic families' would buy one: repeated consultation may have caused its destruction.[15]

The incentives to provide accounts of Irish saints were increased by a papal decree in 1743 elevating the cults of first nine and then another fourteen from Ireland. By 1751 they had been incorporated into and publicized through the printed *Officia Propria Sanctorum Hiberniae*. The most recent was Laurence O'Toole, archbishop of Dublin between 1161 and 1180.[16] The concentration on distant and, it might be supposed, less controversial times was also evident in another influential publication circulating in mid-eighteenth-century Ireland.

Richard Challoner, vicar-general of the London district, wrote and published copiously. Among his works was *Britannia Sancta*, first published in 1745, a compendium of British and Irish saints.[17] Challoner had a vision of shared Christianity that united the neighbouring islands. He happily gave prominence to Patrick, Bridget, Kieran, Malachi and Declan, and credited Ireland with being an island of saints.[18] Challoner drew heavily from Ussher, Colgan, the Four Masters and Giraldus Cambrensis.[19] That he was in contact with Catholics living in Ireland is implied by his description of St Patrick's Purgatory: 'whatever it may have been heretofore, at present, as I have learnt from such as have been there on pilgrimage, it is remarkable for nothing else

---

15 J. Gother, *A papist mis-represented and represented* (Dublin, 1750), advertisement. **16** *Officia propria sanctorum Hiberniae* (Dublin, 1751); T. Wall, 'An eighteenth-century Dublin life of St Patrick', *Reportorium Novum*, 3 (1961–2), 122–7. **17** 2 volumes (London, 1745). **18** R. Challoner, *Britannia Sancta*, 2 vols (London, 1745). **19** On Colgan and the seventeenth-century precursors: B. Cunningham, *The Annals of the Four Masters: Irish history, kingship and society in the early seventeenth century* (Dublin, 2010), pp 223, 229, 242–3; B. Cunningham, 'The culture and ideology of Irish Franciscan historians at Louvain, 1607–1650' in C. Brady (ed.), *Ideology and the historians: Historical Studies 17* (Dublin, 1991), pp 11–30, 223–7; B. Cunningham and R. Gillespie, '"The most adaptable of saints": the cult of St Patrick in the seventeenth century', *Archivium Hibernicum*, 49 (1995), 82–104; C. Giblin, 'Father John Colgan OFM (†1658) and the Irish school of hagiography at Louvain', *Franciscan College Annual* (1958), 23–32.

but its being a place of devotion'.[20] The two volumes of Challoner's 'Saints' were substantial and therefore costly, limiting the impact, especially in Ireland, of his vision of a unified Britannic Catholicism.

As in the apparently official listing of 1751, the Irish saints to be venerated belonged to remote centuries. St Patrick, that most versatile of saints, was celebrated in brief printed lives. Thanks to earlier treatments in the seventeenth century, his cult was spread widely through Catholic Europe.[21] An opportunist decided to exploit the Irish market with a duodecimo, published first in 1746. To give the holy life a greater appeal it was soon supplemented incongruously with detail about Dublin and its environs. The rising interest among Catholics in their national saints also appears with the publication in 1756 of an ambitious engraving of Patrick. If the Patrician iconography was predictable, with the snakes slithering into the sea, other details were not. Patrick was flanked by the seated figures of the king bishop of Cashel, Cormac MacCullinan, and St Ethnea. Dublin pride was flattered with two of its kings and two of its saints being prominently portrayed. The image was dedicated to a leading Catholic peer, Lord Cahir.[22] Patrick, like the early Christianity with which he was credited, was claimed by both Protestants and Catholics as their own. Trading on his appeal across confessions promised profits to booksellers.[23] John Murphy, as has been noted, was deemed a fitting companion for Patrick among the ranks of saints.[24]

Murphy did not join that elevated company. Not until 1992 were seventeen Irish martyrs from the sixteenth century beatified.[25] Oliver Plunkett waited until 1920 to be beatified and was canonized only in 1975. As Peter Burke has stressed, martyrdom was not an essential feature in those made saints between the sixteenth and eighteenth centuries. Elsewhere within post-Tridentine Catholicism, models were found and burnished for beatification and canonization. And yet, no Irish equivalent of John Nepomuk, Carlo Borromeo, Philip Neri, Ignatius Loyola, Theresa of Avila, Francis Xavier or Rose of Lima was found.[26] Murphy's cause, almost casually indicated in the

---

20 Challoner, *Britannia Sacra*, 1, p. 181. Challoner's knowledge may have been based on the recent publication: J. Richardson, *The great folly, superstition, and idolatry, of pilgrimages in Ireland, especially of that to St Patrick's Purgatory* (Dublin, 1727). **21** Cunningham and Gillespie, '"The most adaptable of saints"', 82–104; L. Gougaud, *Les saints irlandais hors d'Irlande* (Louvain, 1936); G. Mesmer, 'The cult of St Patrick in the vicinity of Drackensetein', *Seanchas Ardmhaca* (1961–2), 68–75; T. Messingham, *Florelegium Insulae Sanctorum* (Paris, 1624); A. Tommasini, *Irish saints in Italy* (London, 1937), C. Whistler, 'Tiepolo's Saint Patrick altarpiece', *Irish Arts Review*, 2/1 (1985), 32–5. **22** Wall, 'An eighteenth-century Dublin life of St Patrick', pp 121–36. **23** B. McCormack, *Perceptions of St Patrick in eighteenth-century Ireland* (Dublin, 2000), p. 103. **24** The *Funeral oration* also imagined Murphy residing with 'the saints above', p. 4. **25** P.J. Corish and B. Millett (eds), *The Irish martyrs* (Dublin, 2005). **26** Burke, 'How to be a Counter-Reformation saint', pp 44–55; A.R.G. De Ceballos, 'The art of devotion: seventeenth-century Spanish painting and sculpture in its religious context' in X. Bray (ed.), *The sacred*

published biography, seems never to have been developed or sustained. Its fate is emblematic of the condition of the Irish Catholic church in the 1750s. It was now prepared to celebrate outstanding devotees (not martyrs), but it refrained from directing too close attention onto what it had suffered since the sixteenth century. To do so might endanger tentative moves towards gentler treatment and even provoke new rigour.

---

made real: Spanish painting and sculpture, 1600–1700 (London, 2009), pp 45–57; T. DaCosta Kaufmann, *Court, cloister and city: the art and culture of central Europe 1450–1800* (London, 1995), pp 344–5; E. Levy, *Propaganda and the Jesuit baroque* (Berkeley, Los Angeles and London, 2004); Louthan, *Converting Bohemia: force and persuasion in the Catholic Reformation*, pp 279–316; H. Louthan, 'Tongues, toes and bones: remembering saints in early modern Bohemia' in A. Walsham (ed.), *Relics and remains*, Past and Present supplement, 5 (2010), 177–80.

Sir John Gilbert (1829–98): historian of the Irish bourgeoisie

CIARAN BRADY

I

Until it was most deservedly conferred upon the honorand of the present collection, the title of doyen of the historians of early modern Dublin undoubtedly belonged to Sir John T. Gilbert. The author of the standard three-volume *History of Dublin* (1854–9), editor of the documentary record of two of the city's great monastic settlements, the principal force behind the great project to preserve the civic records of Dublin, and editor of the first seven volumes of the *Calendar of ancient records of Dublin* (1892–8), Gilbert can be credited with doing more than any other individual to make the history of Dublin from the fifteenth century to the eighteenth century available for scholarly examination.[1]

Yet while his achievement as an historian of Dublin has been frequently recorded, there are curious features of Gilbert's scholarly career that have largely gone unnoticed.[2] One concerns the unusual breadth of his intellectual interests. While Gilbert's authority as an urban historian has been amply recognized, his substantial contributions to other phases and aspects of Irish history – his passionate concern with the preservation and publication of pre-conquest Gaelic Irish sources and his intense preoccupation with the events of the 1640s – have never been satisfactorily integrated with his principal interests in the history of Dublin. This neglect of Gilbert's remarkably

---

[1] For a full but not exhaustive list of Gilbert's publications see Máire Kennedy, 'Contribution towards a bibliography of the writings of John T. Gilbert' in Mary Clark, Yvonne Desmond and Nodlaig P. Hardiman (eds), *Sir John T. Gilbert, 1829–1898: historian, archivist and librarian* (Dublin, 1999), pp 141–7. [2] Rosa Mulholland, Lady Gilbert, *Life of Sir John T. Gilbert LLD, FSA* (London, 1905), is the standard biography; based upon personal knowledge and on manuscript materials subsequently lost, it is unlikely to be completely superseded. Despite its quasi-official standing it is not altogether uncritical or bland, notably in relation to Gilbert's early family life, and his early days as a scholar. Nodlaig P. Hardiman, 'The entire Gilbert: the life and times of John T. Gilbert' in Clark et al., *Gilbert*, pp 9–24, is more interrogative and adds some very interesting biographical detail not to be found in Mulholland, *Life*. Brendan Twomey, *Sir John T. Gilbert: life, works and contexts* (15th Annual Sir John T. Gilbert Commemorative Lecture, Dublin, 2012), supplies some valuable comparative perspectives; Toby Barnard's insightful and illuminating, 'Sir John Gilbert and Irish historiography' in Clark et al., *Gilbert*, pp 92–110, is the only attempt to provide a critical estimation of Gilbert's vast output.

broad scholarly endeavour is related to a second, and rather less positive, feature of his career as an historian. This was his early and almost total abandonment of historical writing in favour of editorial work.

Arising from a series of essays he published in the *Irish Quarterly Review*, the great *History of Dublin* was largely complete in the early 1850s when Gilbert was still in his twenties. His next major work, a *History of the viceroys of Ireland ... to 1509* (1865), was intended to be merely the first volume in a larger multi-volume enterprise designed to offer a comprehensive study of the viceroyalty down to modern times.[3] But it turned out to be his last full-scale historical study. Despite his early insistence that the production of a grand historical narrative based on fidelity to the historical evidence was to be the great intellectual task to be undertaken by his generation, Gilbert himself, apart from a few scattered essays, elected to withdraw from historical writing and to devote his massive energies to the task of producing scholarly editions of a huge number of manuscript documents.[4]

He did not, of course, cease to write. Gilbert remained an intense and often bitter controversialist for most of his life. But unlike so many of his disputatious contemporaries in British and Irish historical scholarship – Lecky, Froude and Prendergast, Freeman and Round, for example – his engagement in controversy did not find expression in lengthy critical reviews, or in the construction of alternative *re*-interpretations of his opponent's topics. More prosaically Gilbert chose to air his dissent and complaint directly in public or in private letters largely restricted to the exposure of the technical incompetence of those whose work he was condemning.[5]

Such a pedantic and quarrelsome approach to controversy, coupled with an increasing unwillingness to engage in actual historical writing, has lent itself easily to psychological explanation, especially within a community familiar with the phenomenon. But the nature of the psychological impulse influencing Gilbert's approach to the study of Irish history is far from easy to estimate. That John Gilbert was of a delicate disposition – nervous, shy, extremely sensitive and prone to depression – was acknowledged by his first and only biographer, his wife. As a child and youth he was shy, solitary and abnormally bookish. He made few friends, and those relationships, such as his

---

3 Gilbert, *History of the viceroys of Ireland with notices of the castle of Dublin* (Dublin, 1865), 'Preface', p. ix.   4 Kennedy, 'Contribution towards a bibliography', esp. pp 145–6.   5 See *inter alia* the series of public letters published by Gilbert under the thinly veiled pseudonym of 'An Irish archivist', *Record revelations: a letter on the public records of Ireland* (London, 1863); *Record revelations resumed: a letter on the public records of Ireland* (London, 1864); *English commissioners and Irish records: a letter* (London, 1865). While each of these pieces first appeared in Irish periodicals, Gilbert had them published as individual pamphlets at his own expense in London and supplemented them by a series of letters sent to parliamentarians and other public figures: see his private letter book in the Gilbert MSS, NLI, MS 1599.

close friendship with the poet, Denis Florence McCarthy (who was twenty years' his senior), seemed characterized by an intense emotional pressure. As a youth, and for most of his adult life, he remained immensely close to, and dependent on, his widowed mother and his three sisters with whom he lived in the family home at Blackrock. On the death of his youngest sister, Mary, in 1886, a female cousin was called in to care for him until 1891 when, unexpectedly and to the surprise of most of his acquaintances, Gilbert, aged 62, became engaged to and married the well-known popular novelist, Rosa Mulholland. Though the marriage was apparently a happy and a successful one, Gilbert never became a father.[6]

In adult life, Gilbert's shyness dissolved, and he moved in a wide circle of friends and acquaintances. But his inveterate tendency to take offence involved him repeatedly in disagreeable spats and more serious enmities. The initial rejection of his application to be elected to the Royal Irish Academy at the age of 23 rankled deeply. Even though he was elected without dissent three years later, and thereafter advanced to positions of great influence within the Academy, winning in 1861 the distinction of becoming honorary librarian, he never forgave the initial rebuff.[7]

Gilbert's quarrel with the Academy paled into insignificance in contrast with his assault on the clerks of the Irish Chancery's Rolls Office upon the publication of *Calendar of patent and close rolls* in the early 1860s. His exposure in a series of articles and pamphlets of the incompetence and dishonesty of James Morrin and his team was part of a broader campaign to wrest responsibility for the preservation and organization of the Irish public records away from the law courts and to secure the establishment of an Irish Public Records Office, a project in which several other scholars apart from Gilbert were energetically involved.[8] But the invective of Gilbert's attack not only on the unskilled and ignorant editors, but on their colleagues, their superiors, on those innocent third parties who had been rash enough to praise the *Calendars*, and even on the special commissioners appointed by the crown who largely upheld his allegations, was of such a degree of intensity as to undermine the righteousness of his cause.[9] It certainly damaged Gilbert's rep-

---

6 Mulholland, *Life*, esp. pp 8–17, 316–20, 351–3; Mulholland was 51 at the time of their marriage. Some indication of Gilbert's hypochondria is to be found in his correspondence with his friend and doctor Sir William Wilde, see Wilde to Gilbert, 15 Sept.; 1 Oct. 1866, NLI MS 10722.   7 Mulholland, *Life*, pp 34–6; Siobhan O'Rafferty, 'Gilbert and the Royal Irish Academy' in Clark et al., *Gilbert*, pp 45–58.   8 Greágoir Ó Dúill, 'Gilbert and the Public Record Office of Ireland' in Clark et al., *Gilbert*, pp 25–44; Herbert Wood, 'The public records of Ireland before and after 1922', *Transactions of the Royal Historical Society*, 4th series, 13 (1930), 17–39.   9 See in particular Gilbert's particularly biting but tactless *English commissioners and Irish records*; for an indication that Gilbert's invective was counterproductive, see W.H. Hardinge to Gilbert, 12 May 1864, quoted in Mulholland, *Life*, p. 127.

utation, and may also have been responsible for the second deeply-felt rebuff of his career: the cancelling of his expected appointment as deputy keeper of the new Irish Record Office when it was at last established in 1867, and the offer of the junior post of secretary of the PRO. To this humiliation was added the injury of a paltry salary. In 1874, when a proposal to abolish the post of secretary was mooted, Gilbert concluded, largely without foundation, that this was a deliberate attempt to oust him from the Record Office. He suffered a complete mental collapse that disabled him for more than two-and-a-half years, during which his friends feared not only for his permanent sanity but his immediate safety. On his recovery he was (re)appointed to the post of inspector of the Royal Records Commission within the Office which had been intended for him in the first place.[10]

Gilbert's mid-life crisis also affected his relations within the Royal Irish Academy. His sustained absence from the Academy's committees and council from January 1875 on left the library unattended and unserviced, and allowed the preparation of an edition of The Book of Leinster to proceed without supervision. In March 1876 the council decided that, as he was not in a position to stand for re-election as librarian, he should be replaced (temporarily), and that his replacement, Robert Atkinson, should assume responsibility for supervision of the new edition. On Gilbert's recovery and return to the Academy in 1878, Atkinson graciously resigned. But, understandably, he assumed that he should continue the work of supervision which was already well-advanced and see the Book of Leinster through the press. Gilbert objected and demanded that Atkinson withdraw. An unseemly row ensued and while Gilbert appears to have lost, he continued to provoke controversy within the Academy. Even as he was objecting to Atkinson, Gilbert was mounting an attack on proposals to divert the accumulated funds of the Cunningham Prize away from prizes for essays to the subvention of publication. Gilbert's insinuations that prejudice lay behind the failure of the Academy to award essay prizes provoked considerable discomfort, and, as in the case of his struggle with the Rolls Office clerks, the savagery of his attack lost him support. Similarly, Gilbert's remarkable and quite contradictory action in unilaterally investing funds raised for the establishment of professorship in honour of the late Trinity scholar James Henthorn Todd into the Court of Chancery caused a furore within the Academy. As with the Atkinson and Cunningham cases, Gilbert lost. His actions resulted in a formal censure, and may have seriously damaged his chances of becoming president of the Academy.[11]

10 Ó Dúill, 'Gilbert and the Public Record Office of Ireland', pp 38–9; Mulholland, *Life*, chapters x–xi; though passed over delicately by Mulholland (pp 206–10), the depth and duration of Gilbert's breakdown is fully attested to by contemporary documentation: see the testimonials supplied in NLI, MSS 5929–30; and Mary Gilbert's letter of 11 Mar. 1876, included in the Council Minutes of the Royal Irish Academy. 11 See, in general, O'Rafferty, 'Gilbert and the Royal Irish Academy'; also R.B. McDowell, 'The main nar-

Such instances of Gilbert's super-sensitivity, fragility and lack of sympathy for other persons give ample grounds for assuming that psychological factors are of some importance in accounting for the peculiar character of Gilbert's public career, its rancour, its intensive pedantry, and its determination to establish him as an unassailable authority. But of itself such a conclusion is speculative, inconclusive and insufficient. Because, at the very least, these features of Gilbert's personality cannot be separated from his inherited social and cultural circumstances. For this reason it seems more profitable to explore the character of Gilbert's scholarly life through the more pedestrian – and more verifiable – avenues of social and cultural history.

II

Born in 1829 – the year of Catholic Emancipation – Gilbert was the fifth of a family of six surviving children. He was the second of only two boys, his older brother Henry having preceded him by eight years. His father, John Gilbert, was the son of Henry Gilbert, a Devonshire-man who first came to Ireland and settled in Dublin in the 1780s, setting up as a wine and beer merchant. John was born in 1791, and in 1821 he married Mary Anne Costello, eldest daughter of Philip and Mary Costello who occupied a floor in the Gilbert's own dwelling place at Jervis Street. The Costellos were moderately well-to-do. A carpenter by trade, Philip had moved up into the higher end of the craft as a coach-maker. They were, by Mulholland's account, close to the Gilberts before the marriage and remained so afterwards. But they were Catholic, and Mary Anne was determined that any children of the marriage should be brought up as Catholics and educated in Catholic institutions. Thus, following his other siblings, young John Thomas received his education first in the recently established St Vincent's seminary in Usher's Quay, then in Bective College, Dublin, and finally at the Christian Brothers' College in Prior Park, Bath.[12]

At this point the tensions issuing from Gilbert's dual identity as the product of a mixed marriage, made more complicated by his father's strong attachment to his English heritage and his mother's no less strong attachment to Irish Catholicism, were augmented by those arising from a thwarted and aborted formal education. From early childhood young John had displayed a remarkable intellectual precocity. He regularly came top of his class at Prior Park, won the school's silver medal for academic distinction, and his prize examination

rative' in Tarlach Ó Raifeartaigh (ed.), *The Royal Irish Academy: a bicentennial history, 1785–1985* (Dublin, 1985), pp 56–69.   **12** Mulholland, *Life*, chapters i–iii; but see also the important additional detail about the family property and business supplied in Hardiman, 'The entire Gilbert: the life and times of John T. Gilbert', esp. pp 14–16, 19.

papers were kept as family trophies. A letter to his mother, the only one preserved by Mulholland, dated while Gilbert was still aged 13, is a testimony both to his intellectual potential and his intense concern with academic study.[13] But despite his achievements (celebrated in the family archive) and his evident desire to develop his scholarly ambitions, his mother interposed. As a Catholic Gilbert would still, at mid-century, have been prevented from taking a degree in Oxford and Cambridge, but would have been permitted to attend Trinity College, Dublin, or seek admittance to the King's Inn.

Instead, his mother, according to Mulholland,

> who had resisted the desire of her husband to give the boy to the church approved by law and smiled on by fortune, was now quite as resolved to him taking a step which, in her opinion would have been spiritually disastrous. Her son complied with her wishes, pursuing his chosen studies outside the walls of the University [sic], and in like manner he restrained his desire to give himself solely to ideal aims, again yielding to the mother who had destined him to assist his brother in the management of their late father's business.[14]

Gibert was to remain in the family business as a wine and spirit merchant for around twenty-two years until, significantly perhaps, at age 40, he sold the business outright in 1869.[15]

Even as he entered the Dublin commercial world, however, Gilbert plunged into the parallel world of Irish historical scholarship. In 1848, aged 19, just out of Prior Park, he joined the Irish Celtic Society, and within four years he had become its secretary. During this period the Society was in a state of considerable turmoil. Members seeking amalgamation with the Irish Archaeological Society were opposed by those insisting on independence. The conflict resulted in secession, as a minority split into the short-lived Ossianic Society. But the union was successful and, a stalwart for union, Gilbert became secretary of the new Irish Archaeological and Celtic Society in 1852.[16]

It was against this background that the young Gilbert agreed to allow his name be put forward by Sir William Wilde and others for election to the

---

13 Gilbert to 'Mama', 24 May 1842, quoted in Mulholland, *Life*, pp 9–10.   14 Mulholland, *Life*, p. 16.   15 Mulholland, *Life*, pp 9–12. On Gilbert's intense involvement in the family business as late as the late 1860s, see the correspondence preserved in NLI MS; also Gilbert's statement that in 1867 he was worth almost £1,000 p.a., NLI MS 10722. Despite his withdrawal from the family business, Gilbert continued to manage his financial affairs energetically, e.g., Gilbert to Rosa Mulholland, 12 Apr., 1891, NLI MS 8261.   16 Mulholland, *Life*, pp 20–1; for Gilbert's activities as secretary of the combined society see the 'Letter book of the Celtic Society, 1854', NLI MS 9842; and his correspondence concerning the society in NLI MS 8261; on the general context see, Damien Murray, *Romanticism, nationalism and Irish antiquarian societies* (Maynooth, 2000).

Royal Irish Academy. The result was initial disappointment. Gilbert attributed this rejection to his confessional affiliation. But in addition to this, and to the question of his age – Gilbert at 23 had just about begun on the remarkable series of publications that characterized his early years – a third factor, hinted at by the embarrassed assistant secretary of the Academy, may also have been at play. While seeking to lay the blame on Gilbert's sponsors who failed to rally their ranks on the day, Assistant Secretary Clibborn also hinted at class snobbery. Gilbert's profession having been labelled as 'Merchant' (the term 'General Merchant' having been revised from an earlier draft) may, Clibborn suggested, have given 'a misconception as to the identity of the party proposed.'[17] If so, Gilbert's initial rejection by the Academy would appear to have offered, in epitome, all of the features which characterized Gilbert's relationship to the scholarly community to which he so anxiously sought admission. He was too young, he was a Catholic, and also he was a merchant, a man in trade, the particular instance of which was neither long enough established, nor sufficiently respectable to allow immediate acceptance into polite society.

If such prejudices existed in 1852, they were sufficiently allayed by 1855 to allow for a full reversal by the Academy. But there is a further aspect of the young Gilbert's public character which, though it was never referred to in the Academy's deliberations, may have been an added factor in their suspicion of the amazingly talented and energetic young upstart. This was his intense involvement in the *Irish Quarterly Review*, a journal established just a year before his application to the Academy.

III

Now largely forgotten, the first issue of *Irish Quarterly Review* appeared in March 1851 and ran through thirty-six issues until 1859. Despite the echoes of its title of the Tory *Quarterly Review*, *The Irish Quarterly Review* was strongly reformist in purpose and Liberal in its political sympathies.[18] Many of its contributions concerned the reform of the law, the judiciary and prisons, suggesting a strong association with the legal profession. It was also very strong in its assertions of equitable tenant right over the legal claims of (often absentee) landlords. And while it explicitly adopted a firm anti-sectarian stand, it was also distinctly Catholic in its sympathies. The *Quarterly*, in short, was very close in its attitudes to those of the Independent Irish Party with whose establishment its first appearance coincided and on whose demise the journal also ceased to publish.

17 Mulholland, *Life*, p. 35. 18 On the principles of the *Irish Quarterly Review* see Prefatory Note to vol. 2:1, n.p.; also Tom Clyde, *Irish literary magazines: an outline history and descriptive bibliography* (Dublin, 2003), pp 116–18.

In addition to articles on political, legal and social reform, however, the *Quarterly* also featured contributions on cultural and scholarly topics. Articles concerning Irish art, literature and history appeared in each issue, and it was in this category that Gilbert's first publications appeared. These were a connected series of essays on 'Irish historical literature', 'The historical literature of Ireland' and 'The Celtic records of Ireland', which were published in the second, third and fourth issues of the journal. Other essays on Irish church history, on the Brehon codes, on the Down Survey of the 1650s, on the Danes and Norwegians in Ireland, and on the life of Samuel Madden appeared under Gilbert's pen in the journal in 1852 and 1853. But it was his series of eight articles on 'The streets of Dublin' which appeared in the same years that established Gilbert's scholarly reputation. In an extraordinary spurt of creativity while aged between 22 and 23, Gilbert had published no less than seventeen substantial articles in the journal, an achievement that encouraged him to allow a proposal for his election to the Royal Irish Academy in 1852.

After 1853, however, Gilbert published nothing more with the *Irish Quarterly*. There are some signs that the parting with the journal with which, as Mulholland frequently suggests, he was so closely associated, was less than happy.[19] Significantly, perhaps, it coincided with a split within the movement between those who chose to return to the Whig/Liberal party in the early 1850s, and those who wished to stay independent. If so, Gilbert was perhaps one of those who rejected the independents – those who under the leadership of John Sadleir and William Keogh were soon to be labelled 'the Pope's brass band'.[20] However that may be, the hundreds of pages that he produced in so short a time not only give a clear indication of the kind of grand historical narrative that he envisaged would be written in his lifetime, but also make evident the profound and intense ideological forces which underlay his engagement with Irish history, and which in his later scholarly productions he sought so carefully to conceal.

Gilbert's earliest published words demonstrate his conviction that the history of Ireland had been deliberately transformed into an ideological battlefield.

> As the power of England gradually extended in the country, it became the policy of the more unenlightened and short-sighted of the successful party to endeavour to obliterate every trace of the former state and ancient Celtic institutions of the kingdom. Hence the old historical volumes written in the Irish language were industriously sought and systematically destroyed.[21]

19 Mulholland, *Life*, pp 66, 81.   20 J.H. Whyte, *The Independent Irish Party* (Oxford, 1958); also R.V. Comerford, 'Churchmen, tenants and independent opposition, 1850–6' in W.E. Vaughan (ed.), *A new history of Ireland*, v: *Ireland under the Union, Part I* (Oxford, 1989), pp 396–414.   21 Gilbert, 'The Celtic records of Ireland', *Irish Quarterly Review*,

This deliberate obliteration of the history of the defeated was only one part of the programme. Into the vacuum caused by the destruction of the native Irish historical record, English writers moved to assert that there had been no history there at all, the natives being merely 'wrapped in savagery and barbarism'. It thus became

> politic with the successful colonists to represent themselves as the introducers of civilization and justice and the magnanimous expellers of barbarism and rapine. These partisan views were embodied and propagated by servile authors who composed histories of this country, under the surveillance of a tyrannous oligarchy, by whom patronage and emoluments were distributed in proportion to the amount of plausible misrepresentations and adulation exhibited by those venal scribes.[22]

The scholarly editions of ancient Irish texts now being produced by the Irish Archaeological and Celtic Society were, therefore, more than mere exercises in gentlemanly antiquarianism. They were a central part of a great campaign to undo a great wrong perpetrated by the Anglo-Norman conquest and all subsequent English conquests of Ireland.

From this it is hardly surprising that Gilbert took an extremely positive view of pre-conquest Irish society. He argued that those manuscripts that survived the depredations of the conquerors demonstrated both in the centuries before the coming of the Normans and in several succeeding centuries, that, far from being wrapped in barbarism, the Gaelic lordships were centres of sustained stability and considerable cultural sophistication. Surviving literary, historical and medical texts showed beyond doubt a familiarity with continental literature. The genealogies and annals functioned as nothing short of 'the charters of individual Gaelic families', affirming their rights to residence and ownership in particular places in a manner no less authoritative than the charters of contemporary England. The Brehon law codes, far from being 'an arbitrary compound of barbarity and impiety', as Spenser, Cox and others claimed, were the guiding rules of a sophisticated political and social system which were consciously designed to maintain the stability of Irish society by protecting the freedoms of each sub-unit – the clan – while insisting on the obligations of each clan to their acknowledged superior, the chieftain of the region.[23]

This was a rather roseate picture that modern scholars would hardly endorse. But Gilbert's account of 'Celtic Ireland' was also hedged with certain concessions which were absent from more romantic popular histories of the old

---

1:4 (1851), 588–700; the quotation is from p. 589; also 'The historic literature of Ireland', *Irish Quarterly Review*, 1:3 (1851), 469.   22 Gilbert, 'The Celtic records of Ireland', 593.
23 Gilbert, 'The Brehon Law Commission', *Irish Quarterly Review*, 2:7 (1852), 559–676, quotations from p. 660.

Irish world, and which also lent a greater nuance and persuasiveness to his account. First, Gilbert did not seek to discount the amount of political discord that existed in Gaelic Ireland. Fratricidal conflicts abounded, and much blood was spilt (though hardly more, Gilbert hurried to remind his readers, than was the case in large parts of medieval Europe).[24] In their indulgence in these wars the Gaelic lords were not infrequently the authors of their own misfortunes by the often irresponsible manner in which they drew on the costly support of foreigners – Danes, Scots, Normans and English. The leaders of the Irish nation, moreover, showed themselves on occasion to be willing to abandon aspects of their tradition through the adoption of English customs, English laws, and even for a short time reformed English religion.[25] Finally, at the beginning of the seventeenth century, the Gaelic world collapsed altogether, and was never to revive: its 'ancient institutions, destined by Providence to give place to a system of government which has eventually conduced to promote the liberties and welfare of the human race.'[26] Thus Gilbert's nostalgia for the lost Celtic world was sharply tempered by a keen acceptance of the idea that the history of liberty was also a history of irreversible progress.

The qualified nature of Gilbert's attachment to old Ireland was somewhat obscured by a further element in his view of Irish history. This was his intense, and exceptional, distaste for the other social group in later medieval Ireland, the Anglo-Normans. In contrast to 'the love of freedom implanted in the breasts of the men of Erin', the Anglo-Normans brought to Ireland the accursed system of feudalism.[27] Gilbert quoted the French historian Guizot with passionate enthusiasm:

> Feudal despotism has always been repulsive and odious. It has oppressed the destinies, but never reigned over the souls of men ... the feudal system has been as much opposed to the establishment of general order as to the extension of general liberty. Under whatever point of view you view the progress of society, you find the feudal system acting as an obstacle.[28]

This was the system the Anglo-Normans imposed on Ireland, and from it all the ills of subsequent Irish history ensued. Their violence, their greed, their

---

24 Gilbert, 'The Celtic records of Ireland', 588–700, esp. 646–7; Gilbert, 'Irish church history', *Irish Quarterly Review*, 2:1 (1852), 196–216, esp. 214–15.   25 In addition to sources cited above, see also Gilbert, 'Mr Worsaae on the Danes and Norwegians in Ireland', *Irish Quarterly Review*, 2:4 (1852), 817–28.   26 Gilbert, 'The Celtic records of Ireland', 588–700, the quotation is from p. 691.   27 Gilbert, 'The Celtic records of Ireland', 626.   28 Gilbert, 'The Celtic records of Ireland', 625–6; though Gilbert does not supply the reference, the quotation is from Guizot's *Histoire générale de la civilisation en Europe depuis la chute de l'empire romain jusqu'à la révolution française* (1838), p. 94; an English translation appeared in 1846, and a comparison between both texts suggests that Gilbert supplied his own translation of the original.

duplicities destabilised Irish society more than the occasional excess of individual Gaelic lords had ever done. And to make matters worse, they fought ceaselessly among themselves. Selfish and incapable of honour they foolishly assisted the English in the Elizabethan wars against the Ulster Irish but

> soon found cause to repent of having combined with the enemies of their country. Promises made in the hour of danger were now publicly revoked, oppressive Penal statutes were enacted and the last days of the natives who had assisted to crush O'Neill and his brave adherents were embittered by the reflection that their own conduct had involved themselves in the ruin which they had brought upon those who had bravely stood forth in defence of their ancient liberties.[29]

The Anglo-Irish, moreover, were not merely the victims of English treachery. They were themselves the principal source of that wilful distortion of Irish history which had brought such ruin to the island.

> From their first settlement in Ireland, a section of the colonists found that vilification and ridicule were the most effective modes of depriving their opponents of the sympathy and justice to which they were justly entitled; the language of the Irish was ... pronounced to be barbarous, their laws impious, their ancient history a mass of fabrications, and every effort made to eradicate those sentiments of national pride which dignify and exalt the human character. The colonial oligarchy ... combined to represent the Irish as a nation of fools, blunderers, drunkards and assassins. By thus exciting the fears of the English government, they contrived quietly to appropriate to their own uses the entire spoil of the plundered Irish ... Pausing at no falsehoods, however monstrous, the ascendancy faction succeeded in convincing the neighbouring country that the Irish were little better than cannibals ... whereas if these unscrupulous traders upon national animosities had been divested of the power of retarding the progress of the country, and prevented from intercepting the administration of even-handed justice to all, the people of both islands would have become more conversant with each other and learned mutual respect and forbearance.[30]

Gilbert contrasted the Irish case with that of Scotland 'where the history of the subjugated Highlanders ... was invested with a dignity which evoked a wise nationality', that enabled all sides to join in a celebration of a shared her-

29 Gilbert, 'The Celtic records of Ireland', 691.   30 Gilbert, 'Reminiscences of a Milesian', *Irish Quarterly Review*, 3:1 (1853), 179–92, the quotation is from p. 180.

itage.³¹ But the lies of the 'ascendancy faction' brought their own nemesis: 'Their own suicidal acts at length broke the power of the Irish colonial ascendancy, and their career of profligacy and oppression having finally stripped them of station and influence, the propagation of falsehood became no longer a State object.'³²

This was a view of the history of the Anglo-Irish and of the Act of Union which contrasted sharply with that of his closest associates in scholarship. For Young Irelanders, such as Davis and Mangan, as well as for scholars such as J.P. Prendergast and the young author of *Leaders of public opinion in Ireland*, what distinguished the history of the Anglo-Irish was their repeated ability to empathize with the cause of the native Irish, their willingness to adapt to the best features of Gaelic culture and above all their willingness to assume leadership of a united Irish movement against the exploitation and oppression of the English.³³ For these writers – up until the 1880s at any rate – the Union was a disaster forced upon Ireland by an uncaring English government for short-term exigencies, and the principal aim of Irish politics should be its repeal. But Gilbert refused ever to commit publicly to such a view; and his unqualified condemnation of the historical role played by the Anglo-Irish suggests that behind his refusal to endorse the re-opening of the parliament in College Green lay motives more serious than mere temerity.

A second feature of Gilbert's ideological position as revealed in his periodical writings is his equal refusal to espouse the strongest available alternative to colonial nationalism: Catholic nationalism. Though Gilbert was extremely sensitive to the atmosphere of sectarian prejudice in which he worked, and of the damage which he believed it had wreaked on his career; and though he asserted 'as a singular fact that one of the most neglected departments of our literature is Irish ecclesiastical history', it is remarkable how little attention he devoted to the topic in his own massive scholarly output.³⁴ His later editions of the chartularies and registers of the abbeys of St Mary and St Thomas in Dublin might on the surface be considered contributions to the subject. But the primary materials there presented, and the editorial introductions that accompanied them, emphasized the municipal, social and political character of these institutions rather than their religious or cultural importance.³⁵

---

31 Gilbert, 'Reminiscences of a Milesian', 181.   32 Gilbert, 'Reminiscences of a Milesian', 182.   33 The Young Irelanders' celebration of the Anglo-Norman tradition, redolent throughout the pages of *The Nation* in the 1840s, is epitomized in Davis' poem, 'The Geraldines'; Lecky's veneration for his forbears is fully explored in Donal McCartney, *W.E.H. Lecky: historian and politician, 1838–1903* (Dublin, 1994). For a further discussion of the Anglo-Irish construction of Irish history, see Ciaran Brady, 'An old kind of history: the Anglo-Irish writing of Irish history, 1840–1910' in Carrie Berbéri and Martine Pelletier (eds), *Ireland: authority and crisis* (Bern, 2015), pp 237–86.   34 Gilbert, 'Irish church history', 196–216, the quotation is from p. 196.   35 Gilbert (ed.), *Chartularies of St Mary's Abbey, Dublin with the register of its house at Dunbrody and annals of Ireland* (2

Sir John Gilbert: historian of the Irish bourgeoisie 261

The one sustained consideration of the subject of 'Irish church history' which appeared in the *Irish Quarterly Review* in 1852 contains some surprising observations.[36] First, the essay, the occasion of which was a notice of the E.P. Shirley's decidedly Anglican *Original letters and papers in illustration of the church in Ireland*, was unreservedly (and uncharacteristically) laudatory. Shirley was already an acknowledged scholar whose 'present work gives him another claim to the respect of all students of our literature': Gilbert looked forward to more.[37] Second, Gilbert's terminology is remarkably ecumenical. Despite the tactful nature of Shirley's title, Gilbert throughout the essay refers to the early or the post conquest 'church of Ireland', a concession which ecclesiologically minded orthodox Catholics would have found quite unacceptable. But most importantly of all, and in contrast to many contemporary and subsequent Catholic nationalists, Gilbert conceded that the sixteenth-century Reformation would have had a real chance of success. Several of the leading Gaelic lords were quite favourable to its acceptance. It was consistent with 'their inclination to form friendly relations with the English crown as manifested by their acceptance of patents of nobility and adoption of English customs.'[38]

But once more this possible mode of accommodation between Gaelic Ireland and England was diverted by 'mercenary officials ...[who] foreseeing that the destruction of their own importance would be the consequence of the general pacification of the country, early devised measures for rendering the Reformed religion [Gilbert's capital] repulsive to the natives'.[39] The systematic exclusion of natives from ecclesiastical office, the refusal to spread the evangelical message in 'the Irish tongue' and the rapacious confiscation of ecclesiastical property by private individuals all contributed to the alienation of the Irish from the Reformation.

Gilbert's brisk interpretation of the causes of the failure of the Reformation in Ireland will have proved convincing neither to Catholic nationalists, who have regarded it as a foregone conclusion, or to more modern scholars who have largely taken a more nuanced view of the process.[40] But,

---

vols., London, 1884); *Register of the abbey of St Thomas, Dublin* (London, 1889). Gilbert's editorial emphases are made clear in his extensive introductions to these texts.   36 Gilbert, 'Irish church history', 196–216.   37 Ibid., 216.   38 Ibid., 214.   39 Ibid.   40 It was this unorthodox attitude that may have given rise to the assumption among certain Catholic ecclesiastics that Gilbert was, in fact, a Protestant, see Mulholland, *Life*, p. 274: 'About this time he began to find his position in his work somewhat anomalous ... While facing the fire of the enemy on one side, he was looked on coldly from a distance by many on the other. A letter remains written to him by a priest, his friend, relating with humour, a recent conversation with a Catholic dignitary whom he had met in the street, and greeted with "Have you seen Gilbert's latest book?" "Read Gilbert", cried the Catholic dignitary, "I would not read a word the fellow writes. He is a Protestant and a bigoted Trinity College man!".' Modern scholarship, pioneered by Colm Lennon, has provided a rather

taken in relation to his excoriation of the Anglo-Irish, and his sympathetic but none-the-less emphatic view of the irreversible collapse of Gaelic Ireland, it raises curious questions as to his own understanding of the direction of Irish history. Why should the failure of the Celtic world be registered as regrettable but historically inevitable while an opposite but no less momentous historical force as the failure of the Reformation be accounted largely as an accident?

IV

At the back of this apparent paradox lay a conviction, rarely stated explicitly by Gilbert, but most obvious in his early writings, that there was, after all, a pattern to be discerned in human history. That was the ceaseless striving of humanity to attain the greatest possible liberty. He believed that, 'destined by Providence', 'a system of government which has eventually conduced to promote the liberties and welfare of the human race' had at length been established in Europe.[41] That such a tendency was by no means vouchsafed, Gilbert readily conceded. It could be disrupted, perverted, stifled by the forces of reaction such as the Anglo-Norman feudal magnates, corrupt administrators and ecclesiastics, the decadent and self-serving colonial ascendancy, and of course the hosts of 'venal writers', propagandists masquerading as scholars, who provided an utterly false account of history. But in the end the drive for liberty once represented by the old Irish would break through, in differing form but serving the same purpose of human liberty.

In asserting that the essential imperative of history was the drive toward freedom, Gilbert was, of course, very much in keeping with the dominant philosophy of history of the mid-nineteenth century conceptualized by Hegel and made concrete in the great historical works of Leopold von Ranke.[42] But while he had clearly read and admired Ranke, Gilbert derived his own specific version of the idea that all history was the history of liberty not from Germany, but from France, in the form of the great French historians of the early nineteenth century – Sismondi, Guizot, Barante and, above all,

---

more complex account of the failure of the Reformation than Gilbert's curious simplicity. 41 Gilbert, 'The Celtic records of Ireland', 691.   42 See Leonard Krieger, *Ranke: the meaning of history* (Chicago, 1977); and more generally Krieger, *The German idea of freedom: history of a political tradition* (Chicago, 1957); for French historians' variations on this liberal tradition to which Gilbert was more directly attracted, see Linda Orr, *Jules Michelet: nature, history, language* (Ithaca, 1976); Lionel Gossman, *Between history and literature* (Cambridge, MA, 1990); and Ceri Crossley, *French historians and Romanticism: Thierry, Guizot, the Saint-Simonians, Quinet, Michelet* (London, 1993).   43 Gilbert, 'The historic literature of Ireland', *Irish Quarterly Review*, 1:3 (1851), 409–68, at p. 409; see also 410, 416.

Augustine Thierry, whose names are celebrated in one of the earliest paragraphs Gilbert ever published.[43]

The importance of Thierry, the author of the highly influential *History of the Norman conquest*, to the Young Irelanders of the 1840s has often been noted. The chapters he devoted to Ireland in which he extolled the virtues of the Celts over their brutal Norman conquerors were an inspiration to Davis, Mitchel, MacCarthy, Clarence Mangan and Gavan Duffy.[44] And a key medium by which he praised the vitality of the old Irish culture – their poems, songs and annals – was taken over by them as the essential mode of their programme of cultural revival and historical revision. In his own evocation of the songs and stories of ancient Ireland that he conducted in his journal writings of the early 1850s Gilbert, then, may be seen as a somewhat belated Young Irelander. But a further investigation of the thinking underlying Thierry's celebration of these materials gives a greater depth to Gilbert's more sustained historical campaign.

Two, apparently opposite but related, motives underlay Thierry's rehabilitation of the Celts. One was his deep and abiding hostility toward the Normans and all of those who imposed a feudal regime by conquest. The conquerors, so Thierry's argument ran, may have imposed their will by brutal force. But they could never suppress the culture they exploited completely, and the enduring resistance of a people to their exploiters was expressed in the creations of their common culture. Thus far Thierry's position may be seen as so much impotent sentimentality: an elegy for the vanquished.[45]

But a second and more subtle element in his approach was also more politically subversive.[46] This was his understanding of the medium through which the culture of the oppressed was transmitted to later generations. It was no accident of history; indeed, the historical odds seemed set against it. It occurred only because there had emerged, at another stage of post-con-

---

44 For a contemporary homage see Thomas Davis, *Literary and historical essays* (Dublin, 1845), pp 37, 60, 238; also Marmion Willard Savage's novel, *The Falcon family or Young Ireland* (London, 1845), p. 348; Richard Davis, *The Young Ireland movement* (Dublin, 1988), chapter 4; Malcolm Brown, *The politics of Irish literature: from Thomas Davis to W.B. Yeats*, pp 46, 86, 121.   45 First published in French in 1825, Thierry's *Histoire de la conquete l'Angleterre par les Normands* was almost immediately translated into English as *History of the conquest of England by the Normans* trans. C.C. Hamilton (3 vols, London, 1825). It is likely, however, that most Irish readers of Thierry, including Gilbert, read him in the original. The phrase is actually that of Thierry's early biographer, Ferdinand Valentin, quoted in R.N. Smithson, *Augustin Thierry: social and political consciousness in the evolution of an historical method* (Geneva, 1972), p. 104.   46 Among several studies of Thierry's ideological purposes and historical method see K.J. Carroll, *Some aspects of the historical thought of Augustin Thierry (1795–1856)* (Washington DC, 1951); Stanley Mellon, *The political uses of history: a study of historians in the French Restoration* (Stanford, CA, 1958); Smithson, *Augustin Thierry*; Lionel Gossman, 'Augustin Thierry and liberal historiography' in Gossman, *Between history and literature*, chapter 4.

quest history, a further group of people who found themselves no less oppressed by and hostile to the descendants of the feudal aristocratic conquerors. This new historical group, according to Thierry, which emerged gradually through the later Middle Ages and achieved its independence toward the close of the eighteenth century, was the Third Estate, and in particular, the professional and commercial groups that constituted the bourgeoisie. Like the ancient people, the Third Estate was characterized by a love of liberty. Though bodied forth in different terms in the language of freedom to trade, and to manufacture, freedom to practice law, freedom to think anew about society and to act on those thoughts, the underlying principle of resistance to the dead hand of feudalism united them with their ancient ancestors. In the establishment of this communion between the freedom-loving opponents of feudalism, a special group among the Third Estate provided a crucial service. This was the circle of poets and scholars who, acting independently of the monarchy, the aristocracy and the church, provided the means for the imaginative reconstruction of a sense of a continuous historical community dedicated to the assertion and the defence of liberty. This was not for Thierry (nor for Gilbert) an ethnic connection. It was what later commentators would describe as an ideological one; but which Thierry and Gilbert and so many European Romantics would have expressed as an imaginative one.[47]

Gilbert's deep immersion in the work of the French Romantic historians is most evident in the many references and quotations from their work that pepper his early writings.[48] Less obviously, but more interestingly, it is evident in several textual and paratextual features of his work. Paratextually, it is expressed in the several instances in which his textual discussions of events, dynasties or practices in old Ireland are supported by footnotes where, in addition to source citations, current poetic associations are also supplied. To give a few examples among many, Gilbert in support of his account of the disunity which erupted among the Gaelic Irish in the aftermath of the defeat at Kinsale, quotes in an extensive footnote a poem by Samuel Ferguson, purportedly a translation from 'an old poet'.[49] His account of the Graces of Kilkenny is supplemented by a modern translation *Graesagh-abo*; and a discussion of the manner in which Gaelic chieftains were inaugurated is illus-

[47] Thierry, 'Sur l'esprit national des Irlandais' in *Dix ans d'etudes historiques* (Paris, 1835), ch. vii, pp 128–9. For a detailed critical analysis of Thierry's understanding of the role of racial characteristics in history which discounts the previous assumptions that Thierry was a racist see Martin Seliger, 'Augustin Thierry: race thinking during the Restoration', *Journal of the History of Ideas*, 20 (1959), 273–82. [48] In addition to examples above, see also Gilbert, 'The Celtic Records of Ireland', 607, 617, 620, 625, 629, 681, 692; 'Brehon Law Commission', 669, 676; 'Irish historical literature', *Irish Quarterly Review* 1:2, 220. [49] Gilbert, 'The Celtic records of Ireland', 595, 600, 631, 657, 673, 686–7; 'The historic literature of Ireland', 412, 435–6; 'Irish historical literature', 211.

trated by a lengthy footnote quoting extensively from Thomas Davis' poem 'The True Irish King'.[50]

A further and no less curious feature of Gilbert's mode of writing is his use of genealogy and family history. In a manner that would seem at odds with the principles of scholarly history he so passionately espoused, and similar to the gentlemanly antiquarianism he pretended to dismiss, Gilbert frequently extended his discussions of Gaelic dynasties to record the status of later descendants of the families. Thus in a passing notice of the O'Gara dynasty as sometimes patrons of Micheal O'Clerigh, he thought it relevant to provide in an elaborate footnote details of the subsequent fortunes of the family down to the eighteenth century.[51] A discussion of the Annals of Kilkenny attributed to the Franciscan James Grace prompts a lengthy note on the history of the Graces of Gracecourt, tracing their luminaries down to the nineteenth century; a notice of O'Donovan's edition of the *Tribes of Hy-Many* gives rise to a brief history of the O'Kellys; while a single mention of the Mullalleys occasions a note tracing the ancestry of the great Lally-Tolendal (Louis XV's soldier) back to that family.[52] An essay devoted to a review of the scholarly writings of Samuel Madden is prefaced by a lengthy genealogical history of the O'Maddens – even though Madden himself claimed Scottish origins.[53] Later Gilbert would denounce Brewer and the other Record Commissioners for failing to recognize Art Mac Murrough Kavanagh Esquire of Borris Idrone as a living direct descendant of Diarmaid mac Murrough, or that the line of the ancient princes of Ossory was represented by the 'Right Honorable John Wilson Fitzpatrick, a member of Her Majesty's Privy Council in Ireland and Lieutenant and Custos Rotulorum of Queen's County'.[54]

Gilbert's *excursi* on the subsequent history of the great Gaelic families, however, did not always concern stories of survival and success. He noted also the defeat and disappearance of other families, notably around the time of the Williamite confiscations. The point is most obviously made in Gilbert's brief excursus on the O'Driscolls in 'Irish historic literature', where, while noting that 'the O'Driscolls who remained in Ireland have lost every vestige of the possessions of their ancestors', he goes on to trace the illustrious careers of several members of the family elsewhere, and concludes with a reference to John O'Driscoll, 'Chief Justice of the island of Dominica who has distinguished himself by his *Views of Ireland* (1823) and his *History of Ireland* (1827) works remarkable for the liberal and enlightened views of the author'.[55] Thus Gilbert was not simply concerned to celebrate the resilience of those who survived. His point rather was to demonstrate the reality of continuity

---

50 Gilbert, 'The historic literature of Ireland', 422–5; the lengthy quotation of Davis' poem is at 436.   51 Gilbert, 'The Celtic records of Ireland', pp 590–2.   52 Gilbert, 'The historic literature of Ireland', pp 429–31.   53 Gilbert, 'Rev. Samuel Madden', *Irish Quarterly Review*, 3:2 (1853), 693–7.   54 Gilbert, *English commissioners and Irish records*, pp 11–12.   55 'Irish historical literature', pp 197–204.

and survival well beyond the time of the feudal conquest, and in doing so to diminish its claims of historical finality.

V

It is in relation to this determination to devalue the significance of the feudal conquest that a further facet of Gilbert's distinctive view of Irish history emerges. This was his pioneering work in urban and municipal history. 'The history of the municipal, middle and trading classes in Ireland under or in relation with the rule of England in the twelfth and four subsequent centuries', Gilbert complained, 'has hitherto remained in almost entire obscurity'.[56] This was in 1870, when Gilbert, both in his *History of Dublin* and in the selection of *Historical and municipal documents of Ireland*, which he was then editing, had already done much to redress the balance. But this concern with the history of citizens and merchants was also expressed in his earliest historical writings. In the conclusion to his own manifesto declaiming the vital importance of the records of Celtic Ireland, Gilbert nonetheless added that 'the true history of this nation' would not be written until the recovered history of the Gaelic families was supplemented by that of the 'Anglo-Norman chevalier in his embattled keep' and 'the stout burghers in their walled towns ... the resort in the Middle Ages of the trading French, Spaniards, Portugals and Flemings'.[57] Thus, while the great Celtic scholars whose work he had been celebrating were labouring away at the reconstruction of pre-conquest Irish history, this further dimension of the island's past would be Gilbert's especial contribution to the new national history.

Gilbert's essays on 'The streets of Dublin' were published in the *Irish Quarterly* between March 1852 and December 1853, even as he was engaged on his tireless propaganda in support of Gaelic Irish records. His break with the *Quarterly* around this time put a stop to the planned publication of instalments. But the studies began to appear in book form almost immediately in 1854. Publishing economics frustrated Gilbert's hopes for the publication of further studies. But Gilbert persisted both in researches and in his negotiations, and a further two volumes were added to the original one in 1859.[58]

---

56 Gilbert (ed.), *Historic and municipal documents of Ireland, AD 1172–1320* (London, 1870), p. v.   57 Gilbert, 'The Celtic records of Ireland', 698–9.   58 The publication dates for the series entitled 'The streets of Dublin' in the *Irish Quarterly Review* are vol. 2:1 (Mar. 1852), 1–175; 2:2 (June 1852), 284–347; 2:3 (Sept. 1852), 494–562; 2:4 (Dec. 1852), 701–72; 3:1 (Mar. 1853), 17–50; 3:2 (June 1853), 259–98; 3:3 (Sept. 1853), 541–625; 3:4 (Dec. 1853), 937–89. The first publication in book form was issued under the imprint of McGlashan and Gill, vol. 1 (1854), vols 2–3 (1859); a corrected reprint was published in the three volumes by James Duffy in 1861. It is to this most accessible edition to which reference is made hereafter.

Gilbert's history of Dublin was not the first to appear. In the middle of the eighteenth century, the antiquarian Walter Harris had undertaken to revise and expand a fragmentary manuscript history of the city that had been begun by the seventeenth-century antiquarian (and forger) Robert Ware. Harris' *History and antiquities of the city of Dublin*, which was published posthumously in 1767, was also incomplete. In the early nineteenth century a further attempt at a history was similarly frustrated. Collaboration between James Warburton, Keeper of the Records at Dublin Castle, and James Whitelaw, a clergyman, was ended by their deaths, and the eventual publication of their work by Robert Walsh. The *History of the city of Dublin from the earliest accounts to the present time*, which appeared in 1818, was not only incomplete, it was presented in a rudimentary state, with the documents produced by Warburton strung together with greater or lesser coherence.[59]

It was this inchoate character of the existing histories of Dublin that Gilbert set out to redress. But he did so in a deliberately different way. Whereas the histories of Ware, Harris, Warburton and Co. were conventionally chronological in structure, largely built around the sequential presentation of municipal documents, Gilbert resorted to an alternative, and by now rather old-fashioned mode: he chose to write a topographical history.

With its roots stretching back into the classical world, modern topographical history – the organization of historical information not by temporal sequence but by spatial contiguity – was revived in a significantly altered form in the Renaissance.[60] Whereas classical topographies were characteristically designed as guide-books for travellers, the Renaissance version – most notably in its English form – was conceived as a mode of rediscovery of a place, a region or a space by that location's own inhabitants. Coinciding with the emergence of the gentry as a powerful political class, and with the formation of a sense of 'the county community', 'the Elizabethan discovery of England' was conducted through the composition of a large body of county histories, which were organized on strictly topographical lines, and in the following centuries the topographical model became the standard form in which county histories were composed.[61] It was the model followed

---

[59] Gilbert supplies a brief and critical historiography of Dublin in the Preface to the first volume of his *History*, pp v–xiv; that he was somewhat unfair at least to Warburton and Walsh is suggested in David Dickson, *Dublin: the making of a capital city* (London, 2014), p. 269.   [60] See O.A.W. Dilke, 'Itineraries and geographical maps in the early and late Roman Empire' in J.B. Harley et al. (eds), *Cartography in prehistoric, ancient and medieval Europe and the Mediterranean* (Chicago, 1987); William Rockett, 'Historical topography and British history in Camden's *Britannia*', *Renaissance and Reformation*, 26 (1990), 71–83.   [61] Rockett, 'Historical topography'; Richard Helgerson, *Forms of nationhood: the Elizabethan writing of England* (Chicago, 1992), chapter 3; Mark Brayshay (ed.), *Topographical writers in the south-west of England* (Exeter, 1990); a pioneering and still valuable essay on this topic is to be found in A.L. Rowse, *The England of Elizabeth* (London, 1950), chapter 2.

by the great project in local historical research, *The Victoria County Histories*.

Within this dominant genre, histories of cities or towns organised on topographical principles were rare. Significantly, John Hooker's *Antient history and description of the city of Exeter* was ordered on chronological rather than topographical grounds.[62] But there was one signal model of a topographical urban history produced during the English Renaissance with which the erudite Gilbert would have been totally familiar. This was John Stow's monumental *Survey of London*, first published in 1603.[63] Intended as a demonstration and a celebration of the municipal independence and civic virtues of London, Stow's mode of organizing his materials reinforced this central message. Organized on a ward by ward basis, readers would have had to have prior knowledge of these spaces and their relationship to one another in order fully to appreciate the historical material being supplied to them. They would have had to have been 'insiders', already sharing in the civic values and virtues of which Stow was reminding them. This confirmation of identity was reinforced by the text's topographical structure. The topographical form not only fractured chronological narrative, its necessary re-iteration of historical events as they affected different spaces, served also to privilege continuity over change, stability and order over disruption and accident.[64]

The attractions of Stow's model to the ideologically engaged and historiographically-aware Gilbert are evident. The assertion of the enduring strength of civic values served an important purpose in his campaign against the hated feudal inheritance. It was all the more powerful because, unlike the remains of old Irish civilization, they were not mutilated, marginalized, and rendered recondite by cultural oppression: the evidence of civic culture was vibrant, regenerative, and, above all, palpable in the streets, churches and institutions of the city to whomever wished to experience it. It is this pedagogic – or more precisely, constructivist – element in the topographical mode that is, in Gilbert's case, the most significant. Like Stow, who told his readers that he regarded his book as a kind of 'perambulation', Gilbert suggested to his readers that he wished his work to be seen as a kind of 'handbook'.[65] It would be

---

62 Hooker was the author of a major topographical text, the *Synopsis corographical of the county of Devon* (c.1577), but he made no attempt to adapt this mode to his history of Exeter.   **63** The standard modern edition is C.L. Kingsford (ed.), *A survey of London in the year 1598 reprinted from the 1603 text* (London, 1908).   **64** For critical commentaries on Stow see Ian Gadd and Alexandra Gillespie (eds), *John Stow (1525–1605) and the making of the English past: studies in early modern culture and the history of the book* (London, 2004); William Keith Hall, 'A topography of time: historical narration in John Stow's "Survey of London"', *Studies in Philology*, 88:1 (1991), 1–15 and Edward T. Bonahue, Jnr, 'Citizen history: Stow's Survey of London', *Studies in English Literature, 1500–1900*, 38, *The English Renaissance* (1998), 61–85.   **65** Gilbert, *History of Dublin*,

a *vade mecum*, a text to be taken as the reader actually walked the streets of Dublin. But it was not to be merely a tourist's guide. It would be an intensive educational course in the continuous history of the streets that the readers were integrating into their own experience of their own streets in a manner to make them more acutely aware of the distinctiveness of their own civic tradition.

That Gilbert's *History of Dublin* was a deliberate exercise in what would later be described as 'consciousness-raising' is evident in the very sequence of his topography. Beginning with a survey of Castle Street and Werburgh Street it moves out in ever-expanding circles to address the outer and later streets of the expanding urban settlement; and in following the schema, either in reality or imaginatively, readers would have acquired the conscious experience of being in a historically and culturally distinct environment that was both expanding yet constantly renewing itself within the same framework.

There is a further, but more implicit, manner in which the topographical design also cultivated a sense of community. While the pages of Gilbert's chapters are rich with anecdote concerning accident, violence and disturbance, such events are firmly enframed within the history of the streets and the municipal and civic buildings, including churches, whose stability and endurance diminishes the significance of the occasional events that occurred around or within them. Thus, in contrast to his propagandist writings in regard to Gaelic historical sources, and to his fearsome polemics against the keepers and editors of the Irish public records, the tone of Gilbert's *Dublin* is consistently consensual, eirenic and reaffirming. It is a celebration of the values of the bourgeoisie

Gilbert's concern with shaping an engaged, active readership with modern middle-class values and aspirations has been obscured by several factors, the most obvious being the abandonment of the *History of Dublin* itself. Like so many of its predecessors, Gilbert's *History*, despite its considerable length, remained incomplete. Publication costs were prohibitive, and publishers unenthusiastic, and despite his hopes to add yet other circles to his perambulation, Gilbert was compelled to abandon the work.[66] A second obscuring factor was Gilbert's next (and last) monographic project, his *History of the viceroys in Ireland*, upon which he had begun to work in the later 1850s and which appeared in book form in 1865.[67]

Gilbert's *Viceroys* could hardly have contrasted more sharply both in structure and in substance with his *Dublin*. Whereas the former was topographical, the latter was relentlessly chronological, chronicling the successive actions, reversals and recalls of a sequence of English governors over 400 years largely without overt or intrusive comment. Just as the streets of Dublin

i, Preface, p. xiii.   66 Mulholland, pp 51–2, 55.   67 Mulholland, p. 55.

reaffirmed the central continuity and contiguity of the civic community, so the central trope of the second book, the *Viceroys* by their very transient, discontinuous and contradictory conduct, underlined the central theme of the book which was the ceaseless turbulence, chaos and pointless violence of the anarchic Anglo-Norman feudal colony.[68] Far from marking a departure from his urban history, Gilbert's *Viceroys* thus served as a kind of an alternative panel in Gilbert's vision of the course of Irish history, contrasting the potential for freedom and progress that the island's inhabitants had shown in all ages with the opposing subversive forces of anarchy and reaction which so frequently interposed between them.

A third factor serving to obscure Gilbert's determination to engage an alert reading public to the ideological issues underlying the interpretation of Irish history was the rancorous controversy over the Irish Record Commission that consumed so much of his time and energy in the 1860s. The recondite, not to say pedantic, nature of so many of his allegations might seem from this distance to have repelled rather than attracted the kind of reader Gilbert sought to recruit. But this would be to misunderstand Gilbert's own conception of his readership. It was, in fact, his intense and unceasing efforts to get his objections out to a wider audience, often by funding the re-publication of his contributions on the subject in pamphlet form, that can now be seen as an attempt to raise the consciousness and stimulate the outrage of his intended audience.

A final source of the apparent, but hardly real, diminution in the force of Gilbert's ideological campaign was his deep immersion in editing and calendaring work for the Historical Manuscripts Commission, which preoccupied him for so many years after 1870. His reports on the Charlemont papers and the Haliday papers, and his massive work on the Ormonde papers, were characterized by the most restrained and austere editorial style.[69] There was nothing to be found here of the young encomiast of Irish language records, the subtle celebrant of civic culture, the polemicist against Anglo-Norman anarchy, or the archival polemicist of the 1860s. These,

---

68 The theme of disruption and radical discontinuity is returned to throughout the text (see, *inter alia*, pp 115, 128-9, 163, 176-80, and for a summary, pp 288-92), and is on occasion contrasted with the supposed order and continuity of the Gaelic lordships: 'Harassed by the natives, and disregarded by absentee proprietors, the colonists also suffered in the warfare, which continuously prevailed between the resident Anglo-Norman lords who enforced all the severities of feudalism on their dependants. The natives, meanwhile, were governed by the minute Gaelic code, administered by their Brehons or judges, according to the ancient precedent', p. 114. 69 See the dry and, in contrast to his other writings, extremely brief nature of his editorial comments in his detailed reports for the Historical Manuscripts Commission on the papers of the marquis of Ormonde: *Reports of the deputy keeper of the Public Records of Ireland*, vol. ii, pp 209-10; vol. iii, pp 425-30; vol. iv, pp 539-73; vol. vi, pp 719-80, vol. vii, pp 537-834; vol. viii, pp 499-552; vol. ix, pp 126-81; vol. x, pp 1-106; vol. xiv, pp 1-455.

instead, were texts of an impeccably scholarly standard supplied with the minimum of commentary, and have frequently been regarded as Gilbert's principal achievement.

But Gilbert's official editorial work also contributed to his personal propagandist agenda in a rather subversive way. Even while he was at work for the HMC, it was suspected that Gilbert was using both his position and his salary as a means of furthering his own personal projects.[70] Certainly it is true that in this period – that is in the later 1870s and 1880s – Gilbert embarked on a major programme of historical publications which were to be a model for most of his later scholarly output. First, under the auspices of the Irish Archaeological and Celtic Society, but largely at his own expense, Gilbert published in 1880 a massive three-volume text entitled *A contemporary history of affairs in Ireland from 1641 to 1652*. Then between 1882 and 1891 he succeeded this large documentary publication by an even larger, seven-volume, project entitled baldly *History of the Irish Confederation and the war in Ireland, 1641–1643*.[71]

Their chronological focus apart, these major projects have a number of features in common. They are each built around one central manuscript text hitherto unpublished – the anonymous 'Aphorismical discovery of treasonable faction' in the first instance, and Richard Bellings' manuscript account of the early days of the Confederate government at Kilkenny in the second. But while both of these texts were relatively short, they were surrounded in Gilbert's editions with a vast amount of editorial matter and commentary. A simple quantitative analysis will make the point. The text of the 'Aphorismical discovery', for example, covers some 640 pages spread over the three volumes. But it is accompanied by no less than 880 pages of introductory commentary and documentary appendices: 58 per cent of the work is editorial. The disparity between the text of Bellings' account of the Confederation and the editorial matter into which it is set is even more marked. Over the seven volumes, Bellings' 'History' accounts for some 420 pages. In some volumes no more than twenty pages of text are supplied, and in one instance nothing is printed at all. But the editorial matter amounts to an astonishing 2,850 pages, representing almost 85 per cent of the entire publication.

Such abstract figures may suggest nothing more than a severe case of editorial logorrhoea, a further indication of Gilbert's neurotic character. But closer examination reveals a more considered intent. The texts Gilbert chose were part of no official collection, housed in either the British or Irish state

---

70 Barnard, 'Gilbert and Irish historiography', pp 93, 97–8.   71 Gilbert, *A contemporary history of affairs in Ireland from 141 to 1652 now for the first time published with an appendix of original letters and documents* (3 vols, Dublin, 1879–80); *History of the Irish Confederation and the war in Ireland, 1641–1643* (7 vols, Dublin, 1882–91).

archives. They were rare items whose very scarcity, like that of the Gaelic records, was a direct consequence of their opposition to the official story. They were unpublished, largely uncopied, and survived by chance. They both pointedly denied the veracity of the official record on crucial points. The 'Aphorismical discovery' was an account of the tumultuous 1640s by an author whom Gilbert surmised to be a Catholic priest of Gaelic Ulster origin; Richard Bellings, sometime secretary to the Confederate administration at Kilkenny, was a scion of an old English family, Oxford educated, and enjoying connections at the Caroline court.[72] Each came from very different backgrounds. But both were, in their different ways, loyal royalists, neither irreconcilable rebels nor Romanists, but representatives of those whose true attitudes had been purposefully distorted by a calculating elite at the centre of Irish government of a kind with those who had, in Gilbert's view, so systematically suppressed the literary evidence of Gaelic culture.

Thus in publishing these documents and discussing in great detail their provenance, Gilbert was furthering his war against evidential suppression. But he did more. His massive appendices not only contained items corroborating the evidence of the edited texts, they were also filled with official documents – plantation surveys, state correspondence and memoranda, inquisitions post-mortem, government-inspired pamphlets – whose veracity was to be critically assessed in relation to all the opposing evidence that was now being set before the readers. Gilbert's huge – and financially prodigal – publications of the 1870s and 1880s were all of a piece with his first propagandist publications of the 1850s. But whereas previously he had been content simply to awaken readers as to the magnitude of the great historical fraud that had been perpetrated by the victorious colonial elites and their clients, now he was determined to place the actual materials demonstrating this fraud in front of his readers, allowing, and indeed encouraging, them to discover the extent of the deception on their own by a steady tour through the relevant documents, just as they would have taken their tour through the streets of Dublin.

It was this technique of carefully contrived reader discovery that was to become characteristic of Gilbert's final publications, though the element of manipulation became even stronger. His *Jacobite narrative* of 1892 was ostensibly an edition of the rare Jacobite text, 'A light for the blind'. But Gilbert silently excluded more than half of the original text – the latter portion dealing with King James' exile in France – in order to reinforce his preferred theme, which was what he regarded as a flagrant misrepresentation of Viceroy

---

[72] The identity of the author of the 'Aphorismical discovery' has not yet been established by scholars, thus Gilbert's claim that, like Bellings, he was both a Catholic and a royalist, and a bitter enemy only of the colonial exploiters remains as contested as ever. See *A contemporary history of affairs*, vol. i, pp ix–x.

Tyrconnel's conduct in office.[73] And such space as he saved by his silent excisions was occupied by some 140 pages of commentary and appendices, against 192 pages of the central text. His *Documents relating to Ireland, 1795–1804* was even more contrived in its intended effect. Ostensibly an edition of the memoirs of the United Irishman, William Mc Nevin, Gilbert not only silently edited the text, leaving out all the material that, despite his title, extended beyond 1797, he supplemented this edited reprint of an already published text by printing for the first time a manuscript detailing secret service payments in Ireland over the period 1795 to 1804, which he had discovered by accident in the Royal Irish Academy.[74] The point of this deeply contrived composition was to show once again and in times far different from the sixteenth century, the 1640s, and the 1690s, that a recurrent pattern in Irish history lay in the manner in which the natural tendencies toward individual freedom and social progress, which were displayed in the ancient Irish, later within the ranks of the Old English, and once more revived in the commercial, manufacturing and professional classes of the towns, were being constantly threatened and subverted by a small clique of colonial self-servers who were the real descendants of the self-seeking Anglo-Norman colonists.

VI

An underlying consistency of commitment can thus be uncovered beneath the fractured, rancorous and apparently obsessive scholarly career of John Gilbert. The internal strains and contradictions within Gilbert's understanding of the development of Irish history are abundantly evident. How did the tendency toward liberty of the old Irish, if it ever had been there, transmit to the bourgeois of Irish cities? Perhaps it had no need to: the love of liberty was a natural instinct. But if so why was Ireland so susceptible to its perversion and subversion in the hands of successive generations of colonial oligarchs and time-servers? How did this innate love of freedom among the Gaelic Irish and later among the Old English relate to the equally strong allegiance to Catholicism and a no less fervent loyalty to the crown of Ireland?

Such tensions, however, did not really apply from Gilbert's own perspective. Armed with a view of history as an inevitably progressive force, in which progress was measured by the gradual extension of individual freedom, Gilbert, following his French Romantic mentors, was not blind to the challenges of reaction and counter-revolution. Rooted in the weaknesses and sus-

---

73 Gilbert, *A Jacobite narrative of the war in Ireland, 1688–91 with contemporary letters and papers* (Dublin, 1892); for a critique of Gilbert's editorial practices see J.G. Simms, 'Introduction' to the 1971 facsimile reprint; Shannon, Irish University Press.   74 For a revealing analysis of the text see Maureen Wall's 'Introduction' to the 1970 facsimile reprint of Gilbert's text.

ceptibilities of human nature, such regressive tendencies were pervasive and Ireland had exhibited more than its share. But the means by which they were to be transcended were no less universal. They lay in the ever-vigilant determination to resist oppression and usurpation in whatever guise they appeared, political, economic or cultural. The methods to be adopted in this struggle against inequality varied as much as the nature of the challenges. In extremity, war and rebellion might be all that would serve; but in more moderate circumstances, accommodation with a power that seemed most likely to protect freedom against unlawful encroachment – such as a monarch, an empire or even a reforming Liberal Party – might be the most prudent and most effective course. In such vital calculations, it was imperative that the representatives of freedom should be as deeply informed as possible about the origin and character of the struggle before them, and that by careful and sustained criticism of the evidence before them they should not be misled or distracted from their task. In this ceaseless defence of their values, the freedom-lovers found succour in the custodians of culture – the poets, genealogists and annalists in one epoch, and historians and archivists in another – whose task, expressed in different modes in different ages, was always the same – to celebrate, to encourage, and to warn.

Contributors

TOBY BARNARD is emeritus fellow of Hertford College, Oxford. His *Brought to book: print in Ireland, 1680–1784* will be published in 2017.

CIARAN BRADY is professor of early modern history and historiography in the School of History and Humanities, Trinity College, Dublin. His recent works include *James Anthony Froude: an intellectual biography of a Victorian prophet*, published by Oxford University Press in 2013 (paperback ed., 2014), and *Shane O'Neill* (Dublin: 2nd, enlarged, ed., UCD Press, 2015).

GAEL CHENARD is archivist of the Department des Hautes-Alpes, France. His PhD thesis on *L'administration d'Alphonse de Poitiers en Poitou et en Saintonge (1241–1271)* was awarded at the Sorbonne in 2014.

MARY ESTHER CLARK is the Dublin City archivist and curator of the Dublin Civic Portrait Collection. Her book, *The Dublin Civic Portrait Collection: patronage, politics and patriotism, 1603–2013*, was published by Four Courts Press in 2016.

BERNADETTE CUNNINGHAM is deputy librarian at the Royal Irish Academy, Dublin. She is author of *The Annals of the Four Masters: Irish history, kingship and society in the early seventeenth century* (Dublin: Four Courts Press, 2010).

STEVEN G. ELLIS has taught history at NUI Galway for the past forty years and recently published *Defending English ground: war and peace in Meath and Northumberland, 1460–1542* (Oxford: Oxford University Press, 2015).

ALAN FORD is professor of theology in the University of Nottingham. He has recently published 'High of low? Writing the Irish Reformation in the early nineteenth century', *Bulletin of the John Rylands Library*, 90 (2014).

RAYMOND GILLESPIE teaches in the Department of History, Maynooth University, and has written widely on early modern Ireland. He has recently edited (with Salvador Ryan and Brendan Scott) *Making the Book of Fenagh: context and text*, which was published by Cumann Seanchais Bhreifne in summer 2016.

JACQUELINE HILL is professor emeritus of history at Maynooth University. She has a particular interest in the history of Dublin. She is co-editor (with Mary Ann Lyons) of *Representing Irish religious histories: historiography, ideology, and practice* (London: Palgrave, Macmillan, 2016).

HENRY A. JEFFERIES is the head of history at Thornhill College, Derry, Northern Ireland, and an associate member of the Arts & Humanities Research Institute, Ulster University. He is the author of *The Irish church and the Tudor reformations* (Dublin: Four Courts Press, 2010).

MARY ANN LYONS completed her doctorate on Franco-Irish relations in the sixteenth century under the direction of Colm Lennon and is professor of history at Maynooth University. Her forthcoming publications include 'Religion in Ireland, c.1460–1550: observance and the onset of reform' in Tom Bartlett (ed.), *Cambridge history of Ireland* (Cambridge University Press: Cambridge, 2017), vol. i, and *Representing Irish religious histories: historiography, ideology and practice*, co-edited with Jacqueline Hill (London: Palgrave Macmillan, 2016).

NESSA MALONE completed her doctorate, funded by the IRCHSS, on the Burnell family of Dublin, 1565–1664, at NUI Maynooth, where she was supervised by Colm Lennon. She has subsequently worked as a librarian at the Royal Irish Academy, University of Oxford, London School of Hygiene and Tropical Medicine, and currently the Warburg Institute, London.

RORY MASTERSON teaches at Colaiste Choilm, Tullamore. A past student at St Patrick's College, Maynooth, Colm Lennon supervised his doctoral thesis. He has recently published (in 2014) *Medieval Fore, County Westmeath* with Four Courts Press.

THOMAS O'CONNOR holds his doctorate from the Sorbonne and teaches European history in the Department of History, Maynooth University. His most recent book is *Irish voices from the Spanish Inquisition: migrants, converts and brokers in early modern Iberia* (London: Palgrave, 2016).

SALVADOR RYAN is professor of ecclesiastical history at St Patrick's College, Maynooth. He has recently edited (with Henning Laugerud and Laura Katrine Skinnebach), *The materiality of devotion in late medieval northern Europe* (Dublin: Four Courts Press, 2016). His *Death and the Irish: a miscellany* will be published by Wordwell Press in 2016.

CLODAGH TAIT is a lecturer in history at Mary Immaculate College, University of Limerick, and has published widely on sixteenth- and seventeenth-century Irish social and religious history. Her forthcoming publications include 'Society, 1550–1691' in Jane Ohlmeyer (ed.), *The Cambridge history of Ireland, 2: early modern Ireland*, Cambridge University Press, 2017.

Index

Act to prevent the further Growth of Popery (1704), 167, 204, n.54
aldermen, 35, 69, 82, 198, 203
All Hallows' priory, 32, 34–5, 49
Anglo-Irish, 19, 110–11, 152, 156, 259–60, 262
Anglo-Normans, 141, 153, 258
Armagh, 11, 54, 71, 111, 153, 170, 173, 225, 238, 241
antichrist, 113–14, 116–17, 119–32
Arthur, Thomas, 70, 72, 74, 76, 82, 86–7
Athlone, 142, 143–4, 159–60
Atkinson, Robert, 252
Augustinians, 55–6, 58, 145–6, 150, 155–6, 158, 170, 172

Ballina, Co. Tipperary, 80
Baltinglass rebellion, 99
Banishment Act (1697), 167
Barnewall, Christopher, 96, 104
Barnewall, Patrick, 105–6
Battle of Knockdoe, Co. Galway, 33
Bayle, Pierre, 113, n.16, 117–18
Belfast, 173–92
Bellarmine, Robert, 113–14, 116, 120, 130–1
Bellings, Richard, 272
Benedictines, 135, 138, 170
Bilbao, 160, n.19, 163–5, 212, n.16
Book of Common Prayer, 63–4, 66
Book of Howth, 93
Book of Leinster, 252
Book of Revelation, 113
Bordeaux, 72, 170–1
Bristol, 53
Brotherhood of Arms of St George, 34
Brouncker, Sir Henry, lord president of Munster, 71
Browne, George, archbishop of Dublin, 31
Browne, Mother Mary Bonaventure, 160
Burghley, Lord (*see also* Cecil, William), 94–6, 98, 103
Burke, Lady Margaret, 237–8, 241
Burnell, Henry, 89, 91–107

Cambridge, 86, 109, 111, 254
Camden, William, 52
Carew, Sir George, 67
Carrickfergus, 174, 176–7, 183
Castle Chamber, court of, 96, 104, 106
Castleknock, Dublin, 91–2, 107, 135
Cecil, William (*see also* Burghley, Lord), 104
cess, 89–91, 93–9, 101–2, 105–6
Challoner, Richard, 246
chantries, 19, 31, 55–6, 60, 63
Charles I, king, 76–7, 82
Charles II, king, 194–5
Chichester, Sir Arthur, 75, 105
Christ Church, Cork, 53–6, 60, 62–3
Christ Church Cathedral, Dublin, 11, 19
Church of Ireland, 19, 32, 59, 65–6, 76, 155, 174, 178–81, 183, 187, 189, 219, 230, 234, 242, 244, 261
church papistry, 64, 196
churchwardens, 179, 182
Cistercians, 134, 137, 140, 143, 149–51
Clanricard, earl of, 150, 157–8
Clonmacnoise, 134, 142–4, 150, 153
Coleraine, 173, 177
College of Physicians (Ireland), 76, 86, 177
Confederate wars, 83
confraternities, 103, 231
conversion, 219–24, 233
Coote, Sir Charles, 77, 84
Corish, Monsignor Patrick, 13, 15,
Cork, 51–69, 73, 173, 221, 223, 237, 239
Corporation of Belfast, 174, 183–6
Council of Trent, 113, 162, 226, 244–5
Counter-Reformation, 11, 19, 31, 63–7, 105, 108–10, 157–8, 196, 199, 226
Creagh, Dermot, 64, 67
Creagh, Richard, archbishop of Armagh, 11, 15, 71, 73–4, 78, n.41
Cromwell, Henry, 84
Cromwell, Oliver, 84
Cromwellian wars, 82, 85
Crutched Friars, 150

Derry, 173, 177, 181, 189
Desmond, earl of, 58, 101
Digby, Sir Robert, 104
disease, 76, 85, 161, 176, 215
disputation, 109, 111–12, 113, 115, 117, 119
Dissenters, 181, 183, 198–9, 204–5, 230, 242
Dominicans, 55–6, 58, 83, 156, 158, 160–72
Donegall, earl of, 173–4, 180–2
Drogheda, 92, 169, 172, 190
Dublin Castle, 76–7, 96–8, 101, 108, 111, 114, 118, 266
Dublin Chain Book, 194
Dublin Corporation, 35, 90, 94, 105, 194, 196, 199, 201, 203–5, 209

Edward IV, king, 34–5, 154
Edward VI, king, 11, 36, 58
Elphin, diocese of, 57
Elizabeth I, queen, 19, 35–6, 52, 58–9, 63–6, 68, 91, 97, 105, 195–6, 244
English Test Act (1673), 201, 204
excommunication, 35, 82–3

fines, 71, 94, 178, 198, 205
Fitzgerald, Garret Óg, 93
Fitzgerald, James Fitzmaurice, 59, 99
Fitzsimon, Henry, SJ, 108–33
Fleetwood, Sir Charles, lord deputy, 84
Fore, priory of, 138
France, 53, 157, 198, 202, 213, 238–9, 262, 272
Franciscans, 55–8, 71, 156, 161, 165–6, 172, 265

Galway, 66, 84, 87, 156–73
Gaelic Irish, 85, 249, 264, 266, 273
George I, king, 205
Gilbert, Sir John T., 10, 249–74
Gregory VII, pope, 113
Guild of St Anne, Dublin, 9, 11, 31, 92, 103
Guild of St George Martyr, Dublin, 10, 31–50

Henry VII, king, 33, 35
Henry VIII, king, 35, 53, 56–7, 64, 108

Historical Manuscripts Commission, 270
Hospitallers, 136
Huguenots, 59, 198

Ireton, Henry, 84
Irish Archaeological and Celtic Society, 254, 257, 271
Irish Articles (1615), 114
Irish Quarterly Review, 250, 255, 261
Irish Remonstrance (1661), 195–6

Jacobites, 178, 188–90, 198, 201–2, 205–6, 213, 238–9, 272
James I, king, 36, 106, 200
James II, king, 86, 165, 171, 196–7, 202–4, 230, 238
Jesuits, 59, 71, 73, 105, 108, 110–11, 113, 116–18, 131, 200, 236

Kilcrea friary, Co. Cork, 54
Kildare, earl of, 33, 90, 92, 94, 99–101, 103–4
Kildare rebellion, 56, 152
Kilkenny, 82, 86, 92, 150, 162, 173, 223, 264–5, 271
Kilmainham, 136
Kilmallock, Co. Limerick, 71
King, William, bishop of Derry, 189

Limerick, 10–11, 18, 51, 58, 66–7, 70–84, 87–8, 173, 181, 218, 240
Loftus, Adam, lord chancellor, 100
Lyon, William, bishop of Cork and Cloyne, 60, 64

MacDonnell, Sir Randal mac Sorley, earl of Antrim, 75, 77, 79
Magna Carta, 96, 101
Magrath, Miler, archbishop of Cashel, 64–5
martyrdom, 11, 15, 71, 73, 243, 247
Mary I, queen, 36, 58
Mass, 31, 34, 49, 53, 56, 58, 65, 111, 167–8, 177, 200, 245, 250
Mayo, bishop of, 71
medicine, 72, 86, 175
mental reservation, 200, 205, 208
monasteries, dissolution of, 57–8, 134–55, 157

Index 279

Netterville, Richard, 89–107
New English, 11, 17, 51, 66, 70, n.2, 101
Nine Years War, 65–7, 102, 105, 111, 202
Nugent, William, baron of Delvin, 95
Nun's Island, Galway, 161–2

oaths, 65, 68, 71, 75, 106, 177–8, 182, 184, 187–8, 190, 193–209
Oath of Supremacy, 71, 106, 177–8, 195–7, 199
O'Brien, Donagh, fourth earl of Thomond, 74
Observantism, 56
Ó Dubhthaigh, Eoghan, 60
O'Healy, Bishop Patrick, 71
O'Heyne, John, papal bishop of Cork and Cloyne, 57
Old English, 10, 11, 17, 19, 70, 72–9, 81, 84, 87–8, 90, 92–3, 96, 98, 102–3, 106, 110, 238, 271, 273
O'Neill, Hugh, 68, 102–3, 105
Ormond, earl of, 80, 99, 136
O'Rourke, Conn, OFM, 71
Oxford, 86, 109–11, 254

Pale, the, 11, 17, 33–4, 62, 89–90, 93, 95–6, 98–9, 102, 105–6, 169
Paris, 70, 72–3, 110, 243
Paul III, pope, 57
perjury, 193
Perrot, John, lord deputy, 101
Petty, Sir William, 85
Philip IV, king, 164
pilgrimage, 246
Pius V, pope, 35
Plunkett, Oliver, 243
Poor Clares, 156, 158–66, 170–1
poor relief, 179–80
Popish Plot (1678), 197
Poynings' Law, 101
Presbyterians, 174–5, 178–85, 187–92, 204–5, 225, 233–4
printing, 14, 108, 226, 228, 239, 242, 273

Quakers, 176–7, 198–9, 203, 205, 216, 218, 234

recusancy, 11, 19, 68–9, 102, 104, 106, 157–8, 196, 241

Red Book of Kilkenny, 10
Reformation, 11, 13, 19, 31, 35, 51, 55–8, 60, 62, 69, 108–13, 243, 261–2
revisionist debate, 18
Rheims, 70, 72
Richard, duke of York, 33
Rider, John, dean of St Patrick's Cathedral, 111
Rinuccini, Giovanni Battista, papal nuncio, 82, 162–3
rosary, 163
Roscommon, 147, 221, 223
Royal Irish Academy, 251–2, 255–6, 273

sacraments, 65, 68, 167, 184–6, 191, 204
Salamanca, 163, 229, 233
Shandon Castle, 52, 68
Sheyne, Mathew, bishop of Cork, 59
Sidney, Sir Henry, lord deputy, 52, 58, 92, 94–9
Sloane, Hans, 175–6
sodalities, 12, 110, 244
Skiddy, Roger, bishop of Cork and Cloyne, 57–8
Spain, 65, 157, 163–4, 169, 210–24, 229, 231–3, 239, 243
Spanish Armada, 64
Spanish Inquisition, 210–24
Stanihurst, James, 93
Stanihurst, Richard, 10–11, 17, 32, 35, 111
St Audeon's church, Dublin, 92,
St Lawrence, Christopher, Lord Howth, 93, 96
St Patrick's Cathedral, 33, 111
St Patrick's Purgatory, 246

Tanner, Edmund, bishop of Cork, 59
Test Act (1704), 181, 184, 187, 204
Thierry, Augustine, 262–3
Thirty-Nine Articles, 114
Tipperary, 59, 80, 221, 223, 225
Todd, James Henthorn, 252
Toleration Act (1719), 191
Tower of London, 97
transubstantiation, 199
Trinity College, Dublin, 72, 108, 113, 254
Tyrry, Dominick, bishop of Cork and Cloyne, 57

Ussher, James, archbishop, 76, 79, 108–33, 242

Valladollid, 163
Virgin Mary, 32, 110, 163, 200

Wallop, Henry, 100, 103
Walsingham, Francis, 95, 98–100
Warbeck, Perkin, 33
Ware, Sir James, 77, 240
Waterford, 51, 67–8, 170, 172–3, 237

weavers, 210–24
Wentworth, Sir Thomas, lord deputy, 70, n.2, 79–80
Westminster Confession, 191
Wilde, Sir William, 251, n.6, 254
William III, king, 204
Williamite revolution, 199, 201
wills, 10, 52, n.6, 53–5, 59–64, 66, 87, 92, 107, 175, 179, 188, 215
Wolfe, David, SJ, 51, 59